The Visitor's Guide
to the
Birds of the
Eastern
National Parks

UNITED STATES AND CANADA

Roland H. Wauer

ILLUSTRATIONS BY MIMI HOPPE WOLF

John Muir Publications
Santa Fe, New Mexico

John Muir Publications, P.O. Box 613, Santa Fe, NM 87504

First edition. First printing October 1992

Library of Congress Cataloging-in-Publication Data
Wauer, Roland H.
    The visitor's guide to the birds of the eastern national parks:
    United States and Canada / Roland Wauer ; illustrations by
    Mimi Hoppe Wolfe. — 1st ed.
        p. cm.
    Includes bibliographical references and index.
    ISBN 1-56261-039-2
    1. Birds—East (U.S.) 2. National parks and reserves—East
(U.S.) —Guidebooks. I. Wolf, Mimi Hoppe. II. Title.
QL683.E27W38   1992
598.2974—dc20   92-19638
                                                        CIP

Design: Ken Wilson
Illustrations: Mimi Hoppe Wolf
Typeface: Minion
Typography: Ken Wilson, John Muir Publications
Printer: Publishers Press

Distributed to the book trade by
W. W. Norton & Company, Inc.
New York, New York

Cover photo: Wood duck courtesy of Photo Reseachers, Inc.
Interior photographs by Roland H. Wauer

Contents

Foreword

It is with much pleasure that I write this foreword to *Birds of the Eastern National Parks: United States and Canada*. The Humane Society of the United States (HSUS) is proud to provide, through this important book, an expanded opportunity for wildlife appreciation to those who visit our national parks.

The HSUS has been known widely for its proactive and advocacy-oriented programs to protect animals. We have championed the cause of companion animals, urging those who acquire pets to treat them with consideration and care. We have worked to eliminate the suffering of animals used in laboratories and have aggressively advanced the use of alternatives. We have challenged the all too prevalent inhumane rearing of farm animals and successfully helped promote reforms within this industry while at the same time urging a reduction and replacement of meat and other farm products in one's diet.

Our wildlife programs have been equally forceful and proactive. Among them are the elimination of commercial killing of fur seals on Alaska's Pribilof Islands and the slaughter of the world's great whales; halting the sale of elephant ivory; protecting from destruction animals that would have been destined for fur fashions; and saving millions of animals from brutal elimination caused by predator control programs.

The HSUS, an organization of more than a million and a half constituents, is equally committed to promote an appreciation and enjoyment of wild animals and wild places. This book opens the doors to that appreciation in a unique and authoritative way. Ro Wauer, drawing amply on his lifelong interest in the love for ani-

mals, walks each visitor through the national park units of the eastern United States with the skill and accomplished grace of a dedicated bird-watcher and naturalist. Firsthand, the reader is drawn
into the habitat and environment of each park and its bird life.
Through these pages, the reader feels the interrelations and interaction of the animals and plants and the enjoyment of a lifetime spent
in studying the intricacies of nature.

For my family, this book, with its invitation to sight a particular
bird and then move quickly on to discover another, is far more
important than a field guide. This book encourages knowing a park
and understanding its animal life in a way that all concerned citizens must if the essential qualities of our parks are to be preserved
for future generations.

Finally, the HSUS is pleased and gratified to have a book of this
quality which actively encourages wildlife enjoyment and environmental appreciation. To protect wildlife, people need to understand
wild creatures more thoroughly and to appreciate the subtleties of
their interaction with the environment that sustains them. This
book provides the knowledge and information that can make these
values truly available to each reader.

Ro Wauer has done a magnificent job of integrating his own
special interest in wildlife and his personal commitment to environmental quality into a readable text that will make park exploration a delightful and unique experience. I wish you many delightful visits.

April 17, 1992   John A. Hoyt
Washington, D.C.   Chief Executive,
                              The Humane Society of the United States
                                President, Humane Society International

Preface

The national parks of the United States and Canada possess the best examples of the continent's natural heritage, complete with the grandest scenery and most stable plant and animal communities still in existence. In a large sense, North America's national parks represent a microcosm of our last remaining wildlands.

Birds of the Eastern National Parks: United States and Canada describes the bird life within each of the eastern national parks. This book is intended to introduce the park visitor to the most common and obvious birds and also to provide an introduction to the fascinating world of bird identification and behavior. This book can be used as a reference to the park and its bird life during a park visit as well as a valuable tool in preparing for that visit.

Birds of the Eastern National Parks is not intended to be used as a field guide or a book on bird identification per se. Several excellent field guides are already available; they should be used as companion volumes to this book. Nor is this book intended to help the birder find the rarities or the out-of-the-way specialties. Its purpose is to help the park visitor better appreciate the park and its bird life. If in making new acquaintances, the park visitor should become interested in birds and more concerned about their well-being, all the better.

Thirty-seven national parks are included in this book, from Forillon on Canada's Gaspé Peninsula south to Fort Jefferson beyond the tip of the Florida Keys, east to the U.S. Virgin Islands, and west to Mammoth Cave, Kentucky. The thirty-seven national parks are divided into four broad geographic or biotic regions: those that occur in the Atlantic Maritime region, the Appalachian

Mountains, the coastal plains, and the southeastern United States and Virgin Islands. The four categories provide continuity in discussion of both the natural park areas and the biotic communities they contain, as well as a perspective for anyone planning a trip.

Each chapter begins with a personalized experience that might occur to anyone visiting the park. At Everglades National Park, for example, the reader is introduced to that park through an early morning visit to the Anhinga Trail with its fascinating anhingas and its associated wildlife. Each chapter then continues with a description of the national park itself, including the plant and animal communities that exist there, visitor facilities available within the park, interpretive activities, and where one can write or telephone for additional park information. The chapter then returns to the bird life, describing common birds within several of the most popular and accessible places to visit. Each chapter ends with a summary of the park's bird life and a list of a few key species.

A visit to any of the national parks should begin with a stop at the park's visitor center or information station to obtain a park brochure and activity sheet. These will contain basic information about the roads and trails, location of camping and picnic sites, hiking routes, details of interpretive activities, descriptions of some of the park's key resources, and so on. The numerous sites mentioned in the book can best be located by using the map found in the park brochure.

Common bird names that are used throughout the book are taken from the most recent checklist of birds published by the American Ornithologists' Union (AOU) and used in all the up-to-date field guides. In the case of plants, because common names vary so much from one part of the country to another, a list of all common plant names used, along with their scientific names, is included in Appendix A.

The bibliography includes the works used in the writing of this book and provides the reader with sources for continued study of birds of the eastern national parks.

Enjoy!

Acknowledgments

This book would not have been possible without the kind assistance of dozens of employees of the U.S. and Canadian national park systems: superintendents, rangers, naturalists, resource specialists, and a few other individuals. I especially want to thank the following individuals: Shirley Beccue, Seth Benz, Allen O'Connor, and Superintendent Bob Reynolds at Acadia; Brenda Coleman, Howard Duncan, and Sue Holaborda at Big South Fork; Superintendent Gary Everhardt and Eileen Nieme at Blue Ridge Parkway; Irvin Ailes, Gordon Olson, and Larry Points at Assateague and Chincoteague; John Stiner at Canaveral; A. F. Gibbs and Tim Reynolds at Cape Breton Highlands; Frank Ackerman, Kyle Jones, and Dan Seally at Cape Cod; Marcia Lyons and Bob Woody at Cape Hatteras; Superintendent Bill Harris and Michael Rikard at Cape Lookout; Nancy Cox Beck, Jerry Hightower, and Mari Hayden at Chattahoochee River; John Cissell and Superintendent Pat Reed at Chickamauga-Chattanooga; Kathryn Brett at Congaree Swamp; Jack Collier, Wes Leishman, and Superintendent Charles Vial at Cumberland Gap; Z. T. Kirkland at Cumberland Island; Beth Johnson, Superintendent Dick Ring, and Randy Turner at Delaware Water Gap; Sonny Bass, Jonathan Bayliss, Superintendent Bob Chandler, Gene Cox, Bill Loftus, John Ogden, Mike Soukop, Bill Robertson, and Pat Tolle at Everglades; R. P. Barrett and Kathleen Gillen at Fire Island; Diane Attendu, Denise Gagne, and Maxime St-Amour at Forillon; Edward Hoar, Meredith Reeve, and Rob

Walker at Fundy; Kevin MacCready, Don Riepe and John
Zuzworsky at Gateway; Don Defoe, Kitty Mancill, and John Peine
at Great Smoky Mountains; Roger Burrows, Michael Evens, Anne
Marceau, and Dave Morrow at Gros Morne; Superintendent Jerry
Eubanks and Ted Simon at Gulf Islands; Gisele Doucat, Cliff
Drysdale, Peter Hope, Millie Evans, and Superintendent William
Wambolt at Kejimkujik; Bert Crossman, Benoit Richard, and
Semida Stewart at Kouchibouguac; Verdie Abel, Jeff Bradybaugh,
George Gregory, Stephanie Hibbs, and Superintendent Dave
Mihalic at Mammoth Cave; Superintendent Joe Kennedy, Carol
Pollio, Jodi Schrader, Reba Scott, and Wayne Snyder at New River
Gorge; Heather Rossele and Bill Rudolph at National Capital Parks;
Barbara MacDonald at Prince Edward Island; and Larry Hakel,
Terry Lindsay, and Keith Watson at Shenandoah.

I also want to thank Jan Hartke and President John Hoyt of the
Humane Society of the United States (HSUS) and Earthkind. The
monetary assistance provided by HSUS was necessary for the travel
and research required in the production of this book. Their contributions were most appreciated.

This project was the idea of my friend Bob Cahn, who provided
encouragement throughout. Pat Cahn also lent her editorial exper-
tise in the initial development of ideas and review of early chapters.
Other manuscript reviews and suggestions were provided by Gary
Noel Corbett, wildlife biologist with the Canadian Parks Service;
Bob Duncan of Gulf Breeze, Florida; Mark Elwonger of Victoria,
Texas; Judy Toups of Gulfport, Mississippi; and Henning von
Schmeling of Atlanta, Georgia.

Last and certainly not least, I thank my wife, Betty, who supported this project with editorial advice and assistance as my "trail-
er slave" throughout the 35,000-plus miles we traveled.

1

Birds—What They Are and How to Find Them

The bond between birds and man is older than recorded history. Birds have always been an integral part of human culture, a symbol of the affinity between mankind and the rest of the natural world, in religion, in folklore, in magic, in art —from early cave paintings to the albatross that haunted Coleridge's Ancient Mariner. Scientists today recognize them as sure indicators of the health of the environment. And as modern field guides make identification easier, millions of laymen watch them just for the joy of it.

—Paul Brooks

How often I have wished I could fly. To soar high over the mountains and valleys. To explore secluded places that are impossible to reach any other way. To escape this earthbound existence with the ease of a bird. These were among my secret desires as a youngster. How I envied the hawks and the swallows and even the tiny hummingbirds. They were the masters of my universe.

Only birds and bats, of all the warm-blooded creatures, can fly for more than a few yards. Only birds possess the combination of feathers, powerful wings, hollow bones, a remarkable respiratory system, and a large strong heart. They are truly magnificent flying machines. The power of a wing beat, due to the marvelous flight feathers, allows a bird to cruise at speeds of 20 to 40 miles (32-64 km) per hour while flying nonstop across the Gulf of Mexico or the Arctic tundra. The tiny hummingbird has been clocked at 50 miles (80 km) per hour. And the powerful peregrine falcon is thought to stoop at speeds up to 200 miles (322 km) per hour.

A blue-winged teal banded in Quebec, Canada, was killed by a hunter less than four weeks later in Guyana, South America, more than 2,500 miles (4,023 km) distant. A Manx shearwater, taken from its burrow on Skokholm Island, Wales, and carried by airplane to Boston, Massachusetts, returned to its burrow on the 13th day, having flown 3,000 miles (4,828 km) across the Atlantic Ocean. And a lesser yellowlegs banded in Massachusetts was captured six days later 1,900 miles (3,058 km) away on Martinique, in the Lesser Antilles. That bird had averaged 317 miles (510 km) per day.

Migrants usually fly below 3,000 feet (914 m) elevation, but observers at 14,000 feet (4,267 m) elevation in the Himalayas reported storks and cranes flying so high overhead, at an estimated 20,000 feet (6,096 m), they could barely be seen through binoculars.

Other marvelous features of birds are their bill shapes and sizes. Anyone who has watched birds for any time at all cannot help but notice the diversity of feeding methods. Hummingbirds, for example, have long thin bills that they utilize to probe into flowers to feed on nectar, sometimes deep inside tubular flowers. Their bills are especially adapted to this type of feeding. Many shorebirds, such as dowitchers and common snipes, also have long bills, but they are much heavier for probing for food in mud. The long-billed curlew's bill can reach into deep burrows to extract its prey.

The many insect feeders have dainty bills for capturing tiny insects. Vireos and warblers are gleaners that forage on trees and shrubs, picking insects off leaves and bark. A careful examination of feeding warblers will further suggest the size of their preferred food on the basis of their bill size. Flycatcher bills are wider to enhance their ability to capture flies in midair. Woodpecker bills are specialized so they are able to drill into insect-infested trees and shrubs to retrieve the larvae there.

Finch bills are short and stout, most useful for cracking seeds. Crossbills are able to extract seeds from conifer cones. And grosbeaks are able to feed on much larger seeds, actually stripping away the husk from some fleshy seeds.

Fruit becomes particularly abundant in late summer and fall and provides food for a host of birds, many of which feed on insects at one time of year and fruit at other times of the year. One has only to spend a short time within the coastal bayberry thickets to under-stand the importance of berries to the fall migrants.

And then there are the predators with their variety of bill shapes and sizes. Raptors possess short and stout bills with a specialized hook used for tearing apart their prey. The wading birds possess large, heavy bills for capturing their prey. And diving birds possess bills that are hooked for catching fish and serrated on the edges for a better grip.

Feet are another fascinating feature of a bird's anatomy also helpful in understanding a bird's requirements. Webbed feet suggest its adaptation to water for swimming, and flattened toes help birds walk on soft mud. Tiny, flexible toes suggest an ability to perch on small twigs and branches. And large, powerful feet with sharp talons are required to capture and grip prey.

There are approximately 9,000 kinds of birds in the world; about 900 of those are found in North America. And every one has slightly different characteristics that permit it to utilize a slightly different niche (the combination of its needs) from any other species. Whenever two or more species have the same needs, in all likelihood only one will survive.

A bird is a very specialized creature, indeed, but its bill and feet are usually less obvious than its plumage, the sum total of its feathers. A bird's plumage is unquestionably its most obvious and usually most attractive characteristic. This is especially true for the more colorful and contrasting birds, such as warblers, hummingbirds, some waterfowl, and some finches. Birds are the most colorful of all vertebrates.

Feathers reveal every color in the rainbow. The colors we see are the product of pigments and the reflection and refraction of light due to feather structure. The concentration of pigments produces the intensities of color, as in the vivid red of a scarlet tanager and the diluted red of a female northern cardinal. The total lack of pigment production results in white plumage. Many of the colors we see are due to the light that may be reflected or absorbed by the feather. The bright blues of the blue jay or indigo bunting are due to a particular arrangement of cells of the feather. Iridescence is also due to structure and not pigments. A dull velvet color is the reversal of iridescence.

Of all the aesthetically pleasing characteristics of birds, bird song may be the most enduring. Louis Halle wrote, "As music is the purest form of expression, so it seems to me that the singing of birds is the purest form for the expression of natural beauty and goodness in the larger sense, the least susceptible of explanation on ulterior practical grounds."

Who has not paused to watch an American robin or cedar waxwing feeding on berries, or the wild dives of an osprey, pelican, or tern? Who has not watched a soaring red-tailed hawk or turkey vulture as it circles high in the sky? And who has not stopped to admire a hummingbird feeding from a particularly colorful flower?

But birds have additional values that are sometimes ignored, perhaps because they are often taken for granted. For instance, certain birds are extremely adept at catching and consuming large quantities of insects, many of which are considered pests. These include obnoxious insects as well as those that are a serious threat to various crops on which we humans depend for our sustenance.

Human beings have utilized birds from earliest history. Birds were worshiped by many early civilizations. Cormorants were ringed for catching fish. Pigeons carried our messages. Songbirds were taken into mines and brightened our homes. The concept and development of manned flight was derived from our observations of birds. Every state and province has an official bird, many of which highlight official flags and seals. The majority of Canadian coins and paper money display common bird species. Postage stamps often feature pertinent birds. And the most powerful country in the world utilizes a bird as its symbol: America's bald eagle is one of the most visible symbols in the United States.

Birds truly are an intricate part of the human ecosystem, an important link to nature. Birds, more than any other creatures, are obvious and omnipresent members of our human community.

Birding for Fun

There comes a time when those of us with a natural curiosity and appreciation for the outdoors want to know the names of the various creatures we see around us. The initial spark to identify birds may be kindled by some exceptional happening or a special sighting. Watching a family of gray jays at a campground as they actively investigate you and your food supply or suddenly being attacked by a flock of common terns at the beach must certainly foster an interest in those species and what they are about.

But identifying those birds can be somewhat difficult unless you know where to begin. Although the average park visitor usually can identify more birds than he might at first assume, further bird identification requires some basics, just like any other endeavor. With bird identification, the basics include two essential pieces of equipment: a field guide and a pair of binoculars.

There are several very good field guides available which utilize the bird identification technique developed by Roger Tory Peterson. Peterson's field guides and those published by the National Geographic Society and the Golden Press, as well as Herbert Raffaele's *A Guide to the Birds of Puerto Rico and the Virgin Islands* (for the Virgin Islands), utilize bird paintings. These guides are preferred over those with photographs, because the paintings highlight key features that only occasionally are obvious in photographs.

Binoculars are absolutely essential for identifying and appreciating most birds. They vary in power and field of vision, as well as price. The most popular birding binocular is an 8x35 glass ("8" is the power or magnification, "8x" magnifies a bird eight times, and "7x" magnifies a bird seven times, etc.; "35" is the diameter of the objective lens in millimeters and is used to illustrate the field of view; generally, "50" provides a wider field of view and brighter image than "35"). The 7x50 binocular,which provides a brighter image than the 8x35 binocular, is also good but it is usually too heavy for a full day in the field. Binoculars 9x and above are often too powerful for beginners who are not yet comfortable with holding binoculars perfectly still. Pocket-sized, lightweight binoculars are good for occasional use, but continuous use can cause eyestrain. Also, central-focus binoculars are a must. And the minimum focusing distance is important as well, for focusing on a bird that may be as close as 10 to 12 feet. Binoculars come in all prices, but the moderately priced ones usually work just as well as the most expensive, which may be more water resistant, less inclined to fog, and armored for rough use.

Using binoculars usually requires some experimentation, but

the skill is easy to learn. First make sure that the right ocular is set at "0" for 20-20 vision. Then while looking directly at an object, bring the binoculars up into position without changing your position or looking elsewhere, and use the center wheel to focus on the object. A few tries will produce immediate results.

The next step is to get acquainted with your field guide. Start with leafing through the entire guide and locating the first page of tyrant flycatchers. All the illustrations beyond are of the perching birds. All the nonperching birds (seabirds, waders, waterfowl, raptors, shorebirds, gulls and terns, grouse, hummingbirds, woodpeckers, etc.) are located within the first portion of the book.

Next read the introductory section, especially the discussion about field marks. Your field guide will also include a drawing of a typical bird showing basic field marks. Look these over, so that you acquire a good idea of where the bird's crown, eye line, eye ring, chin, upper and lower mandibles, flank, upper tail and under tail coverts, wrist, wing bar, and so on, occur. And be ready to refer back to this illustration for help when necessary.

Now that you have discovered the value of a field guide, it is time to start identifying real-life birds. You should now have an idea of what features to look for in live birds. The following suggestions provide an identification strategy of sorts:

1. Size. It is a good idea to relate bird size to those species you already know. For instance, consider five categories: sparrow-size, robin-size, pigeon-size, duck-size, and heron-size. With a few exceptions, such as the common raven, any bird the size of a duck and larger is a nonperching bird and will be found in the first half of the field guide. By thinking size, you can immediately know where to start your search. Also, one can often pick out odd-sized birds in a flock for further attention or recognize different species that might be foraging together. For example, a tiny bird within a party of warblers will more than likely be a chickadee, kinglet, or brown creeper.

2. Shape and behavior. Does your bird possess any outstanding features? Is it a wader with long legs and an upright posture? Possibly a heron. Is it walking along the shoreline? Possibly a shorebird. Is it swimming on a lake or bay? Probably a duck or seabird. Is

it soaring high in the sky? Possibly a hawk or gull. Is it perched on a wire or tree limb? Probably a perching bird. Is it a perching bird eating seeds at a feeder? Probably a sparrow or finch. If it is smaller than a warbler, is creeping up a tree trunk, and is all brown, it is sure to be a brown creeper.

3. Color and pattern. Many birds possess an obvious plumage that is an immediate giveaway. Cardinals, robins, indigo buntings, red-winged blackbirds, and American goldfinches are the first to come to mind. These are easily identified species requiring only the minimum of observation time. Their bold and obvious color and/or pattern stand out like a sore thumb. But many of their neighbors will require a little more study. For those less obvious species, pay attention to the pattern of colors. Does the all-white underpart extend onto the back, or does your bird possess only white wing bars? Does its white neck extend onto the face and include the eye, or does the white extend only to the lower mandible? Does its reddish color extend onto the back, or is it limited to the tail and rump? Do the yellow underparts include the throat and belly or only the chest? The answers to these questions will eventually become second nature.

Field Techniques

Bird-finding techniques are often personal ones, and you will need to discover your own preferred methods. For example, I like to move very slowly through a particular habitat, trying to discover all of the birds present within that immediate area. I personally find that part of birding to be a very special challenge. Other birders often prefer to move along at a faster clip, stopping only to watch those birds that become obvious. This plan is based on the concept that they will find more birds by covering more ground. That is definitely the reason for visiting as many habitats as possible, but I believe that the largest number of species can be found by slowly moving through each habitat, making yourself part of the scene, both physically and mentally.

There are definite clues to bird finding that can be used to your advantage. First and foremost are bird sounds. During the breeding season, bird song is the very best indicator of a bird's presence and location. Songbirds often sing throughout the day. They almost always sing at dawn and dusk, but a few species sing only at dawn. The more serious birders will find themselves out at dawn while other birders are still asleep. The majority of the birds, however, can usually be found throughout the day.

A rustling of dry leaves in the underbrush can be another important clue. Leaf rustling can be caused by numerous creatures, but when the leaves seem to be thrown back as if being cleared away for finding insects underneath, the originator is likely a brown thrasher, rufous-sided towhee, or fox sparrow.

Songbirds tend to ignore intruders who are quiet and move slowly, unless they get too close to a nest or fledgling. You can get surprisingly close to songbirds by moving slowly and not making any sudden motions. Also, wearing dull clothing, instead of bright and contrasting clothing, helps you to blend into the bird's environment, usually permitting closer viewing.

Some of the nonperching birds will permit a slow, cautious approach, but the wading birds, ducks, and raptors are not as trusting. You will need to observe these birds from a distance, and you may want to use a spotting scope for these observations. Or you may be able to use a blind, sometimes installed at bird-viewing sites.

During the nonbreeding portion of the year, birds often occur in flocks or in parties. Flocks of waterfowl or blackbirds can number in the hundreds or thousands and be readily visible from a considerable distance. But a party of songbirds moving through the forest will require quiet study for identifying all of the members. It is possible to wander through the woods for some time before discovering a party of birds that may include a dozen or more species. Migrant songbirds usually travel in parties that can include hundreds of individuals of two or three dozen species. When finding such a party, it is best to be still and let the party continue its feeding activities without disturbing it. In the few cases when a bird party is just beyond good viewing distance, you can sometimes attract a few of the closer individuals by spishing—making low, scratchy sounds with your teeth together and mouth slightly open—a few times; attracting the closer individuals often entices the whole flock to move in your direction. However, I find that spishing within a bird party tends to frighten some species off or to move the party along faster than it might otherwise go.

At times, a bird party is concentrated at a choice feeding site, such as fruiting cherry or bayberry plants. So long as they are not frightened or unduly agitated by noises or movement, they may remain and continue feeding for some time. Also, their activities will tend to attract other birds, allowing you to see a broad spectrum of birds at one spot.

Generally, birding along a forest edge, often along the edge of a parking lot, can produce the best results in the early morning. Bird parties prefer sunny areas then, to take advantage of greater insect activity. Within two or three hours, feeding declines rapidly, especially on hot, sunny days.

Birds may then need to be enticed into the open. And many species respond well to some sounds. Spishing works very well. Squeaking sounds made with your lips against the back of your hand or finger may work at other times. Birds are curious, and these kinds of sounds can be very effective. At other times, they seem to frighten birds away. And some species, such as a mourning warbler, will be attracted once but will be difficult to fool twice. So always be prepared to focus your binoculars on the bird immediately when it pops up from the brush or out of a thicket.

As mentioned above, the best way to find a large number of birds is to visit a variety of bird habitats. All birds occur in distinct habitats, especially during their nesting season. But they tend to frequent a broader range of sites in migration and in winter. Learning where species can most likely be expected is very helpful. For instance, a boreal chickadee occurs only in the northern coniferous forests; this species cannot be found in the Everglades. A new birder should learn to take advantage of the range map and habitat description for each species that are included within the field guides. It can save considerable embarrassment.

Birding by song is often left to the experienced birder, but many novices are better equipped to utilize bird songs than many of the experts. Some birders have poor hearing or a "tin ear." So for anyone with an ear for melody, there is a wide range of records, tapes, and CDs available to help you learn the bird songs. And during the spring and summer, there is no better method of bird identification. When tiny warblers are singing from the upper canopy of the forest, finding and observing those individuals can be tough. But their songs are an instant method of recognition that does not involve eye and neck strain from staring into the upper canopy for hours on end. And observing rails in a marsh can also be trying, if not outright dangerous. But rails and other marsh birds sing their own unique songs that can usually be easily identified.

Much of the knowledge required to make quick bird identifications must come from field experience. An excellent shortcut is spending time with an experienced birder who is willing to share his or her knowledge. That person can pass on tidbits of information that otherwise might take years to acquire. Most national parks have staff naturalists who give bird talks and walks during the visitor season. This kind of assistance can be extremely worthwhile for bird finding and bird identification.

Birding Ethics

As with any other activity, there are certain rules to follow. Birding should be fun and fulfilling. It can be a challenge equal to any other outdoor sport. But it should never reach the point that seeing a bird is so all-consuming that the bird's health and habitat are threatened. Any time that we are in the field we must realize that we are only visitors to that habitat on which a number of birds depend for their existence. We must not interfere with their way of life. Disturbing nests and nestlings, for whatever reason, cannot be tolerated. Tree whacking to entice woodpeckers and owls to peek outside should not be allowed.

Most national parks are adequately posted, but there may be times that just plain thoughtlessness can lead to severe impacts on the environment. These acts range from shortcutting to actually driving over a tundra or meadow. Respect closures within the park; there is a very good reason. The survival of nesting piping plovers or peregrine falcons may depend on it. The hobby of birding can be a most enjoyable pastime. And it is one that costs very little and can be done with little or no special training. It can be done alone or in a group and at any time of the day or night. And there is nowhere on earth where birds are not the most obvious part of the natural environment.

Early naturalist Frank Chapman, in his *Handbook of Birds of Eastern North America*, summarized the enjoyment of birds better than anyone else. Chapman wrote that birds "not only make life upon the globe possible, but they may add immeasurably to our enjoyment of it. Where in all animate nature shall we find so marvelous a combination of beauty of form and color, of grace and power of motion, of musical ability and intelligence, to delight our eyes, charm our ears and appeal to our imagination?"🐦

2

Parks as Islands

The wild things on this earth are not to do with as we please.
They have been given to us in trust, and we must account for
them to the generations which will come after us and audit
our accounts.
— William T. Hornaday

The last known peregrine falcon aerie anywhere in the Appalachians was at Alum Cave Bluff in the heart of Great Smoky Mountains National Park. The last viable peregrine population anywhere within the entire southern United States was at Big Bend National Park in West Texas. The discovery that populations of this and several other high-level predators were being decimated by DDT and other chlorinated hydrocarbons and the eventual banning of DDT use in the United States in 1972 were too late to save any of the eastern peregrines. The entire population of that subspecies became extinct in three decades. The West Texas peregrines, however, were well enough isolated and in sufficient numbers that an adequate breeding population remained.

The value of national parks is clear. For peregrines, the parks provided a last stronghold for their populations to withstand those human-induced pollutants. In the case of the West Texas peregrines, the population was adequately buffered so that birds survived long enough to restore that population to pre-DDT conditions, once the principal cause of the decline was eliminated. In the case of the Great Smoky Mountains population, insufficient buffers existed, and the eastern peregrine was lost forever.

During the 1980s, when peregrine restoration programs were being implemented, the Great Smoky Mountains habitat was one of the first selected. By 1990, peregrines again began to frequent their old haunts, including the actual nesting of one pair at Chimney Rock, Blue Ridge Parkway, in North Carolina.

In spite of an apparent peregrine "fix," many other bird populations are continuing to decline. The most serious losses are occurring in Neotropical species, birds that nest in the United States and Canada and winter to the south in the Greater Antilles, Mexico, Central America, and, to a lesser extent, South America. According to U.S. Fish and Wildlife Service Breeding Bird Survey data, 44 of 72 Neotropical species declined from 1978 to 1987. These include almost all the warblers, five vireos, five flycatchers, and various thrushes, buntings, orioles, tanagers, cuckoos, grosbeaks, and blue-gray gnatcatchers.

The reasons for the declines in Neotropical species are varied. These birds are less adaptable than most resident species. They have a shorter nesting season, with only enough time to produce one brood before they must depart on their southward journey. They also produce smaller clutches than the full-time residents. And most of the Neotropical species place their nests in the open, either on the ground or on shrubs or trees. Their nests, therefore, are more susceptible to predators than those of the full-time residents, many of which are cavity nesters (woodpeckers, chickadees, titmice, wrens, and bluebirds). If a raccoon, skunk, or fox were to destroy the nest of a full-time resident, the bird could start over again, but one episode of predation or parasitism can destroy an entire breeding season for a Neotropical bird.

Breeding bird studies within the fragmented environment of Washington, D.C., from 1947 through 1978 revealed that six Neotropical species (yellow-billed cuckoo, ruby-throated hummingbird, yellow-throated vireo, northern parula, hooded and Kentucky warbler) could no longer be found. And several other species, including the Acadian flycatcher, wood thrush, red-eyed vireo, ovenbird, and scarlet tanager, had declined by 50 percent. Conversely, at Great Smoky Mountains National Park, breeding bird censuses conducted in the late 1940s and repeated in 1982-83 "revealed no evidence of a widespread decline in Neotropical migrants within the large, relatively unfragmented forest" of the park, according to the National Fish & Wildlife Foundation. These divergent examples, peregrines in Big Bend and Neotropical breeders in the Great Smoky Mountains, demonstrate the value of large natural parks as preserves for the perpetuation of wildlife resources.

Threats to the Parks

North America's national parks are not immune to abundant threats. Every park has experienced impacts that threaten its ecological integrity. Although the exterior shell may appear unchanged, and the average visitor may find the scene pretty much the same year after year, the parks' fragile ecological web possesses a number of damaged strands.

During the early days, most of the natural parks had sufficient buffers around them that the hearts of the parks were adequately insulated from development and pollution that occurred outside their borders. But with continued population growth and increased adjacent land uses, the parks' buffer zones dwindled. Many of today's parks are bordered by farmlands that are maintained by chemicals, forests that are clear-cut, industrial centers, malls, and housing developments. Widespread air pollution reaches great distances and affects even the most remote parkscapes.

Inside the parks can be found roadways, trails, campgrounds, and other facilities, all designed to permit greater human use of the resources. But they are often poorly sited and designed so that they increase fragmentation and stress resources already threatened by the abundance of external perturbations.

Habitat degradation within the parks by improper management can have serious consequences to the park's bird life. Any fragmentation reduces the integrity of the unit, lowering its value for wild species. New sites increase access to the forest interior for predators that feed on birds and their eggs; parasitic cowbirds that lay their eggs in other species' nests; exotic house sparrows, European starlings, and other invaders that compete for nesting space and food; and exotic plants that can drastically change the habitat. Cuts into the forest interior also increase populations of native open area birds, such as American crows, blue jays, and grackles, that prey on other birds.

Once a park's natural ecosystem has been damaged by fragmentation and pollution, all the resources are much more susceptible to impacts from natural disasters such as hurricanes, floods, fire, and diseases. These catastrophes can seriously affect small, fragmented bird populations that already have been reduced by pollution, predators, parasites, and competitors.

Nature is never static. Environmental changes are part of every natural system. But a healthy bird population is better able to withstand those changes. Wildland fires, which occur within most of our forest, shrub, and grassland communities, are one example. Indeed, many plants and animals are fire dependent. Some pinecones must burn to open, drop their seeds, and regenerate. Woodpeckers frequent freshly burned sites to feed on various wood-boring beetles that inhabit host trees weakened by natural fires.

Native insect infestations can also cause major changes in an environment and can have a significant influence on an area's bird life. For instance, Cape May and bay-breasted warblers are sometimes referred to as "spruce budworm warblers" because of their response to spruce budworm invasions. Cape May warbler population growth may accelerate from one season to the next, from being uncommon or rare to being the single most abundant bird in the forest, soon after the start of a spruce budworm outbreak.

There also are examples of behavioral changes due to environmental opportunities. Examples include Assateague's tundra swans, which have discovered an easier wintertime food supply in the grain fields on Maryland's Eastern Shore and no longer totally depend on aquatic vegetation in the seashore's freshwater ponds. And several species of ducks and some Canada geese no longer migrate but remain all year in one area to take advantage of readily available food supplies without the risk of extensive journeys. Many of these species frequent city parks and other protected sites to avoid hunters.

Black-backed and herring gulls also have taken advantage of new food supplies at dump sites developed along the entire eastern seaboard. Populations of these aggressive species have increased substantially, to the point that several species of terns are threatened by the gulls, which feed on tern eggs and chicks.

North America's eastern forests also are affected by a number of nonnative organisms that have been either accidentally or purposefully introduced. The most profound environmental change occurred when chestnut blight, a fungus native to Chinese chestnut trees, was accidentally introduced into North America's eastern deciduous forests. It radically transformed the composition and appearance of the entire eastern North American landscape. At one time, one out of every three forest trees was an American chestnut, often towering over the canopy higher than any other species. Today, American chestnuts exist only as immature trees within the forest undergrowth, no longer the forest dominant that was able to produce the large valuable fruits that fed an array of wildlife and supported a commercial enterprise.

Other nonnative organisms that affect our eastern forests include balsam woolly aphids, gypsy moths, Dutch elm disease, white pine blister rust, European elm bark bettle, and European-Asiatic fungus. Balsam woolly aphids (adelgid) were accidentally introduced into the Appalachians about 1900. They have since spread throughout the Appalachians and are causing massive die-offs of the native Fraser fir, a dominant tree of the spruce-fir habitats that occurs only in the extreme highlands of the Appalachians. Toxins released into the trees by the feeding insects disrupt the nutrient flow and literally starve the trees to death. The loss of Fraser firs not only has affected the unique spruce-fir communities in the eastern highlands but also has destroyed the Fraser fir Christmas tree industry.

Although extinction is part of the natural process, the rate of extinction has never been so swift as it is at present. The International Union for the Conservation of Nature and Natural Resources (IUCN) predicts that by the year 2000 the world will have lost 20 percent of all extant species.

The greatest losses are occurring within the tropical forests, where many of our songbirds spend their winters. *The Global 2000 Report to the President* stated, "Between half a million and 2 million species—15 to 20 percent of all species on earth—could be extinguished by 2000, mainly because of loss of habitat but also in part because of pollution. Extinction of species on this scale is without precedent in human history. . . . One-half to two-thirds of the extinctions projected to occur by 2000 will result from the clearing or degradation of tropical forests."

In North America, more than 500 kinds of plants and animals have become extinct since the arrival of the first Europeans. Seven species have disappeared since 1973, when the U.S. Congress enacted the Endangered Species Act. Canada established the Committee on the Status of Endangered Wildlife in Canada in 1977. Since then, more than 560 species have been listed as "threatened" or "endangered," and 4,100 more are "candidate species." Endangered species are those in danger of becoming extinct; threatened species are those on the verge of becoming endangered.

Today, the concept of threatened and endangered species is an accepted part of our world. Significant decisions are based on whether a species is "listed" or not. And many of our "T and E" species have become household terms. Who has not heard of the plight of the peregrine falcon, humpback whale, and snail darter?

The shortcoming of the Endangered Species Act is that it addresses individual species instead of communities of plants and animals. It attempts to restore species without giving adequate attention to the natural processes on which they depend. And at a time with inadequate funding and moral support, only the more charismatic species are considered.

An endangered ecosystem act would have much greater success in protecting species if large tracts of landscape that contain several threatened and endangered species were given adequate protection. These larger areas are the essence of the national parks.

The bottom line is that our North American birds are losing their breeding grounds, winter habitats, and all of the stopover places in between.

What Is Being Done within the Parks

Much has been written about the threats to park resources. The National Park Service itself has been in the forefront of expressing concern about those threats. A major "State of the Parks" initiative was undertaken in 1980 and 1981 to identify the threats and to establish a program for preventing additional threats and mitigating current impacts. Parts of that strategy continue to the present, but other portions were eliminated, reduced, or ignored due to in-house bureaucracy or insufficient funding.

In Canada, the National Parks Act was amended in 1988 to require the minister of the environment to report to the Parliament on the "State of the Parks" every two years. In response, Canada's "Green Plan" was developed and includes the goal of setting aside 12 percent of Canada's total lands and waters as protected space. The Green Plan includes targets and specific actions, including five new national parks by 1996 and completion of the Canadian Parks System by the year 2000.

The majority of the eastern national parks, from Forillon on Canada's Gaspé Peninsula to Fort Jefferson off the southern tip of the Florida Keys, are involved in one way or another with bird-oriented research, monitoring, and restoration activities. Research studies are varied and include human impacts on shorebirds along the Outer Banks, migratory birds' use of barrier islands at Gulf Islands, common loons as indicators of the health of park lakes at Kejimkujik and Cape Breton Highlands, ecology and distribution of harlequin ducks at Acadia, the longest-running peregrine falcon banding study in existence at Assateague, the longest-running tern banding study in existence at Fort Jefferson, and the effects of spruce-fir forest decline on breeding songbirds in the Great Smoky Mountains.

Monitoring projects include an abundance of Christmas Bird Counts; numerous breeding bird surveys; many hawk watch projects; several waterfowl, colonial water bird, and shorebird censuses; black-legged kittiwake and associated seabird surveys at Forillon; a secretive marsh bird survey at Assateague; wood stork surveys at Everglades; and a wide array of projects designed to monitor populations of various threatened or endangered species. These include wintering bald eagles along the Delaware River and at Canaveral; piping plovers at most of the coastal parks; roseate, common, least, and arctic terns at several coastal parks, including the largest common tern colony in eastern North America at Kouchibouguac; and red-cockaded woodpeckers at Big Cypress and Congaree Swamp. Restoration programs include bald eagles at Gulf Islands and peregrine falcons at Acadia, Blue Ridge Parkway, Forillon, Fundy, Great Smoky Mountains, New River Gorge, and Shenandoah.

In addition, the U.S. National Park Service and Canadian National Parks Service are participating in the Neotropical Migratory Bird Conservation Program, as coordinated by the

National Fish and Wildlife Foundation. The primary focus of this program will be to "integrate research, monitoring, and management (including ecological restoration activities) on behalf of migratory nongame birds" for "the conservation of Neotropical migratory birds."

Early emphasis has been placed on the development of a network for parks and protected areas in the Western Hemisphere that are linked by Neotropical migratory birds. A migratory bird watch program has begun in more than 30 parks as one way to develop linkages between pertinent park units.

Yet in spite of the parks' mandates for unaltered ecosystems, the dual charge of "protection and enjoyment" has too often been interpreted to mean that the parks are meant primarily for people instead of the resources they contain. And so even the largest of the parks have undergone changes to benefit the human visitor while at the same time creating more chinks in the parks' ecological integrity. These incremental bites may seem insignificant separately, but together they have eaten into the very fabric that keeps parks viable. Many of our national parks are little more than skeletons of their former selves.

Today's national parks more and more are becoming islands within a great sea of disturbance. They can be equated with sea islands, with few connections to continental sources for species renewal. The longer an island is isolated, the less its flora and fauna have in common with other communities, and the greater likelihood of species loss.

The Value of National Parks

How important are national parks for the perpetuation of our North American bird life? Except for a very few of the largest and most remote of the public forests and refuges, and an insignificant scattering of private preserves, only the national parks are dedicated to the preservation of complete ecosystems. The vast majority of other managed areas are primarily dedicated either to the perpetuation of only one or a few species or to the area's multiple use values. The perpetuation of unaltered ecosystems too often is of secondary importance.

In spite of changes, the national parks still represent some of the finest of our natural environments in existence. Many of the units contain some of the least disturbed habitats in North America. And

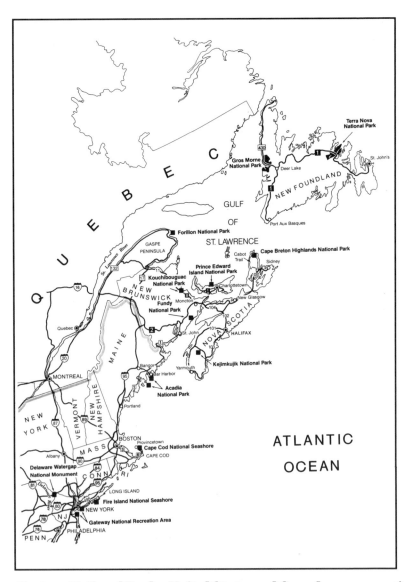

Eastern National Parks, United States and Canada, upper portion

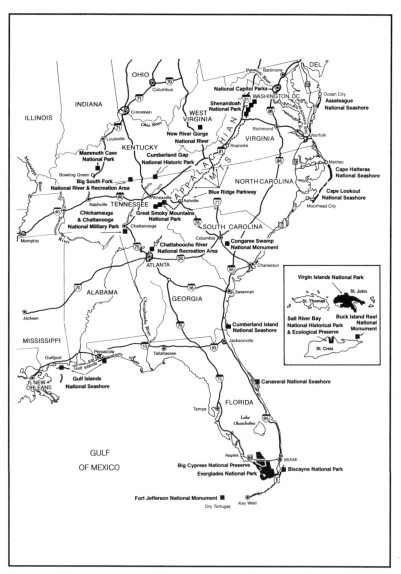

Eastern National Parks, United States and Canada, lower portion

each national park increases in value with every passing day.

The national parks contain far more than tracts of natural landscape, scenic beauty, and places of inspiration. The parks literally serve as biological baselines for the continent. There can be found gene pools of diversity that have disappeared almost everywhere else. The national parks contain our last remaining outdoor laboratories in which we can learn about the past so as to understand the future. There can be found the last reasonably intact examples of what North America was like before our resources were exploited for the benefit of a few.

A survey of the national parks quickly reveals that the park system is far from complete. Many of North America's major biotic communities have been left unprotected. Both the United States and Canada have recognized this shortcoming, have taken steps to identify the needs, and are trying to complete the system.

In addition, only a few of the parks and reserves are large enough to represent a complete ecosystem. Few parks contain a complete spectrum of natural processes that shape the ecosystem, so that the nutrient, hydrologic, fire, and other natural cycles are allowed to function unfettered by human constraints.

The key to long-term perpetuation of native species is the complete protection of intact ecosystems. They must be fully protected from all degrading activities, including grazing, timber cutting, mining, all forms of pollution, fragmentation by overdevelopment or overprotection (such as fire roads), and various forms of recreation that are not compatible with the purpose of the park.

C. F. Brockman understood the greatest value of the parks when he wrote,

> The national parks are charged with the obligation of preserving superlative natural regions, including wilderness areas, for the benefit of posterity. Attentiveness to the pleasure and comfort of the people is essential but it cannot mean catering to absolutely unlimited numbers unless the second function is to destroy the first. In a theatre, when the seats in the house have been sold out and the available standing room also has been preempted, the management does not jeopardize the main event by allowing still more onlookers to crowd upon the stage and impede the unfolding of the drama.

ATLANTIC MARITIME

One swallow does not make a summer, but one skein of geese, cleaving the murk of a March thaw, is the spring. . . . A chipmunk, emerging for a sunbath but finding a blizzard, has only to go back to bed. But a migrating goose, staking two hundred miles of black night on the chance of finding a hole in the lake, has no easy chance of retreat. His arrival carries the conviction of a prophet who has burned his bridges.

—Aldo Leopold

3

Acadia National Park, Maine

Common eiders and black guillemots were common below Otter Point that summer morning. More than a dozen eiders, mostly youngsters, were swimming in the surf about 100 feet below my rather precarious perch on the granite shore. I could almost look down their throats as they searched among the brown algae that covered the rocks for blue mussels, a sea snail known to make up an extremely high percentage of their diet. They also feed on clams, whelks, crabs, and an occasional fish. Swallowed whole, the shellfish are broken into fine pieces by the birds' powerful gizzards.

The common eider is the largest North American duck, and the breeding male is one of the most striking of all waterfowl. Its black, white, and lime green head pattern is unique. A heavy black line extends through the eye and onto the upper mandible, forming an edge to the lime green bill. Its body is black below and light above except for a large white patch on the wings and greenish sides of the neck. In flight, the wings resemble black-and-white triangles. It is a very colorful bird. The female, however, is drab and colorless, well camouflaged for nesting under shrubs, spruce foliage, and beach litter. Both sexes possess the same profile: stocky and thick-necked, with a bill featuring a bare frontal plate.

Mount Desert Island (the heart of Acadia National Park) and adjacent Penobscot Bay are the southern edge of the common eider's nesting range. It is more a duck of the Arctic than the temperate United States. Eiders migrate south of their breeding range only when they are forced to do so to find adequate food.

The dozen birds in front of me were all females and immatures. Males flock together after nesting and depart for the open sea by late

Common eider

July, leaving the family chores to the females. One of the adults was perched on the algae-covered sea rock, preening. Several slightly curled feathers had been plucked, and I watched as the slight breeze moved them off the rock into the surf where they remained afloat, as light as eiderdown. I couldn't help but wonder how many feathers it would take to stuff one pillow. Eider feathers are the best natural substance known for insulating jackets, sleeping bags, and such.

As I watched the eiders maneuver in the surf, two all-black guillemots, only half eider size, suddenly came into view. These black guillemots possess all-black bodies except for large, conspicuous, bright white wing patches. I also could see their bright red legs and feet that angled out to the side of their bodies. I switched my attention to these two birds, probably a male and female. I couldn't help but wonder why these two species of seabirds lead such different lives. Eiders apparently have little male-female bonding, while the smaller guillemots often mate for life. They certainly seemed to be enjoying each other's company that day. One suddenly dived underwater and was gone for almost a minute before surfacing alongside its mate. I assumed it had detected food somewhere below and had gone down for a quick bite. Black guillemots have been reported to dive to 165 feet for marine worms and other seafood.

They can "fly" underwater, propelling themselves with their short, strong wings and steering with their legs and webbed feet. A favorite food is rock eel, a small fish that lives under loose rocks.

I sat at Otter Point for an hour or more watching these and other birds visible from the overview. The herring gull was the most numerous species that day. This is a very large gull with a white body, gray mantle (top of wings), and red spot on the lower mandible. A couple of great black-backed gulls were perched on the rocks off to my right. They possess very black mantles, in contrast to those of the gray herring gulls. Several smaller laughing gulls, also with black foreheads, cruised by as well.

Double-crested cormorants also were present. Most were perched upright along the cliffs, but those in the water showed little more than their long dark necks. Their bright yellow throats were evident through binoculars. These birds spent a lot of time underwater where they, I knew, were swimming down their fish prey. I watched one cormorant flying across the near horizon, and I could actually see the double crest of its head feathers, which has given the bird its name.

Otter Point was a wonderful place to watch birds that morning. It also provided an Atlantic perspective of the Schoodic Peninsula to the far left and Little Cranberry and Baker islands to the right. And the view northward into the park included Cadillac and Dorr mountains behind the calm waters of Otter Cove.

The Park Environment

For anyone who arrives at Acadia National Park from the south, it should be obvious that here is a much different environment than can be found in the southern parks. The dominating broadleaf forests of the Appalachian region have given way to a mixed forest of conifers and hardwoods. Mount Desert (pronounced De-zert) Island is a land of spruce-fir forests, northern hardwoods, villages and fields, and bare rock. It contains numerous lakes, ponds, and wetlands, all surrounded by the Atlantic Ocean.

Mount Desert Island is actually situated within the Gulf of Maine, where the gulf waters maintain a maritime climate with moderate air temperatures, producing pleasant summers and moderate winters. More inland areas have warmer summers and much colder winters.

A part of the Canadian life zone extends south of the border along the coast of Maine and on smaller areas of mountaintops in New England and New York. The dominant trees of this zone at Acadia include red and white spruce, balsam fir (often grown commercially for Christmas trees), and lesser amounts of red maple and white birch.

The northern hardwood forest occurs primarily on the eastern half of Mount Desert Island and is largely the result of a 1947 forest fire that burned for 26 days over 18,000 acres (7,285 ha) of mature forest, almost one-third of the island. The recovering vegetation is dominated by the hardwoods, especially quaking and big tooth aspens, paper and gray birches, and pin cherry, with an understory of low blueberry. A spruce understory is now present in many areas.

The two sides of the park are literally split by Sommes Sound, which is the only true fjord in the continental United States. Sommes Sound was formed during the last Ice Age (between 10,000 and 13,000 years ago) when ice scooped out a deep depression in what is now Mount Desert Island. Most of the park's topography shows evidence (U-shaped valleys, rounded mountaintops, and striations on the rock itself) of the effects of the receding ice sheet.

Acadia National Park was initially established as Sieur de Monts National Monument in 1916, the same year in which the National Park Service itself was established. But three years later Congress redesignated the monument Lafayette National Park, making it the first national park east of the Mississippi River. Finally, in 1929, the park's name was changed to Acadia, derived from the French term for most of the northeastern United States.

The park's total size is approximately 40,000 acres (16,188 ha) and includes Mount Desert Island and Isle au Haut and a portion of the Schoodic Peninsula to the north. The largest park unit of more than 30,000 acres (12,141 ha) is on Mount Desert Island, where there are more than 150 miles (241 km) of hiking trails and 50 miles (80 km) of "carriage roads." These delightful trails were constructed as horse and carriage routes by John D. Rockefeller, Jr., who donated one-third of the island to the National Park Service.

The park's summertime visitor center, located near the northern entrance, contains an information center, exhibits, and a sales outlet for publications, including several books on the park's bird life, bird field guides, videos, and the like. A wintertime visitor center is maintained at park headquarters. A checklist of the park bird life is available at no cost. In addition, the park maintains seasonal charts of bird activity that provide good up-to-date information about the best places in the park to find the birds.

Interpretive programs are provided throughout the summer season and include evening bird talks at various locations and bird field trips that start at Sieur de Monts. Up-to-date information on interpretive programs is published monthly in the park's newspaper, *Beaver Log*, available at all visitor contact sites.

Camping is available in the park only at Blackwoods and Seawall campgrounds. Additional campgrounds and lodging are available at many of the nearby communities.

Additional information can be obtained from the Superintendent, Acadia National Park, Bar Harbor, ME 04609; (207) 288-3338.

Bird Life

Water, rock, and forest merge together at Acadia in a way that is all-prevailing. There are few places where the forces of nature create such a harsh but gentle land. And so it is with the bird life. Tiny, delicate warblers sing their songs within the northern forests that grow right up to the booming surf, where seabirds search for food among the tidal surges.

Acadia National Park has been called the "warbler capital of the United States" for a very good reason. At least 21 species of warblers are known to nest there, more than in any other national park except Great Smoky Mountains and Blue Ridge Parkway. And although there are numerous localities within the park where one can find a good variety of warblers during their nesting season, none is as popular as the Wonderland Trail. This easy trail, located in the southwestern portion of Mount Desert Island, passes through a beautiful spruce-dominated forest festooned with lichens. Numerous mosses and other wetland plants form lush green carpets.

Warbler songs literally fill the air along the Wonderland Trail during May and June. The most numerous warbler is the **black-throated green warbler**, a name that suits this beautiful bird exceptionally well. Its most striking features are its black throat and bright yellow face with greenish ear patches. It seems to prefer the treetops, and from there it fills the air with its very distinct song, a wispy but slightly hoarse "zee zee zee zee zoo zee." Frank Chapman wrote, "There is a quality about it like the droning of bees; it seems to voice the restfulness of a midsummer day."

The **American redstart** also is common in summer along the Wonderland Trail, but it prefers a mixed habitat with conifers and deciduous vegetation. Males are black and orange-red, and females are black and yellow. Both can be very obvious, due to their showy plumage and method of fly catching on the wing. They will often drop from limb to limb in pursuit of some insect, with tail and wings spread like a butterfly. This behavior, and their habit of spreading their wings and tail when perched, shows off their brilliant colors better than any of the other warblers.

In Latin America, where this warbler usually spends its winters, it is called *candelita*, or little torch. Its song is a thin, almost hissing "see-see see-see-see," rising slightly at the end. Its call is also rather distinct, a loud, sharp, and slightly slurred "chick." See chapter 18, Blue Ridge Parkway, for additional information on this species.

The other warblers that nest within the park include the black-and-white, Nashville, northern parula, yellow, magnolia, Cape May, black-throated blue, yellow-rumped, Blackburnian, chestnut-sided, bay-breasted, blackpoll, and ovenbird in the forests or forest edge habitats; the Tennessee, Wilson's, northern waterthrush, and common yellowthroat in wet areas with alders; and the palm warbler in bogs.

A few of the other songbirds that nest along the Wonderland Trail include the yellow-bellied flycatcher, black-capped chickadee, red-breasted nuthatch, gray catbird, American robin, wood thrush, dark-eyed junco, and white-throated and song sparrows. Almost everyone knows what a **chickadee** looks and sounds like. It is one of those birds that everyone knows intuitively, from Christmas cards, household symbols, or whatever. But Acadia possesses two species, black-capped and boreal. Black-caps occur in a wide east-west belt across central North America, but the boreal chickadee is found only in northern North America. A resident of the boreal forests, it reaches the United States in only a few places. The two species are about the same size, and both have a black bib, but the boreal is much browner in color and sings a very different song than the clear "chick-a-dee-dee-dee" of the black-cap. The boreal chickadee's song is a wheezy and drawled "tseet-a-dee-dee."

Another common song of spring and summer is that of the **wood thrush**, a robin-sized bird of the forests. This reddish-colored bird with boldly marked black spots on a white breast is more often heard than seen. Its beautiful, flutelike song, "ee-o-lee," echoes from the forests, especially during early mornings and late afternoons throughout spring, summer, and into early fall.

Fall migration at Acadia begins with the arrival of the earliest shorebirds that have already completed nesting on the tundra and are heading south for the winter. By mid-August the mud flats can be teeming with shorebirds. Most numerous are greater and lesser yellowlegs, spotted, semipalmated, and least sandpipers, northern phalarope, and short-billed dowitcher.

Starting in late August and lasting until mid-November, with a peak in mid-September, raptors move across Mount Desert Island, utilizing the available thermals from the north-south ridges. Sharp-shinned and broad-winged hawks and American kestrels make up the bulk of the migrant raptors.

Wintertime can produce a very different set of birds. All of the warblers, vireos, thrushes, and other summer resident songbirds are far south in the West Indies, Mexico, Central America, or South America. But winter is when the hardier waterbirds, those that are able to find food at the northern edge of the open water, persist within the Gulf of Maine. Among them is one of the most bizarre of all the waterfowl, the harlequin duck.

The **harlequin duck** male is almost gaudy. It possesses an overall slate blue body with chestnut stripes on the head and sides; white markings scattered here and there over its body; a large crescent on the face; and stripes and spots on the neck, including a collar that almost fully circles the head, and scapulars. The name "harlequin" was derived from a comical Italian character of the theater who wore a mask and multicolored tights.

Approximately 400 harlequins overwinter on Isle au Haut and associated islands. They are sometimes found feeding with eiders and black scoters along the shore of Mount Desert Island as well. This habitat is much different from the torrential streams on which breeding harlequins are found in Labrador, Greenland, and Iceland. Recent monitoring activities in winter, undertaken by NPS biologist Judy Hazen and colleague Glen Mittlehauser, suggest that although the overall Atlantic Coast population of these sea ducks has declined in recent years, the Isle au Haut population has remained about the same.

However, Acadia's **bald eagles** declined from 1960 to 1975 and have not yet recovered. These large, white-headed symbols of America reside within the park throughout the year. Although bald eagles occasionally visit Mount Desert Island, the greatest opportunity for seeing this bird, as well as nesting ospreys, is to take the two-hour Frenchman's Bay boat trip aboard the *Acadian*, which leaves Bar Harbor three times daily. On the longer whale watcher trip, which covers a more extensive area, one is likely to spot some of the hard-to-find seabirds, such as greater and Manx shearwaters, Wilson's storm-petrel, and even the Atlantic puffin.

Christmas bird counts have been taken on Mount Desert Island for more than twenty years and provide the best indication of winter species that may occur there. Counters regularly find 55 to 60 species and about 4,800 individuals. In 1991, the dozen most numerous of those were (in descending order of abundance) the common eider, herring gull, mourning dove, American black duck, black-capped chickadee, great black-backed gull, dark-eyed junco, blue jay, oldsquaw, American crow, European starling, and mallard.

The first sign of spring, often by late March, is usually the soft cooing of the mourning dove or the "chick-a-dee-dee-dee" songs of the black-capped chickadee. And within a few days, open blue water appears in the larger lakes and ponds and magically attracts common loons and ducks. The hysterical laughter of the common loon is one of the the park's most notable springtime melodies. Its black-and-white body and green head give it a truly majestic appearance.

Of Acadia's more than 340 bird species, none are better harbingers of spring than the **American woodcocks**. These chunky, robin-sized shorebirds are among the earliest to commence courtship. Woodcocks prefer dense woods and are crepuscular in nature, going about their territorial activities at dawn and dusk. They select open

American woodcock

grassy places in which to court. The woodcock's incredible sky dance was best described by Frank Chapman:

> He begins on the ground with a formal, periodic *peent, peent,* an incongruous preparation for the wild rush that follows. It is repeated several times before he springs from the ground, and on whistling wings sweeps out on the first loop of a spiral which may take him 300 feet above the ground. Faster and faster he goes, louder and shriller sounds his wing-song; then after a moment's pause, with darting, headlong flight, he pitches in zigzags to the earth, uttering as he falls a clear, twittering whistle (actually produced by the wings). He generally returns to near the place from which he rose, and the *peent* is at once resumed as a preliminary to another round in the sky.

The American woodcock is a most unusual member of the sandpiper family. It is one of the few sandpipers that do not occur on the beach or mud flats and rarely are found in marshes. It is instead a sandpiper of the bottomlands and wet woods. It most often feeds in clearings and brushy areas, often in small congregations, where it may eat more than its weight of earthworms—up to 55—daily. It pokes its long bill deep into the mud and uses the tips of its flexible mandibles like tweezers to feel for and extract earthworms, which it swallows whole. Hundreds of probe holes can sometimes be found in the mud of choice feeding sites, a feature that can be used to detect this species.

Other sounds of early spring at Acadia include the hollow booming of ruffed grouse within the old growth forests, the deep honking of passing Canada geese, the clear whistle notes of American robins, the liquid gurgling of red-winged blackbirds at cattails, and the musical trill from the forest of singing dark-eyed juncos.

Those sounds mark the time for the National Park Service interpreters to change their bird locating tables from winter to spring and to prepare themselves for the rush of visitors who will arrive to enjoy the late winter nights and warmer days.

The trails through the better bird habitats again will be trod by those who want to partake of Acadia's most exciting attractions. Southern land birds are best found at Sieur de Monts, within the old burned area that now contains a good stand of more southerly deciduous hardwoods. Northern land birds are best found in Otter Point's forest, which was missed by the 1947 burn. Other good areas for these birds include the Western Mountain Road, Ship Harbor Nature Trail, and Wonderland Trail. Water birds can best be found at Long and Jordan ponds. Seabirds are most numerous at Otter Point, Hunters Head, and Bass Harbor Head.

Seth Benz or another of Acadia's seasonal rangers will again lead visitors on bird walks. These programs, aimed at the beginner, provide wonderful opportunities to learn about birds and to see some of the park's best bird habitats. I spent one rainy morning in August with Seth and six other hardy souls, and in spite of the bad weather, we found more than two dozen species within three hours. Everyone in the group saw all of the birds.

It also is the time of year to watch and see if Acadia's most exciting bird—the peregrine falcon—will again reclaim its ancestral nesting sites on the high, inaccessible cliffs of Mount Desert Island. A peregrine restoration program was undertaken in the park from 1984 through 1986, and hacked birds returned to nest by 1988. Finally in 1991, three young were fledged, the first successful nesting in the park since 1956. See chapter 23 on Assateague and chapter 19 on Great Smoky Mountains for additional information on peregrines as migrants and their status within the Appalachians.

In summary, Acadia's bird checklist includes 344 species; 147 of those have been confirmed to nest since 1965. Of the 147 breeding species, 31 are water and marsh birds, 11 are hawks and owls, and 21 are warblers. Ten are winter visitors only: northern pintail, king eider, Barrow's goldeneye, gyrfalcon, common black-headed gull, snowy and short-eared owls, northern hawk-owl, bohemian waxwing, and common redpoll.

Birds of Special Interest
Common eider. Acadia National Park is at the southern edge of this bird's nesting range, and it occurs at saltwater areas all about Mount Desert Island. Males are colorful and obvious but move out to sea by early August.

American woodcock. One of the park's first birds to display in spring, the woodcock's courtship behavior is classic. Males perform a spectacular courtship flight. It is otherwise a heavy-set little shorebird with an extremely long bill used for probing for earthworms.

Black guillemot. Pairs of these birds occur along the coastline. It is readily identified by its bright white wing patches, which contrast with its all-black body.

Bald eagle. This majestic bird is most often seen at Frenchman's Bay. Its all-white head and tail and dark body make it one of America's best-known birds; it is the symbol of the country.

Peregrine falcon. Recent restoration activities inside the park will undoubtedly increase the chances of seeing this large, remarkable raptor.

Black-throated green warbler. This common warbler possesses a black throat and bright yellow face with a greenish ear patch. It prefers conifer treetops, where it sings its slightly hoarse song all summer long.

American redstart. The males are black and orange-red, and the females are black and yellow, but both are very showy in their feeding behavior. They are most common in mixed forests.

4

Fundy National Park, New Brunswick

A ruffed grouse stood motionless at the side of the trail. It did not realize that it had been discovered. I slowly raised my binoculars and focused on the bird. And what a wonderful bird it was. It was much redder than those I had seen farther south at Shenandoah and the Great Smokies. Its small crest was partially raised, a show of alertness, no doubt. The fan-shaped tail was in good light; I could see the trim, narrow bands and the broad, very dark terminal band. The blackish feathers of the neck were smooth, not ruffed as they are during the nesting season. The ruffed neck has given this bird its name.

It apparently decided that I was not a danger, and it began to walk very slowly away from me down the middle of the trail. It was not until then that I detected other grouse within the low shrubbery, nearby. There were at least three additional birds. And when a young grouse suddenly walked out into the open trail, I realized that I had found a hen and three rather large chicks. The two birds continued down the trail, with the other two youngsters snaking through the undergrowth on a parallel course. They suddenly veered to the left and disappeared.

The ruffed grouse is one of the truly spectacular birds of the northern forest, and it is reasonably common, too. I had walked the Whitetail Trail for only about a hundred yards beyond Fundy's Chignecto Campground before discovering this family group. One of the park's full-time residents, it occurs in all habitats and at all times of the year.

Ruffed grouse

Ruffed grouse are easiest to find during early spring. That is when the males "drum," an act of marking territory as well as attracting a mate. The thumping noise produced can be heard at a considerable distance. It begins with a loud and measured thump, then gradually speeds up before dropping off in volume. It has been written as: "thump—thump—thump—thump, thump, thump-rup rup rup rup r-r-r-r-r-r." The male produces the drumming sound by beating the air with his wings while standing upright and bracing with his broad tail feathers. During courtship the bird's shiny black ruff is conspicuous as a showy, feathery collar that apparently helps to arouse its mate. The hollow, accelerating booming sound of the ruffed grouse is one of nature's most exciting melodies.

There were several other birds present that August morning. The high-pitched calls of the seemingly ubiquitous golden-crowned kinglets resounded throughout the forest canopy. In the understory, dark-eyed juncos and white-throated sparrows were busy finding food and feeding young. And high overhead could be heard the musical warbles of white-winged crossbills, busy in their very late nesting season.

The Park Environment

The most notable feature of New Brunswick's Fundy National Park is the remarkable tides, which produce the world's greatest variation in their twice daily occurrence. The average tide range at the park is 30 feet (9 m), but spring tides (twice monthly when the sun and moon are aligned to produce a greater gravitational pull) can be over 43 feet (13 m). Tidal variation increases the farther up the bay one travels. Fundy National Park is located on the northern shore of Chignecto Bay, one of the subdivisions of the Bay of Fundy. The word "Fundy" is derived from *fendu*, French for "split." These remarkable tides affect all life within the park, from the hardy creatures that live within the intertidal zone, directly influenced by the rising or lowering water, to the forest species that experience only secondary effects.

The Acadian forest, characteristic of Canada's Maritime Provinces, makes up 93 percent of the park's landscape. At Fundy, this forest has been divided into four distinct communities: disturbed forest (37%), mixed softwood/hardwood forest (49%), hardwood forest (6%), and softwood forest (2%). The disturbed forest is composed largely of mixed forests that have been affected by the spruce budworm (which left many dead and dying red spruce and balsam fir trees), in conjunction with extensive glades of ferns and raspberry.

Fundy's mixed forest, composed chiefly of red spruce, balsam fir, yellow and white birch, red and sugar maple, and a lush ground cover dominated by mosses and ferns, is the best representation of the original Acadian forest. Since wildland fire is virtually nonexistent within this moist environment, the opening of the forest to permit the various stages of succession to commence is left to the spruce budworm and, to a lesser extent, to flooding from beaver dams.

Spruce budworms are, in their adult stage, a small brown moth. The population is cyclic, reaching a peak every 35 years or so when the caterpillars are so numerous that they consume enough young needles to kill many of their hosts. The 1968-1982 outbreak significantly reduced the area of the park covered with spruce-dominated mixed forest. That forest is being replaced by a very different disturbed forest that is dominated by birch, maple, balsam fir, red spruce, and raspberry.

Nonforest communities make up only 3 percent of the park, but these areas (wetlands, old fields, and human-use areas) are of some interest. The wetlands are particularly valuable for their diversity of flora and fauna.

Fundy National Park was established in 1948 to preserve 80 square miles (30 sq km) of the upper Bay of Fundy shoreline and adjacent coastal forest environment. Elevations range from sea level to 1,200 feet (366 m) on the hilly top of this highland outlier of the Appalachian Mountains. Topography consists of steep cliffs along the shoreline, rugged slopes, and broad, rolling ridge tops. Numerous tributaries join to form the two principal park rivers, the Upper Salmon and the Point Wolfe.

The park contains plenty of campgrounds at Chignecto, Park Headquarters, and Point Wolfe, as well as lodging, gift shop, restaurant, and recreation facilities, including 68 miles (109 km) of hiking trails. Information stations are located at the Wolfe Lake and Alma Beach entrances. Park literature, including the *Bird Guide* with a bird checklist, is available at these two information stations and at park headquarters near the village of Alma. Interpretive activities; talks and walks, including weekly bird walks; and a variety of recreational programs are provided in season. Schedules are available for the asking.

Fundy winters, which begin late due to the maritime influences, can be extreme, with 3 feet (1 m) or more of snow on the ground. Spring is equally late, so the park's visitor season does not begin until late May. July can be foggy along the coast, but September, October, and November are usually mild and beautiful.

Additional information can be obtained from the Superintendent, Fundy National Park, P.O. Box 40, Alma, New Brunswick E0A 1B0; (506) 887-2000.

Bird Life

The spruce budworm phenomenon has major influences on the park's bird life. In fact, there are two species—bay-breasted and Cape May warblers—that are widely known as "budworm warblers" because their populations are so influenced by budworm infestations and resultant spruce and fir die-offs. When outbreaks occur at Fundy, the spruce budworm caterpillars trigger a population explosion of both warblers. They become the park's most common bird species.

The **bay-breasted warbler** male can be striking in good light, with its deep chestnut crown, throat, and sides and bold black mask. William Bartram called it a "little chocolate-breasted titmouse." Females are duller and lack the black mask. This is one of the largest warblers. Conversely, it has a rather short, weak song that is similar to that of the black-and-white, a "seetzy seetzy seetzy see." Frank Chapman wrote that the song is "liquid and inarticulate." When there is plenty of food, bay-breasts can be found singing their strange songs from near the tops of hundreds of doomed spruce trees.

Bay-breasts respond immediately to spruce budworm outbreaks; they are otherwise one of the uncommon forest residents. Nests are built on horizontal branches of spruce and other trees as high as 50 feet (18 m) above the ground. The number of eggs (4 to 7) depends on the abundance of spruce budworms. Adults feed on these caterpillars, often searching high on the spruce trees, foraging

Bay-breasted warbler

along the branches and twigs, continuously wagging their tails. They also fly catch for flying insects.

The **Cape May warbler** male is a very handsome bird that is best identified by its very distinct chestnut cheek patch surrounded by bright yellow, by large white wing patches, and by heavy black streaks on its bright yellow chest. It also has a yellow rump. This warbler apparently reminded Alexander Wilson of a tiger, for he gave it the specific name of *tigrina*. Cape May songs are similar to those of the bay-breast but higher and on the same pitch, "seet seet seet seet."

Cape May nests are usually placed in the dense crown foliage of spruce or fir trees, sometimes as high as 60 feet (18 m) above the ground. They are next to impossible to find. Female Cape Mays approach the nest by creeping up the tree trunk, not flying directly to it. And they dive downward from the nest when departing.

David Christie, author of the park's *Bird Guide*, pointed out that in 1979, the park's 20 nesting warbler species "accounted for three-quarters of the estimated 110,000 pairs of birds breeding in Fundy National Park." Each species has its preferred niche, from mature forest to secondary forest to old fields and wetlands.

Coppermine Trail, which begins at Point Wolfe and makes a 2.8-mile (4.5-km) loop along a high forested slope, is one of the park's best birding routes. It passes through a beautiful stand of red spruce and balsam fir intermixed with birch and maple. This is a mature forest that is little affected by spruce budworm outbreaks because of its proximity to the coast. Springtime can be a riot of bird song. Nesting warblers to be expected include Tennessee, Nashville, northern parula, magnolia, black-throated blue, yellow-rumped, black-throated green, Blackburnian, bay-breasted, black-and-white, American redstart, and ovenbird.

The Coppermine Trail also is one of the better localities to experience the wonderful and varied melodies of the **Swainson's thrush**. This denizen of the forest, brownish with distinct buff eye ring, cheeks, and breast, more than makes up for its rather drab appearance by the character of its song. It has been described as an ascending spiral of whistles. Wayne Peterson wrote that its song is an "upward-rolling series of flutelike phrases, like wip-poor-wil-

wil-eez-see-see." The Swainson's thrush usually builds its nest in a low evergreen tree or bush.

Rob Walker, of the Fundy National Park staff, informed me that both the Swainson's and hermit thrushes are found along the Coppermine Trail but prefer very separated habitats. Swainson's occurs along the moist slopes, and the **hermit thrush** occurs on the drier ridge tops. It, too, has a wonderful flutelike song, a series of clear notes often repeated at different pitches. This little reddish-tailed bird is not spectacular, but, as Chapman wrote, "Its notes are not remarkable for variety of volume, but in purity and sweetness of tone and exquisite modulation they are unequaled." Hermit thrushes nest on the ground, often in fern glades.

The American robin is also a thrush that frequents these same woods. It, too, has a wonderful song and will often sing long into the evening hours. And during spring migration, the wood thrush also can be heard singing from these same slopes. The combination of these four thrushes vocalizing at the same time along the sylvan halls of the Coppermine Trail is almost more than can be imagined.

The Coppermine Trail also is a good area to see some of the more boreal (far northern) species with regularity. The **gray jay** is undoubtedly one of the best examples of the northern character of the Fundy landscape. This is the robin-sized, gray, black, and white jay that in many northern parks is called "camp robber" because of its habit of stealing food off campers' tables. Its silent, gliding flight and downy appearance, like a giant chickadee, make it hard to resist sharing a piece of bread or some other tender morsel.

Then there is the abundant **red-breasted nuthatch**, more often heard than seen. It is usually detected first by its nasal "toot," like a toy horn. It frequents conifers throughout the park, including the campgrounds. Seeing this little reddish-breasted bird walking head-first down a tree trunk or upside down under a tree limb makes one wonder about the law of gravity.

Caribou Plain Trail provides another good birding site with a varied environment that ranges from mixed forest to wetlands. Two small freshwater lakes, dammed by beavers, are bordered by alders and rushes. Early morning visitors may see moose feeding in these boggy ponds, although the woodland caribou, for which the trail was named, were extirpated from the region by overzealous hunters by the 1920s. The smaller of these lakes is a good place to find post-nesting American black and wood ducks. Also, this is the only location in the park where hooded mergansers raise their young.

Rusty blackbirds nest around the pond and bogs along the Caribou Plain Trail. They are of typical blackbird size and possess yellow eyes. Fall adults have rusty backs and wings, but much of that color wears off by the next nesting season. Swamp and Lincoln's sparrows nest along the pond edges, and an olive-sided flycatcher usually is singing its clear "quick-three-beers" song from the top of one of the snags.

The bulk of the nesting activity occurs in June and July, although there is some late nesting by species such as the **white-winged crossbills**. I found numerous pairs singing from the tops of the tallest conifers in mid-August. Rob Walker referred to this bird as a "boreal nomad" that can be common some years and completely absent others, utilizing cone crops (they extract the seeds with their crossed mandibles and tongue) over widespread areas of northern forest. They nest near the very top of spruce trees, so nesting is almost impossible to detect until they are feeding young. But their very lovely song, soft, sweet, and melodic, much like that of the American goldfinch, was common throughout the forest.

The park headquarters area is another excellent place to find birds throughout the year, and I found this area good for fall migrants. Hundreds of pine siskins, those mites of the coniferous forests, were already busy as I walked through the headquarters campground. Their thin, ascending trills were everywhere, blending with the wispy songs of the golden-crowned kinglets and toy horns of red-breasted nuthatches in the adjacent forest. Suddenly a couple of dozen warblers swept across the trees and landed in the open birches at the entrance station: Tennessees, black-throated blues, black-and-whites, and others that I missed when they abruptly moved on toward the coast.

I followed those songbirds across the open, manicured lawn that surrounds the headquarters area, where about three dozen barn swallows were out searching for breakfast. I heard a belted kingfisher call from the pond next to the amphitheater, and several

American crows took flight in front of me. Farther off was a pair of common ravens; one of these was a young bird that made very odd, squeaky, begging sounds. I saw the adult stuff something into the squeaker's throat.

Ahead was the edge of the bluff overlooking Alma Beach and Bay. I could see small birds busy among the birches and conifers that border the lawn. And as I drew closer I found myself observing literally hundreds of songbirds. Some were actively feeding among the foliage, but others seemed more intent on chasing one another about. I had hit the songbird jackpot! Migrants were everywhere.

During the next two hours, until the activity began to subside, I stood almost in one spot watching a parade of birds moving southwest along the bluff in front of me. I had a wonderful observation position to watch the birds in the adjacent trees as well as in the birches and shrubbery on the slope below me. At times the birds were as near as 30 or 40 feet. I recorded 45 species that morning within two hours, without moving more than 100 feet up and down the bluff.

Warblers made up the bulk of my sightings. Black-throated green and Tennessee warblers were the most numerous, but I also found substantial numbers of yellow, magnolia, yellow-rumped, and black-and-white warblers. And smaller numbers of Nashville, northern parula, chestnut-sided, Cape May, black-throated blue, and bay-breasted warblers, American redstarts, and common yellowthroats were there also. In addition, yellow-bellied, alder and least flycatchers, solitary vireo, and northern oriole were present in what seemed to be one huge bird party. I watched dozens of these southbound birds as they went about finding sufficient food to fuel their six- to eight-week journey to tropical climes where they would spend the winter.

These migrants had to be ever-alert to avoid becoming a meal for the sharp-shinned hawks and other birds of prey that nest and migrate along the Fundy shore. This area also is within the territory of a pair of **peregrine falcons**. Peregrines pose only a minimal threat to songbirds but are much more attracted to the hundreds of thousands of shorebirds (mostly semipalmated sandpipers) that use the Bay of Fundy as a refueling stop between their Arctic breeding grounds and their South American wintering homes. Peregrines are present thanks to a 10-year (1982-1991) release program carried out by Canada's Environment Department. Of 193 young peregrines allowed to fly free, the park falcons and four other pairs have taken up residency along New Brunswick's Bay of Fundy coastline.

The principal fall migration is complete at Fundy by mid-September, although a few late breeders may still be trickling through into November. Winter birds are few and far between compared with the summer birds. David Christie pointed out, "Bird populations vary greatly from one winter to the next. About 25 woodland species overwinter . . . but the population is small—only 2% to 10% that of summer."

Rob Walker compiles the park's annual Christmas counts and has reported an average of 43 species and approximately 850 birds each year. In 1990, the dozen most numerous species found were (in descending order) black-capped chickadee, golden-crowned kinglet, red-breasted nuthatch, snow bunting, American goldfinch, evening grosbeak, pine siskin, blue jay, American black duck, herring gull, common raven, and (even at Fundy) house sparrow.

In summary, a total of 285 bird species have been recorded for Fundy National Park and vicinity, according to Christie's *Bird Guide*. Most interesting are the boreal species that breed there: northern goshawk, yellow-bellied flycatcher, gray jay, boreal chickadee, Tennessee warbler, and Lincoln's sparrow. And the 20 species of nesting warblers make Fundy the warbler capital of Canada. Only 5 bird species are listed solely as winter residents/visitors: Barrow's goldeneye, golden eagle, gyrfalcon, thick-billed murre, and snowy owl.

Birds of Special Interest

Common eider. This is the common, large, black-and-white duck that dives for mussels close to shore in summer. The groups are composed mostly of molting males; the females and their young summer in the island-strewn lower bay.

Gray jay. Small family groups of this soft gray, black, and white jay can be found throughout Fundy's coniferous forests, particularly in the area of Chignecto Campground and Kinnie Brook Picnic Area.

Swainson's thrush. It usually is detected first by its beautiful song, an ascending series of flutelike phrases. Its buff eye ring, cheeks, and breast are distinct.

Cape May warbler. This bird has a distinct chestnut cheek patch surrounded by bright yellow; large, white wing patches; and heavy black streaks on its bright yellow chest.

Bay-breasted warbler. During spruce budworm invasions, this can be the park's most abundant bird. It has a deep chestnut crown, throat, and sides and a black mask.

White-winged crossbill. This boreal finch is abundant some years and absent other years. It is most often seen at the very top of a spruce, singing its distinct song. The male's red body and white-on-black wings help with identification.

5

Kejimkujik National Park, Nova Scotia

There is a mystical quality about the quavering song of the common loon. Once heard, it can never be forgotten. It can be very lonesome, almost soul-wrenching, or a soft and pleasing echo. But whichever the interpretation, it is undoubtedly nature's best representation of the northern lakes. And there is nowhere in the 152 square miles (59 sq km) of Kejimkujik National Park where the song of the common loon cannot be heard from early spring through late fall.

Larger than a duck, the loon flies with its neck and head stretched out and somewhat lower than the rest of its body, a seemingly awkward posture but one that can be recognized from a considerable distance. It swims low in the water, with neck curved and heavy, straight bill pointed slightly upward. A loon in breeding plumage is very striking, with a deep green head and neck, black-and-white spotted back and sides, and white chest and underparts.

Common loons are among the earliest birds to appear on the park's thawing lakes in April. Their arrival is a welcome signal that spring has finally arrived. Their presence begins the daylong and far-into-the-night chorus of loon songs. Park Ecologist Cliff Drysdale told me of an experience that he and a friend had one April night. The quiet darkness was shattered by "a sudden cacophony of loons all at the same time. Maybe two dozen. They sang a variety of songs for about two minutes, then suddenly they all were silent again." What connection do loons on different lakes have that triggers that sudden urge to sing in chorus?

Common loon

For me, the song of the loon represents the true essence of the northern wilderness. Each time that I hear that wild song, it reawakens my appreciation of the northern lakes surrounded by dense boreal forests. Louis Halle wrote, "The wildness of the loon, however, is not dependent on antiquity. It is a wildness uncontaminated by human associations."

Not until nesting is well under way do the loon calls subside. But by late summer, when the adults are accompanied by fledged young, the chorus commences once again. Only when the lakes freeze and the birds move to open water at sea or to the south are they silent. The young will remain in salt water until their third year, when they find their own freshwater lakes to nest and raise families.

A Canadian Wildlife Service survey revealed that twenty-two of the park's lakes contain at least one pair of common loons but that only birds utilizing lakes of more than 100 acres (40 ha) in size produce young. Kejimkujik Lake supports two to four pairs that produce young every year.

Drysdale also explained that common loons are monitored in the park as a way to assess the health of the lakes. Acid rain is known to affect the number and densities of fish species. So long as the loon's food base of brook trout, white perch, and white sucker (species that disappear with high levels of acidity) is present, the loons' continued nesting is assured.

The Park Environment

"Gentle waters and lush forests" reads the Canadian Parks Service brochure for Kejimkujik National Park, the southernmost of the maritime parks, 250 miles (402 km) directly east of Maine's Acadia National Park. Kejimkujik is composed of lakes and rivers (about 12 to 14% of the area) surrounded by Acadian forests that are more like those of northeastern Maine than forests elsewhere in Canada's Maritime Provinces.

The park's forests, usually divided into mixed and hardwood communities, are all-pervasive. The mixed forests make up about three-fourths of the landscape. Major softwood species include red spruce, eastern hemlock, white pine, and balsam fir. Major hardwoods include red maple, white birch, beech, and red oak.

Softwood forests cover less than one-third of the landscape but include a few stands of eastern hemlocks that may be more than 300 years old. Hardwood stands are rare and favor the ridges and drier portions of the park. Canopy trees are dominated by yellow birch and sugar maple.

Kejimkujik National Park was opened to the public in 1968, primarily as a wilderness park for recreational values. It has a network of both hiking trails and canoe routes. Vehicular access is available only from the northeastern entrance near Maitland Bridge, Nova Scotia. The park visitor center, just inside the entrance, contains an information station and exhibits. A small number of publications are sold. A bird checklist for the park is available, as are excellent interpretive brochures on the forests, waters, and other key elements. Several self-guided trails are available. Nature walks with a park interpreter are scheduled throughout the season; a schedule is posted at all key locations. Camping is available inside the park at Jeremys Bay, but lodging must be obtained in several adjacent communities.

In addition, there is a coastal section of the park, located west of Liverpool, Nova Scotia, between Port Joli and Port Mouton Headlands. The Seaside Adjunct contains coastal forests, wetlands, lakes, bays, and beautiful white sand beaches.

Additional information can be obtained from the Superintendent, Kejimkujik National Park, Maitland Bridge, Nova Scotia B0T 1N0; (902) 682-2770.

Bird Life

The Mersey Meadows Trail and overlook at park headquarters is a good place to begin a birding visit to the park. The meadow and open pond, visible from the overlook, can attract a surprisingly large number of birds in spring and summer. Common along the shore are great blue herons, waiting to stab unwary fish or frogs with their heavy bills. Red-winged blackbirds sing their gurgling "conk-ka-ree" song from the adjacent cattails and willows. The "witchity witchity witchity" songs of common yellowthroats can be abundant. And dozens of tree and barn swallows search the air over the meadow and pond for insect prey.

A careful observer can sometimes discover an **American bittern** among the cattails. This is a relatively large bird, about half the height of a great blue heron, but it is seldom seen fully in the open. It stalks its prey among the tall grasses or cattails at the pond's edge, and if startled, it will freeze perfectly still with its bill pointed skyward. It is otherwise a rather plain brown bird with dark brown streaks on its throat and chest and an elongated black patch on each side of its white throat. Its springtime song is like a distant pump, a deep "oonk-a-lunk-lunk-lunk."

Just across the Mersey River, behind and to the left of the visitor center, is the 1.3-mile (2.1-km) Beech Grove Trail. This trail passes through a rather dense stand of eastern hemlocks in the lower area and transects a lovely beech forest along the upper section. The beech grove is one of the best and most accessible hardwood forests in the park and can produce a good variety of birds in spring and summer. Pileated woodpeckers; least flycatchers; veeries; hermit thrushes; solitary and red-eyed vireos; chestnut-sided, black-throated blue, and black-throated green warblers; northern parulas; American redstarts; ovenbirds; and rose-breasted grosbeaks can all be found there.

The **rose-breasted grosbeak** male is one of the park's most colorful birds. Its deep rose-colored breast and wing lining, black back, white belly, and heavy bill make this bird unmistakable. In addition, its loud, joyous song, somewhat resembling that of an American robin, is without equal. Chapman wrote, "There is an exquisite purity in the joyous carol of the Grosbeak; his song tells of all the gladness of a May morning; I have heard few happier strains of bird-music."

The Grafton Lakes Trail, at the far end of the paved roadway, provides the greatest variety of habitats and birds. This one-mile (1.6-km) trail is used for weekly nature walks by park interpreters. It skirts the edge of the lake, crosses the far end where there is a low observation tower, and then circles back over a low ridge.

I walked this trail one early morning in August, after a very rainy night. Fog covered the distant slopes, and patches of mist were scattered along the shore. I could hear ducks before I reached the lakeshore, and it took me several minutes to locate the **American black ducks** some distance to the left among a scattering of water lilies. A flock of twenty-three suddenly appeared out of the mist and settled down with the first two among the water lilies. I was amazed how well they blended into the dark waters.

The black duck is a mallard look-alike but with darker plumage, like that of a mallard hen. Unlike the mallard, the black duck sexes are identical. In flight, the violet-blue speculum of the wings lacks the white borders of the mallard's. This is eastern Canada's most common duck, utilizing abundant wetlands like those at Kejimkujik. According to Chief Park Interpreter Peter Hope, more than 20 broods are produced in the park annually. Farther south in the United States, however, populations have experienced a drastic decline since the 1950s. (See chapter 22 on Gateway and Fire Island for a description of this species in the New York area.)

Three wood ducks suddenly took off from the water, reasonably close to where I was standing. And I discovered a lone great blue heron on the opposite shore. **Belted kingfishers** were fishing there, too. Apparently there were plenty of fish along the shallow shore, because I counted a total of six kingfishers. All were making short flights out over the water, diving headfirst after prey, and usually emerging with a fish grasped tightly in their large bills. They then returned to a snag to swallow their catch. I could detect both males and females in the group. They are reasonably large, bluish-gray birds, with white underparts and a heavy bluish chest band. Females possess a rusty belly band that is lacking in males.

A pair of **eastern kingbirds** were perched on a little island in the lake, and I could see their dark backs and white underparts from a distance. The broad, white terminal tail band was visible each time they made a flight out over the lake. I hoped they were catching some of the large flies that swarm around during the summer months. Their stuttering song, interpreted by Wayne Peterson as "kip-kip-kipper-kipper; dzee-dzee-dzee," was evident with each flight as well. And when I moved farther down the shore to the section with more snag perches at water level, eastern kingbirds were more numerous. I counted 18 of these flycatchers, a surprisingly high number, all going about their business of finding breakfast. I wondered if they also take small fish, as their gray kingbird cousins do in the West Indies.

At the water's edge was a combination of tall green sedges and scattered shrubs, where both song and swamp sparrows were present. These birds respond to spishing or squeaking very well, and I was able to get good looks at these common nesting birds. The **swamp sparrow** is a particularly lovely bird, with its reddish cap and wings, gray face, and streaked back. Its very loud, metallic chip call was evident each time I spished. One bird came so close that I could no longer use my binoculars. In spring and summer, birds sing their songs over and over again, "a simple, sweet, but somewhat monotonous tweet-tweet-tweet, all on one note, and sometimes running into a trill," according to Frank Chapman.

Behind me in the forest I detected a number of songs, calls, and other sounds. Most obvious were the "chick-a-dee-dee-dee" of black-capped chickadees, the rather nasal "yank" of white-breasted nuthatches, the drawn-out "peeeee" of an eastern wood-pewee, and the tapping of a pair of downy woodpeckers that were working on a couple of birch trees less than 35 feet (11 m) from me. Farther away, I detected a pileated woodpecker, an American robin, and a solitary vireo.

As I moved back into the woods and continued along the trail, I suddenly came face to face with a chipping ball of yellow feathers that I recognized as a **magnolia warbler**. This little warbler apparently was still caring for youngsters and did not appreciate my presence. I was amazed at such a tiny creature's ferocity. I remained perfectly still and watched it through my binoculars from about 25 feet for several minutes while it continued its defensive behavior. It was an adult female, with a gray head, a bright yellow underside with thin, black chest streaks that formed a collar, and a distinct white bar across its black tail. The male is brighter and possesses a black mask, which gives it an even more ferocious appearance. I never did hear its "weety, weety, weety" song, but the female's aggressiveness convinced me of its nesting status. This bird is considered to be the most common nesting bird within Kejimkujik National Park.

Midsummer is best for finding birds. It is when all of the park's breeding birds are present and in full song. The forests literally ring with music. Most impressive are the thrushes. Five species can be present along the Grafton Lake Trail. Hermit thrush, veery, and American robin are most numerous. Wood thrush also can be common, but Swainson's thrush is less numerous.

The song of the **hermit thrush** is undoubtedly one of nature's most exquisite melodies. It is full of richness of spirit, with several short phrases of five to twelve notes, the first one loudest and longest. Each phrase is similar to the others but on a different pitch, interspersed with rather long pauses. Eugene Bicknell, in Frank Chapman's *Handbook of Birds of Eastern North America*, wrote that the hermit thrush's song is "not remarkable for variety or volume, but in purity and sweetness of tone and exquisite modulation they are unequaled."

The hermit thrush is a rather secretive species that prefers the deep woods. In good light its reddish tail can be obvious, but in the deep shadows its olive-brown upperparts and whitish underparts marked with large, dark breast spots provide excellent camouflage. It was very different from the other thrush family members that summer at Kejimkujik.

Woodpeckers are also common in the park forests in summer. Six species nest there: downy, hairy, black-backed, and pileated woodpeckers; yellow-bellied sapsucker; and northern flicker.

Some other common nesting birds that might be expected along the Grafton Lake Trail, include the red-tailed hawk; ruffed grouse; barred owl; common nighthawk; blue jay; black-capped chickadee; ruby-crowned kinglet; chestnut-sided, yellow-rumped, palm, and black-and-white warblers; ovenbird; and dark-eyed junco.

The Peter Point Trail is another of the park's better birding routes and more isolated than the other trails. The mixed forest on Peter Point provides good habitat for a wide variety of songbirds, including thrushes, red-eyed vireos, ovenbirds, scarlet tanagers, and rose-breasted grosbeaks.

The complete list of birds for Kejimkujik's two units amounts to 220 species, including 77 water birds and 23 warblers. Many of these can be found in only one of the units, so it is a good idea to visit both. Perhaps the most important bird of the Seaside Adjunct is the endangered piping plover. Annual monitoring of this little shorebird since 1975 has revealed a steady decline in numbers from a high of 27 nesting pairs in 1976 to only 10 to 12 nesting pairs in 1990. Drysdale informed me that their greatest adversary is habitat competition and predation from gulls and raccoons, both of which have increased dramatically in correlation to the pollution of the adjacent lands and waters.

In summary, the 220 species include 90 nesting birds, of which 16 are water birds, 6 are hawks and owls, and 13 are warblers. Three species occur only in winter: dunlin, dovekie, and black guillemot.

Birds of Special Interest

Common loon. Its wavering, mystical song can be heard at almost any time and place in the park. Its black-and-white body and green neck help identify this large water bird.

American bittern. It prefers to hide in the tall grasses and cattails in wetlands, often with its bill pointed skyward. In flight, its very broad wings and striped body help to identify this wetland specialist.

American black duck. This is the park's most common nesting duck. It looks very much like the drab female mallard, which does not occur at Keji.

Barred owl. This is the large owl with brown eyes and an amazing song. Its very loud hoots and screeches can be heard after dark almost anywhere in the park, including the Jeremys Bay Campground.

Eastern kingbird. This black-and-white flycatcher is fairly common at Grafton Lake and along Stillwater River. It sings a stuttering "kip-kip-kipper-kipper; dzee-dzee-dzee" song.

Hermit thrush. It is usually detected first by its lovely, flutelike song, a series of short phrases, each on a different pitch. Its most distinct physical features are its reddish tail and spotted breast.

Magnolia warbler. It is one of the park's most common species in spring, summer, and fall, nesting among the broadleaf trees inside the forests and along the edges. Its bright yellow underparts, black back and collar band, and white tail band help identify this lovely creature.

Rose-breasted grosbeak. The male possesses a rose-colored breast and wing linings, black-and-white belly, and heavy bill. These birds frequent the hardwood forests in summer.

6

Cape Breton Highlands National Park, Nova Scotia

Great black-backed gulls were everywhere, along the rocky coast-line as well as soaring over the forests and the highland barrens. I counted more than 450 birds on Warren Lake, near Broad Cove Campground, one fall morning. Mostly adults with a few immatures, they were concentrated near the center of the lake, where they were bathing, preening, and talking to one another in their "gruuw-gruuw-gruuw" calls, apparently enjoying themselves. Forty to fifty birds suddenly took off and circled upward into the sky. Some veered off toward the coast, but the others made a huge three- or four-mile-wide circle and settled back onto the lake. They cried, "gruuw-gruuw," and "couwp-couwp," and a deeper drawn-out groan that sounded to me more like gull arguments than friendly greetings.

I stood on the lakeshore and watched through my binoculars. On one flight, half a dozen birds passed fairly close overhead. I could actually see their cream-colored eyes and crimson eye rings as well as their yellow bills with a red-orange spot on the lower mandible. Their pure white heads, tails, and underparts contrasted with their very black upper parts with neat white wing edges. It gave them a really stately appearance. The great black-back is an admirable bird, and one that Cape Breton Highlands National Park can claim as its most obvious resident.

The black-backs were not alone on the lake that morning. A pair of common loons was also present. Their hysterical laughing calls echoed across the water, heard even above the abundant gull sounds. It took me several minutes to find these two adults, black and white with green heads, probably summer residents of Warren Lake. I wondered if they had produced young that year, but I couldn't find any others. In searching the far shore I did discover a lone great blue heron. Its very slow flight pattern was obvious even at that distance.

Great black-backed gull

Another flock of black-backs took to the air, circled for altitude, and then headed in my direction. I watched them fly over. As the earlier groups had done, some of their party veered off, and the others circled back several hundred feet above the lake. But one bird was larger, with the opposite black-and-white pattern. An adult bald eagle! Its bright white head and tail and dark body and wings were obvious. I could even see its yellow legs and beak. It was quite different from the black-backed gulls with which eagles often are confused. How this one bald eagle got mixed into a flock of gulls I'll never know; only passing by, no doubt. It was a most welcome bird that August morning.

The Park Environment

Cape Breton Highlands National Park consists of 380 square miles (147 sq km) in the northern portion of Cape Breton Island, Nova Scotia. The park is 42 miles (168 km) north of Sidney, Nova Scotia, and is bordered on the east by the Atlantic Ocean and on the west by the Gulf of St. Lawrence. Cape Breton and Newfoundland are separated by 70-mile-wide (113-km) Cabot Strait.

Most of the park's landscape consists of rolling plateau uplands (White Hill is the highest, at 1,756 ft., or 535 m, elevation) that are dissected by 17 major watersheds and a spectacular coastline with rocky cliffs, small, sandy beaches, and deep bays. The park has two very distinct sides, the gulf and the Atlantic. They are connected by a single road, the Cabot Trail, which follows the coastline and the highland plateau. The gulf slope is more precipitous, with deeper tributaries. Views from the Cabot Trail are truly spectacular.

Cape Breton's vegetation is a mixture of transition and boreal landscapes. The boreal forest, which occupies the upper slopes or approximately 55 percent of the land surface, is an even-aged coniferous forest that is dominated by balsam fir and lesser amounts of white and black spruce, intermingled with small bogs and other wetlands. A taiga landscape dominates the plateau (about 22% of the park) with "windswept barrens, blanket bogs and stunted forests," according to the park's *Fact Sheet.* This region is dominated by dwarf balsam fir and black spruce, blueberry and sheep laurel shrubs, and reindeer lichens.

The lower and warmer valleys and other protected places, about 23 percent of the park's land surface, possess a transitional landscape of Acadian vegetation. Most of this habitat is a mixed forest of conifers and deciduous hardwoods that the Canadian Parks Service further divides into three separate habitats: deciduous canyon with almost pure hardwoods (sugar maple, yellow birch, beech); deciduous slope with a mixture of white birch, white spruce, yellow birch, and pin cherry; and Atlantic slope with a mixture of balsam fir, black spruce, jack pine, white birch, and red maple.

The national park was established in 1936, the first for Atlantic Canada. There are two entrances, Cheticamp on the west and Ingonish on the east, connected by the 84-mile (135-km) northern loop road, dubbed by the Nova Scotia Department of Tourism the Cabot Trail. Several campgrounds exist along the Cabot Trail, and primitive campsites are also available in the interior. Lodging is available at both entrances, including the Keltic Lodge, a large Department of Tourism resort inside the park near Igonish. Park information centers are located at both entrances, although the park's only visitor center is located on the Cheticamp side. The Cheticamp visitor center also houses an outstanding natural history bookstore, considered the best in the maritime parks, which includes numerous books, videos, and tapes on birds. General informational materials, including a bird checklist for the park, can be acquired at both sites. The park *Fact Sheet* is also available and contains considerable information about the location, climate, topography, flora, and fauna. Talks on broad ecological topics are provided by park interpreters throughout the summer. Park activity sheets that describe the interpretive activities are available for the asking.

Additional information can be obtained from the Superintendent, Cape Breton Highlands National Park, Ingonish Beach, Nova Scotia B0C 1L0; (902) 285-2691.

Bird Life

The majestic **bald eagle** can be found at a number of locations within the park. It is especially common along the coast where large rivers flow into estuaries, such as Cheticamp, Aspy, Clyburn, and Ingonish. It fishes the park estuaries all summer. Most winter to the south in the Annapolis Valley in southern Nova Scotia, but some remain throughout the winter; 15 adults and immatures were present for the 1990 Cheticamp Christmas Bird Count. Others return in early spring, even before breakup. Young birds look very different from the majestic adults, and because of their overall brownish plumage and large head and bill, they can be mistaken for golden eagles, which rarely occur there. See chapter 31 on the Everglades for a description of this species in the Southeast.

An adult bald eagle was perched on a tall spruce tree at the high point along the Middle Head Trail. I was initially attracted to it by a great black-backed gull that circled around and around the eagle, calling a high-pitched "kyhaa" again and again. The morning sunlight highlighted the clean white color of both birds. The bald eagle finally gave in and flew off across Ingonish Bay. The gull, instead of following, seemed to forget all about the eagle and flew off in the other direction. It appeared to be a case of pure gull harassment.

The Middle Head Trail provides superb views of the coast, including the high cliffs that rise 150 feet (46 m) or more above the sea and Tern Rock, a small, rather flat island a few hundred yards beyond the rocky point at the end of the trail. This little island is the only site in the park where common and Arctic terns nest. About 80 pairs of these colonial seabirds annually utilize this site, which they are forced to share with the larger, more aggressive gulls. The latter not only compete for space but also feed on tern eggs and chicks.

Common and **Arctic terns** are two of the most glamorous of the more than 50 terns worldwide. They are almost swallowlike in their courtship flights and can be extremely courageous in defense of their nesting sites. These two birds look very much alike at first but can be distinguished by a few key features. Adult birds of both species possess bright red bills, but the tip of the common tern's bill is normally black. Also, common terns seem to stand taller than Arctic terns; they possess longer necks and legs. In flight, they can best be distinguished by the upper side of their wings. Kenn Kaufman describes this feature best in *Advanced Birding*. He wrote that the "adult Arctic Tern in summer has uniformly pale gray upperwings. In the Common Tern the outer five or six primaries are noticeably darker than the inner five, and where these darker and paler gray areas meet, there is a dark wedge pointing in from the trailing edge of the wing; this becomes even more apparent in later summer and fall."

During the nesting season in May and June, the Canadian Parks Service usually closes the upper tip of Middle Head to protect the terns. Both terns can become very distraught when approached too closely. They will leave their nests open to marauding gulls to attack any human being that gets too close and will actually strike the aggressor.

The Tern Rock colony has been monitored for the last ten years by parks staff in cooperation with the Canadian Wildlife Service. Chief Park Warden A. F. Gibbs told me that the Tern Rock colony has experienced a modest decline in recent years.

There are several other birds that usually are visible from the end of Middle Head. Most common is the **double-crested cormorant,** a large bird that is all dark except for its yellow-orange throat. This long-necked diver, locally called a "shag," fishes the surrounding waters, diving into the depths to swim down a fish and capture it with the hooked bill. Then it surfaces and manipulates its catch into position to swallow it headfirst. I found one cormorant that had captured a fish much larger than normal. It took a considerable time to swallow; the fish formed a huge bulge in the bird's throat. That it had been able to get it that far down is hard to believe. But cormorants have fantastic elasticity in their mouths and throats and are able to consume prey greater than the diameter of their throats.

Double-crested cormorants possess a double crest of feathers on their heads, hence their name. They also spend an inordinate amount of time standing on sea rocks, often in a spread-eagle posture, with several neighboring cormorants. There is a very good reason for this. Unlike those of most other water birds, the cormorants' feathers are not fully waterproof, and they must come out of the water often to dry their plumage.

Another very common seabird that is usually below the cliffs that border the Middle Head Trail is the **black guillemot,** an all-black bird with large, white wing patches. They are most often found in pairs and seem to spend an inordinate amount of time underwater. They feed on rock eels and other small fish under loose stones and have been reported to dive up to 165 feet (50 m) below the surface. See additional information in chapter 3 on Acadia National Park.

Chickadees are also common along the Middle Head Trail, and there is no better place to compare the two resident species. The **black-capped chickadee** is the better known because of its wide range throughout northern North America. This is the chickadee common at feeders during the winter months that sings the typical "chick-a-dee-dee-dee" song. But the other, slightly larger and numerous along the Middle Head Trail, is the **boreal chickadee.** It has a black bib as does the black-cap, but its cap is a gray-brown color, not black. And its song is also very different, at least to anyone who truly listens. The boreal chickadee's song is more of a nasal drawl, like "tchick, chee-day-day." In addition, it rarely if ever comes out of the spruce trees, while the black-cap frequents conifers, broadleafs, and shrubbery and even feeds on the ground if the occasion arises.

The bubbly song of the **fox sparrow** is also common there in summer. This species has the finest voice of all the sparrows. It begins with an introductory whistle, followed by a series of sliding notes, whistles, and slurs. Bicknell states that its song is "an emotional outburst rising full-toned and clear, and passing all too quickly to a closing cadence, which seems to linger in the silent air." Its appearance is also rather special. It is not only one of our largest sparrows but also one of the most colorful. A fox sparrow possesses a rusty head, back, and wings and gray underparts with bold streaks that converge into a central breast spot.

Broad Cove Mountain provides another mixed forest environment that is farther away from the coast. A rather steep but easy trail winds up the slope to a wonderful overview of the Atlantic, Broad Cove Campground, and Warren Lake. A walk to the top provided a brisk and invigorating start to a beautiful morning. I could even hear the common loons on Warren Lake, their hysterical calls carried up the slope across the forest for more than a mile.

One of the park's most interesting regions is the barrens that occupy the high open ridges of the plateau. The Lake of Islands Trail passes through this region, which is a mixture of low evergreen shrubs and reindeer lichens, sheltered stands of dwarf black spruce and balsam fir, and bare granitic boulders. Sphagnum, Labrador tea, leatherleaf, sundews, and pitcher plants were all present as well, creating a truly colorful mosaic of light and dark greens, yellows, and grays.

Spruce grouse live in this rather harsh community and can sometimes be seen feeding along the trail. They often permit hikers to approach very close before retreating into the heavy shrubbery. This trusting behavior has given this bird the name "fool hen."

The hardy little spruce grouse male drums in April and May in the same manner as the larger ruffed grouse, a bird also found in Cape Breton's mixed forests. The sound of drumming is like the distant roll of thunder. Its appearance is most striking, with white bars on a black breast, white streaks on a gold-brown belly, and a crimson comb above each eye. When it drums, this comb bulges out and gives the displaying bird a menacing but colorful appearance. The female, in contrast, is a rather drab brownish color, better adapted to blend into its ground nesting habitat.

The most common bird of Cape Breton's barrens is the well-known **white-throated sparrow**, which frequents feeders during the winter months. The adult's black-and-white striped head, with a patch of yellow in front of each eye, and white throat make this bird easy to identify. And Canadians are also proud of its very distinct song: "pure sweet Canada Canada Canada." Its loud, sharp "chink" call is another good identifying feature.

The chink calls of white-throats were abundant as I walked through the barrens at midday. A small flock of purple finches flew by, probably a family of adults and young. A sharp chip from the blueberry shrubs was that of a common yellowthroat. I stopped and spished only briefly, and the little warbler immediately responded, hopping to the top of a dwarf spruce and looking me over. I was able to see its overall yellow color, that of a female without the black mask of a male.

Then I detected an excited tinkling sound ahead of me, some distance off the trail from a small stand of spruce trees: a songbird of some sort. I moved forward to a little rise in the trail where I could better see the area. A **peregrine falcon** suddenly arose from the clump of trees, circled once, and flew off ahead of me. It was a reasonably small, brightly marked peregrine tiercel (male). The excited tinkling sounds continued. I decided to stay put, remain quiet, and see what would appear. It took three or four minutes, but suddenly a **pine grosbeak** moved onto an open branch of the spruce from where it had been hiding. I was able to watch it for several minutes as it calmed down after what probably was a close brush with the predatory peregrine. A pine grosbeak is a large finch, larger even than a crossbill, with a heavy but short conical bill. It did not possess the red plumage of an adult male but had a russet head, gray-brown body, and dark wings with two distinct wing bars. Pine grosbeaks are a true boreal species that is fairly common at Cape Breton Highlands throughout the year. Farther south in the United States, this species is only sporadic in nature, being common some years but completely absent other years. It depends on the availability of cone crops on which it feeds.

The canyon bottoms and principal campgrounds possess a habitat similar to that of more southerly broadleaf communities. That is where the southern songbirds, such as eastern wood-pewee, blue jay, red-eyed vireo, black-and-white warbler, northern parula, ovenbird, American redstart, and rose-breasted grosbeak, occur in spring and summer. One of the best of these areas is Corney Brook, where a trail follows the meandering stream for more than two kilometers. The first portion of this trail was built above the floodplain, so that the observer can look into the canopy of maple, birch, and beech almost at eye level.

The **blue jay** is one of the park's most obvious birds because of its preference for the same habitats that humans utilize for their developments. It hardly needs describing. Its blue and white colors and crest give it instant recognition. In spite of its rather bad temper and preference for eating other birds' eggs and nestlings, it is a highly visible species that receives much adoration. See chapter 7 on Prince Edward Island for the status of this species there.

Another member of the broadleaf forest community is the brightly colored **rose-breasted grosbeak**, one more finch with a short, stout bill suitable for eating seeds. The male rose-breast has an all-black head and back except for two white wing patches, a white belly, and a deep rose-colored breast. The rose color extends onto the wing linings, which are visible in flight. Females are brown-black without the contrasting colors. And the rose-breast's song is a rich, deep-throated, robinlike one with a more rapid delivery.

In summary, the park's bird checklist contains 194 species, 107 of which are considered confirmed nesters. Of these, 17 are water birds (waterfowl, shorebirds, gulls, terns, and rails), 10 are hawks and owls, 6 are woodpeckers, and 17 are warblers. Thirty-nine of the 194 species are full-time residents, 64 are summer residents only, and 13 occur only in winter. The latter include the Barrow's goldeneye; bufflehead; oldsquaw; harlequin duck; rough-legged hawk; purple sandpiper; glaucous, Iceland, and black-headed gulls; dovekie; horned lark; common redpoll; and snow bunting.

Birds of Special Interest

Common loon. A resident on the larger lakes in summer and along the coast in winter, it is most evident by its hysterical laughing calls. Its heavy, black-and-white body and greenish head help identify this large water bird.

Double-crested cormorant. These tall, dark birds fish the saltwater and freshwater areas of the park and spend much time standing on the sea rocks with their neighbors.

Bald eagle. It is especially common along the coast at the larger estuaries. Its large size, dark body, and white head and tail make identification easy.

Spruce grouse. Watch for this dark-colored, chicken-sized bird along the barrens trails. In spring the males drum, and their black and white plumage and red combs help to distinguish them from the ruffed grouse of the forests.

Great black-backed gull. The adult is all white, with a black mantle (wing tops and back) and yellow bill with a red-orange spot on the lower mandible. This is the park's most obvious bird, seen along the coast and even flying over the barrens.

Common and Arctic terns. They are present in summer at Tern Rock off Middle Head. Their white bodies, black caps, and bright red bills help distinguish them from the larger gulls.

Rose-breasted grosbeak. The male's black and deep-rose colors and heavy bill help identify this lovely songbird. Look for it in the broadleaf forests along the tributary streams.

Fox sparrow. This large, reddish sparrow has a heavily streaked breast with a large, central spot. It sings a loud and bubbly song in spring and summer.

White-throated sparrow. It is common on the barrens and forest edges in summer and at feeders in winter. It has a white throat, black-and-white striped head, and yellow patch in front of each eye.

7

Prince Edward Island National Park, Prince Edward Island

Great blue herons were common on the numerous ponds and along the inner bay. This tall, blue-gray bird with a huge, yellowish bill and great, long legs is one of the park's most obvious summer residents. The herons arrive from their southern winter range in April or May and nest in colonies, usually on small offshore islands. But they spend a large part of their days loafing and feeding in the park's wetlands.

I watched a pair of great blues fishing Clarke's Pond one afternoon in August. One bird stood perfectly still, gazing at the water patiently, waiting for a fish or other prey to pass by. The other used a different fishing technique of wading along the shore, placing one foot ever so slowly in front of the other, barely disturbing the water. Now and then, one of the birds would suddenly thrust its very sharp bill into the water; more than half of the time it was successful, spearing a fish, or, on one occasion, a rather large, greenish-brown frog. Lunch was flipped into the air, caught headfirst, and swallowed whole.

Great blue herons are so numerous within the park that they were chosen as the national park symbol, and "Harold the Heron" became a prominent part of the park's interpretive program.

The Park Environment
Prince Edward Island National Park extends for approximately 25 miles (40 km) along the north-central coast of Prince Edward Island, between Tracadie Bay on the east and New London Bay on

Great blue heron

the west. This area of 10 square miles (4 sq km) faces the relatively quiet waters of the Gulf of St. Lawrence. Cavendish, near the park's western edge, is only 24 miles (39 km) from Charlottetown, the capital of the province. Charlottetown is 36 miles (61 km) northwest of the Wood Islands Ferry Terminal, the only access point from Nova Scotia. The park is 33 miles (58 km) north of the Borden Ferry Terminal, the only access point from New Brunswick.

The width of the park varies from about 1.8 miles (3 km) to little more than the width of the beach, the dunes (some of which reach 59 ft., or 18 m, high), and a few hundred feet of grasslands. Various ponds and wetlands are scattered about within the wider portions of the park, and infrequent patches of forest occur on drier hillsides.

The park's visitor center, located in Cavendish, has an information desk, various interpretive exhibits, and a sales outlet that carries books on birds. The excellent *Field Check List of Birds* for the entire island province of Prince Edward is available for the asking.

The park newsletter, *The Blue Heron,* available at all visitor contact stations, contains interesting tidbits on the park and its resources, maps, and a list of interpretive activities. In addition, a small radio transmitter in the park provides continual prerecorded information in English and French about park facilities and activities.

Three family campgrounds are available inside the park, at Cavendish, Rustico Island, and Stanhope. There also is a campground available for organized groups at Brackley. Lodging, restaurants, and camping supplies are available just outside the park at a number of locations.

Additional information is available from the Superintendent, Prince Edward Island National Park, P.O. Box 487, Charlottetown, P.E.I. C1A 7L1; (902) 672-2211.

Bird Life

Stanhope Cape, Covehead, Rustico Island, and the cliffs of Orby Head and Cavendish provide the best places to view offshore bird life. Most common are the great and double-crested cormorants, herring, great black-backed, and ring-billed gulls, northern gannet, and black guillemot.

The two **cormorants** look alike at first glance but can be readily distinguished by two key characteristics. The more common double-crested cormorant has an all-yellow, bare throat, while the slightly larger great cormorant has a yellow throat that is outlined with white. In addition, adult great cormorants possess white flank patches, usually visible below the wing tips.

Both cormorants are large, dark-plumaged birds usually found either standing upright on the shore and on various structures along the bay or swimming with only their long necks and heads readily visible above the surface. These birds feed on fish that they capture underwater, then surface to consume. They have been recorded to remain below the surface for as long as 70 seconds, although their average time underwater is usually less than 30 seconds. They can remain in the water for only a few dives before they must emerge and stand spread-eagle so that their plumage can dry. Cormorants have less oil on their plumage than most seabirds and can become waterlogged if they remain in the water without their occasional sunbath. This accounts also for their low profile in the water.

Migrating seabirds often seen from the various vantage points can include oldsquaw; black, white-winged, and surf scoters; common eider; and harlequin duck. The more common migrant shorebirds include semipalmated and black-bellied plovers; killdeers and greater and lesser yellowlegs; spotted, pectoral, white-rumped, least, and semipalmated sandpipers; ruddy turnstones; sanderlings; dunlins; and short-billed dowitchers.

The park's most important shorebird is the endangered **piping plover**. This little, sand-colored plover arrives by May, and as many as 25 pairs nest along the park's 24-mile (39-km) beach, just above the high tide line. Young are fledged by the end of July to mid-August, and the birds begin their southward migration in late August. The park's beaches are some of the last remaining fully protected nesting grounds for this declining species. Only about 1,600 pairs still occur in North America, and so the Prince Edward Island birds represent about 2 percent of that population.

The Canadian Parks Service has recently implemented a monitoring and special protection program to assure the birds' continued survival. Certain priority nesting grounds are closed to public use during the period of nesting. See chapter 10 on Kouchibouguac for further information on Canada's piping plover populations.

The **common snipe**, another nesting shorebird, prefers wetlands along the pond edges to build its well-concealed nest of grass and moss. Usually very secretive, if flushed, it will fly off in a fast zigzag pattern, making rasping "scaipes." When courting, however, the male's display is far from secretive, as it will fly high in the sky and then dart downward with great speed. Its incredible dive, usually undertaken only at dawn and dusk, is accompanied by a low trembling sound known as "winnowing," produced by vibrating the outer tail feathers. The winnowing sound can be heard for a half mile.

Snipes are famous for the proverbial "snipe-hunt," which usually leaves the novice hunter out in the cold, deserted by companions, literally holding the bag. But once this bird of the wetlands has been discovered as a real-life shorebird, it will thereafter be more than a good joke.

The common snipe is a very plump, very heavily striped, and very long-billed sandpiper usually found crouched along the wet grassy shore. Its long, heavy, but pliable bill is used to hunt its food by feel. It probes in the soft mud for various invertebrate foods. The food is ground up with grit inside the stomach, and the remains are disgorged in the form of pellets five to six hours after eating. John Terres reported that snipe pellets consisted of "chitin, mollusk fragments, grit, plant fibers, seeds, and sawdust."

Neighboring marsh birds include the common red-winged blackbird with its bright red wing patches; elusive marsh wrens, which sing a long series of liquid rattles; common yellowthroats with their well-known "witchity witchity witchity" songs; swamp sparrows, identified by their reddish crowns, backs, and wings and their musical one-pitch trills; and bank swallows, which skim the water's surface for insects before returning to their nests in the banks along the beach.

Just above the beach in the dune grasses is where the **savannah sparrow** occurs. This short-tailed, little sparrow is the park's most common songbird. It is most frequently seen flying out of the grasslands ahead of an intruder; it never flies far before dropping back into the grass. Binoculars reveal it as a heavily striped sparrow with pinkish legs and yellow eyebrows. Its song in summer is a melodious trill preceded by a series of high chips.

Savannah sparrows occur in every province and state and nest from Baja, Mexico, to Labrador, Canada. A. C. Bent reported that the species was "more highly insectivorous than other sparrows" and discussed a study of the stomach contents of 119 savannahs from California to Newfoundland. Their food was 46 percent animal matter and 54 percent vegetable matter, mostly seeds.

The park's sheltered bays and ponds are where the greatest amount of action occurs. At least 12 species of waterfowl nest within the park: Canada goose, mallard, American black duck, gadwall, American wigeon, green-winged and blue-winged teals, northern shoveler, ring-necked and ruddy ducks, and hooded and red-breasted mergansers. The most abundant of these is the American black duck, an all-dark, rather plain duck that looks very much like a mallard hen.

Woodland birds include blue jays, black-capped and boreal chickadees, red-breasted nuthatches, brown creepers, evening grosbeaks, and pine siskins, all full-time residents. The most obvious of these is the **blue jay**, a bird that the Prince Edward Island Legislature declared the island's avian symbol in 1977. This followed an islandwide vote in 1976, which was won by the lovely blue jay in a "landslide."

The blue jay is one of the bird world's most adaptable members. It has learned to associate closely with human developments, and because of this tolerance, its population has greatly expanded into urban areas in recent decades. It can feed on an extremely wide variety of foods, from seeds and fruit to insects and other invertebrates, and even small vertebrates, including other birds and their eggs. It is a ferocious nest robber! Forest fragmentation in North America has opened new habitats to blue jays and other nest predators, resulting in serious declines of many woodland bird species.

In summer, a few additional songbirds arrive from their southern wintering grounds and help fill the woods with music. Most common of these are the hermit thrush with its flutelike songs; the tiny ruby-crowned kinglet, which sings a lovely but loud "tee tee tee, tew tew tew, teedadee teedadee teedadee" song; the larger red-eyed vireo, which sings its whistle songs from the canopy of the deciduous trees; the ovenbird, which sings, "teacher, teacher, teacher" and prefers the dense forest habitat; the rose-breasted grosbeak with its bright rose-pink breast and underwing coverts; the striped purple finch; and the white-throated sparrow, which sings all summer long, "pure sweet Canada Canada Canada."

Bald eagles and ospreys are occasionally seen flying overhead. The osprey nests within the park, but the larger bald eagle nests nearby. Both feed along the coast and in the various bays and ponds.

In summary, the island's 1988 bird list contained 303 species, of which 123 are considered to breed, 50 are full-time residents, and 73 are summer visitors only. Of the 123 species, 37 are water birds (one grebe, seabirds, ducks, shorebirds, and rails), 12 are hawks and owls, and 19 are warblers. Five species occur only in winter: lesser black-backed gulls, northern hawk-owls, boreal owls, three-toed woodpeckers, and hoary redpolls.

Birds of Special Interest

Great blue heron. This tall, blue-gray wading bird is common at all of the park's water areas and has been chosen as the symbol for the park's interpretive program.

Piping plover. Approximately 2 percent of North America's population of this endangered shorebird nest on the park beaches in summer. It has whitish plumage with a black breast band and forehead stripe, orange legs, and an orange and black bill. The plover must be protected at all costs.

Common snipe. This long-billed bird of the park wetlands, with a striped back and plump body, performs outrageous courtship flights in early summer.

Blue jay. This blue and white, crested jay has been declared the official bird of Prince Edward Island by the Provincial Legislature.

Savannah sparrow. This little sparrow of the seaside grasslands is best identified by its short tail, heavy stripes throughout, pinkish legs, and yellow eyebrows.

8

Terra Nova National Park, Newfoundland

Splash! The osprey hit the water hard, and for a second it was totally submerged. Then it emerged, flapping hard to get airborne. Once out of the water, it was again the powerful bird it had been seconds before, except now it possessed a surprisingly large fish held tightly in both talons. I could see the fish wiggling to free itself, but with the osprey's strong talons deeply embedded into its catch, the fish's fate was sealed. In another few minutes, the osprey would reach its nest and waiting young, tear the fish apart, and feed the pieces to the hungry nestlings. The osprey would undoubtedly preen itself, do some housekeeping at the nest, and then head back to Newman Sound for another catch to feed its growing youngsters.

Ospreys are commonplace at Terra Nova National Park all summer long, going about their daily routine in full view of park visitors. There is hardly a time from dawn to dusk that one or two of these large fish hawks cannot be found over Newman Sound, a favored fishing ground. They nest on taller spruce trees across the inner bay from the campground, building nests that often are used for several years and become huge platforms of sticks and related debris.

By late summer or early fall, Terra Nova's ospreys begin to drift south, feeding on the coastal fishery en route. Some birds may overwinter within the southeastern United States, but others continue south into Mexico or Central America. But by early the following summer, they will be back at Terra Nova to nest and raise another brood of two to four young off the fishery at Newman Sound.

The osprey is a long-winged raptor that rarely strays far from

Osprey

its fishing grounds while nesting. It is best identified by its whitish belly, chest, throat, and wing lining; usually solid brown-black upper parts, except for a white cap; underwings with a bold, dark patch at each wrist or bend of the wing; and mottling elsewhere. An osprey's flight pattern is quite distinct, like that of a gull, with wings bent back at the wrists.

These birds were in serious trouble over much of their range while DDT and other chlorinated hydrocarbons were being used so widely during the mid-1950s. But they have recovered very well since 1972, when DDT was banned in the United States and Canada. Ospreys feed almost exclusively on fish, which can store large concentrations of DDT by-products. Increased buildup of these long-lived hydrocarbons in bird tissues, a process known as biomagnification, causes eggshell thinning and, therefore, a decline in osprey populations.

Today, the osprey is as common as it probably ever was in the Atlantic provinces, and people can admire this unique bird once more. There is much to admire. First and foremost, it is a remarkable bird that has adapted to the proximity of human beings. And its spectacular feetfirst dives into the water from as high as 100 feet are doubly exciting. The osprey is the only raptor with front talons that turn backward to allow for greater grabbing ability. In addition, it can be very vocal during the nesting season, calling repeatedly in a high, piercing whistle. When disturbed, its call is usually a prolonged series of "kip kip kip kiweek kiweek" sounds. Ospreys are undoubtedly one of Terra Nova's most exciting birds.

The Park Environment

Terra Nova is the most easterly of Canada's national parks, 166 miles (267 km) west of St. John's, Newfoundland, along the inner reaches of greater Bonavista Bay on the Atlantic Ocean. The park encompasses 97,920 acres (567 sq km). The *Terra Nova Sounds* newspaper describes the area as having "gently undulating granite hills, cradling a host of lakes, ponds and bogs; a boreal forest and its shoreline lapped by the cold Atlantic Ocean and Labrador Current; a deeply indented coastline." It is obvious from the deep valleys and rounded hills that the landscape is a result of ancient glaciers.

Today's landscapes are dominated by a spruce-fir forest and scattered heath barrens. Black spruce and balsam fir are the most dominant forest plants, but white birch, quaking aspen, and alder are common as well. Many areas of forest show evidence of significant changes resulting from either fire or insect infestations. In many of these instances, the forests have been replaced by a heath habitat that is dominated by sheep laurel and a number of other plants, such as leatherleaf, Labrador tea, rhodora, and blueberries. Views from Blue Hill or Ochre Hill reveal the resultant checkerboard patterns of vegetation as well as the park's innumerable bright blue lakes and ponds.

Wetlands are reasonably common along the edges of the upper bays, lakes, and ponds. Many of these areas possess large stands of willows and alders; disturbances of these areas often result in extensive sheep laurel associations.

Park headquarters and a visitor center are located at Inner Newman Sound, just off Highway 1 (Trans-Canada Highway), which cuts directly through the park north to south. Another visitor center is located at the south entrance to the park. Newman Sound is where most of the interpretive activities, evening talks, and nature walks, including bird walks, take place throughout the summer. The visitor centers contain publication sales outlets, where a checklist of the common summer birds can be acquired. More thorough bird-finding books for the area, Roger Burrow's *Birding in Atlantic Canada* and *Birding in Newfoundland,* are sold at the visitor centers.

The park contains two large campgrounds at Newman Sound and Malady Head, several wilderness camping areas along the coast, and one wilderness camping area on a pond island that is accessible only by canoe. A store at Newman Sound carries groceries and some camping supplies. Lodging must be acquired at the adjacent communities.

Terra Nova is largely a recreationist's park, with more than 42 miles (68 km) of hiking trails, several good streams and lakes for canoeing and swimming, and an active summer recreation program.

Additional information can be obtained from the Superintendent, Terra Nova National Park, Glovertown, Newfoundland A0G 2L0; (709) 533-2884.

Bird Life

Inner Newman Sound is one of the park's most diverse areas, containing an inner bay with extensive mud flats at low tide, wetlands in the upper estuary, and a surrounding mixed forest habitat. A trail follows the shoreline and provides good access to all of these habitats.

Park interpreters lead weekly bird walks there in summer, beginning at the little overlook built out into the bay at the "day use area" below the campground. A mounted telescope provides good observation of the mud flats from that vantage point. One morning in late summer I attended Greg Stroud's bird walk, which produced a good variety of birds.

Most obvious were the gulls—herring, great black-backed, and ring-bill—either standing on the bay shoreline or walking over the mud flats in search of various creatures stranded by the retreating tide. Common terns also were present, flying back and forth over the bay waters, occasionally plunging after a little fish to feed their young and help build up their body fat for their impending migration south to warmer climes off the coastlines of Mexico or Central America.

Several dozen shorebirds were feeding on the bare mud flats. Most numerous was the **greater yellowlegs**, one of the park's common summer residents, which nests along the lake margins and bogs. I counted more than two dozen individuals scattered across the mud flats or wading knee-deep in the shallow bay waters. The long yellow legs were most obvious, and the white rump, long neck, and slightly upturned bill also helped to identify this otherwise rather plain bird. Earlier in the summer, when they are in their brighter breeding plumage, they are streaked with black. Greg told me that this species is locally known as "twillick" and was once a favorite local food source. It must have been a good sport bird, too, for it is very wary and one of the first to take flight when disturbed; its warning call is a loud and distinct "too-whee," often repeated several times.

The shorter, plump shorebirds feeding nearby were semipalmated plovers. They have bright yellow legs, a tiny dark bill, and a dark collar across a white chest. And the even smaller, rather nondescript shorebird was the least sandpiper. This little gray shorebird also has yellowish legs that are hard to see from a distance. The Newfoundland term for most of the little shorebirds is "beachy birds."

It was fascinating to watch the three species as they went about their very different feeding behaviors. The greater yellowlegs were swinging their bills back and forth, actually skimming their prey from the water or mud flat. The semipalmated plovers seemed to be chasing down their prey, running here and there after some insect or other invertebrate that they located by sight. And the least sandpipers were probing for their prey, walking slowly along and feeling for worms and crustaceans in the soft mud with their thin, delicate bills.

Suddenly, a fourth shorebird appeared along the near shore. Its teetering motion was an instant clue to its identity as a **spotted sandpiper**. Only slightly larger than the least sandpiper, spotties are also local nesters. But the bird in front of us had already lost its spotted breast and was sporting its plain, whitish winter plumage. It flew to another location still visible along the shore. Its quick, stiff wing beats and loud "weet weet" calls were typical of this species. Nesting birds utilize dry ground along the shore, laying eggs in scrapes. But the most unusual characteristic of spotted sandpipers is polyandry; a female is likely to mate with more than one male. The various males also share nest building, incubation, and feeding of the young. This procedure seems to be quite successful for this sandpiper, the most widespread shorebird in all North America.

We found 16 Canada geese and a number of American black ducks farther along the trail in the far reaches of the inlet. These birds had been utilizing this feeding area for several days, according to Greg. Waterfowl often congregate in Inner Newman Sound before winter, and a few overwinter there, staying farther out once the upper sections freeze over.

The Newman Sound forest is home to several songbirds during the summer months. Most common of these are the black-capped and boreal chickadees; ruby-crowned kinglets; hermit thrushes; yellow-rumped, black-throated green, and black-and-white warblers; and dark-eyed junco. Three sparrows frequent the wetlands along the trail: Lincoln's, swamp, and white-throated sparrows. Each responds very well to spishing, although the Lincoln's sparrow can be very shy. The best known of the three is the white-throated sparrow, because of its wide range throughout eastern North America and its use of feeders farther south in winter. Its loud and distinct song, "pure sweet Canada Canada Canada," can be heard throughout the park all summer long.

The Louil Hills Trail passes through a very different environment, an alder thicket at the start of the trail and secondary forest with scattered stands of mature spruce-fir forest en route to a wonderful overlook at the end of the trail. Burrows reported, "This area as a whole is unmatched for number of species anywhere in the park."

The alders provide nesting habitat for five warbler species: yellow, mourning, Wilson's, American redstart, and common yellowthroat. The downy woodpecker, northern flicker, yellow-bellied flycatcher, American robin, black-and-white and blackpoll warblers, and northern waterthrush are common in the secondary forest. And the hairy and black-backed woodpeckers, gray jay, boreal chickadee, hermit thrush, yellow-rumped warbler, fox sparrow, purple finch, and pine siskin nest in the spruce-fir areas.

The **yellow-rumped warbler** is surprisingly common in the park and can be found in any of the forested areas, although it seems to prefer mature forest habitat. Further, it is one of the most widespread warblers in all North America, nesting in the northern coniferous forests and wintering just south of the winter snow line. And yet, in spite of its abundance, breeding yellow-rumps often go undetected by the novice birder. This is largely because of its small size and its preference for the upper canopy of the mixed and coniferous forests.

Yellow-rumps are named for their bright yellow rumps, a feature that has also earned them the name "butter-rumps." The male possesses a white throat and belly and a black chest, face, and head, with yellow spots on the crown, on each side of the chest, and on the rump. The bird's four distinct patches of yellow are easy features to remember. Females possess the same pattern but are not so bright.

This is the warbler that was known as the myrtle warbler until it was lumped with the western Audubon's warbler, the yellow-throated bird. The change was primarily due to the fact that the two forms interbreed wherever their ranges overlap. This name change was initiated by the American Ornithologists' Union, a professional society of scientists responsible for avian nomenclature throughout North America.

But whatever the name, it remains a common yellow-rumped warbler with a distinct personality. Yellow-rumps leave their nesting grounds in late summer and forage among the berry fields, northern heaths and bayberry, and myrtle shrubbery farther south. In fact, their preference for myrtle berries to the south during migration and in winter is what provided their earlier name, myrtle warbler. For further information on this bird in winter, see chapter 25 on Cape Hatteras and Cape Lookout.

The Ochre Hill Trail is a short 1.2-mile (2-km) loop that passes over pondside bogs and along the edge of sparkling Ochre Hill Pond. Palm warblers and Lincoln's sparrows are common bog residents, and the ubiquitous white-throated sparrows are present as well. The **palm warbler** can be obvious as it sings its buzzing trill, all at the same pitch, from the tops of the low shrubs. This is a little bird with a yellow throat, eye line, and under-tail coverts; grayish-brown back; and chestnut crown. But an even more obvious characteristic of this bird is its constant tail wagging.

Palm warblers spend their winters in southern Florida, the Caribbean, and Central America. At Everglades National Park, it is one of the most common wintering warblers of the mangroves and campground habitats.

Watch, too, for the **willow ptarmigan** along the Ochre Hills Trail. This large, grouselike bird lives within the heath habitat but is difficult to find because of its mottled plumage, which blends so well into the environment. Its black, brown, and grayish colors are almost impossible to detect. Most sightings are of birds that suddenly fly up and away, almost at the feet of a startled observer. In flight, its outer wings reveal their bright white primary feathers, rarely visible when the bird is perched. Oddly, the bird's primaries remain white all year long, while the other feathers change with the seasons. Willow ptarmigans possess all-white plumage from late fall through winter to help hide them from predators.

The Ochre Hill road ends at a small parking lot where another short trail leads to an excellent overlook of the entire Terra Nova region, Bread Cove Pond, Newman Sound, and the whole peninsula of ponds and waterways. It is a magnificent scene. And this upland perch also affords an opportunity to see some of the park's soaring birds. Bald eagles, ospreys, sharp-shinned hawks, and common ravens occasionally put in appearances.

Bald eagles can best be observed by taking one of the Ocean Watch Tours that originate from Newman Sound daily from late June through Labor Day. The boat tours travel the length of the bay and explore "the fjords, islands, and wilderness coves."

An adult **bald eagle** is a spectacular bird, with snow white head and tail and a huge yellow bill that are a stark contrast to its chocolate brown body. Its general appearance as a fierce predator also is in contrast to its true character, that of a timid carrion feeder. Bald eagle populations seriously declined during the 1980s, primarily as a result of eggshell thinning brought about by pesticides and heavy metals derived from fish and other foods. The birds were listed as endangered by the United States and Canada. Since DDT was banned, they have made a remarkable recovery in the Terra Nova area. (For more information about this bird in the Southeast, see chapter 31 on Everglades National Park.)

Winter bird populations are very different from those in summer. Christmas Bird Counts have been undertaken in the park for more than fifteen years and provide an excellent perspective on birds that occur at that time of year. The 1990 count listed 2,855 individuals of

42 species. The dozen most numerous species recorded, in descending order of abundance, were herring gull, American crow, common raven, dark-eyed junco, evening grosbeak, black-capped chickadee, common goldeneye, boreal chickadee, European starling, house sparrow, red-breasted merganser, and American black duck.

In summary, the Terra Nova National Park 1985 checklist of birds contained 181 species, 50 of which are considered full-time residents. Eighty-seven of the 181 species nest within the park; 10 are waterfowl, 6 are hawks and owls, and 15 are warblers. Seven species are listed as wintertime residents or visitors only: Barrow's goldeneye, common merganser, purple sandpiper, Iceland and glaucous gulls, dovekie, and northern shrike.

Birds of Special Interest

Osprey. This long-winged raptor is fairly common all summer over the inner bays of the park. It has a black-and-white pattern, including a dark patch at the bend of each wing.

Bald eagle. Its large size and snow white head and tail, in contrast to its chocolate brown body, distinguish it from any other species.

Willow ptarmigan. It is found most commonly along the Ochre and Blue Hills trails and along roadways. The large body of this grouselike bird, which is pure white in winter, is its most obvious feature.

Greater yellowlegs. The long, bright yellow legs of this middle-sized wader and its loud and distinct "too-whee" calls help identify this shorebird.

Spotted sandpiper. Its continual bobbing behavior and quick, stiff flight pattern help to identify this little shorebird. It has a spotted breast in summer.

Yellow-rumped warbler. The park's most common warbler, it can be found almost anywhere. Its bright yellow rump, crown patch, and spots on each side of the chest are its best identifying features.

9

Gros Morne National Park, Newfoundland

The usually quiet gray jays suddenly appeared out of the boreal forest like ghosts and silently floated to a perch on a stunted spruce tree, almost at arm's length from me. The gray jay can be extremely tame. They often become so familiar with hikers that they will actually follow for a short distance. They may even land on a picnic table or enter an open tent for some choice morsel.

Gray jays are not the most colorful of birds, but they are among the most personable. A family of two adults and three juveniles visited me along the Western Brook Trail, calling very gently to one another as they appeared out of the forest. The youngsters stayed at a discrete distance, but both adults landed, one at a time, within six feet of where I stood admiring these wonderful creatures. They seemed completely unafraid but stayed only long enough to look me over and then glided silently back into the forest. I couldn't help but think how appropriate is their scientific name, *Perisoreus canadensis*, Latin for "storer [as in cache of food] of Canada." Until 1983, this bird was known as the Canada jay; then the name was changed to gray jay by the American Ornithologists' Union.

An adult gray jay has a dark gray back and head and white throat, face, and forehead; a juvenile is an overall slate gray with a lighter, almost silver, bill. These jays have a variety of calls, from a loud, whistled "wheeoo" to low twittering sounds. They also are known to mimic the cries of hawks and songs of local songbirds.

Gray jays are full-time residents in Canada's boreal forests at Gros Morne National Park, moving south only in years when their

Gray jay

food supply fails. They normally remain in their nesting territories during the coldest of winters. And in mid-March, while the snow is still very deep, the jays begin building nests of twigs, strips of bark, grass, feathers, and fur. They are able to nest and feed their young so early in the year, prior to a new food supply, because of their habit of storing food the previous growing season. Partly digested caches of fruit, insects, and carrion are hidden in conifers throughout their territory for the coming winter and nesting season.

The gray jay is an extraordinary creature! It is one of the hardiest and most adaptable of all the park's birds. And its abundance throughout the boreal forest makes it an outstanding representative of Gros Morne National Park.

The Park Environment

Gros Morne is the largest of Canada's maritime national parks (448,000 acres, or 2,593 sq km), almost twice the size of Cape Breton National Park. It is located on the Gulf of St. Lawrence in western Newfoundland, 15 miles (24 km) north of Deer Lake, by Highway 430, and 49 miles (79 km) north of Corner Brook, Newfoundland. Gros Morne (French for "big lone mountain") was established in 1973 through a special federal/provincial agreement to protect the best of Newfoundland's western highlands, including fjord valleys, coastal bogs, deep glacial lakes, and wave-carved cliffs. Tuckamore, the park's interpretive magazine, invites the visitor to "hike arctic-alpine barrens and trails travelled by moose, woodland caribou, and arctic hare. Discover the ancient story told by park rocks—of plate tectonics and continental collision."

Gros Morne is world renowned for its geologic history. In fact, its unique geologic and scenic character earned it World Heritage Site status in 1987, making it Canada's only Atlantic maritime national park so listed by UNESCO (United Nations Educational, Scientific, and Cultural Organization), a true honor.

The park is composed of four very distinct zones. These include the bays and estuaries with their related beaches and rocky shores, the rather extensive coastal plains, the midelevation slopes, and the mountaintops. Much of the vegetation on the coast shows the effects of continuous wind, which causes plants to grow in a windblown, flattened posture, locally called "tuckamore" but more widely called krummholz, a German word for "twisted wood." The poorly drained lowlands contain extensive heaths, numerous ponds and bogs, and slightly elevated ridges with dwarfed spruce-fir habitats. A more substantial spruce-fir forest occurs along the bases and lower slopes of the mountains, and a mixed conifer-deciduous forest habitat occurs in a few of the lower, more protected valleys and hills. The mountaintops are usually barren slopes that possess a tundra or arctic-alpine environment dominated by lichens and a few other hardy, low-growing plants.

Dominant forest plants include balsam fir, black and white spruce, American larch or tamarack, quaking aspen, and balsam poplar. Larch, common juniper, and several shrubs (Labrador tea, sheep laurel, blueberries, and crowberry) dominate the heaths and bogs. Common deciduous forest species include mountain and speckled alders and mountain maple. Dwarf birches and willows, diapensia (a tufted evergreen shrub), crowberry, bilberry, and bearberry are common mountaintop species.

Gros Morne National Park has a single visitor center, located just off Highway 430 near Rocky Harbour. It has an information desk, a few exhibits, and a sales outlet for books and videos. A bird checklist for the park is available for the asking. The park also sells Roger Burrows's very thorough book, *Birds in Atlantic Canada*. A schedule of interpretive activities is available; it includes evening talks and guided walks that are offered at various locations.

Camping is available inside the park at five principal sites and numerous backcountry locations. Lodging must be obtained in the various adjacent communities. More than 42 miles (68 km) of trails exist inside the park. They vary from very short walks to the more extensive 10-mile (16-km) James Callaghan Trail to the summit of Gros Morne (2,000 ft., or 610 m, elevation and second-highest peak on the island of Newfoundland) and 11-mile (18-km) Green Gardens Trail. There also are two boat tours available, on Western Brook Pond and Trout River Pond.

Gros Morne is a wilderness park with adequate trail access to its superb backcountry. Its size and relatively undeveloped environment make it one of North America's best examples of an undisturbed natural ecosystem.

Additional information can be obtained from the Superinten-dent, Gros Morne National Park, Box 130, Rocky Harbor, Newfoundland A0K 4N0; (709) 458-2066.

Bird Life

The Western Brook Trail passes through a checkerboard of boreal forest habitats. It meanders past ponds and streams, heaths, bogs, and stands of spruce-fir to the shore of Western Brook Pond. Gray jays prefer the spruce-fir zones, only occasionally venturing out onto the heaths and bogs. Other full-time residents of these spruce-fir patches include the ruffed grouse, downy and hairy woodpeck-ers, black-capped and boreal chickadees, red-breasted nuthatches, golden-crowned kinglets, pine grosbeaks, red and white-winged crossbills, and pine siskins.

In spring and summer, when the songbirds have returned from their southern winter homes, these patches of spruce-fir can be alive with bird song. Most common of the summer residents are the yellow-bellied flycatcher, American robin, blackpoll warbler, oven-bird, northern waterthrush, and white-throated sparrow.

The **yellow-bellied flycatcher** is unique among flycatchers because of its nesting location. Yellow-bellies prefer the cool green moss within the forest. There they construct a burrowlike nest where a little rise or slope exists within the damp spaghnum. They feed mostly on insects (many ants) and spiders but may subsist on berries during stormy weather.

They sing their abrupt "pse-ek" songs from the crowded spruce trees or in the adjacent alders. Their overall yellowish plumage, with a little green on the back and black on the edge of the wings, helps to identify these pert little songsters.

The slightly larger, dark-backed neighbor with blackish streaks on a slightly yellowish belly is the **northern waterthrush**. This war-bler's continual bobbing behavior, evident as it walks on the ground or along a branch, helps to identify it. It is often detected first by its loud, metallic "chink" call, and its even louder song can be heard for a considerable distance. Wayne Peterson described the northern waterthrush song as "loud and clear with accelerating staccato end-ing, sweet sweet sweet swee-wee-wee chew chew chew."

But the most common warbler of the spruce-fir patches is the
blackpoll warbler. It builds a nest of tiny twigs and rootlets, lined
with grass and moss, on dwarf spruce trees at one to seven feet
above the ground. In summer, the forest patches literally ring with
the high-pitched songs of this bird, a series of six to twelve very
high "szee" notes all on one pitch, slightly louder in the middle, and
gradually trailing off. The male blackpoll is mostly black and white,
with a black cap that extends down over the eye, a broad white
cheek patch, and an extended black line below. Its olive-gray back is
streaked with black, except for two white wing bars. Females have a
similar pattern but are greenish instead of black.

Blackpolls travel an annual migration route that may be in
excess of 10,200 miles (16,415 km), farther than that of any other
warbler. A straight line from their Alaskan breeding grounds to
their Brazilian wintering grounds is approximately 5,100 miles
(8,208 km). Migrants, however, do not travel in straight lines.
Southbound blackpolls generally follow the East Coast of North
America and either cross the Caribbean over Cuba and Jamaica or
follow the island chain that includes the Greater and Lesser Antilles
in a great loop to South America. Northbound migrants tend to
stay farther inland, passing through the United States in late April
and May and arriving at their northern homes from mid-May to
mid-June. Blackpolls are among the last songbirds to arrive at their
nesting grounds.

The open heaths and bogs possess an avifauna that is dominated by four sparrows: fox, white-throated, Lincoln's, and swamp.
The largest of the four is the reddish-colored **fox sparrow.** This
northern sparrow prefers thick undergrowth but often sings from
exposed perches. And its song is a pure delight, one of the richest
and most melodic of all sparrow songs, beginning with a clear whistle followed by a series of sliding notes, whistles, and slurs. Paul
Ehrlich and colleagues point out that the "male sings each song
until [the] entire repertoire is sung, then starts over."

The fox sparrow's large size, reddish color, and heavily spotted
breast with a central, triangular spot help to identify it. It is especially common among the coastal tuckamores. This species spends
a great deal of time on the ground. John Terres describes its feeding

habits: "Forages on ground, scratches, kicking backward with both feet simultaneously so vigorously as to dig hole in ground or snow to humus rich in small animal life; however, essentially vegetarian." It also nests on the ground in thickets or at the edge of bogs.

The **white-throated sparrow** is the best known of the four species because it frequents feeders throughout eastern North America during the winter months. Its white throat, black-and-white striped head, and well-known "pure sweet Canada Canada Canada" song are its most obvious features. The sweet notes of white-throat songs can be so abundant along the trail that it can be heard continuously from the parking area to the boat dock at the edge of Western Brook Pond.

Lincoln's sparrows prefer grassy or brushy areas around bogs and often sit on the outer spruce boughs, where they sing their melodic, gurgling songs. They dive for the underbrush at the slightest disturbance but can often be enticed into the open again with some gentle spishing sounds. Then they can be studied with care. For anyone familiar with this little sparrow in winter, it will be a double treat to see it in its bright breeding plumage. Then it is a beautiful bird with a yellow-brown wash across the chest streaked with black, whitish throat, gray collar, white eye ring below a broad gray eye line, and gray-brown streaked head.

Nearby in the low shrubbery at wet places, one can expect to find the little **swamp sparrow**. It is best identified by its overall rusty color, distinct gray eyebrow stripe, chestnut crown, gray throat and chest, and buff belly. It, too, can be enticed into the open by low spishing sounds. Its loud and sharp "cheep" call will almost always give its presence away. Its song is a loud, even-pitched "tweet-tweet-tweet-tweet."

A more extensive spruce-fir forest along the base of the Long Range Mountains can best be experienced along the lower portion of the James Callaghan Trail. This lush forest contains a few birds that do not occur in the smaller, stunted stands. Of special interest are the ruby-crowned kinglet, a tiny, nervous songster; Swainson's thrush of the deep undergrowth; yellow-rumped and black-throated green warblers; and red crossbill.

The **Swainson's thrush** song is unmistakable and one of the unforgettable sounds of the boreal forest. Its song has been described as an ascending and bubbling "wip-poor-wil-wil-eez-zee-zee." The vigorous chorus of Swainson's thrushes can be heard throughout the day and also all night during the nesting season. Seeing this bird is more difficult. It is extremely shy and spends most of its time within the cool, dim forest, usually feeding on the forest floor. Its overall buff-brown color and buff eye ring, cheeks, and breast help it blend into its gloomy environment. At dawn it often perches out in the open and sings "wip-poor-wil-wil-eez-zee-zee." Its call note is a distinct "whait, like a drop of water in a barrel," according to Terres.

The James Callaghan Trail continues to the top of Gros Morne where the hiker is treated to the incredible scenes that usually are used to advertise this spectacular national park. Also near the summit, within the arctic-alpine habitat, is the park's two ptarmigans' summer home. The rare willow ptarmigan is occasionally found along the eastern slopes (Ferry Gulch is a good place to look). But the more common and smaller **rock ptarmigan** is found regularly within the tundra habitat along the trail on the upper slopes and summit. This grouselike bird, with its mottled summer plumage of black and gray and white wings, is unmistakable. In winter the bird moves into

Rock ptarmigan

lower elevations and turns pure white, except for the black tail feathers and the male's black eye line and scarlet comb above the eye. They rarely fly but will walk out of the way when discovered.

Rock ptarmigan males begin to court their mates in May. The male is extremely active, literally running around its prospective bride with tail spread, wings dropped, every feather ruffled, and the bright red, fleshy comb above the eye swollen and erect. It also makes a peculiar, growling "kurr-kurr" sound. Nests are placed on the open ground in scrapes and lined with grasses, moss, and feathers. The clutch of approximately a dozen eggs, the nest, and the hen blend so well into the scene they are difficult to detect. The chicks are precocial and almost immediately on hatching can leave the nest and fend for themselves, feeding on seeds and insects. Leaves, buds, and berries soon become the summertime preference.

Bald eagles and ospreys also occur within the park and are most often seen around Bonne Bay and its inner recesses. The adult bald eagle's white head and tail, which contrast with its dark body, are its most obvious features. The **osprey** can be more difficult to identify. This bird, almost as large as the bald eagle, has white on its underparts as well as the top of its head. But its back and wing tops are dark brown, and a dark line extends to the eye. It also has dark feathers at the bend of each wing.

In addition, its flight pattern is very different from the flat, straight glide of the eagle. Ospreys are one of the most exciting of all birds to watch fishing. They flap back and forth over their fishing territory and will suddenly dive directly into the water from a considerable height. An osprey may entirely submerge itself before flapping back into the air, usually with a fish held tightly in its talons. See chapter 8 on Terra Nova National Park for additional details.

Northern harriers are also present in summer, most often hunting over the coastal wetlands between Sally's Cove and St. Pauls. This marsh hawk's very distinct behavior is revealed in its slow, almost meandering flight, wings often held in a V-shape, as it cruises low over the wetlands, searching for prey that it detects by its keen hearing. It will suddenly pounce on some rodent or bird and often stay on the spot to consume its catch. Or it will haul its prey to waiting young at a ground nest nearby.

This hawk has long wings and tail, an obvious white rump, and very distinct facial disks. Also, unlike most raptors, the sexes look very different. Males are gray and white with black wing tips. Females are cinnamon-brown overall, with a streaked breast. For additional information on the behavior of this species, see chapter 11 on Forillon.

Waterfowl are rarely abundant within the park, in spite of the abundance of wetlands. The pond below the visitor center often contains a pair of common goldeneyes that nest along the shore and produce ducklings by July. And red-breasted mergansers can usually can be found on White Rocks at St. Pauls Inlet. American black and ring-necked ducks, green-winged teal, and Canada goose can usually be found at various other ponds such as Berry Hill, Stuckless, and Pond Point.

Farther up the coast at Shallow Bay, the common and Arctic terns can be found. These seabirds nest on the little island at the mouth of the bay as well as farther off the coast on Stearing Island. However, the terns do not arrive until May, when much of their nesting ground already has been usurped by the larger, more aggressive black-backed and herring gulls. Park interpreter Michael Evans told me that only about 150 pairs of terns still nest on the little islands of St. Pauls Inlet, far fewer than there were a few years ago. The reason for the decline is the considerable increase in the number of gulls, which not only compete for nesting sites but also prey on the terns' eggs and chicks. Only 170 pairs of gulls nested around St. Pauls Inlet in 1976, but that number had swelled to more than 700 pairs by 1990. New fish-processing plants at Cow Head and Rocky Harbour have provided excess food for the gulls, to the detriment of the terns that must rely on small, live fish.

In summary, Gros Morne's bird checklist includes 230 species, of which only 32 occur all twelve months of the year. Ninety-seven species are known to nest, and another 28 are considered possible nesters. Of these 125 species, 11 are waterfowl, 10 are raptors (hawks and owls), and 15 are warblers. Twenty-six are pelagic (oceangoing) species that are only occasionally seen from land. Seven are regular winter residents only, arriving in late fall or early winter and departing by spring: Barrow's goldeneyes; purple sandpipers; common black-headed, Iceland, and glaucous gulls; dovekies; and thick-billed murres.

Birds of Special Interest

Rock ptarmigan. This large grouselike bird spends its summers in the arctic-alpine regions on the mountaintops. Its brown and black plumage blends into the tundra so well that it is often missed by the hiker.

Northern harrier. Its slow, meandering flight over the coastal wetlands, its distinct white rump, and the black and gray of the males or cinnamon-brown of the females help identify this summer resident.

Osprey. This fish hawk occurs over all the lowland waters in summer. Its dark brown and white plumage and its method of fishing make this one of the park's most exciting birds.

Gray jay. Watch for these usually quiet, gray and white jays throughout the spruce-fir forests. They are quite unafraid and will approach within a few feet.

Blackpoll warbler. This rather large, black-capped warbler is common in the park's denser spruce-fir areas. Its high-pitched "szee-szee-zsee" song, all on one pitch, is unmistakable.

Fox sparrow. Its most obvious features are its reddish plumage, heavily striped breast with a central, triangular spot, and large size for a sparrow. It lives in the tuckamores and forest thickets.

White-throated sparrow. Its loud and distinct song, "pure sweet Canada Canada Canada," is commonplace in dense shrubbery throughout the park.

10

Kouchibouguac National Park, New Brunswick

A terrible argument was already under way when I arrived at Sandstone Garden, along the River Trail. The excessively loud and piercing "kee-ar-r-r" calls were those of a common tern that was trying to escape the insistent attack of a much larger herring gull. The gull was in hot pursuit of the tern, apparently trying to entice the tern to drop the little fish that hung from its bill. "Kee-ar-r-r-r," it called, again and again. The tern was just as determined not to give up its meal. I watched these individuals through my binoculars, and I was amazed at the speed, agility, and grace of both birds. The tern's twisting and turning flight was somehow equaled by that of the heavier-bodied gull, which was able to cut corners to stay right behind the tern. I began to wonder if I was watching a real pursuit for food or if the gull was just enjoying the game. I was sure that the tern was very serious about its part. It did not give an inch but continued to twist and dive, at times flying straight up and then down again. Its piercing cries continued all the while. Then, all of a sudden, the gull veered away and departed, as if tired of the game. It flew off upriver, leaving the tern alone with its catch. I turned my binoculars on the tern just as it swallowed the fish. Why it waited until its adversary departed I don't know; I suspect it could have swallowed its prey at any time. Maybe the chase was only a game. But whatever, it was a thrilling three or four minutes.

There were other birds on the river that seemed oblivious to the action I had just witnessed. The largest of these were the great blue herons, standing along the shore, apparently searching for breakfast. One individual flew across the river, its huge wings flapping so very slowly. Several double-crested cormorants were either swimming and diving for fish in the river or perched on an occasional snag. The large, black-and-white raptor soaring over the outer lagoon was an osprey. The black line through the eye and dark patches at the wrists (bend of the wings) were obvious even at a distance. Several gulls were flying along the opposite shore. Most were herring gulls, but at least one was the larger great black-backed gull, and there were a few of the much smaller ring-billed gulls.

Then very close to where I was standing came the loud, dry rattle call of a belted kingfisher. The bird might have been perched there all along, but when it decided to leave, it did so in style. The call of a belted kingfisher is loud, especially so close. I watched that bird cross the river and alight on a snag near the opposite shore. It hadn't been perched there for more than a few seconds before a second kingfisher chased it off, and the two birds flew on up the river, calling to each other with their distinct rattle calls.

The Park Environment

Kouchibouguac (pronounced Koo-she-boo-gwack) is a Micmac Indian word for "river of the long tides," referring to the river of the same name that flows through the center of the park and into Kouchibouguac Lagoon. Within the park boundary, the river is little more than a long lagoon. The highest elevation in the entire park is only 100 feet (30 m) above sea level. The average tide in the park is less than a meter.

Just beyond the river mouth, across the lagoon, is a pass that cuts the barrier island of Kouchibouguac in two parts, generally referred to as North and South Kouchibouguac. Storms sometimes change the island's configuration so that there are three instead of two islands, and sometimes the northern portion of North Kouchibouguac becomes a spit connected to the mainland.

The 96-square-mile (37-sq-km) national park is 82 percent land and 18 percent lagoons and estuaries. The park's landscape can be further divided into five rather distinct habitats, the largest of which is forest (54%) that can best be described as an eastern lowland section of the Acadian forest. This is primarily a mixed forest dominated by black and red spruce and balsam fir on level areas with impeded drainage, and elsewhere by conifers in close association with red and sugar maple, yellow and white birch, and white pine. Other less abundant woody plants include quaking aspen, gray birch, jack pine, and larch.

Peat lands comprise 21 percent of the park's landscape, forming varied-sized areas that contain only a few trees (primarily larch and black spruce) and numerous shrubs, sphagnum moss, and other interesting plants such as pitcher-plant, sundew, and cottongrass. The dominant heath shrubs include small cranberry, blueberry, Labrador tea, leatherleaf, and bog rosemary.

Salt marshes (3%) and freshwater habitats (1%) and the barrier island system (2%), largely sand dunes with Marram grass, make up the remaining terrestrial landscape.

Kouchibouguac National Park is located on the northeastern coast of New Brunswick, 61 miles (103 km) north of Moncton and 24 miles (39 km) south of Chatham, via Provincial Highway 11. The Park Headquarters and Visitor Center is located just inside the park off Highway 117. It has an information desk, exhibits, and introductory slide shows in both English and French. A few books and videos, including bird books in English and French, are available at the sales desk. In addition, the park offers a wide assortment of interpretive activities, including nature walks and evening programs. Most of these programs are of an ecological nature that incorporates birds, and two bird walks are provided weekly. Also, a puppet show is presented that portrays the plight of the endangered piping plover.

All of the park's interpretive activities and additional up-to-date information are described in the *Osprey*, a visitors' guide that is published quarterly and named for the osprey that is also the symbol of Kouchibouguac National Park.

Camping is available at two sites inside the park, although lodging, fuel, and groceries must be obtained at adjacent communities. Canoes and bicycles can be rented inside the park. Kouchibouguac is the only national park unit in the Atlantic provinces with a well-developed biking trail system; the 18-mile (29-km) system provides access to all the key areas. The rivers and lagoons lend themselves to canoeing. The four hiking trails and seven nature trails add 27 miles (43 km) of trails.

Additional information can be obtained from the Superintendent, Kouchibouguac National Park, Kouchibouguac, New Brunswick E0A 2A0; (506) 876-2443.

Bird Life

The **common tern** is one of the park's most charismatic birds. Although the tern has suffered serious population decline throughout most of its range, the park contains one of the largest nesting colonies anywhere in North America. The Tern Islands colony, located just off the southern end of South Kouchibouguac Island, includes approximately 6,800 nesting pairs of terns. Their population swells to about 20,000 individuals toward the end of the nesting period.

Common tern

The park's common terns arrive in mid-May, and breeding activities begin almost immediately. The aerial displays that precede nesting, accompanied by the screaming chorus of 13,000 terns, create pandemonium. In mating, the male struts around the female with a fish in his bill, which is angled upward with neck extended, breast puffed out, and tail cocked. The male will attempt to feed the female, and if the fish is accepted, it signifies her acceptance of him and probable mating. A nest is built on the sand and is little more than a scrape lined with grasses or seaweed. Eggs hatch after about three weeks, and the chicks are fed small fish by their parents for another 30 days. Feeding territories may be miles from the nests, and so the feeding of the chicks is a full-time occupation.

By early to mid-September, the common terns begin to drift south toward their wintering grounds in South America, although a few may winter as far north as southern U.S. coastlines. During migration they can be found many miles offshore.

An adult common tern during the breeding season is a gorgeous creature, with a crimson bill tipped with black, coal-black cap that extends down over the eyes and along the back of the head, and orange-red feet. The bird's underparts are white, and the upperparts are pearly gray. Their graceful, swallowlike flight has provided them with their scientific name, *hirundo*, Latin for swallow.

Park personnel monitor the tern colony every year and close the islands to human use during nesting. Boats can approach reasonably close, but the occupants are subject to tern attacks that can be vicious. Diving terns often strike the intruders, and they also have a habit of defecating at the bottom of each dive. They can be amazingly accurate.

The island beaches also provide nesting habitat for an even more threatened bird, the **piping plover**. This little shorebird does

Piping plover

not have the appeal of the common tern, but it is a lovely creature
nonetheless. Its back and head are almost sand colored, and the
underparts and rump are white. It also has orange legs, an orange
bill tipped with black, and two black streaks: a breast band (sometimes incomplete) and a forehead band that extends from eye to eye.

Only about 20 nesting pairs occur within the park, where they
must use the same beaches used by the human population, the
principal reason for their endangered status. The Canadian Parks
Service, in cooperation with the Canadian Wildlife Service, moni-
tors these populations closely and closes sections of the beach to
protect nest sites when necessary.

Piping plovers remain in the park only from late April to mid-
August (rarely to early September) and then head south to their
wintering grounds along the southern coasts from Florida to
Central America. There is often an overlap with migrating semipalmated plovers during spring and fall, and this poses a dilemma.

Piping plovers look very much like the nonthreatened semipalmated plovers, which occur along the park beaches only as
migrants. Semipalms are dark-backed birds with leg and bill colors
similar to those of the piping plover. Because these plovers can be
so numerous at times, people tend to misunderstand the plight of
Kouchibouguac's piping plovers.

Kouchibouguac National Park does not have the diversity of
habitats that some of the other maritime parks have, but it does
provide better access than most parks to some important habitats,
especially the salt marshes and peat lands.

Kelly's Beach area contains a boardwalk that crosses over a salt
marsh where there are excellent views of that habitat. A summer
morning on the salt marsh can be alive with birds of all sizes and
shapes. Most obvious are the **red-winged blackbirds** with their
bright red shoulder patches and loud, gurgling "kong-quer-ree"
songs. The females look very different; they are heavily streaked,
dark birds that sometimes show slight reddish color on the wings.
These songbirds will often dive at anyone who encroaches onto
their nesting territory, proclaiming their intentions with a shrill
alarm "chee-e-e-e."

Bird sounds often are so loud and intense that some of the quieter songs go undetected. One of these is the short, subtle song of

the **sharp-tailed sparrow**, another summer resident of the salt marsh. Its raspy "te-sheeeeeee" song was described by Wayne Peterson as hot metal plunged into water. The sharp-tail possesses distinct orangish color on its face, neck, and breast, with gray cheeks and crown. It also has a rather large, horn-colored bill.

Early morning birders will find them perched atop marsh grasses singing their strange songs. There may be dozens at a time; they are colonial nesters and can be numerous at choice sites. Otherwise, they can be difficult to see. Sharp-tails spend a good part of their time foraging at the base of the marsh grasses and will run like mice, with their heads held low, when disturbed. They will respond to low spishing sounds and will often climb onto a higher perch to investigate. Populations of these little sparrows have declined over much of their range in recent years due to loss of habitat and environmental pollution. The extensive marshland at Kouchibouguac is one of the few places where they still occur in abundance.

The nearby Salt Marsh Nature Trail offers a similar habitat at the mouth of Major Kollock Creek. One morning in early September I walked this short boardwalk trail. The sharp-tails were silent or already had left for their winter homes along the southeast coast. The sharp chips of common yellowthroats were evident, as were the chink calls of white-throated sparrows in the nearby shrubbery. A few migrant warblers passed overhead, and one yellow-rumped warbler landed in a spruce tree just long enough for a quick sighting.

Several great blue herons were stalking their prey along the edge of the creek. I watched one individual strike down into the water and extract a white fish about three to four inches long. The heron immediately swallowed its prey with only a slight flip of its bill that miraculously sent the fish down its long throat. Just beyond the great blue, a number of ducks muddled around in the water in a surprisingly compact group.

They were a flock of **red-breasted mergansers** that apparently had discovered a school of fish and were in a feeding frenzy to capture and consume as many as they could. This species is known to fish in a cooperative manner by driving prey into shallow feeding areas. I watched as they tipped with their heads below the surface time and time again. Every once in a while, one would move away from the flock with a fish hanging from its bill, seemingly not wanting to swallow it in front of the others. This feeding activity went on for eight or ten minutes but finally subsided, and the red-breasts swam farther on, toward the lagoon.

Red-breasted mergansers are common nesters along the park's rivers and ponds, and they share Tern Islands with common terns. In summer, the male possesses a glossy, green-black head and crest, bright red eyes, and an orange-red bill. Its breast is a reddish-brown color with blackish streaks and topped with a white collar. Its large, white wing patches are obvious both in the water and in flight. Females show a similar but duller pattern. After nesting, several family groups join flocks that usually stay together through the winter. Most of Kouchibouguac's red-breasts go south for the winter, but a few hardy individuals remain to fish the open waters.

The Bog Nature Trail provides easy access into one of the park's larger peat lands. An observation tower at the entrance to the bog provides excellent views of the surrounding area. This is where the palm warbler and Lincoln's sparrow reside during the summer. Neither are easy birds to see, but their association with the peat land environment makes them rather special.

The **palm warbler** usually is detected first by its rapid, buzzy trill song, all on the same pitch. It is almost insectlike. The warbler will sing from the top of a stunted spruce or larch tree, all the time wagging its tail in a most obvious manner. It is not an overly gorgeous bird, mostly grayish-brown with a yellow throat, eye line, rump, and crissum. The crown patch is chestnut and in good light can be very colorful contrasting with the yellow eye line below. Some birds stay until early September, but most move south in August, frequenting open areas that often look very much like the peat lands in which they nest. This bird is one of the common winter residents at Everglades National Park.

The even smaller **Lincoln's sparrow** is rarely so bold as to sit in the open but chooses instead the shrubbery for its summertime residence. Its song is more melodic than that of the neighboring palm warbler. Starting low, it rises and then drops, according to Wayne Peterson, who described the song as follows: "kee kee kee, see see, see-dle see-dle, see-see-see-see." However, its very distinct call note, a low, hard "tsup," is more often the first clue to its presence. Then a low spishing sound will often bring it into the open, although any movement will frighten this shy songster back into cover.

This little bird is rather nondescript at first sighting, but it has some beautiful features. Most notable is its buff, almost yellowish breast with fine black streaks. Its whitish eye ring can be a good identifying feature, as can the broad gray line above its eye and heavy black streaks on its back. In spite of its rather dull features, it is one of the most pert and personable of all the sparrows, and finding this bird on its breeding grounds can be a true pleasure.

Kouchibouguac's forest birds can best be found along the Major Kollock Trail or on the Pines Nature Trail. The Major Kollock Trail provides a good sampling of the mixed Acadian forest habitat where most of the more southern songbirds occur. Although there is considerable overlap of species, the more common summer residents there include hairy woodpeckers; yellow-bellied flycatchers; blue jays; black-capped chickadees; golden-crowned kinglets; veeries; American robins; red-eyed vireos; Tennessee, Nashville, chestnut-sided, magnolia, Cape May, black-throated green, bay-breasted, black-and-white, and Canada warblers; northern parulas; American redstarts; ovenbirds; rose-breasted grosbeaks; and dark-eyed juncos.

The Pines Nature Trail has a large number of conifers where most of the pine land birds reside. The more common summer residents there include yellow-bellied sapsuckers; gray jays; boreal chickadees; red-breasted nuthatches; winter wrens; ruby-crowned kinglets; hermit thrushes; Tennessee, magnolia, Cape May, black-throated green, and bay-breasted warblers; and dark-eyed juncos.

Another notable occurrence is the arrival of thousands of waterfowl and shorebirds in autumn. Canada geese, brants, and several duck species may stay until freeze-up time. One year on the Christmas Bird Count, 2,500 Canada geese were still present.

In summary, Kouchibouguac's checklist of birds contains 223 species, 45 of which occur all twelve months of the year. Ninety-seven of the 223 species nest within the park; 12 are water birds (one bittern, ducks, shorebirds, and seabirds), 4 are hawks and owls, and 19 are warblers. Three species reside in the park only in winter: the snowy owl occurs only during invasion years; the white-

KOUCHIBOUGUAC   **103**

winged crossbill is irregular in occurrence; the common redpoll is common each winter.

Birds of Special Interest
Osprey. This fish hawk can be expected throughout the park and is the symbol for the national park. It has white underparts, dark upperparts, a white crown, and dark patches at the bend of its long wings.

Red-breasted merganser. It is most numerous within the inner bays, often fishing in groups. The adult male possesses a greenish head, red eyes and bill, broad white collar, and reddish breast.

Piping plover. This endangered shorebird nests on the barrier island beaches, often in direct conflict with human users. Since this species is declining throughout its range, there are few places where it can be protected.

Common tern. More than 6,800 pairs of this species nest on Tern Islands and fish all of the saltwater lagoons. Its bright red bill and feet, black cap, and white body help to identify this very special seabird.

Sharp-tailed sparrow. This little salt marsh sparrow can be common in summer. Its orangish breast and face and raspy "tsheeeee" song help identify the little songster.

Lincoln's sparrow. This is the little sparrow of the peat lands, with a buff breast, white eye ring, and black streaks.

Red-winged blackbird. In summer it is usually the most abundant bird of the salt marsh. The male's bright red shoulder patches are obvious to even the most casual observer.

11

Forillon National Park, Quebec

The "kitti-aa, kitti-aa" calls of more than 20,000 black-legged kittiwakes were hardly distinguishable in the combined din of the seabirds, the surf, and the wind. Thousands of kittiwakes leave the cliff at the same time, dive downward toward the sea, and then swirl, like gigantic snowflakes in a blizzard. Then another few thousand drop from their nests on the narrow ledges, another white blizzard. Each wave swirls together and then returns to the nests, the birds always crying the unique call from which their name was derived.

In June and July, the cliffs of Forillon National Park house a seabird spectacle that is second only to that at nearby Bonaventure Island. The 660-foot (200-m) cliff face provides nesting sites for approximately 35,000 seabirds of seven species, each using a slightly different location. The most abundant of these are the black-legged kittiwakes, which nest on unbelievably narrow ledges midway up the cliffs. Higher up are the double-crested cormorant nests, built of sticks and debris placed on wide rocky shelves in those precarious locations. Scattered throughout are the razorbills, heavy-bodied birds who hide their eggs in crevices. Herring gulls also nest throughout but select more open ledges. Below these birds, at the base of the cliff among the rockfalls, are the black guillemot and great black-backed gull nests. And down on the pebble beach but close to the cliffs, common eiders build their downy nests. But the most abundant nesting birds by far are the kittiwakes.

Black-legged kittiwakes are true marine birds. They are the only gull capable of diving and swimming underwater, feeding on small

Black-legged kittiwake

fish as well as animal plankton. Capelin and sand lance are priority seafoods while nesting. All the rest of the year they spend at sea. Their nests are constructed of seaweed, moss, and sod and lined with fine grass. But because of the very narrow space they allot themselves, the birds actually cement their nests in place with mud and guano. Only about half of their nest structure may actually rest on the ledge. Kittiwake chicks, unlike most gulls, stay in the nest until they are ready to fly. The nest is a deep cup, and the chicks possess sharp claws for holding on.

Forillon's kittiwakes begin to arrive in mid-March, nest during May, June, and July, and return to sea in August. Only an occasional youngster remains into September. Maxime St-Amour, the park's chief interpreter, told me that the kittiwake population at Forillon has doubled in the last four years. He believes that the increase is a natural one due to an ensemble of favorable factors.

The buoyant, swallowlike flight of the black-legged kittiwake is very different from that of most of the lumbering gulls. It is a medium-sized, long-winged gull with snow white underparts and a gray mantle. Unlike other gulls, it has wing tips that are solid black. From below, the black wing tips, legs, and eyes contrast with its yellow bill and white body. And when several thousand birds take flight at once, the sky can be filled with black-spotted snowflakes.

The Park Environment
Forillon National Park is situated at the eastern tip of Quebec's Gaspé Peninsula, which extends into the Gulf of St. Lawrence. It does not touch the North Atlantic waters. Highway access to the park is via Provincial Highway 132, which makes a complete loop of the peninsula. Gaspé is derived from *gespeg*, a Micmac Indian word meaning "end of the land." Forillon is an old French word dating back to the sixteenth and seventeenth centuries and referring to a vertical rock structure ("flower pot") surrounded by water. French explorer Champlain in 1626 described such a forillon off the tip of the park's peninsula. Eventually the name Forillon was extended to the whole park area.

Gaspé can refer to more than the end of the peninsula; it also marks the northern end of the Appalachian Mountains. Cap Gaspé is where that continental range literally drops into the sea. However, the park's vegetation more closely resembles that of the more northern boreal forests than of the southern Appalachian landscapes. St-Amour, in his book, *Forillon National Park*, described the park's forest, which makes up 95 percent of the landscape, as "predominantly conifer boreal forests where the forest types 'fir with yellow birch' and 'fir with white birch and wood fern' form the typical climax forest." Forillon's most common forest species include balsam fir, white and yellow birch, sugar and red maple, white and black spruce, and speckled alder.

The remaining 5 percent of the park landscape consists of cliffs, a salt marsh, old fields, small alpine meadows, a peat bog, small lakes, streams, and ponds. Although all of these habitats are individually distinct and possess numerous unique plants, taken as a whole they make up the most insignificant part of Forillon in terms of its unique character.

Forillon, Quebec's first national park, was established in 1970 to protect 98 square miles (38 sq km) of the spectacular scenery, geology, and wildlife of the Gaspé. The park contains an interpretive center in the North Area and two information centers, located at Triat-Carre and Penouille. All three facilities have sales outlets for publications, including books on birds.

During summer, roving interpreters are available at strategic sites. In addition, guided boat tours (up to six daily) are available from mid-June through mid-September, departing from Cap-des-Rosiers fishing harbor and traveling along Forillon's cliffs out to Cap Gaspé and back. This cruise is especially worthwhile during June and July, when the seabirds are so active. One also can expect to see seals and whales.

Camping is available within the park at three principal locations—Des Rosiers, Cap-Bon-Ami, and Petit-Gaspé—and a few backcountry locations. Lodging, groceries, and camping supplies are available outside the park in various communities.

Additional information can be obtained from the Superintendent, Forillon National Park, P.O. Box 1220, Gaspe, Quebec G0C 1R0; (418) 368-5505.

Bird Life

Forillon has few equals for its abundance and array of seabirds. The majority of the park's roads and trails lead to seabird viewing sites. The most important and popular of these is the Cap-Bon-Ami area, where a public telescope is available to study the nesting cliffs.

The **double-crested cormorant is** undoubtedly one of the most obvious of the park's birds. Because of its presence throughout the year, except in midwinter, it was selected as the symbol of the park's interpretive program. These long-necked seabirds are easily observed along the shoreline, often standing spread-eagle while drying their plumage after fishing the adjacent waters. And they are visible almost continuously as they fly from one place to another. They have learned to shortcut across the peninsula at the narrowest depression between Cap-Bon-Ami and Grande-Grave.

The double-crested cormorant, with a brown-black body and a bare, bright yellow throat, is not a particularly handsome bird; immature birds have buff-colored underparts. But it possesses some outstanding characteristics. First of all, it is an underwater-pursuit swimmer that dives forward from a floating position and then swims down its catch. It can reach depths of 100 feet (30 m) and capture its prey with its hooked bill. It must come out of the water often to dry its plumage. Cormorants do not have adequate oil glands, as most seabirds do, to keep their plumage properly water-proofed.

Forillon's other seabird that spends a good deal of its time standing upright is the **razorbill**. This heavyset bird is a member of the Alcid family and is the closest relative to the extinct great auk, which was hunted out of existence in the coastal waters of the North Atlantic. Razorbills also were hunted during the early 1900s, and DDT was responsible for additional declines during the mid-1900s. Today's populations are reasonably stable, primarily because their nesting sites are hard to reach; seabird meat and eggs are no longer in vogue; and DDT was banned in 1972 in the United States and Canada.

The razorbill is Canada's answer to penguins, but unlike that Antarctic bird, the razorbill is capable of flight with its short wings. The French name for this bird is *petitpinguuin,* meaning "small penguin." Although these birds spend most of their life at sea, they must come to land to nest. When leaving their nests to fish, they actually throw themselves off the cliff and torpedo downward into the sea. There they literally fly through the water, propelling themselves with both feet and wings. And like their puffin cousins, razorbills can capture several fish on each trip, leaving the water with fishtails dangling from their bills. They have been recorded at more than 390 feet (65 fathoms).

The razorbill is one of the chunkiest of all birds, possessing a big head, thick neck, and huge rounded bill crossed with a white band. During the nesting season it also has thin white lines that run from its eyes to the top edge of the bill. Otherwise, it is all dark above and white below.

The smaller **black guillemot,** another member of the Alcid family, is very easy to identify. Its coal-black body with large white wing patches and red feet is striking. Because the guillemot is not as shy as most seabirds and often swims below the overlooks, one can actually watch it flying through the water after its prey. The clear waters of Forillon provide exceptional viewing opportunities of this kind. A lucky observer may actually watch a guillemot chase and catch its prey.

Herring and great black-backed gulls also nest on the Forillon's cliffs and are abundant throughout the year. They are some of the hardy birds that are year-round residents. The herring gull is all white with a gray mantle and a yellow bill with a bright red spot on the lower mandible. The black-backed gull is larger and has a black mantle. Neither of these birds matures until its fourth year, and so there always are lots of irregularly marked herring and great black-backed gulls within the abundant gull flocks.

Last, the **common eider** drake is one of the most striking of all the seabirds. This sea duck has a black-and-white body topped by a large head with a sloping forehead. A broad black line extends from the back of the head onto its large bill, forming a V-shape, and the sides of its neck are greenish.

Populations of this large duck have increased since the days when it was hunted for its feathers, which were used for stuffing sleeping bags, jackets, and the like. Eiderdown from farm-raised birds is still used in many products because of its wonderful insulating quality. Today, hundreds of these seabirds can be watched in the park waters from the beaches and overlooks. See chapter 3 on Acadia for additional information.

It is possible to hike from Anse-Qux-Sauvages, the end of the South Area road, for 2.4 miles (3.9 km) to Cap Gaspé by taking the Les Graves coastal trail, or one can follow an old roadbed parallel to the trail. This hike provides wonderful views of the Bay of Gaspé, including Bonaventure Island far across the bay to the south. At the end of the trail, the picturesque Cap Gaspé Lighthouse provides additional incentive, if the grand, scenic views and abundant seabirds are not enough. Also from that viewpoint it is possible to see hundreds of **northern gannets** streaming between their Bonaventure nesting sites and their favorite feeding grounds far up · the St. Lawrence River. This large, all-white bird, with long, pointed tail, black pointed wing tips, and a gold cast to its head and nape, nests on Bonaventure Island in a colony that numbers more than 26,000 pairs. Roger Tory Peterson called this site "one of the greatest ornithological spectacles of the continent."

Northern gannet

The gannets pass by Cap Gaspé all day long, sometimes singly but usually in large numbers, often in stretched-out V-patterns. These birds are very strong fliers and think nothing of traveling a hundred or more miles to fish a particularly choice fishery. They dive headfirst into the sea, wings folded, like a rocket, sometimes from a height of 100 feet (30 m) or more. Their splashes often shoot up 15 feet or more. And when a flock of gannets has discovered a school of mackerel, and dozens of birds are diving together, it is an extraordinary visual treat. Hugh Halliday reported in *The Bird Watcher's America* that a diving bird may reappear with "its throat bulging. It may have swallowed a full-sized mackerel or as many as five herring in just one plunge."

The northern gannet is the only northern member of a family of birds (Sulidae) that prefer warmer waters to the south. And the entire Gaspé population of gannets joins relatives during the winter months, frequenting the coasts of Florida and the Gulf of Mexico. See chapter 29 on Canaveral National Seashore for a description of this bird in wintertime.

Another seabird that fishes by diving into the sea, although never so spectacularly, is the much smaller **common tern**. These black-and-white birds, with black caps and orange-red bills and feet in summer, are observed flying and diving along the park's sandy beaches and salt marsh, but they nest elsewhere in the area.

One day in early September I found dozens of common terns along the beach at Penouille. Their loud, piercing "kee-ar-a-a-a" calls were continuous, and when one individual decided to chase one of the numerous American crows, its calls were even louder and shriller. Herring and great black-backed gulls were common, and lesser numbers of Bonaparte's gulls were present as well. A spotted sandpiper, already in its nonspotted winter plumage, flew along the beach as I passed by. And a small flock of red-breasted mergansers, probably a family group, flew overhead toward the far end of the Penouille salt marsh.

Gazing out over the marsh, I counted more than 300 American black ducks scattered across the wetland. This is the park's most common surface-feeding duck, which looks very much like a mallard hen. It is brown-black overall, with a lighter face and forehead and a yellowish bill. Eight blue-winged teals flew up from the edge of the marsh and retreated to the far shore, where they might feel more secure.

But the most obvious bird that morning in the salt marsh was the **great blue heron**. I counted 22 individuals feeding within the shallow waters or along the shore. This is the park's tallest bird, reaching a height of 46 inches and a wingspan of 6 feet. Its blue and gray colors, long legs, and very large, yellowish bill help to identify this summer resident. Maxime St-Amour told me that these birds nest in tall pine trees in the sheltered canyons along the north coast. The nearby Penouille Marsh is undoubtedly the best place in the park to see them.

Farther out along the controlled access road, beyond the marsh, are a black spruce-dominated forest and open fields. White-throated, song, and Lincoln's sparrows were numerous in the low shrubbery adjacent to the trail. Small flocks of American goldfinches, a few cedar waxwings, and a pair of white-winged crossbills flew over. At one place I encountered a party of songbirds within the mixed forest. Black-throated green, yellow-rumped, and black-and-white warblers were busy foraging for insects among the conifers and broadleafs. Several black-capped chickadees had joined the flock as well. A lone red-breasted nuthatch called its toy horn notes. And a ruby-crowned kinglet put in its appearance, flashing its bright red crown patch.

Then, just ahead, I detected a number of northern flickers feeding on the ground. When those birds flew up into the trees, they joined several others. There could have been more than two dozen of these large, yellow-shafted woodpeckers. Suddenly, they all took flight and scattered in several directions. And there in the midst of where they all had been was a **merlin**, the dominant little falcon of the boreal forest. It apparently had missed its first chance at taking one of the flickers, as it made a tight circle and then took off after another. I heard the flicker's excited calls, then almost a screech, and then silence. I could only assume that the merlin had made a kill; it would spend the next hour or so consuming the greater part of the flicker. That merlin knew very well where to hunt that morning. The Penouille forest was filled with flickers.

Merlins nest within the park's conifer forests and prey almost exclusively on the abundant bird life of the area. They are one of the park's most efficient predators. Only about 12 inches long and with a wingspan of about twice that, they can take birds larger than themselves, although they usually prey on medium-sized birds, such as flickers. Most of their hunting success comes from chasing rather than diving on their prey, the method most often used by their larger cousin, the peregrine falcon.

The adult merlin male has a slate gray-colored back and crown, and buff underparts streaked with dark brown; the female is similar but is dark brown above instead of slate gray. A light tan eye line offsets the dark crown. Its dark tail has two or three grayish bands and a whitish terminal band. In flight it shows the falcon's typical streamlined body and long, pointed wings with their powerful wing beats. Its rapid flight is like that of a wild pigeon, a similarity that led to its earlier name: "pigeon hawk."

Beyond the Penouille forest are open salt meadows. This is where I found the **northern harriers**, flying low over the fields in search of rodents, birds, frogs, or whatever they happened upon; they are far less discriminating than merlins. These raptors actually work a field for prey, flying back and forth as if covering a predetermined grid. Harriers have a unique ability among hawks to use hearing for hunting. They can locate rodent vocalizations (squeaks and squeals) so accurately that they attack prey without visual or olfactory clues. Their hearing ability is within the same range known for owls and at least four times as great as that of other diurnal raptors.

The northern harrier is almost twice the size of a merlin, with a long tail and wings and an obvious white rump patch. Another harrier characteristic is its habit of holding its wings in a shallow V-shape in flight. In addition, it possesses a pair of large facial disks, evident by the pattern of feathers surrounding the face. These relate to the special hearing mechanism that this species utilizes when hunting.

Adult male and female northern harriers possess very different plumages, unlike most birds of prey. Males are pale gray except for their white rumps and underwings and the black trailing edges of their wings. Females are dark brown with streaks of darker brown and buff blotches.

The Le Vallee Trail, on the north side of the park near L'Anse-Au-Griffon, provides a very different environment and an excellent place to find northern harriers hunting the open fields. This area was farmland until acquired by Parks Canada. It still retains much of its former appearance, although conifers and shrubs are beginning to invade. This is where to best find many of the more southern species: American kestrel, eastern kingbird, blue jay, common yellowthroat, chipping sparrow, bobolink, common grackle, and American goldfinch.

It is possible to hike, bike, or ride horseback across the park on this trail; the southern portion is called Le Portage Trail. The total distance is 6.6 miles (11 km). Le Portage Trail passes through a mixed forest habitat that probably is the best and most accessible songbird area in the park. This is where one can expect to find olive-sided and alder flycatchers, gray jays, black-capped and boreal chickadees, winter wrens, ruby-crowned kinglets, veeries, Swainson's and hermit thrushes, American robins, solitary and Philadelphia vireos, white-winged crossbills, evening grosbeaks, and the following warblers: Nashville, northern parula, yellow, magnolia, black-throated blue, yellow-rumped, black-throated green, backburnian, black-and-white, American redstart, ovenbird, northern waterthrush, and Wilson's.

Wintertime at Forillon can also be exciting, although snow covers most of the landscape. The open bay waters attract many water birds. Christmas counts regularly tally forty or more species and approximately 2,000 individuals. The dozen most numerous species recorded each year include the common eider, oldsquaw, common goldeneye, red-breasted merganser, herring and great black-backed gulls, black guillemot, American crow, common raven, black-capped chickadee, European starling, and snow bunting.

In summary, Forillon's bird checklist includes 245 species, 33 of which occur all twelve months of the year. One hundred twenty-four species nest within the park. Sixteen of these are water birds and seabirds, 12 are hawks and owls, and 20 are warblers. Ten species occur only in winter: the Barrow's goldeneye, gyrfalcon, Iceland and glaucous gulls, dovekie, snowy owl (irregular), Bohemian waxwing, Lapland longspur, snow bunting, and hoary redpoll.

Birds of Special Interest
Double-crested cormorant. It is one of the park's most obvious birds along the coast and flying overhead. It has an all-dark body and yellow throat.

Great blue heron. The park's tallest bird, this long-legged wader frequents wetlands and is especially abundant at Penouille Marsh.

Northern gannet. Hundreds of these large, white-bodied seabirds with black wing tips pass by Cap Gaspé from their nesting colony on nearby Bonaventure Island en route to fishing grounds in the inner reaches of the St. Lawrence River.

Northern harrier. It prefers the open fields and meadows, flying back and forth with its wings held in a shallow V-shape. Its large, white rump patch is usually obvious.

Merlin. This is one of the park's most dynamic raptors, preying on medium-sized birds within the forest community. The male's slate gray back and head give it a striking appearance.

Herring gull. This is the abundant, large, white gull with a gray mantle and a yellow bill with a red spot on the lower mandible.

Great black-backed gull. This is the larger white gull with a black mantle and a yellow bill with a red spot on the lower mandible. Although it is commonly seen along the park coastline, few nests have been found.

Black-legged kittiwake. More than 20,000 of these birds nest each year on the seacliffs at Forillon. It is a small, white gull with a yellow bill and black wing tips, eyes, and feet.

Razorbill. Approximately 100 of these large, heavyset seabirds nest on Forillon's cliffs. The razorbill's black-and-white body and very heavy, blunt bill help identify this relative of the extinct great auk.

Black guillemot. This reasonably small seabird is coal black, with large white wing patches and bright red feet. 🐾

APPALACHIAN MOUNTAINS

The Peregrine Falcon is, perhaps, the most highly specialized and superlative well developed flying organism on our planet today, combining in a marvelous degree the highest powers of speed and aerial adroitness with massive, warlike strength. A powerful, wild, majestic, independent bird, living on the choicest of clean, carnal food, plucked fresh from the air or on the surface of the waters, rearing its young in the nooks of dangerous mountain cliffs, claiming all the atmosphere as its domain and fearing neither beast that walks nor bird that flies. It has a legitimate and important place in the great scheme of things, and by its extinction, if that should ever come, the whole world would be impoverished and dulled.

—G. H. Thayer

12

Delaware Water Gap National Recreation Area, Pennsylvania and New Jersey

There is something mystical about a river in the early morning. It may be the placid surface that belies the powerful energy within. Or it may be the continuous flow of the water. But for me the river has long represented a passageway through varied landscapes, a route for man and wildlife, as well as plant life, to expand their range and clothe the landscapes with a more diverse environment. All of these were evident as I stood on the Delaware River shoreline at Dingmans Campground.

The morning mist still hung over the riverway here and there, and portions of the New Jersey slopes across the river were partially hidden. A rattle call of a belted kingfisher broke the tranquillity, and I watched that bird as it sped eastward along the far shore. Honking of Canada geese echoed across the water, and I searched the channel for these large water birds. I found an even dozen individuals at about midchannel, and farther away was a much larger flock. Downriver were an even larger number, at least 200 birds in all. Some were preening, while others were searching for food along the shallow shoreline. The presence of so many of these large birds helped confirm the belief that this section of the Delaware River that lies within the National Recreation Area is one of the cleanest rivers in the eastern United States.

A huge, slow-flying great blue heron crossed the river and landed almost directly across from me. It was then that I noticed the mergansers, eleven in all, fishing near the opposite shore. They all

Canada geese

were common mergansers, about half the size of a Canada goose and built very differently. These are fishing ducks that can swim down their prey underwater. Their bills are serrated to permit them to hang onto their slippery catch. Most of the mergansers that morning were youngsters; only two were adult females. Apparently, I was privy to a merganser fishing class. I watched the adults dive underwater, followed by one or two of the young. The rest, however, instead of following the adult below the surface, stayed on top and skittered along to keep up with the swimming adult. They met her when she surfaced. Clearly, teaching any youngsters can be a difficult task.

A loud "kwock" call sounded behind me, and I turned just in time to see a green-backed heron land on the little island very near to where I was standing. It froze in place, apparently knowing that it had been discovered. I was able to admire this beautiful little heron at my leisure. I could see its deep chestnut neck well in the morning light, and its whitish underparts, green-black crown, and yellow legs were obvious as well. This is the heron of ponds and rivers, unlike most of its long-legged relations that prefer marshes and swamps.

The little, rock-strewn island along the Pennsylvania shore was almost completely covered with the tall stalks of purple loosestrife.

Song sparrows were chasing each other about from one group of plants to the other. And a pair of eastern kingbirds were perched on the far end of the island, occasionally flying up to capture a passing insect and then settling back on a perch after proclaiming their success with a series of stuttering "tzeet" notes.

A Carolina wren song emanated from the undergrowth on the shore. And from the upper vegetation came the nasal "yank" of a white-breasted nuthatch. A well-marked male scarlet tanager suddenly appeared, and I admired its contrasting brilliant red body and deep black wings. A dull-colored scarlet tanager feeding nearby was either a young bird or a female. And then suddenly a bright orange and black bird appeared very near the male tanager. A male northern oriole, and what a beauty it was. The two male birds provided a beautiful contrast against the bright green foliage.

One flock of ten geese suddenly flew up from the river and disappeared over the trees. Almost immediately a larger flock followed. I could hear their loud honks for a considerable distance. The others remained on the river. They would more than likely soon join the departing flock to find fields somewhere in the valley to feed. Daytime at Delaware Water Gap had begun.

The Park Environment

The park is dominated by the Delaware River, which is responsible for the deep valley as well as the tributaries and adjacent forested slopes and ridges. On a broader perspective, the area is part of the Appalachian Valley and Ridge Province that runs for more than 1,200 miles (1,931 km) between Alabama and the St. Lawrence River. Numerous elements of the northern forests also occur in cooler and wetter areas of the park.

Vegetative communities vary with elevation and temperature. The riverbanks and broad floodplains possess a tangle of vegetation owing to the river's annual rise and occasional flooding. Sycamores and cottonwoods are two of the tallest trees there, but silver and red maples, American elms, willows, and black and river birches are numerous as well. Other common woody species include black walnut, butternut, and hickory. Fields and pastures, recovering from agriculture and grazing practices, are dominated by red cedar and white ash.

The somewhat drier slopes of the park possess a very different community, sometimes referred to as a mixed oak forest, that is dominated by a variety of oaks as well as red and sugar maples, tulip-tree, cherry, beech, and hickory. Most of these same species can be found in the tributaries. And eastern hemlock and white pine are dominant in wetter and cooler locations. Some ridge tops possess a drier environment where pitch pine and scrub and chestnut oaks are most abundant.

Approximately 35 miles (56 km) of the river and adjacent landscape, a total of almost 70,000 acres (28,329 ha), were authorized by Congress in 1965 as the Delaware Water Gap National Recreation Area. This included all the lands that were previously acquired for the proposed Tocks Island Dam and Reservoir. According to the NPS General Management Plan (1987), these park lands "are to be used for recreation; the preservation of scenic, scientific, and historic resources; and resource utilization as long as the primary values of the national recreation area are not impaired."

Unlike most national parks, this park permits hunting (required by special legislation) during the normal New Jersey and Pennsylvania hunting seasons. Nature study must take a backseat six days a week during the fall hunting season, when hunting is permitted every day but Sunday.

Two visitor centers are operated by the National Park Service: at Kittatinny Point, just off Interstate 80 in New Jersey at the southern end of the park, and at Dingman's Falls, off Route 209 in Pennsylvania in the northern portion of the park. Each site has exhibits and a sales outlet for publications and videos. A checklist of the park birds is available at both sites. And at Dingman's Falls, an "owl prowl" is sometimes offered during the spring months.

In addition, the Pocono Environmental Education Center (PEEC) provides a wide range of special environmental education programs, including several on birds. These include bald eagle programs in winter, general birding classes in spring, and hawk watch weekends in the fall. Further details on these programs are available by writing PEEC, RD 2, Box 1010, Dingman's Ferry, PA 18328.

Camping is available inside the park at Dingman's Ferry Campground in Pennsylvania, at Worthington State Forest in New

Jersey, and also at primitive sites along the river and on the 25-mile (40-km) length of the Appalachian Trail that transects the park. There are several commercial campgrounds around the park. Lodging is available outside the park at a wide range of locations.

Additional information can be obtained from the Superintendent, Delaware Water Gap National Recreation Area, Bushkill, PA 18324; (717) 588-2435.

Bird Life

The spring migration, especially the first two weeks in May, is the best time to find the largest number of birds at Delaware Water Gap. Northbound birds of all types literally pour through the area, some utilizing the valley, while others follow the ridges. More than half of the park's bird checklist of 263 species can be expected during the spring migration. Thirty-five of those are warblers, an amazingly high number of these brightly colored songbirds that can occur by the hundreds. On a pleasant spring day, the woods can be alive with bird song.

Fall migration can be just as exciting, but in a very different way. That is the time of year when the raptors are so abundant. The flights of hawks over Kittatinny Ridge can be spectacular. Olin Sewall Pettingill wrote, in *A Guide to Bird Finding East of the Mississippi*,

> From northeastern North America—Labrador, Newfoundland, the Maritime Provinces, and New England—hawks by the thousands funnel into eastern Pennsylvania, sailing along the western face of Kittatinny Ridge. They come when the autumn colors are rich and the westerly winds are brisk. Truly there are few avian spectacles in the eastern United States that can excel the hawk movements along the Kittatinny.

The PEEC Hawk Watch Weekends are called the "Greatest Show Above the Earth" and are scheduled during the peak of the fall migration, from mid-September to the first of November. The count site is Sunrise Mountain (1,653 ft., or 504 m), which provides views of Kittatinny Ridge for 8 miles (13 km). Broad-winged hawks, which move through in late September, can number in the thousands on any particular day. The accipiters—sharp-shinned and Cooper's hawks and goshawks—are most abundant in October, and red-tailed hawks can be most numerous in late October and very early November.

The **red-tailed hawk** is one of the park's most common raptors in all but midwinter. It is easiest to identify by its clear red, sometimes brick red, tail and broad wings, although young birds have grayish-brown tails that show faint dark bands. It usually can be found soaring over the ridges as soon as the sun heats the valleys enough to produce thermal drafts on which the birds can soar for hours on end.

The red-tail is the most common raptor in all of North America. It is a very adaptable bird that exhibits a wide range of behavior. For instance, it hunts within the forest, in fields, and along the riverway. Soaring and hovering red-tails are commonplace over the high ridges. Although their preferred foods appear to be rodents, insects, and a variety of other invertebrates, they also eat reptiles, smaller birds, and even bats captured in flight.

Turkey vultures are also abundant during the summer season and use the thermals for soaring as well. While it is rare to see more than one red-tail at a time, except in migration, turkey vultures often soar in groups of a few to dozens. Their dark feathers, bare red heads, shallow-V wing pattern, and constant tilting from side to side help to identify this large scavenger. See chapter 14 on Cumberland Gap for additional information.

Winter at Delaware Water Gap can be extremely cold, causing all but the most rapid currents of the waterway to freeze over. During those periods, the **bald eagles** that spend their winters within the park provide a spectacle that draws people from all parts of the country. The number of bald eagles in winter apparently has increased in recent years, and as many as 25 or 30 individuals are not unusual. These symbols of America roost on large trees within the more protected side drainages, but during the daytime they fish wherever open water allows. The best localities to observe these birds are Dingman's Ferry Crossing, Bushkill Boat Access, and Milford Beach on the Pennsylvania side, and at Kittatinny Point Visitor Center and Poxono Boat Access in New Jersey. See chapter 31 on the Everglades for details about southern bald eagles.

During mild winter days, when there is open water, waterfowl sighting provides another treat that is hard to ignore. Finding 10 to 15 species in a day is not unusual. Most dependable are the mute swan, Canada goose, green-winged teal, mallard, American wigeon, canvasback, ring-necked duck, lesser scaup, common goldeneye, and common merganser. Less dependable are the snow goose, wood duck, northern pintail, bufflehead, and hooded merganser.

Springtime begins in late February or very early March, when the first songs of a fox sparrow or red-winged blackbird, silent during the long winter, echo across the fields or along the river. It will not be long before other birds join the chorus, the river is fully thawed, and the earliest tree swallow is searching for insects along the river.

Approximately 120 of the 263 species on the park's checklist actually nest within the recreation area. Finding a majority of these birds during that period will require visiting each of the communities: the river, floodplain, tributaries, forested slopes, and ridge tops. There are numerous good floodplain areas. Some of the easiest ones to visit are (north to south) Milford Beach, Dingman's Campground, the Old Mine Road, and Smithfield Beach. Upland sites include the PEEC Nature Trail and Blue Mountain and Crater lakes. Dingman's Falls Trail follows a tributary through a varied habitat to the ridge top. Listen for the loud song of the Louisiana waterthrush during the summer months. It is hard to miss when it is in full singing form.

My personal favorite is the **blue-winged warbler** that I found at several locations within secondary growth near old fields. The male blue-wing is one of the loveliest of birds, an overall soft yellow color with light blue wings and tail and a bold black line through the eye. But it is the blue-wing's song that makes it extra special. Actually, it is more of a musical trill than a true song. Frank Chapman stated that its song "consists of two drawled, wheezy notes swee-chee; the first inhaled, the second exhaled." Blue-wings remain on their nesting grounds for only a few weeks before they have fledged their young and are en route south to their winter homes in South America. This bird, more than any other I can think of, reminds me of the relationship between our eastern forests and those tropical areas far to the south. The survival of our nesting blue-wings depends upon the survival of the tropical forests more than 5,000 miles (8,300 km) away.

In summary, the PEEC bird checklist contains 263 species, 73 of which occur all twelve months of the year. One hundred forty-three are summer residents and presumably nest within the park; 20 of those are water birds, 12 are hawks and owls, and 18 are warblers. Thirteen species are listed only as wintertime visitors: long-eared and northern saw-whet owls, boreal chickadees, American tree and white-crowned sparrows, Lapland longspurs, snow buntings, pine grosbeaks, red and white-winged crossbills, common redpolls, pine siskins, and evening grosbeaks.

Birds of Special Interest

Canada goose. This large waterfowl is most common along the river, where it usually is found with a few too many other "honkers." Its gray-brown body, black neck, and white chin help identify this full-time resident.

Turkey vulture. A few to dozens of these large, blackish birds spend much of their summer days soaring over the ridge tops of the park. They hold their wings at a slight angle in flight, not straight out as does an eagle. A closer look will reveal their bare, red heads.

Bald eagle. In winter, up to 30 of these large, beautiful raptors can be found along the Delaware River inside the park. The pure white heads and tails of adults are easy clues to recognition of the official bird of the United States.

Red-tailed hawk. This is the park's most common hawk, which is most frequently seen soaring over the ridges by midday. Its red tail can usually be seen without difficulty.

Blue-winged warbler. This tiny warbler is one of the park's most numerous summertime songbirds, utilizing second-growth wood-lands and forest edges. Its soft yellow body and blue wings help to identify this hard-to-see species.

13

New River Gorge National River, West Virginia

Aloud but very melodic bird song exploded ahead of me to the right of the trail, 20 or 30 feet into the forest. It sounded again, a sweet "tweeta tweeta wee-tee-o." I froze in place, binoculars at the ready. The bird was only three or four feet above the ground and moving toward me. I could detect yellow color through the shrubbery. "Tweeta tweeta wee-tee-o!" Clear notes and an emphatic delivery. Then it suddenly came into view, and what a spectacular bird it was, a brightly colored male hooded warbler. An incredibly beautiful bird with bright yellow cheeks and forehead surrounded by a coal black crest, collar, and throat. The warbler has an olive green back and yellow underparts.

I watched it search for insects among the foliage. Then suddenly it put its head back and sang again, "tweeta-tweeta-wee-tee-o," nine very distinct notes. Frank Chapman once wrote that hooded warblers sing, "You must come to the woods, or you won't see me." Listening to that bird's melodic song, I fully concurred with his interpretation. The hooded warbler is truly a bird of the eastern forests, and it seemed to represent the densely forested slopes of West Virginia's New River Gorge better than any other species I had seen. I found it almost every place I visited, from the lower elevations at Sandstone Falls to the highland forests along Manns Creek at Babcock.

I had camped at Babcock the night before and had awakened to a light rain at dawn. It was only mist as I left the campground and started down the Manns Creek Gorge Trail. Carolina chickadees and tufted titmice greeted me first, and an American robin glided out of the woods into the campground to search the mowed lawn for worms. Off to the right I detected the song of a great crested fly-catcher. And high above, an American goldfinch was en route to some secret destination.

Hooded warbler

It was there, less than 200 yards into the forest, that the hooded warbler had appeared. I stayed within a few yards of that site for the next hour; there was lots of bird activity. I first spent several min-utes admiring the male hooded warbler, but then it departed as suddenly as it had appeared. Only then was I attracted to another warbler song, very close to where the hooded warbler had disap-peared. "Teacher teacher teacher." The song was almost as loud as the hooded warbler's but not so explosive. A second later I located the rather plain ovenbird, sitting at eye level on a tree branch. The ovenbird sang its teacher song again, four times in a row.

I made a low chip sound, and the ovenbird immediately responded. It jumped onto a slightly higher branch and sang again.

It was in better light now, and I could see its brownish-green back and head and its rather distinct whitish eye ring. It took me several seconds to see its orangish head stripe. Its overall brown-green coloration and striped breast provide this little warbler with excellent coloration to help conceal it within the shadows of the forest.

A very high-pitched but melodic song higher in the trees attracted my attention. A pair of black-and-white warblers had joined the party. And not far off, a white-breasted nuthatch, searching the furrowed bark of a chestnut oak tree, called a nasal "yank." Both warbler and nuthatch were in view at the same time, and I was able to compare their very similar feeding habits. Both searched the bark for insects, but the smaller black-and-white seemed to spend more time probing deeper cracks and searching smaller branches. The white-breasted nuthatch, almost twice as large, moved up and down the trunk and heavy branches in a jerky motion.

Then at head level less than eight feet away, a buff little bird with solid black streaks on its head appeared—a worm-eating warbler. It might have been there all the time, but I did not see it until it was almost beak to nose with me. It may have been its faint chips that attracted my attention. But once aware, I watched this forest warbler glean leaves and smaller branches for insects for several minutes before it moved off into the heavy vegetation.

I continued down the trail, walked a loop from the campground to Camp George Washington Carver, and returned via a paved roadway. A few other birds seen included downy and hairy woodpeckers, eastern wood-pewee, blue jay, Carolina wren, gray catbird, blue-gray gnatcatcher, red-eyed vireo, American redstart, and indigo bunting. It was a lovely morning and an excellent introduction to the upland birds of New River Gorge.

The Park Environment

New River Gorge National River includes only a 53-mile (85-km) stretch of the New River and its narrow gorge, which averages 1,000 feet (305 m) in depth, between Hinton and Gauley Bridge, all within southeastern West Virginia. The New River actually begins in the highlands of northwestern North Carolina. It cuts through the Appalachians and Allegheny Plateau of Virginia and West Virginia and eventually flows into the Kanawha River where the Gauley River intersects the New, a total distance of 250 miles (402 km).

Many geologists believe that the New River, considered one of the oldest rivers in North America, is part of the ancient Teays River system. They say the Teays system extended beyond the Kanawha to the west across southern Ohio, Indiana, and Illinois, and into a northern arm of the Gulf of Mexico, now the Mississippi Valley. About 10,000 years ago, Ice Age glaciers filled the Teays above Kanawha Falls, creating the Kanawha and Ohio rivers. Even today the Kanawha River drainage is the nation's largest north-flowing river system; it flows into the Ohio River at Pt. Pleasant.

In spite of the New River's fascinating geologic history, it was its natural character as a free-flowing river popular to river runners and nature lovers that enticed Congress in 1978 to establish New River Gorge National River as a unit of the National Park Service.

The river is undoubtedly the centerpiece of the park, but the surrounding landscape makes up the greatest part of the park's 62,000 acres (25,091 ha). Varying in elevation from 900 to 3,200 feet (274-975 m), the park contains an amazing assortment of habitats. Maurice Brooks, the well-known West Virginia ornithologist who wrote the West Virginia chapter in Pettingill's *A Guide to Bird Finding East of the Mississippi*, included a popular toast to the state:

> Here's to West Virginia: the most northern of the southern states, the most southern of the northern states, the most western of the eastern states, and the most eastern of the western states; but here's to West Virginia, a mighty good state for the shape she's in!

Athough Brooks was actually referring to the state's physical outline, which seems to protrude in all directions, that description also applies to the state's diverse flora and fauna. And the 53-mile (85-km) park provides a microcosm of habitat diversity. All the park lies within the eastern deciduous forest of North America and represents a midelevation landscape of the western slopes of the Appalachian Mountains.

Kurt Buhlmann described five distinct but overlapping communities in his little book, *A Naturalist's View of the New River Gorge National River*: ridge tops, mixed hardwood forests, tributary streams, floodplains, and aquatic habitats.

The river's floodplain seldom extends for more than a few hundred feet beyond the channel. In a few places cliffs rise directly above the waterway. The riparian vegetation, plants that have their roots in wet soils at all times, is usually dominated by sycamore, river birch, silver maple, and honey locust. Just above the floodplain in slightly drier soils, the mixed hardwoods begin and extend almost to the ridge tops.

The mixed hardwood forest is varied, depending on elevation and protection from the drying sunlight. Exposed southern slopes can be hot in summer, while the northern slopes remain much cooler. Black and chestnut oaks and hickory dominate the drier slopes, and beech, tulip-tree, black cherry, white and red oaks, buckeye, and red maple are most numerous elsewhere.

The open ridge tops contain a habitat that is usually dominated by Virginia, white, and pitch pines; chestnut oak; American holly; and sourwood. Great rhododendron forms a heavy undergrowth on most ridge tops. And a few places with adequate moisture have a completely different set of plants. Along the Canyon Rim Trail at Grandview, for example, is a habitat more typical of higher elevations. Catawba rhododendron and mountain rosebay are common, and eastern hemlock, yellow birch, red maple, and ferns enhance the highland appearance.

The tributary stream community provides yet another combination of plant species, although most also grow within the wetter portions of the hardwood forest and in protected places on the ridge tops. Dominant plants along the tributaries include eastern hemlock, yellow birch, musclewood, beech, red maple, buckeye, magnolia, and rosebay rhododendron.

Because New River Gorge is a relatively new unit of the National Park Service, land acquisition and development are still under way. Visitor facilities are few and far between. The most accessible and heavily visited site at present is the park's new Canyon Rim Visitor Center off U.S. Highway 19, just west of Fayetteville. Visitor centers are also planned at Grandview and Sandstone. A temporary visitor center is operated near Hinton. Both sites provide interpretation and limited publication sales.

Only a few on-site interpretive activities are currently available, but Sunday morning bird walks at Grandview, in season, have been well attended.

Camping inside the authorized park boundary is permitted only at Babcock, but there are several campgrounds outside the park. There are several state parks adjacent to the National River and several private sites that provide camping. Lodging is available at Beckley and most of the smaller towns.

Additional information can be obtained from the Superintendent, New River Gorge National River, P.O. Box 246, Glen Jean, WV 25846; (304) 465-0508.

Bird Life

Of all the park's approximately 200 bird species, none are so obvious during most of the year as the **American robin**. Especially during spring and summer, robin songs literally fill the air at all the open places at all elevations. And after the normal nesting season, when most of the other birds are silent, the robin will still be loudly proclaiming each new day from some lofty perch. When evening shadows creep into the forest, the last bird song of the day will be that of the American robin. It is this red-breasted songster that turns over the daytime to the various nighttime species, the owls and nightjars.

The common American robin is one of our most adaptable birds. It frequents a wide assortment of habitats, from forests to gardens, and has greatly expanded its wintering range in recent decades. While it once was found in West Virginia only in summer and during migration, many now overwinter. It relies on the variety of fruits and berries available from gardens and exotic shrubbery. In summer it prefers earthworms, which it hunts by sight on lawns and in fields.

Inside the forest the most numerous songsters, at least in spring and summer, are the **red-eyed vireos**. In spite of its abundance, this five-and-a-half-inch bird is difficult to find. It lives among the upper foliage of the taller broadleaf trees, where it gleans insects from the leaves and smaller branches. Its song, a series of short but deliberate robinlike whistles, with a rising inflection at the end of each phrase, can be heard throughout the day. One interpretation is "You-see-it, you-see-it, do you hear me? do you believe it?" It also holds the record for singing more frequently than any other North American songster. De Kiriline recorded 22,197 songs during one ten-hour summer day. It also possesses a nasal "whang" call in its repertoire.

The red-eyed vireo, like all vireos, is curious and bold and can often be enticed closer with a few drawn-out spishing sounds. Then it may come into the lower foliage and provide the observer with a better look. Its olive green back can be beautiful in the sunlight. The best features for identification are its striped head and red eye. The broad, white stripe above the eye is highlighted by a black stripe above and the ruby red eye below.

The park's most dynamic bird must be the **peregrine falcon**, a species that was reintroduced during a four-year project sponsored by the National Park Service in cooperation with the West Virginia Department of Natural Resources, U.S. Fish and Wildlife Service, U.S. Forest Service, and the Peregrine Fund. A total of 28 peregrines were hacked from 1987 through 1990. "Hacking" is the term used to describe the introduction of chicks into the wild by caring for them at artificial nests, including feeding them natural prey species, until they are able to leave the sites and hunt on their own. The concept is that the youngsters will imprint on the hacking area and return to nest when mature.

Peregrines disappeared from all of eastern North America by the early 1960s because of DDT and PCB poisoning. This large raptor was at the top of the food chain, feeding on a wide variety of birds that in turn fed on insects or smaller predators that had come in contact with the deadly, long-lasting pesticides. The accumulation of pesticides in peregrines, a process known as bioconcentration, caused eggshell thinning and loss. Peregrines were given endangered species status and DDT was outlawed during the early 1970s. With the help of hacking programs, peregrine populations are beginning to recover. There is no sure place in the park to find a peregrine. But because of the bird's affinity for cliffs and waterways, the Canyon Rim Visitor Center overlook, Grandview Overlook, and along the river itself are the most logical places to look.

Grandview is not only a superb place for possible peregrine sightings but also one of the best areas in the park to find a wide assortment of birds. Park naturalist Don Kodak leads bird walks there throughout the visitor season from early June to September and finds approximately 40 species each trip. Don posts the "Birds of the Week" on the bulletin board at Grandview Overlook. By late July, when I reviewed the list, it had a total of 64 species. Don also is one of the authors of *A Guide to the Birds of the New River Gorge Area*, a booklet that describes 26 birding locations in the park, including Grandview. I spent several hours one morning in July at Grandview, walking the edges of the forest and fields and following the Canyon Rim Trail that runs for about two miles between the Grandview Overlook and Turkey Spur Rock. I recorded birds of open fields and edges, open woodlands, and deep forests.

Although the nesting season was over, a few species were still singing. American robins, chipping sparrows, and song sparrows were most vociferous, while lone songs were detected from a northern cardinal and a rufous-sided towhee. The trees surrounding the parking lot were busy with cedar waxwings. Down the service road below the parking lot was a weedy field with lots of blackberry bushes. Gray catbirds, all-gray birds with rufous caps and crissums, were numerous there, chasing one another from clump to clump. At one point a brown thrasher popped up for a look around. At another place I found three prairie warblers among the low-growing shrubbery. And when a male northern oriole alighted on one of the blackberry clumps, I noticed the abundance of ripe fruit. I assumed that the birds were feeding on either the fruit or the numerous insects that would likely be attracted to fruiting shrubbery.

I stood at the overlook for some time, gazing toward the river and watching for a peregrine to go zooming by, but to no avail. I did see a lone red-tailed hawk and a turkey vulture riding the thermals from the deep gorge. A mixed flock of Carolina chickadees and tufted titmice was busy in the adjacent forest. Farther off I could hear a white-breasted nuthatch. And then I detected the soft vocalization of warblers somewhere below the overlook. I searched the treetops for movement. But it was several minutes before I discovered my first warbler, an immature black-throated green. And within the next 15 to 20 minutes, more than two dozen warblers and a few other birds moved out of the canyon, passed the lookout, and continued out of sight. I recorded three black-throated greens; a well-marked black-throated blue male; a pair of hooded warblers; three worm-eating warblers; seven or eight American redstarts; four black-and-white warblers; two ovenbirds; and lone chestnut-sided, yellow-throated, prairie, cerulean, and Canada warblers. Also included in the parade were both scarlet and summer tanagers, four or five red-eyed vireos, lone solitary and yellow-throated vireos, a gray catbird, and a female rose-breasted grosbeak. It seemed very early for migrants, so I assumed that these were local birds that had already formed parties like those that form on their wintering grounds in Mexico, Central America, or South America.

Sandstone Falls, just north of Hinton, is another good area for birds. The habitat is mostly floodplain and river and is the best area in the park to find water birds. I discovered two large flocks of Canada geese while driving up the river road. Four immature wood ducks and a female mallard with eight or nine ducklings were also present.

Cliff and barn swallows were fly catching over the water and adjacent fields. I parked in the roadside parking lot and walked the boardwalk trail to the upper edge of a little island where there are several good views of Sandstone Falls. Several songbirds were present among the sycamores and willows. Song sparrows were most abundant, and several were singing a rather sharp song composed of three or four clear "sweet" syllables, followed by a melodic buzz and a drawn-out trill. It is a lovely song, one that must have impressed early ornithologists sufficiently for them to proclaim its singer the "song" sparrow.

The loveliest bird of the day was a bright red male **summer tanager**. It appeared from the foliage of a spreading sycamore tree, flying up after an insect that it captured on the wing, then flying back to an open perch, where it commenced to devour its rather large prey. I have long admired this beautiful creature, which prefers the broadleaf habitats near wetlands. It seems to me that its black-winged cousin, the scarlet tanager of the upland forests, gets more attention, but I prefer the all-red summer tanager.

Don Kodak had told me that the Sandstone area can be excellent during migration, and I could easily visualize the abundance of waterfowl, shorebirds, and land birds there in spring. Migrants often follow river valleys, and the New River Gorge provides an excellent highway for birds.

Wintertime birds can be abundant in lowland areas like Sandstone as well. The park's best sample of winter species is the annual Christmas Bird Count done at Oak Hill. The 1991 count recorded more than 4,600 individuals of 60 species. Most of those were the common resident birds, but the list included a few species that occur along the New River only in winter: common snipe, black-capped chickadee, brown creeper, winter wren, golden-crowned kinglet, yellow-rumped warbler, American tree sparrow, white-throated sparrow, dark-eyed junco, rusty blackbird, pine siskin, and evening grosbeak.

In summary, Kodak's bird checklist contains 195 species; 121 of those are summer residents that apparently nest. Of those, 8 are water birds, 12 are hawks and owls, and 12 are warblers.

Birds of Special Interest

Peregrine falcon. It will undoubtedly increase in numbers as birds hacked in the park mature and nest. The best spots for sightings are along the river and at the various park overlooks.

American robin. This common, red-breasted bird is one of the park's most abundant species, utilizing a wide variety of habitats.

Red-eyed vireo. Its song can be heard all spring and summer from the broadleaf forest. It is olive green with a striped head, a white stripe above the eye, and black stripes above and below its ruby red eye.

Hooded warbler. It is common in spring and summer within the forested parts of the park. The male's bright yellow cheeks, surrounded with black, and its loud "tweeta tweeta wee-tee-o" song help identify this beautiful bird.

Summer tanager. This all-red bird with a yellow beak prefers floodplain areas along the lower river. In spring and early summer, its staccato call notes can be common.

14

Cumberland Gap National Historic Park, Kentucky, Tennessee, and Virginia

Turkey vultures are by far the most common soaring bird over Cumberland Mountain. Their six-foot wingspan, uniform black-brown plumage, except for the paler trailing half of the wings, and bare, red heads are their most outstanding features. From a distance the bare, red head is rarely evident, and the vulture can be confused with an eagle or smaller hawk. But the latter two birds soar with their wings held more or less straight out from their bodies; turkey vultures soar with their wings extended in a slightly upright or a shallow V-shaped position. And they also rock in flight, tilting slightly from side to side. With this in mind, one usually can identify this bird at a considerable distance.

Turkey vultures are well adapted for soaring over the high ridges and valleys with little or no flapping. They are able to take advantage of the slightest updrafts from wind blowing over the terrain as well as the thermals, which are stronger columns of warm air rising from the lowlands. Vultures using these drafts usually soar in tight circles. Or they can soar long distances on a single updraft or series of updrafts, flapping only when necessary to adjust from one to the other. It is not uncommon to find a dozen or more turkey vultures soaring about the Pinnacle.

The Pinnacle is a high promontory overlooking historic Cumberland Gap, with panoramic views to the west and south. From there it also is possible to watch other soaring birds. The area's most common raptor, the broad-winged hawk, also takes advantage

Turkey vulture

of the updrafts to soar high over the slopes and ridges. This all-brown buteo (broad-winged) is only half the size of a turkey vulture, and it possesses broad wings and a relatively short tail, which is marked with white and black bands. Its head is feathered.

The broad-winged hawk nests within the park's forest. It usually is quiet and secretive, although during the breeding season it will often call, sometimes when soaring high overhead, its shrill and slighty descending whistle, "pee-tee," sometimes over and over again. Broad-wings are sometimes blamed for killing poultry and are persecuted by misinformed hunters. However, this hawk is limited to much smaller prey. Frank Chapman reported that a study of 65 broad-winged hawk stomachs revealed that 30 contained insects; 28, mice and other small rodents; 15, frogs and toads; 11, reptiles; 4, crawfish; 2, earthworms; and 7 were empty.

Four other hawks reside in the park: red-tailed, red-shouldered, sharp-shinned, and Cooper's hawks. The red-tailed and red-shouldered hawks are also buteos and slightly larger than the broad-wing. The red-tail possesses a dull to brick red tail, and the red-shouldered hawk has a long, heavily banded tail and a reddish shoulder patch. The sharp-shinned and Cooper's hawks are accipiters, or bird hawks, with short, rounded wings and long, banded tails. Red-tailed and red-shouldered hawks feed on small rodents and other small critters, while the sharp-shinned (locally called "blue darter") and

Cooper's hawks feed almost exclusively on wild birds. They actually pursue their prey, sometimes in wild flights through the forest. All of these birds take advantage of the air currents to soar, and each can be seen on any given summer day from the Pinnacle.

The Park Environment

Cumberland Gap is a great notch through a mountain ridge that was cut by an ancient stream. Afterward, the stream was diverted northward when the ridge was uplifted, leaving a natural pass east to west. Similar notches in the Appalachians are called "wind gaps." This one provided the best route across the very difficult mountains and therefore was used by wildlife and Indians long before European settlers reached the East Coast. Early American explorers also utilized the gap. After the Revolutionary War and before canals and railroads dominated the transportation scene, Cumberland Gap became the single most important route from the eastern seaboard into Kentucky and westward.

Frederick Jackson Turner described the Cumberland Gap best when he wrote, "Stand at Cumberland Gap and watch the procession of civilization, marching single file—the buffalo following the trail to the salt springs, the Indian, the fur-trader and hunter, the cattle-raiser, the pioneer farmer—and the frontier has passed by."

In 1940, Cumberland Gap and 20 miles (32 km) of the Cumberland escarpment were set aside as a 20,223-acre (8,184-ha) national park. Elevations range from 1,134 feet (346 m) at Middlesboro, Kentucky, to 3,513 feet (1,071 m) near White Rocks. Cumberland Gap is primarily a mountain park with a long ridge and numerous drainages, although some flatlands occur in the north-central portion, at Hensley Settlement, an area that is being maintained as an operating farm.

The entire forest, except on the least accessible ridges, was logged prior to the Civil War to produce charcoal for iron furnaces. The secondary growth now present is generally dominated by hardwoods, including oaks, hickories, and yellow poplars. Virginia pine is abundant on well-drained soils and ridge tops. Eastern hemlock, red maple, and rosebay rhododendron are common along the various streams that drain the steep slopes.

The Cumberland Gap Visitor Center is located off Highway 25E at the edge of Middlesboro, Kentucky. It offers an information center, orientation programs, exhibits, and a sales area for publications, including bird field guides, and local crafts. Interpretive activities are provided throughout the summer and include evening talks at the Wilderness Road Campground, history walks and tours, and various historical exhibitions. There are no programs specifically on the area bird life.

The park contains 40 miles (64 km) of trails, including the 38-mile-long Cumberland Trail, which follows the Cumberland Mountain ridge from Powell Mountain, below Middlesboro, northeast to beyond White Rocks. Camping is limited to the Wilderness Road Campground, but picnic tables are scattered at numerous sites throughout the park. Lodging and supplies must be secured in the local communities.

More information can be obtained from the Superintendent, Cumberland Gap National Historical Park, Box 1848, Middlesboro, KY 40965; (606) 248-2817.

Bird Life

The Cumberland Trail, which runs northeast from the Pinnacle, provides some of the best bird-finding opportunities in the park. The high, rocky promontories and forested slopes contain habitats that support a number of upland species. One of these birds is the **ruffed grouse**, with colors that blend into its habitat so well that a hiker may practically step on one before it suddenly flies up with excited wing beats and sails off through the forest at great speed. Nature has given it a variegated plumage of blacks, browns, grays, and whitish colors. In flight, its most distinguishing features are its heavy body, short but broad wings, dark band at the end of its tail, and dark spots on the sides of the neck. See chapter 4 on Fundy and chapter 17 on Shenandoah for details of its drumming behavior.

A sudden flash of bright red and black in the upland forest is likely to be a male **scarlet tanager**. Its scarlet body and coal black wings are unmistakable. And its loud and cheery song, somewhat like that of an American robin, is a rather short but melodic "querit, queer, queery, querit, queer." It will often sing over and over again from the very top of a high tree. The female is an overall olive green color, better camouflaged to attend the nest and fledglings while the brightly colored male is defending their territory by singing and, if necessary, attacking another male that may venture too close. This bird is one of the park's more common species, especially at higher elevations.

The scarlet tanager also is one of the park's most outstanding connections to tropical America, from Panama to Bolivia, where it spends its winters. The continued existence of the bird at Cumberland Gap in summer depends on the survival of those essential tropical forests.

At open areas along the Cumberland Trail, as well as at lower elevations, the most abundant and obvious songster is usually the little **indigo bunting**. The name is derived from the male's bright indigo-colored plumage. The female is a very dull brownish color. This is one of the most prolific singers of the bird world, vocalizing from dawn to dusk during the spring and summer. The song is a series of varied, high-pitched phrases that Paul Vickery described as "swee-swee zreet-zreet, swee-swee, zay-zay seeit-seeit." And an individual can actually incorporate additional notes and elements into its repertoire of songs. They commonly sing in flight as well. See chapter 17 on Shenandoah for additional information about this species.

Other songbirds that can be expected along the Cumberland Trail in summer include great crested flycatchers; eastern wood-pewees; blue jays; Carolina chickadees; tufted titmice; white-breast-ed nuthatches; wood thrushes; solitary and red-eyed vireos; black-and-white, black-throated blue, black-throated green, cerulean, chestnut-sided, hooded, and Canada warblers; ovenbirds; and rufous-sided towhees. Some of these birds are common throughout the park at all elevations in summer.

The most widespread of these is the **red-eyed vireo**, a species that is more often heard than seen. Because of its preference for the forest canopy, it seldom is found in the lower vegetation, where it can more readily be observed. It has a dark olive back, slightly yellow underparts, a gray crest, a white eye line bordered by black, and a reddish eye. Its most obvious characteristic is its continuous singing from dawn to dusk. Its deliberate whistle notes have been described as "you see it—you know it—do you hear me?—do you believe it?" Further information on this species is available in chapter 13 on New River Gorge.

The Sugar Run Picnic Area is another of the park's better places to find birds. Several additional summering birds can usually be found in the surrounding lowland cove forest habitat: eastern phoebes, Acadian flycatchers, American crows, Carolina wrens, blue-gray gnatcatchers, white-eyed vireos, worm-eating and Kentucky warblers, Louisiana waterthrushes, summer tanagers, northern cardinals, and song sparrows.

The streamside and moist places along Sugar Run contain two of the park's most exciting songsters, the Louisiana waterthrush and the Kentucky warbler. Both are rather secretive but can be located by their very loud and distinct songs. Chapman wrote of the waterthrush song: "It is the untamable spirit of the bird rendered in music. There is an almost fierce wildness in its ringing notes." Its song is a very loud and emphatic "see-you, see-you, see-you, chew, chew, to-wee." The Kentucky warbler also sings its song with vigor, often repeating it numerous times: "turdle, turdle, turdle."

The two birds look very different, although there are similarities: their long legs and habit of walking over the wet ground in search of food. The Louisiana waterthrush is dark above and light below, with heavy dark streaks and buff on the belly and a bold white eye line. The Kentucky warbler is dark olive green above and bright yellow below, with black on the crest and cheeks and yellow above the eyes.

Woodpeckers are also fairly common in the park, and six species were present within the Wilderness Trail Campground during the days I stayed there in early November. Red-bellied woodpeckers, with their light underparts, black-and-white barred backs, and red crowns and napes, were most numerous. Downy woodpeckers were fairly common, and the larger, look-alike hairy woodpecker was seen but once. Small groups of northern flickers, with yellow-shafted flight feathers and white rumps, were searching for insects on the ground. The very large pileated woodpecker was heard several times but only seen once, a lone bird flying overhead with its batlike flight. And below the campground proper along

Skylight Cave Trail, I found a lone yellow-bellied sapsucker. I was attracted to it by its almost catlike "cleur" calls. Its black-and-white body, slightly yellowish belly, and red forehead helped identify this winter visitor.

Hensley Settlement contains a very different habitat than elsewhere in the park. Chief Ranger Jack Collier told me that over the years Hensley has provided a number of unexpected sightings, especially after a cold front moves through. That is where Collier has found a goshawk and a snowy owl. The area also has a thriving population of **wild turkeys**. Although this large bird was absent from the region for many years, reintroduction in 1973 by the Kentucky Department of Fish and Wildlife was a great success. This "historic" species is now present throughout the lowlands of the park. Collier believes that it was eliminated by blackhead virus, a common parasite of poultry, obtained from domestic chickens. Recent years have seen a significant reduction in chickens in the farmlands adjacent to the park.

There are few wild birds with the historic connection of wild turkeys, a native species that played an important role in feeding the early explorers and settlers in the Cumberland Mountains. It is likely that they will increase in numbers and will again provide a significant link between the natural environment and the early peoples that depended so much on the natural resources about them.

In summary, the park's bird checklist contains 127 species; 73 of those are believed to nest. Only one (green-backed heron) of the 73 breeding birds is a water bird, 7 are hawks and owls, and 14 are warblers. Eighteen species on the checklist are listed as winter residents only: northern harriers; long-eared, short-eared, and northern saw-whet owls; yellow-bellied sapsuckers; red-breasted nuthatches; brown creepers; winter wrens; golden-crowned and ruby-crowned kinglets; yellow-rumped warblers; vesper, white-crowned, white-throated, and fox sparrows; purple finches; pine siskins; and evening grosbeaks. Some of these are undoubtedly also migrants.

Birds of Special Interest

Turkey vulture. This is the large soaring bird with a bare, red head, seen over the ridges and slopes. It holds its wings in a shallow V-shaped position and rocks side to side in flight.

Broad-winged hawk. A fairly small hawk with broad wings and a black-and-white banded tail, it is most often seen in the forest or soaring over the ridges.

Wild turkey. Watch for this large bird in clearings and on the lower slopes. The male has a dark, iridescent body, red wattle, and spurred legs.

Ruffed grouse. It is reasonably common but difficult to find because of its variegated plumage, which blends into its surrounds. This is the bird that drums during the spring.

Red-eyed vireo. One of the park's most abundant songbirds, it is heard far more often than it is seen. It is rather plain, with a bold white eye line bordered by black and a red eye.

Scarlet tanager. It is most common on the upper slopes in summer; the males are scarlet with coal black wings and females are olive green.

Indigo bunting. Males are bright indigo, sing all during spring and summer, and prefer clearings at any elevation.

15

Big South Fork National River and Recreation Area, Kentucky and Tennessee

The pileated woodpecker is one of the world's most outstanding birds. Not only is it the largest of our woodpeckers, looking very much like Woody Woodpecker of cartoon fame, but it also is one of the most vocal. And Bandy Creek Campground, at Big South Fork, has one of the largest populations of these wonderful birds of any place I know. Their loud, raucous calls can be heard there at almost any time of day.

A pair of pileated woodpeckers (according to Webster's *Ninth New Collegiate Dictionary*, both "pie-le" and "pill-e" pronunciations are correct) were perched on a huge black oak tree very near our campsite. Their large, black bodies, bright red crests, and the bold white line that extends from their white cheeks down their necks were obvious. The male, evident from the red patch behind the bill, suddenly called out a loud, high-pitched, and rather nasal "kuk-kuk, kuk-kuk." It then took flight, looking almost like a huge bat. Its great, broad wings beat slowly but powerfully enough to drive this large bird in a direct line (although they often exhibit an undulating flight), giving the distinct impression that it was mostly wings. Its flight is so different from that of most other birds that it can be identified at a great distance. It is similar to the American crow, in both flight and size.

Pileated woodpeckers require big trees and large acreage. They have disappeared from many parts of their range due to timber cutting and fragmentation of their habitat. They utilize year-round territories and may mate for life. Nest cavities are constructed in dead trees from 15 to 85 feet (4.5 to 26 m) above the ground but usually 28 to 35 feet (9 to 11 m) high, according to John Terres. And Paul Ehrlich and colleagues described an incident in which a female pileated transferred eggs from a fallen nest tree to another nest, and the pair succeeded in raising their brood.

Huge, gaping holes are often dug into dead and dying trees for insects, which make up about 75 percent of their diet; fruits and nuts make up the remainder. Their winter diet, especially during colder winters when most insects are no longer available, may be mostly dormant ants.

Pileated woodpecker

The female pileated at Bandy Creek Campground remained in place near my campsite, working the deep hole in the oak tree. It probably had found larvae of beetles or some other wood-boring insects, and I watched as it continued to feed. I could only imagine its specialized tongue, equipped with tiny barbs to aid in capturing insects, probing into the cavity it had dug with sharp pounding of its heavy bill. Then suddenly it flew, its broad wings flapping. It called one last time as it apparently joined its mate, uttering a similar but slightly higher pitched "kuk, kuk, kuk, kuk, kuk."

The Park Environment

The centerpiece of the park is the Big South Fork of the Cumberland River, created by the confluence of the Clear Fork and the New River in Tennessee. The Big South Fork flows north for more than 80 miles (129 km) through the Cumberland Plateau from Peters Ford Bridge, Tennessee, to Yahoo Falls, Kentucky, and beyond. Elevations vary from 800 feet (244 m) along the river to 1,800 feet (549 m) along the highest ridges. Of the park's 105,000 acres (42,493 ha), only a thin ribbon is river and floodplain habitat. The vast majority of the park consists of deciduous forest and scattered fields in various states of regeneration.

Dominant woody plants of the deciduous forest include beech, sugar maple, yellow birch, and tulip-tree in the moist soils of coves and ravines; eastern hemlock, river birch, sycamore, and an undergrowth of rosebay rhododendron along the river floodplain; and Virginia pine, white and red oaks, and hickory on the drier, well-drained sites. Old fields contain a variety of grasses and sedges, and the thickets that are common along the old fencerows and deserted yards are comprised of blackberry, winged and staghorn sumacs, honeysuckle, and briars.

The park's visitor center is located at Bandy Creek in Tennessee, although part-time information services are also available at Blue Heron, Kentucky. The Bandy Creek Visitor Center contains a few exhibits and a book/craft store that carries several nature guides, including bird field guides. A list of possible birds is also available for the asking, but the best, most up-to-date list is included in *Hiking the Big South Fork*, by Brenda Coleman and Jo Anne Smith.

Interpretive activities are provided from Memorial Day through Labor Day and include evening talks and guided walks on weekends at various locations. Schedules are posted or can be obtained at the information stations. None of the programs are specifically on birds, but some guided walks are nature oriented. The park's interpretive staff also provides environmental education programs in local communities during the school year.

Campgrounds are located at Bandy Creek and Blue Heron, but backcountry camping is permitted almost anywhere in the park. Only "primitive lodging" is available inside the park, at Charit Creek

Lodge from mid-April to mid-December; reservations are necessary. Other lodging and supplies are available at the adjacent towns.

Big South Fork is primarily a multiple-use recreational area. River trips are most popular from late winter to early summer, when water level allows for favorable canoeing and rafting; check for water levels at the park's visitor center. Free-flowing, the Big South Fork is a renowned river with Class III and above rapids, as well as an abundance of quiet and serene sections. A list of outfitters is available on request.

The park maintains 150 miles (241 km) of hiking trails and 130 miles (209 km) of horse trails. The Coleman and Smith book includes details on all of the park's trails. Horses can be rented at Bandy Creek Stables. In addition, mountain biking on the horse trails and roadways is allowed. Park legislation also permits hunting, an activity not normally permitted within national parks. Deer hunting season runs from late September through the second weekend in December.

Additional information can be acquired from the Superintendent, Big South Fork National River and Recreation Area, Route 3, Box 401, Oneida, TN 37841; (615) 879-3625.

Bird Life

The Bandy Creek Campground and adjacent fields, including the visitor center grounds and stable area, are among the park's best places to find birds. The small cattail pond almost always contains a few **red-winged blackbirds**. The male's black body and red wing patches are its most obvious features; the female is duller, with darker streaks and very faint wing patches. Almost everyone knows the red-wing's song, a liquid gurgling "konk-quer-ree," ending in a trill.

When nesting among the cattails, the males challenge each other with loud "chut, chuck" calls, often voicing a shrill alarm, "chee-e-e-e," and circling the pond with open wings to display their gorgeous epaulets. In fall and winter red-wings may appear in flocks of a dozen to hundreds, often wheeling together like black snowflakes in a driving storm.

The cattail pond attracts a variety of bird life. Park interpreter Howard Duncan told me that he once found a common loon that stayed three days and another time, a red-breasted merganser. Many of the local birds frequent the pond to drink. During my late October visit to the park, there were hundreds of American robins around the pond. They perched in the nearby trees and seemed to take turns at the pond; sometimes a dozen or more would line the edge for a drink. Chipping sparrows were abundant there, too, their reddish caps gleaming in the early morning light.

American crows were the loudest of the many bird species that morning. Their "caw caws" were everywhere. Crows were flying over the forest and fields and walking along the edges of the parking lots and in the picnic area, searching, no doubt, for scraps left by yesterday's visitors. Blue jays were just as numerous, and their "jay jay jay" calls were almost as loud. I watched a small flock of these birds in the shrubbery behind the pond. They were jumping onto the leaf-strewn ground, flipping leaves this way and that, searching for food, and then flying back to the shrubbery while others took their turn. I wasn't sure whether their timing was purposeful or only coincidental. But their blue backs, with white wing bars, and blue, black, and white crested heads, were most colorful.

Hundreds of European starlings are usually present about the compound, as well. These nonnative birds are attracted to the stables and will usurp nesting sites of the cavity-nesting native species. The eastern bluebird is one species that has been affected by the aggressive starlings, but bluebirds were fairly common that October morning, thanks perhaps to the nest box program designed to aid bluebirds but exclude the larger starlings. I found several bluebird boxes along the edges of the fields.

The woods to the left of the visitor center were suddenly alive with birds. The melodic trill of a pine warbler was first to attract my attention. I found this little yellowish bird searching the needles of a short-leafed pine, almost creeping about the boughs. A pair of downy woodpeckers were present at eye level, whacking at the branch of a young pine. Higher up was a red-bellied woodpecker, calling out "chuuur." And a white-breasted nuthatch was also present, creeping along the trunk of another short-leafed pine. I watched it searching for insects in the scaly bark.

"Jimmy, jimmy, jimmy," sang a **Carolina wren** from the undergrowth. I switched my attention to this reddish bird with a bold white eye line as it popped up into view. And another nearby Carolina wren sang a slightly different song, "tea-kettle, tea-kettle, tea-kettle," with an inflection on the first syllable. Frank Chapman referred to this bird as the "mocking wren," because of its variety of calls. He wrote that it has "irrepressible energy, and the bird accompanies his movements by more or less appropriate notes: scolding cacks, clinking, metallic rattles, musical trills, tree-toadlike krrrings—in fact, he possesses an almost endless vocabulary." See chapter 28 on Congaree Swamp for additional details of the Carolina wren's singing ability.

The Carolina wren is common throughout the park, preferring forest edges and thickets. Its nervous behavior is fairly typical of wrens, but few have adapted so well to human habitation. Pairs utilize permanent territories and can usually be found there throughout the year. They nest in natural cavities of trees and elsewhere.

The park's many fields, mostly the old farms that have been sold to the government for public use, are still filled with weedy vegetation that attracts a variety of birds. Common yellowthroats, eastern meadowlarks, and grasshopper and field sparrows utilize the open grasslands, while another group of birds prefer the fencerows and thickets: northern mockingbirds, brown thrashers, rufous-sided towhees, song sparrows, and American goldfinches.

In spring and summer, the **prairie warbler** sings its very high-pitched, ascending song, not a trill but very separate notes, from the tops of the red cedars that are beginning to invade the old fields. This little songster is one of the prettiest and most easily identified of the warblers. Its song is so very distinctive, and it will sing throughout the daylight hours. The male's all-yellow underparts are bordered by black streaks on the face and chest; its back is a yellowish-green color with a chestnut patch that sometimes is difficult to see. It also twitches its tail when foraging for food. Females possess a similar pattern but are not as bright.

The prairie warbler spends its winters in Florida and the West Indies, from Cuba to the Virgin Islands. This bird is another reason it is so important to speak out in support of habitat protection, not only in the United States but also where these warblers spend their winters. The survival of prairie warblers depends just as much on the protection of mangroves and deciduous forests in the West Indies as it does on the perpetuation of natural ecosystems within the United States.

The Angel Falls Trail follows the Big South Fork for two miles through the forested ravine bordered by high cliffs. The thermals rising from the canyon usually support soaring vultures and hawks. **Turkey vultures** are most numerous, with their long, black wings and bare, red heads. This large bird with a six-foot wingspan is often mistaken for an eagle or hawk. But turkey vultures hold their wings tilted upward in a slight V-shape, unlike most hawks. They often soar for hours on end above the cliffs, riding the currents like kites, with rare wing beats. Vultures are true scavengers that depend on dead animals for their survival. They will feed on carcasses that are in the last state of putrification. And they feed their young by regurgitation. In spite of their so-called vile occupation in the web of life, they are a vital strand. See chapter 14 on Cumberland Gap for additional information on this bird's flying ability.

Another of the park's soaring birds is the somewhat smaller **red-tailed hawk**. This is the common broad-winged hawk with a dull red to brick red tail and white or mottled underparts. If its tail has black and light bands, it is not a red-tail but the smaller broad-winged or red-shouldered hawk. Red-tails are full-time residents and can be expected anyplace in the park. They feed primarily on rodents, which they capture by stooping from above, often in a power dive with wings folded and talons extended at the last second. This bird can also hover in the air like an American kestrel and then glide down to capture prey that it has found from above.

When red-tails retire for the night, they may be replaced by one of the nocturnal predators: a great horned owl in the fields and secondary vegetation, a barred owl in the taller vegetation along the waterway, or an eastern screech-owl in the forest. These owls are more often heard than seen. The more common great horned owl song is a series of hoots, "whoo whoo who-who," while the somewhat smaller barred owl song can include a whole range of sounds. Its most distinctive song is a rhythmic series of hoots, "who-cooks-for-you, who-cooks-for-you-all." It is almost a primeval sound. And from up close, as might be experienced by river runners camping along the river, it can be a wonderful wilderness expression. See chapter 26 on Cumberland Island for additional information.

The eastern screech-owl is quite common within the park and sings a very different song from that of the two larger owls. Screech-owls sing a variety of songs, including a rapid trill, all on the same pitch except for a decided drop on the last few notes; a long, horse-like whinny call; and a series of short barks and yelps. This little, eared (feather tufts) owl comes in both gray and red phases.

Another bird of the river is the **belted kingfisher**, a reasonably large bird with a massive bill that it uses to capture its prey. It is usually found flying swiftly along the river or perched on an over-hanging snag or branch. From there it watches for a passing fish, frog, snake, or some other critter. It will then dive headfirst into the water to grab its prey and fly to a perch to feed. See chapter 27 on the Chattahoochee River for a further description of this species.

A kingfisher is slightly longer than one foot and is mostly blue above and white below with a blue chest band. The female has a rusty belly band. This crested bird will often sit very still as it is approached. It will usually allow a closer approach by a boat than by a hiker. Then suddenly it will fly swiftly away, calling in a very loud, dry rattle, usually twice or several times. It will often make a wide circle to let the boaters pass before returning to the same perch.

Several songbirds not mentioned above are present along the river in spring and summer. The long, skinny bird with white under-parts, rufous wing patches in flight, and a yellow bill is a yellow-billed cuckoo. The eastern kingbird is black above and white below with a broad white tip on its tail. Three swallows are likely: the fork-tailed barn swallow; the cliff swallow with its buff rump and chest which builds mud nests on the cliffs; and the nondescript brown northern rough-winged swallow, which nests in burrows in dirt banks. The yellow warbler, all yellow with faint rusty chest stripes, frequents patches of willows. The yellow-throated warbler sings high in sycamore trees. The brown and black orchard oriole also prefers sycamore trees along the riverway. And the all-red bird with a yellow bill is a summer tanager; its call is a loud and continuous staccato "ki-ti-tuck." The all-red bird with a crest is the northern cardinal.

In summary, the Coleman and Smith checklist contains 143 species, 93 of which are permanent or summer residents and are assumed to nest. Of those, only 2 (green-backed heron and wood duck) are water birds, 8 are hawks and owls, and 17 are warblers. Seventeen of the 143 species are considered winter visitors only: pied-billed grebe, Cooper's hawk, common snipe, short-eared owl, yellow-bellied sapsucker, red-breasted nuthatch, winter wren, brown creeper, golden-crowned and ruby-crowned kinglets, hermit thrush, yellow-rumped warbler, swamp and white-throated sparrows, red crossbill, pine siskin, and evening grosbeak. Many of these probably occur as migrants as well.

Birds of Special Interest

Turkey vulture. It is most often seen soaring over the steep slopes. Its flight pattern is unique, and it tips slightly from side to side. A turkey vulture has a six-foot wingspan and a bare, red head.

Red-tailed hawk. This raptor soars as well and is usually identified by its broad wings and brick red, nonbanded tail.

Pileated woodpecker. The largest of our woodpeckers, with a black-and-white body and red crest, it looks much like cartoon character Woody Woodpecker.

Belted kingfisher. It is rarely found away from the river and is identified by its bluish body, crest, and huge bill that it uses to spear its prey.

Carolina wren. This is the reddish songster with a bold white eye line that sings its "tea-kettle" song throughout the daytime.

Prairie warbler. It can be found among the red cedars in the old fields; its distinct song is an ascending series of high-pitched notes.

Red-winged blackbird. It prefers the marshy areas along the river and at ponds. Males are black with bright red wing patches.

16

Mammoth Cave National Park, Kentucky

There is something haunting about the song of the wood thrush. It is a sound of the deep, undisturbed forest, where few humans venture. Yet its beautiful, flutelike song is commonplace within the broadleaf forests at Mammoth Cave. It is, in fact, the dominant bird song there during spring and summer. Anyone walking the park trails can hear the wood thrush's incredible songs, an outdoor experience that will not soon be forgotten. Louis Halle wrote,

> The ease and leisure of the wood thrush's song is one of its characteristics. The singer is never shaken with effort like a house wren. Usually he sits motionless on a branch, at rest. Every few seconds (with the regularity of some marvelous mechanical toy) he lifts his head, opens his bill, and delivers himself of a brief phrase; subsiding then until another phrase has formed and is ready to well up within him.

The wood thrush is a secretive bird, one that prefers the shadows to open sunlight. Except at dawn and dusk, when it frequents the open trails and roadways, it is a bird not easily seen. At these times it feeds on insects, running here and there to capture some juicy morsel, before standing upright and alert, ever watchful for predators. Its cinnamon-rufous back and head and white underparts with large black spots are often difficult to see in the subdued morning light. But when sunlight falls on this lovely robin-sized bird, amid the bright green foliage, it becomes one of the forest's loveliest creatures.

Wood thrushes were in full song as we walked down the path

Wood thrush

that summer morning, beyond the park visitor center, past the hotel to the historic cave entrance, and onward to the floodplain of the Green River. I counted at least a dozen individuals along the way. Their songs seemed even more vibrant as we descended the slope. Their only competition that morning came from the busy Carolina wrens, another reddish-colored songster of the forest. Next in abundance perhaps was the white-breasted nuthatch. Their continual nasal honks provided communications between young birds and adults. But the loudest of the bird sounds came from the much larger pileated woodpeckers. This crow-sized species is the real world's Woody Woodpecker. Its black body and black-and-white head, and the male's bright red crest are difficult to mistake for any other species, especially when it is perched only a few feet away on an open trunk of a tree, as so often occurs along this trail. There are few places where these large, showy woodpeckers are as numerous as in the forest at Mammoth Cave National Park. See chapter 15 on Big South Fork for a description of this woodpecker there.

Verdie Abel, one of the park interpreters, and I had begun our walk at the visitor center at dawn. A white-tailed doe and two spotted fawns were still grazing on the lawn. A lone raccoon was making a last round before retiring to some dark cavity for the day. Several American crows had just arrived in the parking lot and were searching for breakfast. The trumpetlike calls of blue jays echoed from the adjacent forest. Overhead were several chimney swifts, their bodies dark gray with long, swept-back wings, out for their first feeding flights of the day.

Several "edge birds," those species that live along the forest edge instead of inside the forest, were active as well. American robins, close relatives of the wood thrush, were searching for worms on the lawn, and a pair of eastern kingbirds were chasing one another about the tops of the cedars. I detected the soft "chur-ree" calls of eastern bluebirds. Far across the lawns was a singing indigo bunting, sitting atop an isolated red cedar. The trill of chipping sparrows and the "to-whee" call of a rufous-sided towhee were evident as well.

We stopped at the cave's historic entrance to locate an eastern phoebe pair known to nest on the walls there year after year. Tufted titmice and Carolina chickadees were singing in the higher foliage. Suddenly the low whinny call of an eastern screech-owl resounded from the dense foliage higher up the slope. We searched the dim outlines of the open branches for this nocturnal predator without success. This little gray or reddish owl could be calling from a nest hole, or it could be perched against a tree trunk in such a position that finding it from 100 to 200 feet (30 to 60 m), through a network of twigs and foliage, would be impossible.

Farther down the trail, the clean whistle notes of a red-eyed vireo descended from the high foliage of a huge sycamore tree. It took us several minutes to locate this bird, and we watched it gleaning the underside of several leaves for insects. Much closer to where we stood, at about eye level, a smaller bird darted up from its perch to capture a tiny flying insect. It immediately returned to the same perch, pumped its tail once or twice, and then commenced to swallow its catch. I watched this Acadian flycatcher capture three more insects, returning each time to the same perch, before it flew away to another perch. Twice it sang its rather sharp "peet-see-it" song.

Across the wooded ravine, from among the tangle of limbs and shrubs, came a loud, clear warbler song, "weeta weeta wee-tee-o." A second song followed the first. We repositioned ourselves so that we could better see the place where the songs emerged. I made one loud chip sound, my lips to the back of my hand, then another. Suddenly the songster appeared in the tangle of brush, much closer than I had expected—a beautiful male hooded warbler. It undoubtedly had been attracted to my chips, but it stayed only briefly before moving out of sight again to continue its search for insects among the brush and litter.

Movement to the right of where the hooded warbler had disappeared attracted my attention. It was another warbler but not as bright yellow and black as the male hooded. Instead, this bird was buff overall, except for the black head stripes that identified it as a worm-eating warbler. It was, however, less shy and remained in sight for several minutes, all the time emitting a high-pitched, trilling call. We watched as it moved from the ground up to eight or ten feet high, gleaning insects from every object it encountered.

As I observed its very different behavior, I began to realize that I had seen a wide variety of feeding characteristics that morning. Even the two warblers utilize slightly different niches. They find insects on leaves, twigs, branches, and the ground. The red-eyed vireo forages high above in the upper canopy. The smaller chickadees and titmice utilize the higher foliage as well but search for insects at the outer ends of the branches taking advantage of their lighter weight. The screech-owl hunts rodents and large insects on the ground during the nighttime. The larger pileated woodpecker finds its prey within the insect-infested trunks of the larger trees. The white-throated nuthatch searches for insects on the trees' bark. The little Acadian flycatcher captures its prey on the wing after locating it from a perch, and seeds are the preferred food of the indigo bunting. The wood thrush and robin find their insects and worms on and just under the surface of the ground.

Finding a variety of forest birds verifies the significant recovery of the Mammoth Cave forest from the time when the park landscape was farmland and fields. The park's secondary forest is an intermediate step in the eventual return of a mature deciduous forest. The wide variety of forest birds that already nest there, utilizing a diversity of feeding methods, is a good indication of an increasingly stable community.

The Park Environment

The Mammoth Cave system includes more than 330 miles (531 km) of passageways, the world's longest. It was primarily that resource that prompted Congress to establish Mammoth Cave National Park in 1941. Although the vast majority of the park's visitors see only the underground resources, the 51,450-acre (20,822-ha) park contains equally fascinating aboveground attractions. In fact, the park contains some of the finest examples of North America's lowland deciduous forest community.

The forest can be divided into three general habitat types, although differences between the three are becoming less obvious as the vegetation matures. The river bottoms contain a rather lush, tall forest that is dominated by sycamore, maple, sweetgum, blackgum, beech, and willows. The tall, stately sycamores are some of the largest to be found anywhere.

The forest is not so lush above the floodplain and is dominated by several species of oaks and hickories and the tulip-tree. Persimmon, dogwood, redbud, and sourwood are abundant in the undergrowth. And the higher, drier ridges are dominated by pines and red cedars. In general, the park's topography varies from rolling hills to rugged canyons and sinkholes, forested valleys, and narrow river bottoms.

Mammoth Cave National Park, ranging in elevation from 421 to 920 feet (128-280 m), is located on a limestone plateau in south-central Kentucky, halfway between Nashville and Louisville. Hotel accommodations are available inside the park, and more accommodations are available at nearby Cave City, on Interstate 65. Camping is also available inside the park. A restaurant and gift shop are connected to the hotel, and the National Park Service visitor center has a sales outlet for books and other interpretive materials. Field guides to birds and other animals, as well as plants, are available there.

Additional information can be obtained from the Superintendent, Mammoth Cave National Park, Mammoth Cave, KY 42259; (502) 758-2251.

Bird Life

More than 200 species of birds have been recorded within the park, and the greatest number are present during late spring and early summer. Approximately 90 species are known to nest. Early May is the best time of year to find the greatest variety of birds, for that is when all of the park's breeding species are present and the northbound migrants are still passing through the state. Migrant land birds can be especially abundant, as "waves of warblers cross the state," according to Kentucky ornithologist Burt Monroe.

In spring and summer, warblers are some of the park's greatest attractions. These are fairly easy to locate during May and June, when they are actively defending a territory and nesting; the forest can literally be full of warbler songs. But by July, they are less active and usually difficult to locate, especially those species that feed in the upper canopy. In addition, midsummer warblers often sport their less distinctive postbreeding plumage and are more difficult to identify. Also, some species actually begin their southward migration by midsummer.

Kentucky warbler

No one should leave Mammoth Cave without seeing a **Kentucky warbler.** This boldly marked, yellow and black bird, with a broad black "whisker" mark running below the eye onto the throat, can be common at moist places along the rivers and at ponds. It is a fairly large warbler, with long legs and a habit of walking rapidly over the forest floor, then searching methodically for food among the leaves and debris. It often bobs its tail up and down.

The Kentucky warbler song is wonderfully cheery and loud, and although similar to that of the more common Carolina wren, it is a more explosive and clear "churry churry churry" or "tur-dle, tur-dle, tur-dle." Paul Ehrlich and colleagues pointed out, "Each male has only one song type in his repertoire but can alter frequency characteristics of songs to match songs of nearby males when countersinging." Early ornithologist Frank Chapman described a male Kentucky warbler that sang "about 875 times, or some 5,250 notes," within one three-hour period. It also has a distinct call note, a loud "chuck" that is often uttered over and over again when it is alarmed.

Another of the park's streamside warblers is the more subtly marked Louisiana waterthrush. It, too, has a loud and wild character to its song, which Wayne Peterson wrote as "see-you see-you see-you chew chew to-wee." This is another long-legged bird that walks rather than hops, constantly raising and lowering its tail, teetering up and down with a noticeable springing motion of its legs. It has a dark back and white underparts, with heavy black streaks on the chest and buff flanks, and a heavy white streak above the eye.

Then there is the **common yellowthroat**, which, at least along the rivers, is the most numerous of all the park's warblers. Its loud "whitchity whitchity whitchity" song is one of the better-known songs in all the bird world. The male's bright yellow throat and black mask are very distinctive; the female has dull plumage. This is a bird that is easy to entice out of the heavy underbrush with a loud chip sound or by spishing.

The other warblers that are known to nest within the park include prothonotary, blue-winged, northern parula, black-and-white, cerulean, yellow-throated, prairie, yellow, Swainson's, ovenbird, yellow-breasted chat, and American redstart.

Woodpeckers are other significant members of the park's bird community. They are some of the most obvious and easiest birds to find and watch. I was especially impressed with finding seven species within the picnic area next to the busy visitor center parking lot. The most exciting of these were several **red-headed woodpeckers** that were obvious one early morning in July. Their loud "ker-r-ruck, ker-r-ruck" calls actually vibrated throughout the area, and I found three adults calling from the very tops of snags that stood above the high foliage. Five youngsters were present as well, acting like any other youngsters enjoying the early morning. They seemed actually to fall from the foliage out of control, then suddenly glide to another snag or patch of foliage. The immature birds lacked the bright red heads of the adults but showed large, white wing patches even at this early stage. This species, once reasonably common throughout North America, except in the Southwest, has declined throughout its range. The presence of nesting birds within the park provides a special opportunity to see this very distinct and unique species.

Northern flickers were present as well, and once I observed a young flicker join the red-heads. At least three adult flickers called out occasionally; their nasal "kee-yer" calls seemed almost to approve of the youngster's frolics with the red-heads. And a pair of red-bellied woodpeckers tapped away on the midlevel branches of a tall beech tree.

Downy woodpeckers were fairly numerous there as well; their presence was most evident from their thin "peek" calls, less obvious than those of their larger, look-alike cousins, the hairy woodpeckers. Both species continued their tapping patterns, some louder than others, and I was not sure if I could differentiate the two species by pattern or intensity. I could, however, easily separate the loudness of these two birds' pecking from the much heavier tapping of the pileated woodpecker that was also present.

I found the picnic area and adjacent parking lot to be one of the best birding areas in the entire park. Early in the morning, before the masses of park visitors arrive, one can find 30 or more species just in the woodland edges. The area provides an exceptional opportunity for anyone wanting to see birds while waiting for a cave tour.

Verdie and I spent one early morning at Sloan's Crossing Pond, located along the Park City entrance road (State Road 70). According to Gordon Wilson, the first ornithologist to study the park birds, the pond was created by the Civilian Conservation Corps (CCC) but was later enlarged when beavers dammed the entrance. Today, it is one of the few freshwater ponds in the park and the only place where red-winged blackbirds regularly nest.

We found four wood ducks swimming among the water lilies at Sloan's Crossing Road. All were young birds of the year, probably from a tree nest along the edge of the pond. A pair of eastern phoebes were catching flies from woody shrubs in the center of the pond. A red-shouldered hawk screamed off to my right. Blue jays were present, too, and it seemed, from their continuous squawking, that they had found this larger predator and were giving it a hard time.

Following an easy trail around the pond, we encountered a few other bird species. The rich chip note of a Kentucky warbler led us to a good look at this welcome songster. The emphatic "chip-whee-oo" call of a white-eyed vireo was heard on several occasions. Other birds encountered on our walk included eastern screech-owl, downy and pileated woodpeckers, eastern wood-pewee, blue jay, Carolina wren, Carolina chickadee, tufted titmouse, gray catbird, red-eyed vireo, hooded warbler, scarlet tanager, and American goldfinch. We expected to find a prothonotary warbler among the pondside vegetation but did not; Verdie had seen one there earlier in the spring.

Later that morning we took the very short ferry ride across the Green River and drove a wide circle through the northern portion of the park to Temple Hill, just above the Houchins Ferry crossing. We parked next to a small cemetery and walked the First Creek Trail for about a mile and a quarter to First Creek Lake. According to Verdie, this lake is the largest in the park and one of the best places to find water birds.

It was a beautiful walk through fairly rough terrain within a lovely, tall forest. The trail descends into the Nolin River gorge, which it follows for several hundred yards before dropping onto the lakeshore. Sure enough, several green-backed herons and a lone great blue heron flew off as we approached. A number of wood ducks moved into the protective vegetation across the lake. The rattle call of a lone belted kingfisher echoed across the pond. Here we also added broad-tailed hawk and rough-winged swallow to our growing list of Mammoth Cave birds. We visited two backcountry campsites, very close to the lakeshore. Both were empty, and I promised myself that I would return there someday to enjoy the wonderful ambience of this isolated spot.

Finally, there is the very easy, paved Heritage Trail that starts at the hotel and makes a half-mile loop to Sunset Point. My wife and I walked this trail one evening soon after she had shed her cast from a broken ankle. Evening sounds are not as grand as those at dawn, but many of the same birds were singing. A great crested flycatcher and a pair of summer tanagers were evident along the edge of the hotel grounds. A northern flicker called from across the way, and a pileated woodpecker call came from the forest.

We sat for about an hour at Sunset Point, listening to bird songs and enjoying the calmness that prevailed. A family of white-breasted nuthatches was active in the trees nearby. An Acadian flycatcher was singing some distance down the slope, and an eastern wood-pewee added its plaintive song to the chorus. There, too, was the beautiful, flutelike song of the wood thrush.

Suddenly, a doe and two spotted fawns emerged from the forest to feed on the new, green vegetation only a dozen feet from where we sat. They seemed to ignore us, and yet we were aware of the doe's watchfulness.

Down the trail came a number of children, four to twelve years of age, and sounding for all the world like each was trying to outdo the other. The doe and fawns became alert and stared toward the oncoming sounds. Then suddenly the noise ceased. The children had seen the deer. They became different people, quiet, calm, and curious. They stared for several minutes and then walked slowly by, each inspecting the doe and fawns in his own way but each with due respect. The deer stayed and resumed their feeding.

As the children passed by, I told them that they "would see much more of the forest if they would be quieter and watchful." My message was apparently ignored, because as they continued along the trail, they soon were just as noisy as they had been before. But I marveled at how seeing wildlife can truly calm the savage breast. And I thought, too, of the value of the Mammoth Cave forest as a place of refuge and solitude, as well as a valuable resource for all the world.

In summary, the Mammoth Cave checklist of birds contains 162 species, 73 of which are considered to nest. Of these, only 3 are water birds, 8 are hawks and owls, and 17 are warblers. Twelve species occur only in winter: American black duck, mallard, rough-legged hawk, common snipe, yellow-bellied sapsucker, golden-crowned kinglet, cedar waxwing, brown creeper, red-breasted nuthatch, winter wren, hermit thrush, and yellow-rumped warbler.

Birds of Special Interest
Eastern screech-owl. Listen for its wavering song that descends slightly near the end; sometimes the call is a long whinny. Usually heard after dark, these owls also may sing during early morning and late afternoon. They are fairly common behind the visitor center and near the historic cave entrance.

Wild turkey. This large, well-known bird is fairly common within the park, although it was once totally eradicated by hunting and clearing of the forest. Birds were reintroduced to the park, and their numbers have increased. Look for it along the trail below the historic cave entrance.

Red-headed woodpecker. Two or three pairs frequent the far end of the picnic area, and young may be seen in summer. The bright red head and black-and-white wings help to identify this usually hard-to-find bird.

Pileated woodpecker. The largest and showiest of the park's woodpeckers, it is common within the forests throughout the park. It is easiest to find along the trail to the historic cave entrance.

Wood thrush. There is no better singer, and it is common through most of the park in spring and summer. Although it can be difficult to see, its beautiful, flutelike songs are especially common at dawn and dusk.

Kentucky warbler. Watch for this rather secretive yellow and black warbler at wetlands and in moist forest areas where there is good cover. Its yellow throat and spectacles, surrounded with black, are the best identifying features.

17

Shenandoah National Park, Virginia

The early morning mist dissolved in front of me as I made my way through the wet grasses and shrubs of Big Meadows. Bird song was everywhere. And a hundred or more barn swallows were all around, searching the air for their first meals of the day. Eastern bluebirds were almost as numerous; many were youngsters barely off the nest. Song sparrows were perched on several of the low shrubs, each one trying to outdo the other in territorial songsmanship. There, too, were the field sparrows, birds I had long admired for their cheery song that ends with a spirited trill. A brightly colored, male rufous-sided towhee flew across my view, alighted on a taller shrub, and called its very distinct "chreee." Its maroon-red eye was a marked contrast to its coal black head.

Four or five white-tailed deer disappeared into the shrubbery in the center of Big Meadows as I approached. The taller shrubs were primarily spirea and red-panicle dogwood, and numerous blueberry bushes, literally full of lush, rich fruit, were scattered throughout. Gray catbirds were scolding, and when one jumped onto an open twig I could see purple-red stain on its head, a sure sign of blueberry indulgence. The "wichity, wichity, wichity" song of a common yellowthroat sounded from deep in the center of the thicket. And then I detected the sharp double-syllable song of a flycatcher: "fitz-bew, fitz-bew," very towhee-like. I edged around the shrubbery to where I could see the bird. It sat at the top of the tallest shrub, its back to me, singing its two-syllable song again and again. In another few minutes I was able to circle the thicket to where I could see the bird's front side. It had very plain underparts, a slight yellowish belly, a yellow-orange lower mandible, and only a smudge of an eye ring. A willow flycatcher, I was sure, though Empidonax flycatchers are tough to identify. Yet all of its features, including its distinct song and the habitat, were right for a willow. It was not the most beautiful of Shenandoah's more than 200 bird species, but it was an exciting find, nonetheless.

The Park Environment

Shenandoah National Park is largely a mountaintop park, although each of the hundreds of side drainages and dozens of hollows below the ridge top possesses unique characteristics. The 331-square-mile (128-sq-km) park, established in 1935, extends along the northern Blue Ridge Mountains for 80 miles (129 km) from Waynesboro north to Front Royal, all within western Virginia. The famous Shenandoah Valley lies to the west of the Blue Ridge, and the more gradual eastern slopes drain into the Rappahannock and James rivers, which cut through the Piedmont Plateau and flow into Chesapeake Bay.

Skyline Drive follows the ridge tops inside the park for 105 miles (169 km) and is intersected by four highways: at the northern and southern ends of the park and at two more central locations, Thornton Gap between Luray and Sperryville and Swift Run Gap between Elkton and Stanardsville. The Appalachian Trail also follows the ridge top and is an integral part of the park's trail system.

The National Park Service maintains visitor centers at Dickey Ridge, which is at the northern end of Skyline Drive, and at Big Meadows, halfway between Thornton and Swift Run gaps. Each provides information on the park, including introductory films, exhibits, and a sales outlet for books, postcards, posters, and the like, including field guides and a bird checklist.

A wide variety of interpretive activities are available at a number of park locations from Memorial Day through Labor Day. Bird walks are provided weekly in season at Big Meadows and Skyland, and a special "Birds of Prey" program, with live owls and hawks, is given at a wide range of locations ten times each week. The park's *Shenandoah Overlook*, a free newspaper, is published each season and contains information on all of the interpretive programs. It is available throughout the park and at many adjacent sites.

Camping is available in the park during the travel season at four key locations, while lodging is available only at Skyland, Big Meadows, and Lewis Mountain. Numerous commercial campgrounds and motels are available outside the park along all four of the cross-mountain highways.

Shenandoah is the heart of the northern Blue Ridge Mountains. The park's vegetation is dominated by eastern deciduous forest, although remnants of boreal forest occur at the highest elevations and in a few of the moist, cool drainages. The National Park Service has further classified the vegetation into seven rather distinct plant communities. By far the most extensive of these is the chestnut oak forest that makes up 49 percent of the park ecosystem. It occurs on low to midelevation slopes that have a southern or southwestern aspect. The tulip-tree community, with yellow birch, eastern hemlock, white pine, and white oak, occurs on the lower side slopes and is second in acreage (16%). Third is the cove hardwood forest (15%), dominated by ash, red oak, and basswood, which occurs in the hollows and other moist sites. Red oak (10%), pine (6%), black locust (4%), and eastern hemlock (1%) make up the rest of the park's forest communities.

A few additional habitats occur within the park, but their small sizes make them rather insignificant. For example, the summit of Hawksbill Mountain contains a relic stand of balsam fir, and Big Meadows contains a fascinating grassland/shrub community as well as a small wetland.

Additional information can be obtained from the Superintendent, Shenandoah National Park, Rt. 4, Box 348, Luray, VA 22835-9051; (703) 999-2243.

Bird Life

Anyone driving the park's Skyline Drive will undoubtedly stop occasionally at one of the numerous overlooks, many of which are situated at a gap or an open area maintained as a vista. These locations invariably possess a few birds that, although they may be absent or uncommon elsewhere, can be very obvious and elicit excitement from even the least interested visitor.

The bright blue **indigo bunting** (male) is common at all the overlooks at all elevations throughout the summer season. This sparrow-sized songster is undoubtedly one of the park's most readily observed birds. If it does not appear immediately, it can almost always be found by its loud and merry song. John Terres described the song as "sweet-sweet, where-where, here-here, see-it, see-it." And it will often sing the same song over and over again, even in late summer when most of the other birds are silent. Females and immature birds cannot match the bright indigo color of the males; the former are a dull brown color, but all possess a stout conical bill, suitable for eating seeds.

One reason for the indigo bunting's lengthy season of song is that it usually produces two broods. Three to six eggs are laid in a well-woven cup placed in the crotch of a woody shrub 5 to 15 feet high. Nest-building materials include almost anything found locally: dried grasses, dead leaves, strips of bark, weeds, feathers, hair, Spanish moss, snake skins, and an assortment of human debris, from pieces of paper to shreds of clothing.

Rufous-sided towhee

Another bird of the overlooks, often more numerous than the indigo bunting, is the larger **rufous-sided towhee**. It, too, will often perch out in the open and sing its very distinct towhee song, often described as "drink your tea," with a strong trill on "tea." This bird is one of the most curious of all the park birds; it takes very little coaxing, in the form of low spishing or chipping, to attract it into the open. Most park visitors already know the rufous-sided towhee from yards and gardens at home, and seeing one away from home in Shenandoah National Park can be like discovering a longtime friend.

The park overlooks also are good places to watch the numerous soaring birds. Most of the broad-winged raptors do not appear until the sun has warmed the slopes sufficiently to produce upward air currents. The rising columns of warm air are called "thermals." They keep the large soaring birds aloft with a minimum of energy expenditure for hours on end. Most numerous of these are the **turkey vultures**, clumsy scavengers on the ground but agile and graceful when riding a thermal high over the Blue Ridge. Their wingspan is almost six feet, and their bare, red heads and overall blackish color help to identify them even at a distance. The less common **black vulture** can sometimes be found soaring with them. It has shorter and broader wings with a whitish patch near each tip and a black, rather than a red, head.

The most commonly seen soaring hawk is the **red-tailed hawk**, usually identified by its reddish, nonbanded tail. This hawk is widely distributed throughout North America, and it can be expected almost anywhere in Shenandoah National Park. This adaptable raptor uses a variety of techniques in hunting. It may soar or hover over a field and use its excellent eyesight to locate a meadow mouse or other prey, then silently pounce on the unsuspecting rodent. It may perch on a tree or post and glide down to capture its prey. Or it may actually stalk its prey on the ground, jumping on rodents, small birds, snakes, salamanders, grasshoppers, and an assortment of other prey.

Two broad-tailed hawks with banded tails sometimes soar as well: the red-shouldered and broad-winged hawks. The red-shoulder is only occasionally seen but is resident in the park all year, preferring the lower cove hardwood forest areas. Its red shoulder patch is usually only evident when seen from a side view and reasonably close; it is more often identified by its very distinct call, a loud, drawn-out, screaming "kee-aaaah." The more common broad-winged hawk is also a forest hawk but is more inclined to soar in midday. It is a reasonably small hawk with a thin, slightly descend-

ing whistle call, a "pee-teee." The uncommon Cooper's hawk also
soars on occasion. It is an accipiter, or bird hawk, that preys on
smaller birds within the forest. Its flight pattern is quite different
from that of the slow flapping broad-wings; accipiters fly with quick
wing beats and then glide. Their wings are shorter and more rounded than those of the broad-wings.

Of all the park's raptors, none command as much respect and
attention as the **peregrine falcon**. It is one of the fastest and most
exciting birds in the world. But it is a bird that was totally extirpated from the park and elsewhere in eastern North America by pesticides. An estimated 350 pairs existed in 1942, but peregrines had
totally disappeared as breeding birds by 1964. Since then, DDT, the
pesticide that was the principal cause of eggshell thinning, has been
outlawed for use in the United States, and a major restoration effort
has been initiated in a few of the eastern parks. Since 1989, 29 peregrines have been returned to the wild in Shenandoah. It is hoped
that mature birds will return to local nesting sites and establish a
natural population once again.

The **common raven**, another of the park's soaring birds, often is
misidentified in flight. Its coal black color, broad but pointed wings,
and rounded tail can cause it to resemble a peregrine, a hawk, or
even an eagle. This bird is fairly common along Skyline Drive, and
early morning motorists can usually find it patrolling in search of
road kills from the previous night. See chapter 18 on the Blue Ridge
Parkway for further details about this bird.

With its general north-south orientation, the Blue Ridge serves
as an important highway for migrating hawks and other birds. In
fact, every year from September 15 to 25, the Charlottesville Bird
Club conducts a "hawk watch" at Rockfish Gap, at the south end of
the park. Participants count all the raptors that pass south along the
ridge during that period. Totals often mount into the thousands,
with broad-wings the most numerous. Ospreys, bald and golden
eagles, northern harriers, accipiters, and falcons are also included.

The **chestnut-sided warbler** is another of the overlook birds
that can be reasonably common. However, this little songster is easily missed because it is smaller than most other birds and rarely
sings from an open perch. Although it sings with great vigor during

Chestnut-sided warbler

May and June, it usually stays partially hidden among the foliage at the edge of the forest. Its musical song, however, is loud and clear and of a high enough pitch that it often can be heard above the other songsters. Its song is usually interpreted as "so pleased, so pleased, so pleased to meet cha."

Breeding chestnut-sided warblers possess chestnut-colored sides, white cheeks below black eye lines, and a yellow or chartreuse crown. If there ever was a chartreuse-colored bird, it would be the chestnut-sided warbler in late summer and fall, when the bird's back and crown turn that color. It is the only warbler that possesses all-white underparts, except for the chestnut stripes on its sides.

I also found several chestnut-sides along the upper portion of the Limberlost Trail in early August. They and most of the park's other breeding warblers were present within the old apple orchard that morning. I began my walk at the Whiteoak Falls Trailhead, across from Skyland, soon after daylight. An eastern wood-pewee was singing vigorously just inside the forest; I paused to look at that very plain, slightly crested bird. I watched it dash off its perch to capture an insect and return to the same perch, pump its tail once, and then consume its prey.

White-breasted nuthatches were giving their nasal "yank" calls nearby, and farther down the trail I encountered a pair of solitary vireos. The female was scolding, but I could not determine what had disturbed her. The brighter male sat quietly and allowed me to admire its olive green back, white throat, and large eye ring. The solitary vireo is one of the easiest of all birds to watch; it stays calm and collected and rarely is shy and skittish.

The Limberlost area contains a rather extensive stand of eastern hemlocks and red spruce and, therefore, represents quite a different habitat from most other places in the park. **Dark-eyed juncos** were the most abundant bird found there. Although this little, slate-colored bird with a white belly occurs almost everywhere along the Blue Ridge, Limberlost must represent the bird's most preferred habitat. Everywhere I turned were juncos. Several were singing a song that reminded me of the trill of chipping sparrows but more musical. Normally, junco songs are at the same pitch, but on several occasions I detected an abrupt change of pitch in the middle of their trill.

The Limberlost Trail makes a broad turn to the right and then doubles back through what was once an apple orchard. Apples were numerous, but they were small and hard. I decided to leave them to the birds. But I soon discovered that the birds had already discovered the area. The first indication of their presence was a loud chuck call from the undergrowth. I chucked back at the sound, but it took considerably more coaxing before a brightly marked Kentucky warbler emerged from the vegetation. It was a truly gorgeous bird, with its bright yellow and black face pattern, olive green above, and yellow underparts.

While I was admiring the Kentucky warbler, I realized that the trees behind me were literally filled with bird activity. There were at least five American redstarts, three yellow-tailed females and two red-and-black males. Three black-throated green warblers were in the same tree. And a lone worm-eating warbler was gleaning the lower leaves of an apple tree. A female black-and-white warbler was searching the tree trunk for food. A yellow-throated warbler (rare in the park) was present as well. Then a female or immature Blackburnian warbler came into focus alongside the yellow-throat. A chestnut-sided warbler was present, too. A loud "chick" call echoed from the shrubbery underneath the apple trees, and it took me several minutes to finally spot a Canada warbler. It stayed in

view for only a second or two before moving away. I had hit the
warbler jackpot! There were other members of the morning bird
party: downy woodpecker, northern flicker, great crested flycatcher,
American robin, Carolina wren, Carolina chickadee, blue-gray
gnatcatcher, solitary vireo, scarlet tanager, and rufous-sided towhee.

Later that morning I talked with park naturalist Terry Lindsay
about the park's bird life and the best places to find birds. Terry
agreed that the Limberlost area is a good birding locality. He said
that the South River Falls Trail, just north of Swift Run Gap, also
produced a good variety of birds in spring and summer. He told me
that his favorite birding area, especially during the spring migration, was the "Hazel country." The Buck Hollow Trail, which begins
at the Meadow Springs Parking Area a couple of miles south of
Thornton Gap, provides the best access route into that area.

Another good birding area is along the Appalachian Trail itself,
which transects 95 miles (153 km) of the park's ridge top habitats. A
walk along any mile of this trail can produce a good assortment of
birds any time of the year but midwinter. Ruffed grouse, shy birds
that are well concealed by their plumage, are reported more often
along the Appalachian Trail than anywhere else in the park.

I also met with Keith Watson, resource management specialist.
We talked about various bird projects being undertaken within the
park. Keith is the park coordinator for the peregrine restoration
program and is responsible for the annual breeding bird surveys.
Four surveys are done each year within the four districts of the
park. The goal of this monitoring program is to develop long-term
trend information that can be used to detect changes in the bird life
and, therefore, the park environment.

I examined the summary sheets for the recent breeding bird
surveys and discovered a total of 74 species. Thirty-two of the 74
species had been recorded in all four areas, and a dozen of those
stood out as especially abundant: eastern wood-pewee, Acadian flycatcher, American crow, northern raven, wood thrush, gray catbird,
red-eyed vireo, ovenbird, scarlet tanager, indigo bunting, rufous-
sided towhee, and American goldfinch.

We also talked about the winter birds. I had participated in one
of Shenandoah's Christmas Bird Counts years ago, and I had found

only 24 species during one very long, bitterly cold day between Thornton Gap and Skyland. But when Keith showed me a 22-year summary of the park's Christmas counts, I had a much better understanding of the status of the park's winter bird life. The total list amounted to 131 species, and 37 of those had been seen on every one of the 22 counts. The dozen most numerous wintering birds were turkey vulture, rock and mourning doves, American crow, blue jay, American robin, European starling, white-throated and white-crowned sparrows, dark-eyed junco, common grackle, and brown-headed cowbird.

In summary, the park's bird checklist contains 205 species. Only 49 of those are full-time residents within the park, and an additional 63 species occur in summer. Of the park's 112 breeding birds, only two are water birds, nine are hawks and owls, and 21 are warblers. Twenty-four species are considered winter residents only. Several of these, such as northern shrike, white-winged crossbill, and common redpoll, might be considered "invasion" species that appear irregularly.

Birds of Special Interest

Peregrine falcon. Although this species was totally extirpated from the park by the 1950s, a special restoration program released 29 during 1989-91. Watch for it near Hawksbill Mountain (highest elevation in the park, at 4,049 ft., or 1,234 m) and the nearby overlooks.

Ruffed grouse. It is most common along the ridge tops during spring and summer but moves to somewhat lower elevations in winter. Few birds represent the upland forests so well as this large species.

Common raven. It is much larger than the look-alike American crow and often is found soaring over the ridge tops, where it is mistaken for a hawk or an eagle.

Chestnut-sided warbler. Watch for this multicolored songster along Skyline Drive, especially at the edge of overlooks. Its chestnut sides, heavy black eye line, and yellow cap help to identify this little warbler.

Indigo bunting. This is the bright blue songster at the park's numerous overlooks. It sings a loud and merry song, translated as "swee-swee zreet-zreet swee-swee zay-zay seeit-seeit."

Rufous-sided towhee. Its loud "chree" call is common at all the park's open areas. The male has a distinct black head with maroon-red eyes and rufous sides.

18

Blue Ridge Parkway, Virginia and North Carolina

The trees and shrubs behind the Peaks of Otter Visitor Center gleamed in the early morning sunlight. A few leaves were beginning to show autumn color. Bird sound was abundant. Thousands of southbound migrants were passing by, mostly in the upper portion of the vegetation, but others were working the brushy undergrowth, and a few were searching for breakfast on the ground. It was a glorious morning.

The most numerous birds that fall morning were the scarlet tanagers. The scarlet and black-winged males and yellowish females and immatures were moving through the canopy, four or five at a time, sometimes stopping to feed and other times continuing right to left in what seemed like a steady stream. Rose-breasted grosbeaks were common as well, and many were calling to one another in a high-pitched "chink." The male's rosy, actually carmine red, breast and white belly provided a beautiful contrast to its coal black head and back. The female's dark brown back and streaked breast provided better camouflage. Buff-chested juveniles were also present. All had the very heavy "gros" beak.

Blue jays were also there in numbers, but there was no way to distinguish those that were residents from those moving through from more northern breeding grounds. But most of the day's migrants were smaller songbirds, especially warblers and vireos. At times as many as a hundred individuals may have been present. Tennessee warblers were most numerous, identified by their greenish backs, grayish heads, yellowish underparts, and bold white eye line. They seemed to show little preference for habitat, utilizing the canopy vegetation as well as lower shrubs. And once I watched half a dozen individuals searching through the fallen leaves beneath the shrubbery. They would perch in the shrubs, glean the leaves for insects for a while, then drop onto the ground to feed there.

Black-throated green warblers were also common, generally staying among the taller shrubbery and higher tree foliage. Most of these individuals were dressed in their faded winter plumage, but one brightly colored male looked as if it could still be in its breeding colors. Its black throat and breast, olive green back, and bright yellow face with a greenish ear patch were in marked contrast to the duller birds. Most fall warblers lose their bright plumage after nesting; many change so drastically that they look altogether different. Field identification in the fall can be tough. And yet by knowing a few basic features, one can usually readily identify them. Black-throated greens, for example, always possess blackish throats and yellowish faces. No other eastern warbler has those same features.

Magnolia warblers were present at midelevation that morning as well. The magnolia has a yellow throat, gray crown, black to gray cheeks, and a broad, white tail patch that often is its most noticeable feature in fall. And northern parulas were busy searching the foliage for insects. A few of these tiny, yellow-breasted birds showed the black chest band that usually is limited to adult males. Black-and-white warblers were present, too. And there were smaller numbers of chestnut-sided warblers, with their almost chartreuse backs and heads. American redstarts, both black and red males and black and yellow females, were also present. Black-throated blue warblers stayed back among the denser foliage, but I could hear their very distinct "tic" calls now and again. And a lone, immature Cape May warbler suddenly joined the passing parade of warblers. I wondered if this bird was heading for the Virgin Islands, where they are fairly common in winter.

It would be fascinating to know where all the migrants that were following the Blue Ridge that morning were bound. Most of the species spend about the same amount of time at their wintering homes in the tropics as they do on their breeding grounds. In viewing such a variety of songbirds, one becomes aware of the need for their full-time protection, within all of their territories.

The Park Environment

The Blue Ridge Parkway transects 469 miles (775 km) of highland forests, balds, old fields, and rocky outcroppings and links two great national parks, Shenandoah at the north end and the Great Smoky Mountains to the south. The two-lane parkway follows the Blue Ridge Mountains southward for 355 miles (571 km) and then weaves along the Black, Craggy, Pisgah, and Balsam mountains, all part of the southern Appalachians, for another 114 miles (183 km). A unit of the National Park Service since 1936, the 87,500-acre (35,411-ha) Blue Ridge Parkway is one of the world's best examples of a mountain corridor preserve, containing an exquisite matrix of grand scenic vistas and significant natural and cultural resources.

The park can be divided into three rather distinct sections. The northern portion is an extension of Shenandoah National Park. It is narrow and steep, with a rugged terrain; elevations range from 649 feet (198 m) at James River to 3,950 feet (1,204 m) ten miles south at Apple Orchard. The central section south of Roanoke Mountain (Milepost 120) has gentler terrain and is dominated by old fields and adjacent farmlands, although Grandfather Mountain (5,837 ft., or 1,779 m) rises above the parkway at Milepost 303. And beyond Crabtree Meadows (Milepost 339), the terrain becomes higher and more mountainous; a wilderness character prevails. The highest point on the parkway (6,053 ft., or 1,845 m) occurs at Richland Balsam at Milepost 433.

Charlton Ogburn, in his book *The Southern Appalachians: A Wilderness Quest*, in discussing some of the 110 miles of streams, wrote, "North of Roanoke the rivers originate well over on the inland side of the range and, collecting tributaries in the long valleys, break through the mountains on their way to the Atlantic in often striking water gaps." Below Roanoke, he added, the rivers "generally originate on the eastern-most escarpment of the Blue Ridge and cross the whole remainder of the Appalachians to send their waters finally to the Mississippi and the Gulf."

The vegetation along the parkway varies with age and elevation and is moderated by the open or protected locations. Old fields and cutover areas contain red cedar and thickets or pine-oak communities that are dominated by pitch, scrub, and (table) mountain pines and white, chestnut, red, and black oaks. Open areas on the highest ridges are usually referred to as "balds." Grassy balds are dominated by grass, and heath balds are dominated by shrubs of the heath family, such as catawba rhododendron, azalea, huckleberry, blueberry, and a few other species.

Areas of maturing second-growth hardwood forest are dominated by tulip-tree, sycamore, tupelo, black locust, sugar maple, sourwood, yellow birch, magnolia, and hickories. The understory usually consists of mountain laurel, rhododendron, and winterberry holly. The hardwood forests on the ridges, locally called "orchards," are dominated by beech, birch, and red oak trees. The ridges above 5,500 feet (1,676 m), near Mt. Mitchell, Richland Balsam, and Waterrock Knob, contain forests of spruce and fir, primarily red spruce, Fraser fir, and yellow birch.

Eleven visitor centers are situated at strategic sites along the 469-mile parkway, north to south, at Humpback Rocks, James River, Peaks of Otter, Rocky Knob, Cumberland Knob, Moses H. Cone Memorial Park, Linn Cove Viaduct, Linville Falls, Museum of North Carolina Minerals, Craggy Gardens, and Folk Art Center. Each has an information station and sales area for publications, which include bird field guides and other books. Bird checklists are available for various sections of the parkway.

Nine campgrounds are scattered along the parkway, north to south, at Otter Creek, Peaks of Otter, Roanoke Mountain, Rocky Knob, Doughton Park, Julian Price Memorial Park, Linville Falls, Crabtree Meadows, and Mount Pisgah. Lodging is available at Peaks of Otter, Rocky Knob, Doughton Park, and Mount Pisgah. Camping and lodging are also available at many of the adjacent communities.

The park contains more than 100 hiking trails that vary from short walks to more extensive hikes, such as the 18.5-mile (30-km) Roanoke Valley Horse Trail, the 13.5-mile (22-km) Tanawha Trail, the 10.8-mile (17-km) Rock Castle Gorge Trail, and the 7.5-mile (12-km) Bluff Mountain and Mountain-to-Sea trails. The famous Appalachian Trail follows the Blue Ridge for the first 100 miles (161 km) below Shenandoah.

A wide variety of interpretive activities are provided by the park service at the visitor centers from approximately Memorial Day through October. These activities range from orientation programs to evening talks and nature walks. A few of the talks and walks are oriented toward the area bird life. Weekly schedules are posted at strategic locations in the park in season.

Additional information can be obtained from the Superintendent, Blue Ridge Parkway, 200 BB&T Building, One Pack Square, Asheville, NC 28801; (704) 259-0701.

Bird Life
The north-south trending ridges of the southern Appalachians provide a natural migration route for a wide variety of birds. Especially in fall, millions of birds stream south from the northern forests toward their wintering grounds in the warmer southern states or beyond to the West Indies, Mexico, Central America, or South America. Songbirds and raptors, in particular, favor the mountain routes in fall. There is still an ample food supply, and the higher elevations are more like their northern breeding grounds. And their ancestors have utilized these same routes for thousands of years.

The myriad songbirds found that morning at Peaks of Otter are typical of the species that could be seen along most of the Blue Ridge in fall. And as the day becomes warmer and the thermals begin to rise over the ridges, the soaring birds put in their appearance. Most numerous are the **turkey vultures**, the very large, all-dark birds with bare, red heads and a unique flight pattern. They soar with their wings held upright in a wide V-shape and with a slight rocking motion, side to side. See chapter 14 on Cumberland Gap for more details.

The only hawk to be found in numbers along the Blue Ridge in fall is the **broad-winged hawk**, a small forest hawk with a banded tail and white underwings with dark borders. The adult also possesses a barred, reddish breast. This species, more than any other eastern raptor, migrates in large numbers. On days when conditions are right, and before they spiral up and out of sight, flights can be spectacular. The Virginia Society of Ornithology reported a total of 3,717 broad-wings over the Blue Ridge just north of Roanoke on a single day, September 25, 1976. Pete Dunne and his colleagues, in *Hawks in Flight*, point out that eastern hawk watchers' success depends on the number of broad-wings recorded. In describing a soaring bird, they wrote, "The wings are held horizontally and flat, not uplifted or drooped. In a glide between thermals (when wings are pulled in slightly) or when the bird is using an updraft off a ridge, the wings may be angled stiffly downward."

Broad-wings also nest along the Blue Ridge, usually in fairly continuous stands of forest. They frequent openings in the forest, roadsides, and pathways when hunting. Studies suggest that the bulk of their diet is made up of small mammals and birds, including species as large as hares and ruffed grouse. Hunting is generally done by the perch and strike method, in which perched birds wait for prey to pass and then strike, rather than search from the air or hover. This explains why the species is seldom seen away from the forest except later in the day, when thermals are available for soaring.

The breeding season is undoubtedly the most exciting time of the year for birds. That is when their plumage is brightest and they are most active. It is when bird song fills the air. Each of the principal communities along the parkway—the hardwood and spruce-fir forests, old fields, and balds—contains a particular group of species, although there may be some overlap.

Common hardwood forest nesters include red-tailed hawk, chimney swift, northern flicker, red-bellied and downy woodpeckers, great crested and Acadian flycatchers, eastern wood-pewee, blue jay, American crow, Carolina chickadee, tufted titmouse, white-breasted nuthatch, blue-gray gnatcatcher, wood thrush, American robin, red-eyed vireo, black-and-white and hooded warblers, northern parula, American redstart, ovenbird, Louisiana waterthrush, and scarlet tanager.

None of the above are as numerous as the **red-eyed vireo**, but it is rarely obvious; it spends most of its time in the forest canopy and seldom visits the lower foliage where it can be more easily observed. Although it is a fairly large bird, its olive green to gray back and head and whitish underparts help it blend into its variegated environment. Once found, however, it is fairly easy to identify by its distinct head pattern: a bold white eye line bordered with black and a ruby eye.

Most often it can be detected during spring and summer by the male's (only vireo males sing) steady singing from dawn to dusk and sometimes at night. Its song is robinlike, with a series of rising whistles, each separated by short pauses. Its song can be written as, "you-see-it, you-know-it, do-you-hear-me? do you believe it?" John Terres wrote that red-eyes may possess the "record for singing most frequently." One bird was recorded singing 22,197 songs during one 10-hour summer day. Ehrlich and colleagues also point out that a single male has a repertoire of about 40 song types and "rarely sings the same song type in succession." It also has a short, scolding call—a harsh "wheree"—and an alarm note—a nasal "tschay!"

Although red-eyes are abundant during the nesting season, the entire population overwinters in South America, primarily in Amazonia. There they utilize forest edges, shrubby clearings, and gardens that are quite different from the habitat they prefer in the southern Appalachians. And they rarely, if ever, sing on their wintering grounds.

American redstart

Another common nesting songbird of the hardwood forests along the Blue Ridge is the **American redstart**, a warbler that is very reminiscent of a butterfly in its behavior. When feeding, it will spread its wings and tail to flash its contrasting tail and wing patches. This action tends to startle insects and spiders into moving. As a result, the redstart can find them more readily. And the bird will often float downward, with wings and tail spread, like a butterfly or a falling leaf. Adult male and female American redstarts possess a similar plumage pattern but very different colors. Males are coal black except for their whitish belly and orange-red wing and tail patches; females are olive-gray above with yellow wing and tail patches.

The American redstart, unlike the red-eyed vireo, is one of the easiest forest birds to see. Not only does it spend a good deal of its time foraging among the lower, smaller trees in the forest undergrowth but its flashing behavior makes it one of the most obvious birds in the community. In Latin America, it is very properly known as *candelita*, or little torch.

Its song is a shrill, unmusical series of five or six rapid notes that have been described as "zee-zee-zee-zawaah" with a rising inflection, or "zweee" with a downward slur. They also produce a sharp "click" note that they utilize all year.

Bird life of the spruce-fir forests includes several species that are more common in the northern forests than in the southern Appalachians. Their presence is due to the relict stands of boreal forest that occur only on the higher mountaintops south from the Canadian forests into the southern Appalachians. Northern songbirds that nest within these forests include the red-breasted nuthatch, brown creeper, winter wren, golden-crowned kinglet, black-throated blue, Blackburnian, and Canada warblers, and dark-eyed junco.

Of these, the tiny, secretive winter wren and the bold and aggressive dark-eyed junco are the most pervasive. Their songs can usually be heard from dawn to dusk during May and June. The **winter wren**, a four-inch ball of reddish feathers with a very short, barred tail and buff breast, is heard far more than seen. Its song is a rapid series of high, tinkling trills and warbles. Arthur Cleveland Bent described its song as a rising and falling series of high-pitched notes, a fine silver thread of music lasting about seven seconds and containing 108 to 113 separate notes. The songs emanate most often from the moist, moss-draped undergrowth, but males will often sing from some high snag or branch beneath the forest canopy.

Nests are hidden in cavities in rotted stumps and logs or in roots and debris. Males also build one to four "dummy" nests to fool predators. Each consists of a mass of mosses, grasses, twigs, feathers, hair, and the like. Their diet is primarily insects and spiders that they find by poking into every conceivable hole and crevice in their territory. In winter they also consume berries. And like their junco neighbors, they often move to lower elevations during the colder months, a habit that cannot be considered true migration.

The **dark-eyed junco** is seldom as secretive as the smaller winter wren and often can be found singing its single-pitched trill from the very top of the tallest tree. This is the little slate-colored bird with a dull yellow bill, white belly, and obvious white outer tail feathers. Those that migrate to warmer areas to the south are often referred to as "snow birds."

Juncos once were split into five species, according to their general appearance; the eastern bird was then called "slate-colored junco," based on its plumage. There are now only two species, the dark-eyed northern bird and the yellow-eyed junco of southern Arizona and Mexico. All those in the United States and Canada have dark eyes and hop, while the southern juncos have yellow eyes and walk.

The old fields and other openings along the Blue Ridge contain another set of birds that rarely, if ever, occur in the forest communities. A springtime visit to one of the many open fields will likely produce sightings of the northern bobwhite, ruby-throated hummingbird, American crow, American robin, eastern bluebird, common grackle, American goldfinch, and field and song sparrows. The thickets and forest edges support an additional group of birds: Carolina wren, gray catbird, brown thrasher, chestnut-sided warbler, northern cardinal, indigo bunting, and rufous-sided towhee.

Heath balds occupy many of the open areas on upper ridges. These are exciting places to visit but do not have a separate bird life. One of the best examples of this habitat on the Blue Ridge can be found at Craggy Gardens. One day in mid-June, I spent a full morning loafing along the self-guided nature trail, admiring the blaze of colors that surrounded me and walking the Craggy Pinnacle trail to the panoramic view at the summit. It was truly inspiring!

I sat at the summit for an hour or more, admiring the 360-degree vista and watching the aerobatics of various soaring birds.

Several turkey vultures, a pair of red-tailed hawks, and a broad-winged hawk were present all the while. On a couple of occasions, the much smaller chimney swifts zoomed by like winged torpedoes, twisting and turning in their search for high-flying insects. Then they would suddenly drop like bombs into the forest, where I assumed they had a nest within a deep, chimneylike cavity. Perhaps they already were feeding young.

Then five coal black **common ravens** suddenly appeared along the ridge and soared overhead. But instead of continuing, they began to dive and circle reasonably close by, performing an amazing display of aerobatics. As I watched their maneuvers through my binoculars, I began to realize that here were two adults and three juveniles, and I could not help but wonder if I was watching a class in aerial acrobatics. The younger birds trailed the adults, doing many of the same movements, although they did not seem to have perfected the twist as well.

At one time they decided to harass one of the larger turkey vultures, diving sharply downward and coming within inches before pulling out and angling upward for additional height, then twisting over and plunging down again. The turkey vulture soared off toward the south, and the ravens concentrated on another series of rolls and twists.

In flight, the common raven is very different from its smaller cousin, the American crow. The raven is half again as large, and its beak is massive in comparison with that of the crow. In addition, the raven's tail is rounded in flight, like a wedge, not squared off like the crow's. And with my binoculars I could also see loose feathers around the bill that gave it a ragged appearance. By contrast, the American crow has a smooth countenance.

I wondered if the ravens' nest was nearby, on one of the rocky ledges of Craggy Mountain. This species nests early in spring, and young are off the nest by April or May. It was good to know that these birds were again doing well, because their numbers had declined in the East for many years, probably as a result of DDT.

Common raven

There are few birds of the eastern mountains that represent the wild highlands as well as the common raven.

In winter, the high ridges can be cold and the bird life sparse. Christmas Bird Counts are taken annually at various areas along the parkway, but two of these, at Peaks of Otter, Virginia, and Grandfather Mountain, North Carolina, are the best representatives of the parkway itself. The 1991 counts reported 37 species of 943 individuals at Peaks of Otter and 35 species of 1,026 individuals at Grandfather Mountain. The dozen most abundant (combined) species, in descending order of abundance, are the dark-eyed junco, American crow, European starling, Carolina chickadee, golden-crowned kinglet, tufted titmouse, American goldfinch, northern cardinal, white-breasted nuthatch, pine siskin, downy woodpecker, and house sparrow.

In summary, the Peaks of Otter checklist in Catlin's book contains 184 species, 105 of which are known to nest. Only 2 of those are water birds, the green-backed heron and wood duck; 8 are hawks and owls; and 21 are warblers. Three species are listed for winter only: pine siskin, and white-winged and red crossbills.

Birds of Special Interest

Turkey vulture. This all-dark bird with a bare, red head soars over the parkway with wings held slightly upward in a shallow V-shape, and it rocks slightly from side to side.

Broad-winged hawk. The smallest of the broad-winged hawks, it has a short, banded tail and underwings that are white bordered with dark. It prefers the forest but will soar on occasion.

Common raven. It is coal black with a huge beak and long, wedge-shaped tail in flight. It will often soar over the upper ridges and has a series of deep caw calls and a mixture of rumbling sounds.

Winter wren. This is the tiny, reddish bird with a short tail that occurs in the spruce-fir forests in summer. It sings a rapid series of tinkling trills and warbles.

Red-eyed vireo. Probably the most common songbird of the hardwood forest in summer, it is best detected by its robinlike whistles, which have been described as, "you see it, you hear it, do you hear me? do you believe it?"

American redstart. This is the "butterfly" warbler of the hardwood forest that flashes its wing and tail patches while hunting. Males are black and orange-red; females are black and yellow.

Dark-eyed junco. This slate-colored bird with obvious white outer tail feathers is present all year but summers only in the spruce-fir forest community.

19

Great Smoky Mountains National Park, Tennessee and North Carolina

The forest was wet from yesterday's rain, and patches of fog hung along the trail or crept over the ridge from the hollows below. Bird song literally surrounded me that early May morning as I followed the Appalachian Trail west from Clingman's Dome. Dark-eyed juncos were most obvious. Several were perched in treetops around the parking area, singing their musical trills. At least two American robins were in full song as well. And the high-pitched song of an indigo bunting echoed across the parking lot from a mountain ash.

The dense stand of conifers along the observation tower trail was also filled with song. Black-capped chickadees and golden-crowned kinglets were most vociferous. In the woods beyond, a winter wren sang an extensive series of tinkling and tumbling notes that continued all the while I was in hearing distance. And beyond, on both sides of the Appalachian Trail, which probably served as a territorial boundary line, I could hear additional winter wrens. They, too, were in full song, undoubtedly guarding their breeding territories within that boreal habitat. See chapter 18 on the Blue Ridge Parkway for additional descriptions of this little songster.

The slower, rather deliberate whistle notes ahead were those of a solitary vireo. Its song was a series of short but very sweet phrases "chu-wee, cheerio," with pauses between. It sang the same song over and over. I was able to approach the singing bird close to watch it forage among the foliage of a beech tree. Since only vireo males

Solitary vireo

sing, I had expected to find a brightly colored bird, but this male's plumage that lovely morning was exceptional. Its back and head were slate gray to almost blue-gray, a gorgeous contrast to its bright white eye ring and lores; its underparts were a yellow-blush color.

All the while it seemed totally unaware of my presence. It continued to glean the foliage for insects in its deliberate manner. Every 15 seconds or so, it would put its head back and sing. Then suddenly it began to scold, as if my status had changed from that of an enchanted observer to a dangerous intruder. And scold me it did! It used a harsh, nasal "see-ah" sound, and it did not let up. It suddenly dawned on me that maybe I had crossed some invisible line and was too close to its nest, a good enough reason for its belligerence. And sure enough. It took me several minutes of searching the upper branches before I found it, wedged between forked branches about 15 feet (4.5 m) above me. It looked very much like a ball of dried leaves and moss, and when I backed away, I could actually see the top of the female's head and tail protruding from the cup-shaped structure. I was reminded of another solitary vireo nest I had found years before. That nest had been located in vegetation slightly below a trail, so that I was able to approach it within a few inches. I actually photographed the singing male from a foot away while it was sitting on the nest. It remained there all the while.

The Park Environment

Authorized by Congress in 1926, Great Smoky Mountains National Park is currently the most heavily visited of all the national parks. But in spite of the excessive traffic found in summer and fall on the park's principal roadways, there is no finer example of Appalachian wilderness. A hiker does not need to go far off the highway before finding a truly magnificent natural setting. Some of that isolation is due to the fact that only a small percentage of park visitors go beyond the parking lots. But part of the park's wilderness character is due to the closeness of the forest and abundant streams that help to insulate it from the outside world. Add the large size of the park (517,368 acres, or 213,423 ha) to that formula, and it is no wonder that the Great Smoky Mountains remain one of the few places anywhere in the East to possess a significant population of black bears and a reasonably unaltered bird life.

Because of the park's natural character, it has become a principal center for natural science research. More tree species occur in the Smokies than in all of northern Europe. There, too, is one of the largest blocks of virgin temperate deciduous forest in North America. These and other superlatives have earned both Biosphere Reserve and World Heritage Site status for the park.

Many classic forest studies have been done within the park. A total of about 1,500 flowering plants and more than 4,000 nonflowering plants have been identified within seven broad communities. From low to high elevations, these are: fields and pastures at Cades Cove, Sugarlands, and Oconaluftee; small areas of wetlands in Cades Cove; pine-oak forests on the drier lowland ridges; cove hardwood forests within most of the low to midelevation drainages; northern hardwood forests on the higher slopes and "gaps" along the ridges; spruce-fir forests at the cooler summits; and heath and grassy balds on the open ridge tops.

The greatest diversity of plant life can be found within the cove hardwood forests. Dominant canopy trees are white ash, sweet buckeye, red and sugar maples, bitternut hickory, tulip-tree, white basswood, bigleaf magnolia, yellow birch, beech, and eastern hemlock. Common understory trees are ashleaf and mountain maples, flowering dogwood, sassafras, redbud, earleaf magnolia, common witch-hazel, sourwood, and silverbell-tree.

The northern hardwood forest community is dominated by yellow birch and beech, and the spruce-fir forest is dominated by red spruce and Fraser fir. The Great Smoky Mountain heath balds contain the early blooming catawba rhododendron, late blooming rosebay rhododendron, and orange-flowering flame azalea. Blooming wildflowers in springtime can produce an unforgettable sight.

The park extends east to west for 54 miles (87 km); its width is 15 miles (24 km). It is situated along the southern Appalachians crest between Tennessee and North Carolina, a 36-mile (58-km) section of which exceeds 5,000 feet, (1,524 m) in elevation. The highest point is Clingman's Dome (6,643 ft., or 2,025 m), accessible by motor vehicle off the Newfound Gap Road, the transmountain highway between Gatlinburg, Tennessee, and Cherokee, North Carolina.

Although there are no lakes or large ponds inside the park, Fontana Lake extends two to three miles into Hazel and Eagle creeks on the North Carolina side. More than 600 miles (966 km) of streams flow out of the Smokies and into the Tennessee River, which in turn flows into the Mississippi River. Abrams Creek meanders through Cades Cove, where it forms small wetlands and eventually flows out of the park at its lowest elevation (857 ft., or 261 m) into Chilhowee Lake on the Tennessee River.

The park service operates three visitor centers: Sugarlands, near Gatlinburg; Cades Cove; and Oconaluftee, near Cherokee. All three contain exhibits and publication sales, including bird field guides and an excellent 1991 bird book by Fred Alsop. A park checklist of the birds is also available on request.

Interpretive activities include a wide range of programs at various locations which generally run from late spring through October. These include evening talks and nature walks, some specifically on the park's bird life. The Spring Wildflower Pilgrimage in late April also includes bird walks, and the Great Smoky Mountains Institute at Tremont offers numerous nature programs. Birding courses are offered by the Smoky Mountains Field School.

The park also has ten self-guided nature trails and three motor nature trails, scattered around the park at key habitats or historic areas. In addition, a wonderful little book, *Mountain Roads & Quiet*

Places, by Jerry DeLaughter, contains more insights into thirteen park roadways. That book and Robert Johnsson and John Dawson's excellent *A Naturalist's Notebook* are two of the finest interpretive books available on any of the national parks.

Schedules of all interpretive activities, as well as additional up-to-date park information, are available in the official park newspaper quarterly, *Smokies Guide*, available at all contact stations within the park.

An incredible array of hiking trails within the park, approximately 800 miles (1,330 km) worth, vary from short saunters to more extensive and difficult backpacking hikes. Backcountry camping is allowed by permit at numerous locations. Drive-in campgrounds are located at ten scattered sites; reservations are accepted at three: Smokemont, Cades Cove, and Elkmont.

Lodging is available in the park only at the primitive LeConte Lodge, located on Mt. LeConte at the end of a 5½-mile (9 km) hike. Other lodging and supplies are available in the various communities that surround the park.

Additional information can be obtained from the Superintendent, Great Smoky Mountains National Park, Gatlinburg, TN 37738; (615) 436-1200.

Bird Life

The trail from Clingman's Dome to Silers Bald passes through spruce-fir and hardwood forest communities before it emerges onto Silers Bald and its unique world of azaleas and rhododendrons. Bird song was obvious along the trail and continued throughout the morning. Every now and again, the flutelike songs of **veeries** reached my ears from the forested slopes below. The veery's song is outstanding, even among the family of thrushes that is blessed with a special ability for singing. Its song is a series of downward-spiraling phrases such as "whree-ur, whree-ur, veer veer." Winsor Marrett Tyler, in Bent's Life History series, wrote, "We cannot think of it as a song in the sense of its being an expression of joy; it seems to express a calmer, deeper, holier emotion, like a hymn or a prayer." For me, the veery's song expresses the sanctity of the Appalachian highlands better than any other.

Veery

I was fortunate to glimpse the actual singer on two or three occasions during the early morning; individuals ran ahead of me along the forest trail. Once one stopped, turned sideways, and raised its crest ever so slightly. A bit of sunlight formed a shaft of light through the green canopy to highlight its rufous back. I could also see its buff breast with wedge-shaped spots and its thin eye ring. Then it flicked its wings and disappeared. A few moments later, a downward spiraling "whree-ur, whree-ur, veer veer" song reached my ears from below the trail.

I passed a stand of spruce and fir that showed extensive damage from the pervasive balsam woolly aphid. A winter wren song emanated from the devastation. A healthy spruce-fir community usually contains the following species in summer: broad-winged hawk, northern saw-whet owl, ruffed grouse, hairy woodpecker, black-capped chickadee, red-breasted nuthatch, brown creeper, winter wren, golden-crowned kinglet, American robin, solitary vireo, black-throated blue, black-throated green, Blackburnian, and Canada warblers, dark-eyed junco, and red crossbill.

Not far ahead was Double Springs Gap; beech, yellow birch, yellow buckeye, and a few other trees dominated the low point on the ridge. I stopped to admire the yellow flowers of a bluebead lily, one of the park's many unique plants. Then, almost overhead, the husky notes of a **black-throated green warbler** attracted my attention. An adult male sat among the lower branches of a birch tree, singing a song that is one of the hallmarks of the highland forests of the Smoky Mountains. The song of the black-throated green is very distinct—a slow, drowsy series of five to eight notes, "zee zee zee zo zee," ascending at the end. Although this bird moved off into the woods, its song continued all the while I was exploring the beech gap habitat. Bent pointed out that black-throated greens are one of our most persistent singers and that one individual "gave 466 songs in a single hour and more than 14,000 in the 94 hours of observation." Frank Chapman wrote that its song has "a quality about it like the droning of bees; it seems to voice the restfulness of a summer day."

It is also one of the most attractive warblers of the Great Smokies. A breeding male sports a coal black throat and breast, a yellow face with an olive line through the eye, olive green upperparts, two white wing bars, and a white belly. The female is a duller model of the male.

Other songbirds found within and adjacent to the beech gap that morning included a black-capped chickadee, a red-breasted nuthatch with its constant honking call, almost like a Model-T horn, a golden-crowned kinglet that was gleaning the spruce bark for insects, a gray catbird, an American robin, a solitary vireo, chestnut-sided and black-throated blue warblers, an indigo bunting, and a dark-eyed junco.

The most impressive of these birds was a male **black-throated blue warbler**, another of the outstanding warblers that nest within the Great Smoky Mountains. The sides of its face, throat, wings, and tail are an almost leaden black, but its crown, back, and shoulders are deep blue in a shawllike pattern. It also has a white belly and bold wing patch. Females are dull olive green above and olive yellow below, with a partial eye ring. The song of a black-throated blue warbler is also unique. It consists of three or four drawling notes, "zee, zee, zee, ee" or "I am la-zy," usually ending with an upward slur.

Black-throated blues are, perhaps, one of the most appropriate representatives of the Great Smoky Mountains. This is because they utilize such a wide variety of habitats in summer, from the spruce-fir forests to the northern hardwoods and rhododendron thickets. They also are one of the tamest of warblers and will often allow one

Black-throated blue warbler

to approach close enough to really appreciate their gorgeous plumage.

This warbler also may be considered a top candidate for the Smoky Mountains' representative to several Latin American countries. It spends its winters in Central America, South America, and the Greater Antilles, including the moist evergreen forests at Virgin Islands National Park.

Silers Bald, a 4-mile (6.4-km) hike from Clingman's Dome, provides a commanding 360-degree view of the Smoky Mountains. Looking east or west along the ridge helps one understand the significance of the Appalachians as a massive backbone to the entire eastern half of the nation. The grasses and shrubbery on the balds do not possess a distinct bird life, probably due to their recent development. But several species found at other open areas are present there in summer, including gray catbird, indigo bunting, and rufous-sided towhee.

The Smoky Mountains' balds are excellent places to observe various soaring birds. The open views provide good hawk-watching. Red-tailed hawks, with their dull- to brick-red tails, are most common, but the smaller and chunkier broad-winged hawks are regular in appearance as well. Sharp-shinned and Cooper's hawks also soar on occasion. And the endangered peregrine falcon again has begun to appear in the park. Reintroduced birds at the park and elsewhere in the southern Appalachians have begun to reappear at old nest sites, and it is likely that this marvelous creature again will become a regular in summer. The opportunity to watch peregrines courting and adults teaching their young to capture prey, from a natural grandstand along the Appalachian crest, will add a very special quality to the park experience.

Watch also for the two all-black soaring birds—the turkey vulture with its six-foot wingspan and bare, red head and the smaller common raven. A soaring raven is best identified by its large bill, pointed wings, and wedge-shaped tail. See chapter 18 on the Blue Ridge Parkway for more information.

Many of the long ridges that branch off the main ridge contain heath "slicks" that remain bright green through most of the year. And between the ridges, within the varied drainages or "coves," are the cove hardwood forest communities. Here can be found a different group of nesting birds.

Birds of the cove hardwood forest communities are more or less typical of those found throughout most of the eastern deciduous forests. Common nesting species include the yellow-billed cuckoo; eastern screech-owl; red-bellied, downy, hairy, and pileated woodpeckers; chimney swift; eastern wood-pewee; great crested and Acadian flycatchers; blue jay; Carolina chickadee; tufted titmouse; white-breasted nuthatch; Carolina wren; blue-gray gnatcatcher; American robin; wood thrush; yellow-throated and red-eyed vireos; northern parula; back-and-white, worm-eating, and hooded warblers; American redstart; ovenbird; scarlet tanager; northern cardinal; rose-breasted grosbeak; and brown-headed cowbird. And in wet areas, the Louisiana waterthrush, Kentucky warbler, and song sparrow can usually be found.

The trail from Cosby Campground to Low Gap provides an easy 3-mile (5-km) transect through a cove hardwood forest along Cosby Creek. I visited this area in late May, when nesting was in full swing. A pair of eastern phoebes and several American crows greeted me at the parking area, and red-eyed vireo songs were evident in every direction. The "peet-seet" calls of Acadian flycatchers echoed from the adjacent forest. And American robin songs blended into the morning chorus.

Almost immediately, as I started up the trail, I was greeted by the very loud, almost explosive "see-you, see-you, see-you, chew chew, to-wee" song of a Louisiana waterthrush. It sang again, and I was able to focus my binoculars on this large, long-legged warbler, walking along the edge of the creek. It had a dark back, white underparts with brownish streaks, and a bold white eye line. It teetered and bobbed as it walked along the water's edge searching for breakfast. It already had worms or larvae hanging from its bill; it probably was gathering food for a waiting family. Then, with a sharp "chip," it flew up the creek. I followed but could not locate it again. A few minutes later I heard it or another individual singing again, "see-you, see-you, see-you, chew chew, to wee." Unmistakable!

"Teach, teach, teach, TEACH, TEACH" came from the forested slope just ahead. This was the Appalachian dialect of the **ovenbird**, very different from the "teacher" notes of northern birds. Although another ground feeder, it is a warbler of the forest undergrowth instead of the streamsides. It took me several minutes and several more songs before I located this little songster, perched on an open branch about ten feet above the ground. It sang again, "teach, teach, teach, TEACH TEACH," each syllable stronger and louder than the one before.

The ovenbird is one of the Smoky Mountains' most common breeding birds below approximately 5,000 feet (1,524 m) elevation. The female builds a roofed nest of grasses, leaves, and moss on the forest floor which resembles a miniature Dutch oven, hence its name. The nest entrance is hardly more than a narrow slit.

At first glance, the ovenbird looks like a small, chunky thrush, but it is quite different. It has solid olive green upperparts, except for an orange crown stripe bordered with brown and a rather bold whitish eye ring; its underparts are white with heavy brown stripes. In addition, its feeding behavior is unique. The ovenbird walks over the forest floor, poking into every conceivable crack and cranny for insects and advancing with a strange vibratory gait that includes motion of its tail and body. The name "wood wagtail" seems to apply, as does its Jamaican name, "land-kickup."

Other birds found above Cosby Campground that day were hairy and pileated woodpeckers, blue jay, Carolina chickadee, white-breasted nuthatch, veery, wood thrush, solitary vireo, black-and-white and black-throated green warblers, scarlet tanager, rose-breasted grosbeak, song sparrow, and American goldfinch.

Cades Cove, of the many places in the park to see birds, is probably the most productive. The 11-mile (18-km) loop road provides easy access to the various habitats within this lovely valley and is maintained by the park service in its historic setting. Abrams Creek meanders through the fields and pastures and past scattered stands of hardwoods and pines, all surrounded with forested slopes and mountain ridges.

Roadside birds to be expected on an early morning drive in summer include the wild turkey, northern bobwhite, eastern phoebe, eastern kingbird, northern rough-winged and barn swallows, blue jay, American crow, eastern bluebird, indigo bunting, chipping sparrow, eastern meadowlark, common grackle, and American goldfinch.

The **wild turkey** is the largest of the park's birds and can usually be found with little difficulty along the Cades Cove loop road. It is difficult to misidentify a turkey because of its very distinct appearance. Although common today, the population was much reduced in the 1920s by hunting and the die-off of the American chestnut trees, which produced its principal food supply. The protection provided in the park has permitted it to increase once again, and park birds now range to all altitudes and habitats. But they are most obvious along the wooded fringes at Cades Cove.

A stop at almost any of the pullouts or side roads, such as the John Oliver Cabin or Missionary Baptist Church, will likely produce sightings of a number of woodland birds. Listen for the "pee-wee" call of the eastern wood-pewee, the "chick-a-dee-dee-dee" song of the Carolina chickadee, the "peter, peter, peter" song of the tufted titmouse, the wheezy song of the blue-gray gnatcatcher, and the wonderful, flutelike "ee-o-lay" song of the wood thrush.

A short walk into the woods can result in finding a number of warblers. The ovenbird is usually common here, as is the northern parula, an energetic little songster with a blue-gray back marked with a green-yellow patch and a yellow throat and chest with a blackish-orange band (male only). Its song, one of the easiest of all bird songs to remember, is a series of buzzy notes that ascend to a final "hic" note, like "zzzzzzzzeuric."

A stop at the Abrams Creek parking lot and a brief walk along the waterway will expose one to yet another group of songbirds. Listen for the loud, musical song of the **yellow-throated warbler** among the sycamores. Its song delivery is unique in that the syllables become faster as they descend and end with an abrupt higher note, written as "tee-ew, tew-ew, tew-ew, tew-ew, tew-wi." This species and many others found at Cades Cove frequent the Sugarlands Visitor Center area as well. The yellow-throated warbler is an exquisite bird with a bright yellow throat and chest bordered with coal black sides that extend onto the cheeks and below the eyes. It has a white eye line and dark gray back with a greenish-yellow patch, like that of the northern parula. It also has a snow white belly and two white wing bars.

This warbler has the longest bill of any of the wood warblers, enabling it to feed under bark and in deep crevices, from streamsides and cypress swamps to pine and oak forests. It is a true southern warbler, however, summering only in the Southeast and north to the Chesapeake Bay area. In winter it prefers the southern climes from Florida and south Texas into Mexico and Central America. It also is found along the palm-studded beaches of the Greater Antilles.

The Louisiana waterthrush and Kentucky warbler prefer wet areas along creeks or at seepages. Their songs have a similar dynamic delivery, but the Kentucky warbler's song contains more syllables, "tur-dle, tur-dle, tur-dle" or "chur-ree, chur-ree, chur-ree," and is usually repeated a number of times. See chapter 16 on Mammoth Cave for additional details.

Wintertime is very different in the Smokies. The upper slopes can be almost devoid of birds, especially during colder periods. But the lowlands, such as Cades Cove, Sugarlands, and Ocunaluftee, can be very productive. Park naturalist Don DeFoe has been coordinating the annual Great Smoky Mountains Christmas Bird Counts since 1975. These counts usually produce approximately 40 species and about 1,100 individuals. The dozen most common species on the 1991 count, in descending order of abundance, were American crow, European starling, chickadee (Carolina and black-capped chickadees were not separated), golden-crowned kinglet, mourning dove, song sparrow, dark-eyed junco, turkey vulture, white-throated sparrow, tufted titmouse, Carolina wren, and eastern meadowlark.

In summary, Alsop's 1991 checklist contains 236 species, 110 of which are known to nest. Only 3 of those, the green-backed heron, yellow-crowned night-heron, and wood duck are water birds; 10 are hawks and owls; and 22 are warblers. Fifteen species are listed as winter residents/visitors only: American black and ring-necked ducks, mallard, white-winged scoter, common goldeneye, bufflehead, common merganser, herring gull, hermit thrush, dickcissel, white-throated sparrow, snow bunting, house finch, white-winged crossbill, and common redpoll.

Birds of Special Interest

Wild turkey. This is the park's largest bird and can best be seen at Cades Cove. Males possess bright red wattles. When courting in spring, they fluff out their iridescent plumage and spread their tails in broad, colorful fans.

Veery. Its flutelike, downward-spiraling songs are commonplace throughout the forests in summer. Its reddish back and streaked breast are less evident within the shady undergrowth.

Solitary vireo. This is the surprisingly tame little forest bird with a slate gray back, yellowish underparts, and obvious white eye ring and lores, like a pair of eyeglasses.

Black-throated blue warbler. The combination of deep blue, black, and white helps identify this lovely warbler of the Smoky Mountains. Its song is a drawling "zee, zee, zee, ee."

Black-throated green warbler. Its coal black throat and chest, olive back, and yellow face with a greenish ear patch make it unique among North American songbirds.

Ovenbird. This is the chunky, olive green bird with an orange crown stripe. Usually found on the forest floor, it sings a loud "teach, teach, teach" song in the Smokies.

20

Chickamauga and Chattanooga National Military Park, Georgia and Tennessee

The woods behind the restored historic cabin were alive with birds. The "chuuur" call of a red-bellied woodpecker was answered by a second red-belly farther up the slope. Carolina wrens were singing their loud "tea-kettle, tea-kettle" song from the dense thicket below. One of these reddish songsters, sporting a broad white eye line, popped out for a second or two and then disappeared into the undergrowth. Farther away, a rufous-sided towhee sang its characteristic slurred "ch-reee." A larger bird with rufous plumage and a long tail, sitting ever so quietly in the thicket, was a brown thrasher. And the smaller, tan and striped sparrow was a song sparrow. I watched it long enough to see its dark breast spot, resembling a stickpin. Then a bright red male northern cardinal suddenly climbed out of the thicket, jumped onto a long curved branch, and began to devour the little black buckthorn berries that were present by the hundreds.

It was then that I realized why so many birds were at this one spot. The Carolina buckthorn shrubs were full of fruit, and dozens of forest-edge birds were there to take advantage of the readily available food supply.

The nondescript little bird flitting nervously among the foliage was a ruby-crowned kinglet. It moved continuously, especially its wings. Through my binoculars I could see its white eye ring and faint wing bars against its overall yellowish plumage. It took several minutes before it flashed its bright red crown patch, a very showy patch in the center of its crown. Then it called a low, almost scold-ing "je-dit, je-dit." I wondered where it had spent its summer months—somewhere in the spruce-fir forests far to the north, no doubt. Yet here it was at the southern end of the Appalachians. Maybe it was still en route to Florida or elsewhere in the Southeast for the winter.

Another reddish-brown bird moved in the thicket. It appeared at an opening where I could see its black-and-white head and the tiny spot of yellow in front of the eye. A white-throated sparrow! Another visitor from the northern forests. Then several others began to move, and I realized that there was a whole flock of white-throats, at least 12 to 14 individuals. I could see a few adults, but many were imma-ture birds with streaked breasts and brown and gray heads. Then one of the adults sang a clear and cheery "old Sam Peabody, Peabody, Peabody," a delightful song. The same song in the Canadian woods is translated as "oh sweet, Canada, Canada, Canada."

Then overhead came the soft but rich "chur-lee" calls of eastern bluebirds. I moved out into the open where I could better see the surrounding sky and adjacent fields. There were a dozen or more bluebirds, and I watched as they settled onto the top branches of a huge black oak very near where I was standing. Their bright blue backs and russet breasts gleamed in the morning sunlight.

The bluebirds' arrival in the oak had apparently displaced two yellow-rumped warblers, which flew off across the field, proclaim-ing their annoyance with their sharp chip calls. I focused my binoc-ulars on a white-breasted nuthatch in the upper branches, very near the bluebirds, and I watched it search for insects among the fur-rowed bark. And just below was a pair of downy woodpeckers. One uttered a sharp "peek" call. Movement in the foliage below pro-duced both Carolina chickadees and tufted titmice.

I turned back to the field where several American crows were walking along the freshly mown grass. They were searching, no doubt, for insects or whatever else they might find to eat. Perched on one of the stone monuments was an eastern phoebe. It pumped its tail, then flew out after some passing insect and returned to the same perch.

It was a beautiful and serene morning. Bird song was all about, from the open fields and forest edge to deep in the woods. As I

marveled at the scene, I wondered if George Snodgrass had enjoyed
a similar pastoral scene when he lived here. With eight children to
feed, the Snodgrasses may not have taken the time to enjoy the sim-
pler pleasures of life. Life in the 1860s was very different from life
today, but I imagined that the Snodgrasses had also enjoyed similar
mornings and the even greater variety of bird life that existed then.
The historic scene has been re-created to that of 1863. But not even
the most vivid imagination can re-create the great catastrophe that
befell that lovely scene when the Snodgrass farm was suddenly
transformed into the bloodiest battlefield of the Civil War.

The entire family somehow survived. During the battle, they
hid in a nearby ravine, and afterward they helped nurse soldiers
from both sides inside their little one-room house.

The Park Environment

Most of the area's forests were destroyed during the war. Unlike
most Civil War battles, which were fought in open fields, this one
was fought mostly in the thick woods. More than 37,000 Union and
Confederate soldiers were missing, killed, or injured during the
two-day battle, considered the bloodiest engagement in the entire
Civil War. Dead and dying littered the forests and fields. It was a
decisive win for the Union, and by the next spring, Sherman began
his march to Atlanta and the sea.

In 1890, only a quarter of a century after the war, the
Chickamauga and Chattanooga National Military Park was dedicated
"for the purpose of preserving and suitably marking for historical
and professional military study the fields of some of the most
remarkable maneuvers and most brilliant fighting" of the Civil War.
Although 17 separate units (approximately 8,400 acres, or 3,399 ha)
were included, the greater part of the park is encompassed within
two large areas, Chickamauga Battlefield in Tennessee (5,500 acres, or
2,226 ha) and Lookout Mountain, Georgia (2,689 acres, or 1,088 ha).

That act, although designed primarily to commemorate the
great battle that occurred there, also set aside rather extensive tracts
of forestlands that have since recovered to mature forest, as well as
smaller acreages of scattered fields and wetlands. The most impressive forest cover is the hardwoods that are dominated by red oak

and hickories. Zones of white oak, elm, tulip-tree, white ash, sweet-gum, and hackberry are also common. And some of the better-drained sites are dominated by pines.

The two large park units have visitor centers with orientation programs and a bookstore dedicated to Civil War history. A bird checklist is not available. However, a variety of interpretive activities, some of them of a biohistorical perspective, are offered at both units; they include car caravans and walking tours. And from mid-September to mid-October, retired park ranger Ken Dubke coordinates a hawk watch at Signal Point.

No camping or lodging is available inside the park, but both are readily available nearby.

Further information can be acquired from the Superintendent, Chickamauga-Chattanooga National Military Park, P.O. Box 2128, Ft. Oglethorpe, GA 30742; (404) 866-9241.

Bird Life

The **eastern bluebirds** at the Snodgrass Cabin were but a few of the many songbirds that frequent the battlefield through the year. But there are few species with as much appeal as the sweet and dainty bluebird. Frank Chapman wrote, "The bluebird's disposition is typical of all that is sweet and amiable." And Bradford Torrey reported it as "common" at Chattanooga, with "young birds out of the nest, April 28," in his 1896 book *Spring Notes from Tennessee*. Nesting birds utilize natural cavities in trees and shrubs, especially those surrounded by or along the edge of fields. And on the historic battlefield they also nest in the cannon barrels. Bluebirds are the only members of the thrush family that are cavity nesters. Males carry on a courtship behavior that includes much fluttering, with wings draped and tails spread, and singing a "tru-a-lly" song. And they may actually preen and feed their mates. Young from the previous year often help to feed the nestlings.

Bluebird populations were severely reduced throughout the East, by as much as 90 percent, according to Ehrlich and colleagues, primarily due to excessive use of chlorinated hydrocarbons during the 1970s and increased populations of European starlings and house sparrows, which compete with them for nesting cavities.

Eastern bluebird

Although bluebird populations have largely recovered, it took a complete ban of DDT in the United States and the help of many local citizens who placed bluebird boxes at the edges of fields to help build up their populations.

The Chickamauga woods contain a different bird population in spring and summer than in winter. Resident birds, such as the woodpeckers, blue jays, American crows, Carolina chickadees, tufted titmice, white-breasted nuthatches, Carolina wrens, mockingbirds, eastern bluebirds, and pine warblers remain the same. But there are many more species in summer which nest and raise their broods before returning to their more southern wintering grounds.

The **pine warbler** is one of the few members of the colorful warbler clan that lives in the park its entire lifetime. More northern pine warblers migrate south for the winter, but the Chickamauga Battlefield birds are full-time residents. And on sunny days in winter it can often be heard singing its clear, musical trill, a slow succession of soft, sweet notes with little variation. Its song has been compared with the faster and higher-pitched chipping sparrow song.

The pine warbler is an overall yellowish color with a noticeably yellow throat and eye line, two white wing bars, and rather obvious white spots at the corners of the tail. Unlike the names of many warblers, the pine warbler's suits it very well. It is rarely found away from pines. It has a habit of creeping about the pine branches and boughs and gleaning insects from among the needles, often near the very tops of the trees. See chapter 21 on Cape Cod for an additional description of this warbler.

In summer, another warbler is present in the park, the **yellow-throated warbler**. It, too, will nest in the pines. But west of the Cumberland Plateau, it prefers sycamore trees for nesting. This species uses a creeping motion when feeding, often in the upper foliage. The yellow-throated warbler is one of the loveliest of the warblers and one of the easiest to identify. Its bright yellow throat is bordered on the sides with black and with white below. Its black-and-white head pattern includes black cheeks and a bold white eye line. It also has the longest bill of any of the warblers. And its song is very distinct: a loud, ringing sound like that of an indigo bunting or waterthrush. Paul Sykes described the song as "a loud musical series of clear syllables given faster as they descend with abrupt higher note at end: *tee-ew, tew-ew, tew-ew, tew-ew, tew-wi* or *sweet-ie, sweetie, sweetie*; sounds like northern parula's repeated twice."

This warbler winters to the south from the Gulf Coast to Costa Rica and east into the Greater Antilles. There it frequents palm trees, often along a particularly beautiful white sand beach. I have often thought it has a choice existence, summering in the northern forests and wintering along Caribbean beaches.

Other forest songbirds that occur within the Chickamauga forest only in summer include the great crested and Acadian flycatchers; eastern wood-pewee; wood thrush; yellow-throated and red-eyed vireos; black-and-white, northern parula, Kentucky, and hooded warblers; ovenbird; and scarlet tanager.

The overgrown fields and forest edges support a slightly different group of nesting birds. These include the eastern kingbird, gray catbird, white-eyed vireo, common yellowthroat, orchard oriole, summer tanager, blue grosbeak, and indigo bunting.

West Chickamauga Creek forms the park's southeastern border and, along with the adjacent wetlands, provides yet another habitat for birds. This is where the **great blue heron** and the smaller green-backed heron can be found. The great blue is blue, gray, and white; its wingspan is six feet. The green heron is less than half that size and has a green back and chestnut throat. Both species can be found on the banks, patiently waiting for a fish, frog, or other water-loving critter to happen by.

The great blue heron is one of the park's most obvious residents, not only because of its large size but because its flight is special. Its six-foot wingspan and very slow flight pattern stir the imagination.

Watch along the creek, too, for the wood duck, the park's only summering duck. But what a bird it is! The male is a lovely creature with a green, black, and red head and multicolored body. The female is very drab, much like a female mallard. See chapter 24 on National Capital Parks for further details.

Signal Point, high above the northern slopes of the Tennessee River, was used by the U.S. Signal Corps during the Civil War to relay messages. The river gorge has more recently been described as one of America's "five most beautiful gorges." But local birders know Signal Point best as the site for their fall hawk watch. This is where Ken Dubke has monitored the passing raptors from mid-September to mid-October every year since 1973.

The hawk watch results are not spectacular, in comparison with some of the better known hawk-watching programs along the north-south ridges of the Appalachians, but none are done with more enthusiasm. Ken and his 10 to 15 helpers annually record a dozen species and up to 500 individuals on a good day. In 1991, September 21 was their best day, with 134 broad-wings, 4 ospreys, 2 sharp-shins, 2 Cooper's, 1 red-tail, and 1 peregrine. A bald eagle was observed on September 18 as it flew below the overlook. Everyone had a superb look at this magnificent bird.

One reason for Signal Point's popularity is that most of the raptors pass reasonably close, at eye level or below, so that the watchers usually have fantastic views. The **broad-winged hawks** can be practically bill to nose with the observer, but on clear, warm days they prefer the thermals that carry them high above the ridges and out of sight.

Although a few broad-wings nest within the forested parts of the park, the vast majority of birds that pass Signal Point are migrants from farther north along the Appalachian slopes or southern Canada. They are crow-sized broad-winged hawks, chunky with rather short, black-and-white banded tails, and broad wings with white underparts and dark borders. The adult's chest is banded with reddish or brownish bars. Except for a few birds that winter in Florida and along the southern Gulf states, most overwinter from southern Mexico to Brazil. See chapter 18 on Blue Ridge Parkway for additional information about broad-winged hawks.

For several years the battlefield was included in the Chattanooga Christmas Bird Count, and those counts provided a reasonably good index of the wintertime bird life. Approximately 10,500 individuals of 90 species were recorded. The dozen most abundant species in 1979 (in descending order of abundance) were the European starling, American robin, rock dove, red-winged blackbird, mourning dove, common grackle, brown-headed cowbird, white-throated sparrow, American crow, cedar waxwing, rusty blackbird, and song sparrow.

In summary, a very old list of park birds contains 149 species, 78 of which are known to nest. Of these, 3 are water birds, 7 are hawks and owls, and 13 are warblers.

Birds of Special Interest

Great blue heron. This long-legged, blue, gray, and white bird occurs along the creek and other wet areas. It has a six-foot wingspan and flies with slow, deliberate wing beats.

Broad-winged hawk. A small forest hawk, it nests within the park and can be common during the fall migration. It is best seen from Signal Point in mid-September.

Eastern bluebird. It is usually detected first by its soft "chur-lee" calls as it flies overhead. It has an all-blue back and russet breast.

Pine warbler. This resident warbler is an overall yellowish color and is almost always found among the pines. It has a drawn-out, melodic trill for a song.

Yellow-throated warbler. Its bright yellow throat is bordered on the sides by black. It frequents pines during all seasons.

COASTAL PLAIN

We need the tonic of wildness—to wade sometimes in marshes where the bittern and the meadow-hen lurk, and hear the booming of the snipe; to smell the whispering sedge where only some wilder and more solitary fowl builds her nest, and the mink crawls with its belly close to the ground.
—Henry David Thoreau

21

Cape Cod National Seashore, Massachusetts

There were several hundred herring gulls visible from my perch above Coast Guard Beach. These white and gray birds were scattered along the beach singly and in flocks of varying size as far as I could see. They also were numerous on and over the ocean, coming and going in both directions, or following close behind fishing boats. And off to the right on Nauset Marsh, I counted another six dozen or more individuals. Cape Cod's bird life was dominated by this one species. Never before had I realized the prevalence of one bird.

An adult herring gull is a very showy creature. It has an all-white head, neck, and underparts, pale gray mantle with black wing tips with conspicuous white spots, pinkish legs, and a yellow bill with a red spot on the lower mandible. Its eyes are a pale yellow, with a reddish eye ring when breeding. And, except for the great black-backed gull, it is the largest of North America's gulls. Wintering herring gulls show dusky streaks on their otherwise immaculate plumage. And immature birds, until their fourth year, can possess plumage that varies from dark brown to mottled brown and white.

Gulls are superb fliers, able to utilize the strong coastal breeze to fly low at breakneck speed over the waves or to soar high in the sky, often circling to great heights. They also feed on almost any kind of food available, from fish to garbage. I watched several individuals quarreling over the remains of a fish carcass to which one had laid claim; the other three were attempting robbery. The argument was settled when the last of the carcass was swallowed whole. Another individual had found a large moon shell and was attempting to remove the snail. The gull was not having much success. Once it flew up in the air with the shell in its bill, perhaps 30 to 40 feet (9 to 12 m) high, dropped the shell, then followed it down, and pounced on it at almost the second it hit the wet mud. If the surface had been rock or concrete, I am sure the shell would have cracked, and the ingredients would have been eaten. The herring gull had undoubtedly used this technique before. But using the soft mud was a lost cause.

Then across the marsh another chase ensued. This time a herring gull was after a much smaller ring-billed gull. The ring-bill had found some sort of morsel, and the herring gull was in hot pursuit. They flew with surprising agility, swerving this way and that, up and down. Suddenly the ring-bill dropped its burden; the herring gull was on it by the time it hit the mud flat. The ring-bill made one half-hearted attempt to reclaim the object, then gave up, flying off to find lunch elsewhere. The dominant herring gull stayed put and consumed its prize.

This kind of avian bullying or piracy goes on all during the daylight hours between herring gulls and several other birds of the beach and wetlands. The aggressiveness and adaptability of the herring gull is why it is the most abundant "sea gull" of the northeastern coast. Not only does it take advantage of other birds but it has adapted to artificial foods that have been made available through various human activities, often to the detriment of several other avian species. Its population has soared owing to the abundant and easily accessible foods left behind on the beaches and deposited at open landfills. The resultant increased populations of gulls have indirectly led to the displacement of several nesting terns. Furthermore, as omnivores, gulls also feed on tern eggs and chicks. And so tern populations have been seriously reduced all along the northeast coast.

Recent awareness of this interrelationship has created enough concern for the declining tern populations that all three of the open landfills on Cape Cod have been capped. Local residents and the National Park Service hope that this action will help the terns recover to their previously common status.

Acadia's rounded mountaintops, carved by an ancient ice sheet, are reflected in Jordan Pond, summer home of common loons. (Photo by Ro Wauer)

Extensive flats at the mouth of the Salmon River are exposed at low tide at Alma, Fundy National Park. (Photo by Ro Wauer)

The dark waters of the Mersey River reflect the green forest of red maples and eastern hemlocks at Kejimkujik National Park. (Photo by Ro Wauer)

The rugged and rocky shoreline of Cape Breton Highlands National Park is capped with conifer forests. (Photo by Ro Wauer)

Black spruce, balsam fir, and alders dominate the wetlands near Blue Hill, Terra Nova National Park. (Photo by Ro Wauer)

A glacially carved valley provides a backdrop to Western Brook Pond at Gros Morne National Park. (Photo by Ro Wauer)

Kelly's Bog boardwalk provides an opportunity to see a bog and its unique flora and fauna close up at Kouchibouguac National Park. (Photo by Ro Wauer)

Approximately 35,000 seabirds nest on the 600-foot cliffs of Cap Gaspé at Forillon National Park. (Photo by Ro Wauer)

The Delaware River forms scattered wetlands below the forested slopes at Delaware Water Gap National Recreation Area. (Photo by Ro Wauer)

Sandstone Falls of New River is nestled below the forested slopes at New River Gorge National River. (Photo by Ro Wauer)

Fall view of the Big South Fork from the East Rim Overlook.
(Photo by Ro Wauer)

Quiet backwaters of the Green River, below the River Boat Dock, at
Mammoth Cave National Park. (Photo by Ro Wauer)

Fall colors of the deciduous forest dominate the gentle mountain slopes at Shenandoah National Park. (Photo by Ro Wauer)

View southwest from near Apple Orchard on the Blue Ridge Parkway. (Photo by Ro Wauer)

Dawn among the spruce-fir forest on Mount LeConte, Great Smoky Mountains National Park. (Photo by Ro Wauer)

Abrams Creek flows through the lush meadows of Cades Cove in Great Smoky Mountains National Park. (Photo by Ro Wauer)

A fall scene at the historic Snodgrass Cabin, Chickamauga and Chattanooga National Military Park. (Photo by Ro Wauer)

Looking east across Nauset Marsh toward Coast Guard Beach at Cape Cod National Seashore. (Photo by Ro Wauer)

Waterfowl at Jamaica Bay, Gateway National Recreation Area, with the New York City skyline as a backdrop. (Photo by Ro Wauer)

The Washington Monument and Tidal Basin are visible through the cherry trees at National Capital Parks, Washington, D.C. (Photo by Ro Wauer)

View across Swan Pond from the Swan Pool Trail, Assateague National Seashore. (Photo by Ro Wauer)

Cape Lookout Lighthouse rises above the salt marsh and slash pines at Cape Lookout National Seashore. (Photo by Ro Wauer)

The Roller Coaster Trail passes through a mature oak-palmetto forest at Cumberland Island National Seashore. (Photo by Ro Wauer)

Chattahoochee River National Recreation Area and the city of Atlanta, Georgia, from Palisades Overlook. (Photo by Ro Wauer)

The white sand beach and sea oats at Gulf Islands National Seashore. (Photo by Ro Wauer)

Bald cypress trees growing in a slough at Congaree Swamp National Monument. (Photo by National Park Service)

Tidal flats of Florida Bay from the end of Snake Bight Trail, Everglades National Park. (Photo by Ro Wauer)

Cypress swamp habitat, with bromeliads, ferns, and shrubs, along the Loop Road, Big Cypress National Preserve. (Photo by Ro Wauer)

The grounds inside the historic fort, Ft. Jefferson National Monument, Dry Tortugas. (Photo by Ro Wauer)

View of Maho Bay and beach with Mary Point beyond, at Virgin Islands National Park, St. John. (Photo by Ro Wauer)

The coral gardens below the thorn scrub vegetation on the eastern slope of Buck Island National Monument, St. Croix. (Photo by Ro Wauer)

Sugar Bay Salt Pond is fringed with mangroves at Salt River Bay Historical Park and Ecological Preserve, St. Croix. (Photo by Ro Wauer)

Herring gull

The Park Environment

Cape Cod National Seashore is the northernmost of six national seashores located along the Atlantic Coast. Established in 1961, the park embraces a 40-mile-long (64-km) section of the Cape between Provincetown and Chatham. The park is 70 miles (113 km) southeast of Boston, Massachusetts, via U.S. Highways 3 and 6.

Cape Cod is the great hook of land that forms Cape Cod Bay on the west and abuts the Atlantic Ocean on the east. Within the 44,596 acres (18,048 ha) of the park can be found beaches and dunes, freshwater ponds, native cranberry bogs, stands of pitch pines, forest communities, and old fields. The shifting sand dunes sometimes inundate the pine communities. Good examples of this changing environment occur along Race Point Road.

Various forest communities occur within swales or protected areas throughout the cape. These forested areas are usually dominated by pitch pine, white or black oaks, beech, or Atlantic white cedar. Other common trees of these forest areas include black cherry, sassafras, and sour-gum and several woody shrubs such as huckleberry, bayberry, beach plum, bearberry, highbush blueberry, and swamp azalea.

The old fields that once maintained farms are now shrub-dominated habitats. The most common woody plants of these areas include red cedar, domestic apple, black locust, beach plum, salt spray and Virginia roses, common blackberry, and bullbriar. The saltwater marshes are another important habitat of the cape and are dominated by salt marsh cordgrass, salt meadow grass, and sea lavender.

The National Park Service operates two separate visitor centers in the national seashore, at Salt Pond near Eastham and Province Lands near Provincetown. Each center contains an information desk and exhibits. Various introductory films on the park and its resources are shown throughout the day. The visitor centers also have sales areas for publications and videos, including books on birds in general, New England bird life, and the park area specifically. A checklist of Cape Cod birds also is available.

Interpretive programs at the park include talks and walks on a wide range of topics, from broad ecological issues to more specialized ones. Bird walks are designed for various levels of interest, from beginners to more advanced. Monthly activity schedules are available on request. In addition, nine self-guiding nature trails are scattered throughout the park, and there are 36 miles (58 km) of walking trails and 11 miles (18 km) of biking routes.

Cape Cod is also home to a wildlife sanctuary operated by the Massachusetts Audubon Society, one of the country's largest Audubon societies, which offers educational programs, self-guiding trails, and a sales operation at South Wellfleet. And in the town of Orleans is the Bird Watcher's General Store, where the nature lover can find the best assortment of bird-related materials, from bird feed to earrings and tie tacks, that I have encountered.

There are no NPS campgrounds within the park, but several private camping areas operate on private land within the boundary. Lodging, restaurants, and supplies are available along Highway 6.

Additional information can be obtained from the Superintendent, Cape Cod National Seashore, South Wellfleet, MA 02663; (508) 349-3785.

Bird Life

The other large gull of the national seashore is the great black-backed gull. Although larger than the herring gull, it is best identified by its all-black mantle, a feature that usually is obvious from a considerable distance. Populations of black-backs have increased in recent years, and there is some evidence of interbreeding between the two species. Both compete with and prey on the smaller terns.

Four kinds of terns nest within the national seashore: the endangered roseate and the common, Arctic, and least terns. Their nesting colonies are subject to careful monitoring by the park service in cooperation with the Massachusetts Division of Fisheries and Wildlife. Park Resource Management Specialist Kyle Jones told me that the park has been monitoring tern populations for more than 15 years and that during that time, all four populations have suffered a general decline; the most stable of the three is the least tern.

The **least tern** is the smallest of the four species, smaller even than a robin. Its tiny size, bright yellow bill with black at the very tip, yellow feet, and white forehead are its best identifying features.

Least tern

But it usually is first detected by its surprisingly loud and staccato "yip yip yip" calls.

These little seabirds arrive from their South American wintering grounds in early May and almost immediately begin to nest. The two to four eggs, almost the color of the dry sand, are laid in a shallow depression in the sand that is usually lined with shell fragments. Both adults participate in incubation and feeding of the young. When the eggs are subject to extensive sunlight, the adults actually cool their eggs by dipping their feathers into the nearby surf or bay and sprinkling water on the eggs.

Least terns feed on tiny fish and invertebrates that they capture by diving into the surf or skimming the calmer bay waters. They can be extremely active when, of necessity, they must make trip after trip from their nest to their feeding grounds to feed their chicks. Sometimes they fish so close to shore that a swimmer may have an unexpected companion. Their nesting sites, too, are often shared with beach users, often to the detriment of the terns. However, these birds are largely colonial in nature, and several dozen pairs will utilize select areas along the seashore. In those cases, the park service usually fences the areas or restricts use throughout the nesting process. More than 2,500 pairs of nesting least terns have been counted yearly along the Massachusetts coast; the largest colony (almost 900 pairs) occurs on Nauset Beach.

Smaller numbers of the three larger tern species—roseate, common, and Arctic—nest within the national seashore as well. The common tern is the most abundant tern statewide. The Arctic tern is the least numerous; the largest congregation is only eight pairs that utilize New Island near Orleans. These three tern species are similar in appearance, and identification can be a problem at first. However, with adequate binoculars or a spotting scope, they can be readily identified.

Breeding adults possess bright plumage and colorful bills and feet. The most useful identifying feature is the color of the bird's bill. The roseate tern's bill is all black except for red at the base; the common tern's bill is orange-red except for a black tip; the Arctic tern's bill is deep red. When the bird's bill cannot be seen well, identification must be based on other features. The upper wing and underwing patterns are the best features to examine at that point. Kenn Kaufman's *Advanced Birding* book includes the best descriptions of these features.

Several marsh birds can usually be seen from the Nauset Marsh overlooks. Morning views are best from the Coast Guard Beach side, but evening views are better from Fort Hill. **Great blue herons** are the largest of the wading birds visible from the overlooks as they feed along the shore or in the shallow water. Those lanky, blue and gray birds can be quite numerous. With a wingspan of six feet, a heron in flight is graceful and can be amazingly agile if it chooses to dive or to elude a red-winged blackbird or other bird that may be harassing it. Then it may utter a series of loud squawks that can usually be heard far across the marsh.

Other waders of Nauset Marsh include the much smaller snowy egret, a bird that feeds along the narrow channels of the marsh and so is less noticeable. Snowies have all-white plumage with a black bill and legs; their feet are bright yellow. And the even smaller **green-backed heron** utilizes similar habitats but prefers the fresher water areas of the inner bay. This heron often sits very still and uses its coloration to hide it from danger. However, once discovered, it will fly up with a loud, abrasive "kyowk" call and streak off to another feeding site.

Green-backed adults are extremely colorful, especially in sunlight, with their greenish-blue backs, shiny green crowns, and deep chestnut necks and throats. They will perch perfectly still on a snag or the bank and patiently wait for prey (fish, frog, or invertebrates) to come close enough to strike with their heavy bills. They sometimes reach far out over the water in seemingly impossible balancing acts.

In addition, there is a longtime night-heron roost along Nauset Marsh at the end of Hemenway Road. Every evening at dusk black-crowned night-herons and an occasional yellow-crowned night-heron leave their roosts and fly over the parking area to the marsh, where they feed throughout the night. At dawn they return to their roosts.

The adult black-crowned night-heron is a large and very chunky bird with a distinct black crown and back. Its cheeks and neck are white, and the rest of the bird is a grayish color, except for yellow legs. The yellow-crowned night-heron possesses a black-and-white head pattern with a yellow crown and an all-gray back and underparts. Immature birds are more difficult to distinguish. The ability of these herons to hunt after dark is unique for the family of herons. All the other herons are active during daylight hours and roost overnight.

Nauset Marsh is also home to Canada geese and a number of ducks. The American black duck, drab like a mallard hen, is most numerous. Several dozen individuals can usually be found feeding on the shallow waters or loafing along the shore. Less numerous are blue-winged and green-winged teal, mallards, northern pintails, northern shovelers, gadwalls, American wigeons, ruddy ducks, and red-breasted mergansers. The wood duck can often be found at small freshwater ponds. Two family groups were present at the little pond at the start of the Beech Forest Trail one morning in September. The male wood duck (see chapter 24 on National Capital Parks) is one of nature's finest creations.

Killdeers and spotted sandpipers are the only shorebirds that nest within the park's wetlands, but the endangered **piping plover** utilizes the sandy beaches. A total of 28 pairs nested within the national seashore in 1991; 74 chicks were known to have fledged, according to an NPS report by John Meisel. This bird has been subject to considerable attention since it was listed as threatened in 1986. Not only does the park service monitor the birds that utilize the park beaches but nesting sites are closed to pedestrians, dogs, and kite flying. Beaches are closed to ORVs after hatching occurs. Most of the nests are also enclosed in predator-proof fencing.

Piping plovers are well adapted to care for themselves in the wild. Their sand-color plumage provides excellent camouflage, and they distract predators by pretending injury, dragging a wing as if it were broken. These techniques worked well enough until human beings appeared. After they had to compete for beach space with recreationists and their pets, their populations declined to a point where they began to disappear altogether. Once their plight became known, and they were added to the list of threatened and endangered species, federal and state wildlife agencies began recovery programs. These include on-site management as well as public awareness. By using radio spots, brochures, and word of mouth, the wildlife agencies have made the public aware of the birds' problems. These activities have apparently begun to pay off. Piping plover populations have begun to stabilize, and in a few areas with greater protection, such as Cape Cod National Seashore, they actually are on the increase.

Migration time on the cape can be exciting beyond the beach and marsh. More than 60 species have been reported in spring and fall as migrants. And because of the seashore's position far out in the Atlantic Ocean, many stray species are found after strong weather fronts move through. Northbound migrants begin to appear in late March, and migration is in full swing by mid-April. Among the species present only as migrants are olive-sided, yellow-bellied, Acadian, alder, and least flycatchers; cliff swallows; gray-cheeked and Swainson's thrushes; solitary, yellow-throated, warbling, and Philadelphia vireos; 18 species of warblers; summer tanagers; blue grosbeaks; and Lincoln's sparrows.

The park's forests and woodlands provide habitat for a host of songbirds during the nesting season. None of those are as numerous as the tiny **black-capped chickadee**. This personable little bird with the "chick-a-dee-dee-dee" song is barely five inches in length and has a black bib and head and white cheeks and breast. Nesting birds utilize cavities in trees, and the male feeds the female throughout incubation. During the winter they join flocks of songbirds that roam the woodlands together. One of the best ways to find winter songbirds is by listening for the constant songs of the black-caps.

Other common woodland songbirds in summer include eastern wood-pewee, great crested flycatcher, eastern kingbird, American crow, tufted titmouse, Carolina wren, American robin, red-eyed vireo, pine warbler, ovenbird, and common grackle.

Breeding bird surveys initiated by Kyle Jones reveal that of all the above species, the **pine warbler** is the most obvious. This is undoubtedly due to that bird's continuous singing at that time of the year; it even sings during midday the rest of the year. Its song is a musical trill that varies only slightly in pitch. Paul Sykes described its song as "like a chipping sparrow's song but softer, lower, and less rapid: zit, zit, ziz-ziz-ziz-ziz-ziz-ziz-ziz-ziz-ziz-ziz."

The pine warbler is well named because it rarely ventures out of the pines. An adult male has yellow underparts, olive green upperparts, yellow eyebrows, and two prominent white wing bars. Females have a similar pattern but are duller. These birds also join the winter bird parties but usually stay in the pines even when the rest of the party is feeding in adjacent hardwoods. See chapter 20 on Chickamauga and Chattanooga for an additional description of this bird.

Then there are the old fields with scattered junipers and brushy edges. This habitat usually contains another very different group of songbirds, although there may be some overlap. For instance, black-capped chickadees seem to utilize almost any habitat to search for food. One day in September along the Nauset Marsh Bicycle Trail, I found this bird in pines, junipers, oaks, several species of shrubs, in the tall cane growing along the shore, and on the ground.

Some of the more common old-field birds in summer include the gray catbird, northern mockingbird, yellow and prairie warblers, common yellowthroat, northern cardinal, rufous-sided towhee, chipping and field sparrows, and American goldfinch. Of these, none are as obvious as the **gray catbird**. Every thicket seems to house a pair of these rather nondescript songsters. Their catcalls, very much like a house cat's meow, can be heard from each pile of shrubbery. But their song is much softer, although rather disjointed, almost like that of a mellow mockingbird.

In sunlight, gray catbirds can be quite lovely birds. The brightly plumaged male is a deep gray color with a slaty cap and rusty crissum. Their coloration is well suited to their secretive behavior, as they prefer the deep shadows of the underbrush to a perch in the sunlight. However, they also are among the most curious of birds, and a low spishing sound will almost always bring the curious catbird into the open.

Wintertime at Cape Cod is very different from the rest of the year. Forest and field birds are scattered in small parties and are seldom conspicuous. The marshes are usually frozen. Harbors and the open ocean provide the best birding. Annual Christmas Bird Counts produce approximately 65 to 70 species of about 7,000 individuals. The dozen most numerous species listed for the 1990 Christmas Count, in descending order of abundance, were the northern gannet, common eider, red-breasted merganser, herring gull, loggerhead shrike, American black duck, great black-backed gull, razorbill, bufflehead, black-capped chickadee, black-legged kittiwake, and ring-billed gull.

In summary, the Cape Cod checklist of birds contains 312 species, 49 of which occur all twelve months of the year and 109 that nest within the national seashore. Thirty-six of these are water birds (waterfowl, seabirds, shorebirds, and marsh birds), 9 are raptors (hawks and owls), and 11 are warblers. Eight species are listed only as winter residents or visitors: Barrow's goldeneye, gyrfalcon, skua, dovekie, snowy owl, pine grosbeak, white-winged crossbill, and common redpoll.

Birds of Special Interest

Great blue heron. This is the tallest of the marsh birds and is easily identified by its size, long legs, heavy bill, and blue-gray and white plumage.

Green-backed heron. Watch for this little green, blue, and chestnut-colored heron in the upper marshy areas of the bays in summer. When surprised, it will utter a loud "kyowk" call.

Herring gull. This is the large, gray-backed gull that is so numerous on the beach and marshes and over the ocean. It is so adaptable that it has learned to take advantage of human refuse.

Least tern. It nests on Cape Cod beaches in large colonies and fishes the surf and calmer waters of the bay. Its small size, black cap, yellow bill, and white underparts help to identify this threatened species.

Gray catbird. It is common in summer at all the brushy areas on the cape. It has an overall gray body with a black cap, a rusty crissum, and a call that sounds like the meow of a house cat.

Pine warbler. Look for it among the pines throughout the year. Its overall yellow color and two distinct white wing bars are its best identifying features.

22

Gateway National Recreation Area and Fire Island National Seashore, New York and New Jersey

I counted more than two dozen glossy ibis at the far end of West Pond. Judging by their constant preening, they all seemed extremely concerned about their personal appearance. I watched as they groomed each feather with their long, curved bills. Evidently, they had already eaten. Their glossy, dark green backs, from which their name is derived, gleamed in the midmorning sunlight, outdone only by the deep chestnut throats and breasts of the adults. The mottled brown birds were immatures; one individual with an obviously shorter bill was undoubtedly a bird of the year. Otherwise, they all had long, down-curved, gray-brown to yellowish bills of about five and a half inches in length.

Suddenly another eight ibis appeared, landing in the shallow water alongside the busily preening birds. As far as I could tell, they were completely ignored. The new arrivals apparently had not completed breakfast, because they immediately began feeding along the muddy shoreline. They seemed to be using two very distinct methods, probing into the soft mud or moving their bills back and forth over the shore. The probers seemed content to stand in one place, but the others walked forward, moving their bills back and forth as if vacuuming. I was not close enough to assess their success, but I knew that they were searching for food, from almost any invertebrate to some larger creatures such as fish, frogs, and snakes.

Glossy ibis

The glossy ibis is a medium-sized water bird with an unusually long, curved bill that would be more expected in the tropics than in temperate wetlands within sight of the New York City skyline. It is, however, one of Gateway's more common resident birds, actually nesting on the small, more isolated islands within Jamaica Bay. They spend much of their time loafing and feeding at places such as West Pond, returning each evening to roost on the islands.

A similar pattern of daily movement is followed by most of the other long-legged waders that utilize Jamaica Bay: great blue and tricolored herons and great and snowy egrets. All five of these colonial water birds were visible from the 1¾-mile (3-km) loop trail that morning at Jamaica Bay.

The Park Environment

The greater New York City area includes a 32-mile-long (51-km) barrier island, long spits, and great estuaries. Portions of Fire Island, Long Island, Rockaway Peninsula, and Jamaica Bay in New York and Sandy Hook in New Jersey are included within the two national parks that extend for approximately 60 miles (97 km) from the

William Floyd Estate on Long Island southward to the base of Sandy
Hook. The combined 45,579 acres (18,438 ha) include 19,579 acres
(7,924 ha) within Fire Island National Seashore, established in 1978,
and 26,000 acres (10,522 ha) within Gateway National Recreation
Area, established in 1972. In 1980, 1,400 acres (567 ha) of Fire Island
were designated as wilderness. Gateway's name was derived from the
two arms of land that extend into the greater New York-New Jersey
estuary like a natural gateway to the New World.

These park areas lie within the Atlantic plain east of the
Piedmont and contain extremely important habitats for birds
throughout the year. Vast numbers of North America's migrants
following the Atlantic flyway pass through these areas in both
spring and fall. The undeveloped portions of the parks, especially
the 9,155-acre (3,745-ha) Jamaica Bay Wildlife Refuge, provide
increasingly important stopover sites.

Jamaica Bay is a man-made sanctuary with ponds, mud flats,
salt marsh, old fields, and scrub thickets. Northern bayberry,
winged sumac, poison ivy, blackberry, wrinkled rose, red cedar,
gray birch, and black cherry are most evident in the thicket habitats
that will someday be a secondary forest. Large stands of reed grass
grow at various places along the shore.

The extensive dune system of the islands, usually only a few
hundred feet wide, is dominated by American beach grass, seaside
goldenrod, and false beachheather, with pockets of woody vegetation. These thicket habitats are dominated by northern bayberry
and beach plum, with lesser amounts of Juneberry, black cherry,
and vines such as poison ivy, greenbrier, wild grape, and Virginia
creeper.

The William Floyd Estate (named after a signer of the
Declaration of Independence), a detached 613-acre (248-ha) area
on Long Island, contains a mature oak-hickory forest community
that possesses many of the original forest species: red, black, scarlet,
white, and chestnut oaks; pignut, mockernut, and bitternut hickories; flowering dogwood; sassafras; hophornbeam; hackberry; green
hawthorn; and several other trees. Mountain laurel, blueberries,
mapleleaf viburnum, and deerberry are common understory
species.

National park visitor centers are located (north to south) at Smith Point West, Sailor's Haven, Watch Hill (these latter two are accessible only by ferry or private boat), Fire Island Lighthouse, Jamaica Bay, and Spermaceti Cove at Sandy Point. Each of these facilities contains an information desk and sales outlet for publications. Bird checklists are available for Jamaica Bay and Sandy Point.

A wide variety of interpretive activities are scheduled throughout the summer season. These include ranger-guided nature walks, including several bird walks, and evening programs; schedules are free on request. In addition, the two parks have several self-guided trails that are well worth the time and effort, as they are located at the more natural areas and provide sound information about the individual ecosystems found there.

No camping is available in the national parks, but adjacent state parks provide no-service sites. Lodging and supplies are abundant within adjacent communities.

Access to all the national park areas, at least for the nonresident, requires careful planning with attentiveness to direction en route. A word of advice: use the main routes and refrain from shortcutting.

Additional information can be obtained from the Superintendent, Fire Island National Seashore, 120 Laurel Street, Patchogue, NY 11772; (516) 289-4810; and Superintendent, Gateway National Recreation Area, Jamaica Bay Wildlife Refuge, Floyd Bennett Field, Bldg. 69, Brooklyn, NY 11234; (718) 338-3338.

Bird Life

Jamaica Bay Wildlife Refuge is without doubt the best place in both parks to see the largest number of birds with the least amount of work. This birding hot spot was described by Arthur Morris in an excellent 1989 article in *Birder's World*.

One three-hour visit in mid-September produced 58 species of residents and migrants. Several hundred birders were present that morning, strung out along the path either alone or in small groups. There was also a large tour group of about 80 people. The glossy ibis always got a lot of attention, but some of the neighboring birds received long looks as well.

West Pond contained several thousand ducks and geese. Most abundant was the **American black duck**, a mallard hen look-alike with dark plumage, a violet speculum bordered with black, and white wing linings that are best seen in flight. This duck interbreeds with the closely related mallard, which also was common that morning. Hybrids with white-bordered speculums are increasing. During my visit hundreds of black ducks arrived from all directions, coming in large flocks or small family groups to join the others. At one time I counted more than 200 individuals flying over the marsh and open water from the northwest.

Fewer numbers of blue-winged teals, American wigeons, and ruddy ducks were present, and **Canada geese** were quite numerous. These large, stately birds were grazing on the grassy shores at scattered locations around the pond. I was surprised how close they fed to the graveled pathway. They no doubt knew they were protected within the park, and people there enjoyed the presence of these amazing creatures. Although the species is a full-time resident at Jamaica Bay, nesting at weedy areas throughout, the population undoubtedly increases during spring and fall when migrant Canada geese stop to feed and rest on their long journey.

The large bird with a long, gracefully curved neck was the **mute swan**, a gorgeous, all-white bird with an orange bill with a black knob. Two pairs were present on West Pond, but I found 26 additional birds across Crossbay Boulevard in the east pond. Several of those birds were immatures, evident from their brown-mottled plumage. Mute swans were introduced from Europe in the mid-nineteenth century and for years were found in only a few localities along the East Coast; their numbers increased dramatically in the 1980s. One cannot help but wonder if they will replace one of the native species that is being threatened by various changes in the environment. See chapter 23 on Assateague for a description of this swan in that more southern location.

Double-crested cormorants were also present in substantial numbers, mostly lined up on a dead tree limb that poked out of the water at the far shore near the ibis. A couple of the cormorants stood spread-eagle with their wings out to dry. They apparently had already been fishing and were drying their waterlogged plumage

American oystercatcher

before they reentered the water to swim down another fish dinner.

At the far end of the loop trail is a short secondary loop trail that provides access to the flats and channels to the west. This area is where I found **American oystercatchers**, large and bizarre-looking shorebirds. Their black-and-white plumage is set off by their long, heavy, orange-red bills and red eyes in their coal black heads. There were five individuals along the little islet across the channel. Through my binoculars, I watched them feeding on the exposed mussel beds. I could not tell for sure what they were eating, but the species is known to feed on a wide variety of marine life, including oysters. Ehrlich and colleagues pointed out that this bird can open an oyster shell in less than 30 seconds. They wrote,

> The trick, in part, lies with having the right tool—a long, stout bill with mandibles that are triangular in cross section and reinforced so that they do not bend easily. But the success of the oystercatcher depends mainly upon use of one of two learned techniques. Oystercatchers are either stabbers or hammerers.
>
> Stabbers sneak up on open mollusks and plunge their bills between the shells, severing the abductors before the bivalve can "clam up." The meat is then neatly chiseled away from

each shell, shaken free, and eaten. Hammerers, in contrast, loosen the bivalve from its moorings, and then shatter one shell with a rapid series of well-directed, short, powerful blows. The bill is then inserted through the hole, the abductors are cut, the shells pried apart, and the mollusk removed and devoured.

The park's most threatened shorebird is the tiny, sand-colored **piping plover.** These little birds nest on the outer beaches in April and May, remain through August, feeding in the intertidal zone, and leave for their southern wintering grounds by early September. While nesting they are extremely vulnerable to human activities, and so nesting sites in the park are usually fenced for their protection. See chapter 10 on Canada's Kouchibouguac National Park concerning the status of this species farther north.

Shorebirds can be plentiful during migration along the shore and at mud flats. The inner bays usually provide the greatest numbers. The most common species include semipalmated and black-bellied plovers, killdeers, greater yellowlegs, short-billed dowitchers, ruddy turnstones, least and semipalmated sandpipers, and dunlin.

Migration also produces the largest number of songbirds. These little and often colorful birds can be found almost anywhere that vegetation provides adequate cover and food. Sandy Hook's Old Dune Trail and Fire Island's Smith Point Trail can be superb in spring or fall. Northern mockingbirds; gray catbirds; brown thrashers; American robins; white-eyed and red-eyed vireos; yellow-rumped, blackpoll, and palm warblers; northern waterthrushes; American redstarts; dark-eyed juncos; and white-throated sparrows can be common at these sites. Overhead, tree, bank, and barn swallows can be abundant.

Gray catbirds were abundant along the Smith Point Trail in September. Every thicket produced a half dozen or so as I progressed around the boardwalk loop trail. If a catbird was not already visible, a low spishing sound would immediately attract two or more of these very curious birds. They possess slate gray plumage with black caps and rusty crissums. But when they poke out of the thicket, it is their black eyes and long tails that seem most obvious.

By late summer, the low barrier island thickets are ready for the southbound migrants that will stop to feed and rest at select sites along their route. Most of the shrubs are rich with fruit, from the tiny grayish berries of bayberry to the large purplish plums of beach plum. Even poison ivy contributes to the smorgasbord. And during the few weeks while the myriad songbirds pass through the area (early September to mid-October) they will consume the bulk of the fruit. Even many species that normally are insectivorous will take advantage of the readily available nutrients.

The shrub thicket habitat also supports a number of nesting birds in summer. Most numerous of these are the mourning dove, gray catbird, brown thrasher, yellow warbler, rufous-sided towhee, and song sparrow. The **rufous-sided towhee** is a robin-sized bird with an all-black head, a red eye, dark back, white underparts, and rufous sides. It can be abundant and readily visible during early mornings, when it often sits atop the shrubs and sings its well-known, loud "towheeee" song. Actually, to me, the song is more of a "threee," with the inflection on the "eee." If startled, towhees will dive for cover with a flash of their white-tipped tail feathers. But they also are very curious birds and usually can be enticed back into the open with low spishing sounds. See chapter 17 on Shenandoah for a description of this species there.

The **song sparrow** is much less obvious but even more numerous within the dune thickets, and it can be enticed into the open just as readily. This little sparrow is rather drab, with brownish plumage marked by darker streaks that come together on the chest like a stickpin. What this bird does not have in color it makes up for in personality. It is one of the perkiest and most active birds of the dune communities. It seems always to be on the move from one clump of shrubs to another. And its song has few equals.

Ernest Thompson Seton (in Chapman) described its song as a "merry chant—which has won for it the name of song sparrow." He further wrote, "It is a voluble and uninterrupted but short refrain, and is, perhaps, the sweetest of the familiar voices of the meadow lands." Although this species has more than the ordinary number of songs, each begins with clear "sweet sweet sweet" notes, followed by a trill that drops in pitch and is highly variable.

The mature forest at the William Floyd Estate, perhaps more than anywhere else in the joint parks, supports a breeding bird population closer to that which probably existed on much of Long Island prior to European man's influences. Paths lead through the forest, starting from the field in front of the house, and provide easy access into this very tall and diverse habitat. However, because the estate is closed a good part of the time, anyone wishing to visit the area should first contact the park manager at (516) 399-2030.

A summer visit to these woods, especially during the early morning hours, would more than likely result in finding many of the following birds: mourning dove; whip-poor-will; northern flicker; hairy, downy, and red-bellied woodpeckers; eastern wood-pewee; great crested flycatcher; eastern phoebe; blue jay; American and fish crows; black-capped chickadee; tufted titmouse; white-breasted nuthatch; house and Carolina wrens; gray catbird; brown thrasher; American robin; wood thrush; blue-gray gnatcatcher; Philadelphia, yellow-throated, and red-eyed vireos; blue-winged, yellow, chestnut-sided, pine, prairie, and black-and-white warblers; ovenbird; American redstart; northern cardinal; common grackle; brown-headed cowbird; scarlet tanager; and chipping sparrow.

Wintertime birds can be just as spectacular as those during other times of the year. Christmas Bird Counts have included portions of both areas for many years, but because they also cover areas outside the park, they are not good indicators of what might occur within the parks. However, the park undertakes waterfowl counts at Jamaica Bay each January. These censuses account for approximately 7,500 individuals of 20 to 22 species annually. The various species recorded, in order of abundance, include the American black duck, greater scaup, Canada goose, bufflehead, brant, snow goose, red-breasted merganser, American wigeon, mallard, double-crested cormorant, ruddy duck, great cormorant, horned grebe, mute swan, gadwall, canvasback, northern pintail, northern shoveler, oldsquaw, American coot, and common goldeneye.

In summary, the two parks have a combined list of about 330 species, of which more than 100 are known to nest. Eleven of those are waterfowl, 11 are wading birds, only 3 are hawks and owls, and 7 are warblers. Seven species occur only in winter: the red-necked grebe, tundra swan, harlequin duck, purple sandpiper, snowy owl (irregular), northern shrike (irregular), and snow bunting.

Birds of Special Interest

Glossy ibis. This bird with a long, curved bill, glossy greenish back, and chestnut neck and breast can be found at Jamaica Bay's West Pond all year; it is rare in winter.

Mute swan. Its all-white plumage, long, graceful neck, and orange bill with a black bulb distinguish it from all other birds. It is a full-time resident at Jamaica Bay.

Canada goose. This large waterfowl is best identified by its black neck and head and broad white throat. It also has a deep, musical "honk" call.

American oystercatcher. Its heavy, orange-red bill, all-black head, brown back, and white underparts are a sure giveaway. This is one of the largest of the shorebirds.

Gray catbird. This large sparrow-sized songbird lives in the thickets but is not shy and will come out to investigate any strange sound. It is slaty gray with a black cap and rusty crissum.

Rufous-sided towhee. It also lives in thickets and sings the familiar "towheee" song. This songbird has a black head with a red eye, black back, rufous sides, and white-cornered tail.

Song sparrow. This is the most common songbird of the dune thickets. It can best be identified by its reddish-brown plumage, streaked with black, and dark blotch in the middle of its breast.

23

Assateague Island National Seashore, Maryland and Virginia

The brown pelican is without doubt one of nature's strangest creatures. One moment it can be ungainly and awkward, and the next, it can be all control and grace. On the one hand, when a pelican becomes airborne after one of its incredible dives, especially if its pouch contains a larger than average fish, it looks like part of a circus act. On the other hand, when this bird, which is of considerable size, skims only inches above the water without a wing beat, it is an act of near-perfection.

A dozen or more brown pelicans were visible from the Bayside picnic area, either flying over the deeper portions of Sinepuxent Bay or fishing the shallower waters near shore. I focused my binoculars on one of the closer individuals just as it plummeted downward from 35 to 40 feet (11-12 m) above the water. It folded its wings and dropped beak first like a torpedo, hitting the water with a force that sent spray at least 20 feet (6 m) high. A few seconds later, there was a great flurry of wings and water as it worked to get airborne again. It actually pushed itself out of the water with its wings and took several strides with its broad, webbed feet to clear the surface. I wasn't sure if its dive had been successful or not; it may have swallowed its catch immediately. Within 30 seconds, it was again in the air and ready for its next dive.

I watched that same brown pelican for about an hour. It seemed to follow a pattern; it made three or four dives and then flew a wide circle, perhaps to check on a mate or fishing opportunities elsewhere.

It then returned to the same area, flying above the water at about 40 feet (12 m) and plummeting into the bay once again. Splash!

The bird I was watching was an adult, probably one of those that nest on the little islands just off South Point. It still possessed deep brown color on the neck, although its forehead was dirty white, not the bright white of a breeding bird. Some of the other pelicans in the vicinity were immatures that still had dull brown plumage overall. But they all possessed the great pelican bill, complete with the distensible pouch that they use to scoop up their prey. A specialized hook at the tip of the bill aids in capturing fish.

Brown pelican

What a marvelous bird is the pelican! Its seven-foot wingspan is the greatest of any of the local nesting birds. And yet this North American endemic almost followed the great auk and passenger pigeon into oblivion. Pelican populations were so reduced by the effects of DDT obtained from fish that some brown pelican populations disappeared altogether. Following the ban on DDT in 1972, many populations made unprecedented recoveries. By 1986, they began nesting off South Point, and by 1991, that colony had grown to 140 birds, representing the northernmost nesting colony on the Atlantic Coast. It appears that Assateague's brown pelicans are healthy once again and that visitors to Assateague Island can again enjoy their fishing antics as I did.

The Park Environment

Assateague Island is a 37-mile-long (60-km) barrier island extending from the Ocean City, Maryland, inlet to Toms Cove Hook just below Chincoteague, Virginia. Its width varies from a quarter of a mile at the northern end to 2½ miles (1-4 km) just north of Toms Cove. The island is managed by three separate agencies: the National Park Service (NPS), U.S. Fish and Wildlife Service (FWS), and the Maryland Park Service. The Assateague Island National Seashore portion, established in 1965 and managed by the NPS, is limited to 7,897 land acres (3,196 ha) in Maryland. The NPS is also responsible for 32,716 water acres (13,240 ha) around the entire island. Chincoteague National Wildlife Refuge (9,460 acres, or 3,828 ha) continues to the south. The refuge was established in 1943 to maintain and improve the wintering grounds for the snow goose. However, the Toms Cove Hook area of the refuge is managed by the NPS through a unique cooperative agreement between these sister agencies that requires the NPS to manage a visitor recreation program within the refuge.

In addition, the Maryland Park Service operates a 680-acre (275-ha) state park with a campground within the national seashore boundary south of Ocean City. Two NPS campgrounds also exist in the immediate area. There are no agency campgrounds in the Virginia portion of the island, but there are several commercial campgrounds nearby. All lodging, restaurants, and supplies must be acquired within adjacent communities.

Three visitor centers exist on the island: the Barrier Island Visitor Center along Highway 611 below Ocean City, the Toms Cove Visitor Center, and the Chincoteague Refuge Visitor Center near Chincoteague, Virginia. The latter is operated by the FWS. Each of these centers contains an information desk and sales outlet where videos and publications, including a variety of bird books, are sold. A single bird checklist is available for the refuge but pertains to the entire island.

Interpretive activities include talks and walks throughout spring, summer, and fall by both the NPS and the FWS. These include several programs specifically on the island's bird life. Schedules are available at the visitor centers. In addition, the refuge operates a "wildlife safari" bus trip that runs 7 miles (11 km) into the refuge and "evening cruise" boat trips into refuge waters throughout the season.

Assateague Island is like most barrier islands, having a beach, primary dunes, lesser dunes or a flattened sandy area or swales behind the dunes, followed by an area of thickets and/or forest, and, finally, bayside salt flats or marshes. The plant communities behind the dunes—shrub thickets, forests, and marshes—are important habitats for birds.

The shrub thickets are the most diverse of the three and form extended areas along the bay side or patches within the dune swales. These habitats are dominated by northern bayberry, common waxmyrtle, highbush blueberry, red cedar, black cherry, winged sumac, and several vines: poison ivy, greenbriar, Virginia creeper, and Muscadine grape are most prominent.

The forest communities vary a great deal from dense loblolly stands with few other woody plants to taller and more open forest habitats, such as those present along the Wildlife Loop and Swan Pool Trail at Toms Cove. Loblolly pine and a few hardwoods, such as sweet gum, red maple, and various oaks, are dominant. The understory often includes arrowwood, serviceberry, highbush blueberry, and poison ivy and greenbriar vines.

The bayside marsh community is extremely important to many wildlife species, although it does not have a high plant diversity. Most areas are dominated by saltmeadow cordgrass, although a few other salt-tolerant plants grow there, as well.

Additional information can be obtained from the Superintendent, Assateague Island National Seashore, 7206 National Seashore Lane, Berlin, MD 21811; (410) 641-1441.

Bird Life

The bay and marshes contain innumerable large, white birds. Among these are the tall, yellow-billed great egret and the smaller snowy egret, with its black bill and legs and bright yellow feet. The most common of the mostly white gulls is the herring gull, with its all-white underparts, gray mantle, and bright yellow bill with a red spot on the lower mandible. The smaller ring-billed gull has a gray mantle like that of the herring gull, but its yellow bill has a black ring near the tip. The even smaller laughing gull possesses a black head that is highlighted by a liver-red bill during the breeding season. The other summer gull, the great black-backed gull, is the largest of the four and similar to the herring except for its very black mantle. This bird stands out among a flock of gulls because of its size and black back.

The nonbreeding appearance of gulls is very different from their bright, sometimes showy breeding plumage. Wintering herring, black-backed, and ring-billed gulls lose their snow white heads, which become mottled with browns; however, all three retain their bill colors and characteristics. It is a different matter with the laughing gull, which loses not only its black head, which becomes mottled, but also its bill color. Fall and winter laughing gulls have all-black bills. They look almost forlorn, standing on the beach in their drab winter plumage. Most laughing gulls migrate to the southeast coast for winter.

The Toms Cove approach road was built on an embankment that separates the saltwater Toms Cove from freshwater Swan Pool: salt water to the right and fresh water to the left. There are several pullouts along this roadway to encourage wildlife observation. A stop there can be productive any time of the year.

Swan Pool was named for the tundra swans that spend their winters in the freshwater empoundment. But there is an addendum to the Swan Pool designation. Tundra swans have wintered along the East Coast long before parks and wildlife refuges were invented. Each year, 1,000 to 2,400 birds arrive in November and stay until late March. Until very recently, Swan Pool was devoid of swans until they returned the following November. Then, all of a sudden, the mute swan put in its appearance and has since become a common summer resident of Swan Pool. Approximately 40 individuals can be found there all summer long. The mute swan population declines in winter about the same time the tundra swans arrive. So now, Swan Pool is never without swans.

The native **tundra swan** is another all-white bird with a black bill and legs. A careful examination will also reveal a small yellow spot in front of each eye. Some birds also show a rusty stain on

Tundra swan

their heads and upper necks. That results from minerals in the marsh soils where they nest. A swan's neck is about the same length as its body. A graceful and beautiful bird, it also must be respected for its long migration. Tundra swans nest on ponds and sloughs on the tundra north of the Arctic Circle from northern Alaska to Baffin Island and winter along the East Coast from Massachusetts to Florida. Few large birds undertake such an extensive migration.

The migration routes of tundra swans, earlier called whistling swans, have been well studied. The Chesapeake Bay population, which includes those at Assateague Island, comes all the way across the continent from Alaska's Seward Peninsula. Southbound birds fly east to the Mackenzie River, then southeast to central Minnesota and Wisconsin, and then nonstop to the East Coast, a journey of about 3,000 miles (4,828 km).

The call of a tundra swan is a mellow "hoo-ho-hoo," a little like that of a snow goose. Swans can be very vocal during migration, communicating with one another in flight and while feeding, but they are less vocal in midwinter. They feed largely on leaves, stems, and tubers of aquatic plants, usually in shallow water so that they need only to immerse their heads and upper necks. However, beginning in the winter of 1969-70, Assateague's tundra swans began to feed in the fields on Maryland's Eastern Shore, flying several miles inland each day to eat "waste corn and soybeans and browse on shoots of winter wheat," according to Frank Bellrose. This behavioral change may ensure their continued use of the area during colder winters.

The **mute swan** is an even larger bird, all white with a red-orange bill with a black knob. This bird was introduced into North America in the mid-1800s, and it took almost 150 years to reach Swan Pool. As a nonnative species, it competes with native waterfowl for nesting space and food. The American black duck, the most abundant resident duck, has declined dramatically in population since the mid-1980s, about the time mute swans first appeared, according to a report by Roy Kirkpatrick. Refuge Biologist Irvin Ailes told me that the FWS has begun to manage mute swans by controlling reproduction to keep their population from expanding any further.

Canada geese also use Swan Pool in summer and often sit along the southern shore, where motorists can get a close-up view of these black, brown, and white birds. This goose has an all-black neck and head with a snow white chin. It is interesting, too, that at least two races of Canada geese can usually be seen at Swan Pool: large and medium birds that once only wintered along the East Coast and then migrated north to Newfoundland and James Bay to nest. These very adaptable birds can now be found at Swan Pool all year long. However, the relatively small summer population of 300 to 400 individuals expands to about 3,500 birds when their northern cousins arrive. They all make daily flights inland to feed on the available seed in the fields. It is likely that the Canada geese showed the tundra swans this easier method of feeding.

Winter is also when the **snow geese** arrive. As many as 21,000 snows overwinter within the refuge and often dominate the scene. Some years, however, that population may be as low as 3,000 to 4,000 birds, depending on weather patterns along the East Coast. Warm winters allow the birds to winter farther north.

Although snow geese cannot compete with swans in size and glamour, they represent another beautiful, all-white bird, except for their solid black wing tips and pinkish bills. They, too, can have rusty stains on their faces and necks from their northern habitats. And snow geese are among the most vocal of all waterfowl, communicating with one another almost continuously. Bellrose describes their call as a "shrill, scratchy *uh-uk*, somewhat similar to yelp of a fox terrier."

Assateague's wintering snow geese arrive in October and begin to depart in January; only a few remain into March. They move north along the same route they followed south, stopping on the St. Lawrence River below Quebec City and then continuing north across the frozen tundra to the Thule District of Greenland, arriving there in early June. Egg laying begins immediately, long before the winter snows have melted. The young are fed almost 24 hours a day, fledged in six weeks, and flying by August. Adults molt their flight feathers in July, and so both adults and young are ready for their journey south by late August.

NPS and FWS biologists and volunteers do weekly censuses of geese, swans, and ducks by driving the principal dikes and roads. In this way they keep track of the 9 dabbling ducks and the wood duck, the 6 diving ducks, the 5 sea ducks, and the 5 geese and swans. Several years of data were summarized by Kirkpatrick in 1991 and provide a good overview of these populations. Seven species of waterfowl nest at Assateague: the wood duck, American black duck, mallard, blue-winged teal, gadwall, mute swan, and Canada goose. Fifteen species are primarily winter residents: the northern pintail, American wigeon, ruddy duck, lesser scaup, redhead, hooded merganser, bufflehead, common goldeneye, surf and white-winged scoters, oldsquaw, snow and Canada geese, brant, and tundra swan. And four species are primarily migrants or occasional visitors only: the green-winged teal, northern shoveler, and red-breasted and common mergansers. According to the Kirkpatrick report, the greatest variety of waterfowl can be expected from December into January, with another peak of spring migrants in March.

Shorebirds also can be common on the mud flats of the back bays in May and June and again during August. Common spring migrants include the black-bellied and semipalmated plovers; greater yellowlegs; willet; whimbrel; ruddy turnstone; red knot; sanderling; semipalmated, western, least, pectoral, and stilt sandpipers; and short-billed dowitcher. The red knot's arrival, and that of other shorebirds to lesser degrees, coincides with the availability of masses of horseshoe crab eggs during May.

The most numerous southbound birds include the black-bellied and semipalmated plovers; greater and lesser yellowlegs; ruddy turnstone; sanderling; semipalmated, western, least, pectoral, and stilt sandpipers; dunlin; and short-billed dowitcher.

As soon as the shorebirds begin to move through the area, it is time to expect the predatory birds that follow. Most important of these is the **peregrine falcon**. The swiftest and most powerful of the North American falcons, it can fly up to 200 miles (322 km) per hour in a stoop, or descent. At the bottom of a long stoop, it kills its prey by striking a swift blow with a doubled-up fist to the base of the skull. Peregrines are dark-backed birds with light underparts that are streaked with brown or black. They have a broad, mustache-like stripe (wedge of black on their cheeks below the eyes). Few birds have been studied so extensively; Assateague Island has been the focal point of the longest continuous study of peregrine migration. See chapter 13 on the New River Gorge for a description of peregrines within the Appalachians.

Only six shorebirds nest on the island: the Wilson's and piping plovers, killdeer, American oystercatcher, willet, and American woodcock. The most significant of these is the little sand-colored **piping plover**, which is listed as threatened because of its sudden decline throughout its range. In 1991, 38 pairs of these beach-nesting birds fledged 30 young. Their productivity has increased in recent years, due to the efforts undertaken to ensure their survival. Nesting areas are now closed to all recreational uses, and nest sites are fenced from predators. See chapter 10 on Kouchibouguac for additional information on this species.

Another shorebird that becomes obnoxiously obvious when nesting is the **willet**. This medium-sized, rather plain, brownish bird with gray legs shows obvious black-and-white wing patterns in flight. It often holds its wings up when it first lands as if to display its most distinct characteristic. It nests in the salt marshes but seems to claim a rather extensive territory, often extending onto adjacent trails, which it will sometimes defend against any intruder. Its incessant call, a loud "pillo-willo-willet," from which its name was derived, and its continual circling just above the intruder can be most effective.

Willets are semicolonial in nature, often defending joint nesting sites as well as much larger feeding areas, sometimes even during winter. Although both sexes incubate and feed the chicks, the female abandons her mate and brood during the second or third week after hatching; the male attends the brood for an additional two weeks.

One of Assateague's most visible shorebirds is the **greater yellow-legs**, with its long, yellow legs, brownish upperparts, whitish belly, and long, very slightly upturned bill. Like the willet's, the yellow-leg's call can be heard throughout the day. Claudia Wilds described the call as "clear, ringing *whew-whew-whew*, usually 3-5 notes; sometimes single, loud cry. In spring, a yodeling, repeated *tu-whee* or *whee-oodle*." This species nests only from south-central Alaska across the prairies to Labrador, but it is usually present in small numbers throughout its range.

Spring and summer on Assateague Island can be difficult if the area has experienced normal or above normal rainfall; the mosquitoes can be maddening. That is, however, the best time to find the woodland birds. Northbound songbirds are most abundant when the weather is rainy, foggy, or even windy enough to force the birds to stay within the protection of the vegetation. At other times they pass over the island to take advantage of the southern breezes.

Nesting songbirds can be obvious from their abundant songs within the woodlands, thickets, and marshes. The more common nesting woodland and thicket songbirds include the eastern wood-pewee; great crested flycatcher; eastern kingbird; tree swallow; American and fish crows; Carolina and house wrens; blue-gray gnatcatcher; American robin; gray catbird; brown thrasher; European starling; white-eyed and red-eyed vireos; yellow, pine, and prairie warblers; American redstart; northern waterthrush; northern cardinal; rufous-sided towhee; song sparrow; and boat-tailed grackle. Other common woodland/thicket birds in summer include the northern bobwhite, mourning dove, yellow-billed cuckoo, and chuck-will's-widow.

The more common songbirds that nest in marshes and open fields include the common yellowthroat; field, seaside, and song sparrows; red-winged blackbird; eastern meadowlark; and American goldfinch. The little **common yellowthroat**, once called

Maryland yellowthroat, is the black-masked, yellow-bellied warbler that sings its "witchity witchity witchity" songs throughout the day. Frank Chapman pointed out that this songbird also has a flight song in its repertoire, which it usually "sings toward evening, when the bird springs several feet into the air, hovers for a second, and then drops back into the bushes." It is a most curious bird, and although it frequents dense brushy areas and marshes, it can usually be attracted into the open with a low spishing sound. The males are beautiful black and yellow birds, but the females are much duller, the better for hiding from predators during incubation. This species spends considerable time in family groups, and so calling one individual will usually attract two or more.

The fall migration of songbirds can be like the spring movement in that the thickets can be filled with little, colorful birds at one time but almost completely vacant the next day. On two mid-September mornings in a row, I walked through the Bayside Campground. The first morning was alive with songbirds; the second morning I managed to find only a dozen or so individuals. Most abundant on the first morning were warblers. I recorded ten species: the northern parula, yellow, magnolia, prairie, palm, black-and-white, American redstart, northern waterthrush, mourning, and common yellowthroat. Additional songbirds included the least flycatcher, eastern kingbird, tree swallow, house wren, hermit thrush, gray catbird (probably the most numerous of all), brown thrasher, white-eyed and red-eyed vireos, field sparrow, and northern oriole.

Many songbirds may linger in the area until January if food is available and mild temperatures prevail. This phenomenon results in high numbers for the Christmas Bird Count most years. Two counts include national seashore areas. The 1990 Ocean City, Maryland, count reported 69,911 individuals of 136 species; the 1990 Chincoteague National Wildlife Refuge Count reported 33,773 individuals of 138 species. The dozen most numerous species found on the Ocean City count were (in descending order of abundance) European starling, ring-billed gull, snow goose, red-winged blackbird, Canada goose, yellow-rumped warbler, herring gull, mallard, dunlin, common grackle, white-throated sparrow, and house finch. The dozen most numerous species found on the Chincoteague count were (in descending order of abundance) snow goose, brant, European starling, American black duck, dunlin, yellow-rumped warbler, common grackle, Canada goose, northern pintail, ring-billed gull, sanderling, and mallard.

In summary, the Chicoteague checklist contains 296 species, 79 of which have been found all twelve months of the year. Ninety-eight species are known to nest; 7 of those are waterfowl, 16 are marsh birds, 7 are hawks and owls, and 5 are warblers. Ten species occur only in winter: the white-fronted goose, rough-legged hawk, Iceland gull, snowy and long-eared owls, American tree sparrow, Lapland longspur, red crossbill, common redpoll, and evening grosbeak.

Birds of Special Interest

Brown pelican. It is found along the coast and back bays, where it feeds by diving into the water after fish. A nesting colony on the islands off Smith Point is the northernmost on the Atlantic Coast.

Tundra swan. This all-white bird with a long, graceful neck is a winter resident only, using Swan Pool and adjacent fields to feed.

Mute swan. This is the all-white summer swan that frequents Swan Pool. It has as orange-red bill with a black bulb.

Snow goose. Several hundred to as many as 21,000 individuals spend their winters on the refuge, flying out daily into adjacent fields to feed. It has white plumage with solid black wing tips.

Greater yellowlegs. This is the shorebird with long, yellow legs and a slightly upturned bill. It is easily disturbed and has a loud call.

Willet. Its black-and-white wing patterns and obnoxious behavior when disturbed help to identify this otherwise indistinguishable shorebird.

Peregrine falcon. This large, dark-backed falcon visits the island each spring and fall, preying on the abundant shorebirds and other migrants.

Common yellowthroat. It was once called Maryland yellowthroat because of its abundance in the coastal marshes of Maryland. The male possesses an all-yellow body with a black mask.

24

National Capital Parks, Washington, D.C., Maryland, and Virginia

Bird songs were everywhere that early May morning. I walked slowly along the towpath between the great Potomac River and the historic Chesapeake and Ohio (C & O) Canal, stopping now and again to identify or watch a bird among the fresh greenery. Migration was well under way, and many of the songbirds I found that morning were transients only, en route to more northern habitats to nest and raise families before returning in fall to their southern winter grounds. The Potomac River has been an important highway since their ancestors first began their migrations in the distant past.

Many of the resident birds were busy nest building, and wood duck hens already were indoctrinating their chicks to the world outside their nest chambers. Four female wood ducks with sets of 12, 14, 15, and 8 youngsters were observed during the morning. Wood duck nest boxes were scattered along the canal, back in the woods at ponded areas. I could not help but wonder if these birds had used the nest boxes or if they had preferred the natural tree cavities. But the four families had done well, whatever the choice. The date was May 3, and the chicks were already a week old or older. Add an average of 30 days for incubation and the fact that the hen usually lays only one egg daily, and this places the start of nesting in early March, when winter is still clinging to the wetlands.

The hen wood duck is a rather drab, mottled brown bird with a large, elliptical, white eye ring. Drake wood ducks, however, are extra special. Few birds anywhere are as striking as the wood duck

Wood duck

male. Its glossy, colorful plumage, especially the head, can properly be described as gaudy. Its iridescent green to purple crest is highlighted by a white line that runs from the back of the red bill to the tip of the crest, which extends halfway down the burgundy-colored neck. A second white line forms the base of the crest, running from behind the eye to the tip of the crest. Additional white lines extend from the white throat onto the cheeks and halfway around the neck. The large red eye seems to punctuate its velvety black cheeks. The body is an assemblage of white, black, burgundy, buff, and blues.

The gaudy males were nowhere to be seen that morning. Apparently, they were already molting in out-of-the-way places, less susceptible to prying eyes. Fledgings are the sole responsibility of the more subtly colored hens. I wondered if the clutch of eight had already been reduced by predators. Or maybe all of the clutches had originally been larger. Wood ducks are known to brood up to 50 eggs in a single nest, with many of the eggs contributed by other hens. The "dumping" of eggs into a single nest is a fairly common occurrence in wood ducks. Up to five hens are known to participate, but only one hen and drake will incubate the clutch. The drake stays involved only until all the eggs are hatched. He then leaves to join bachelor flocks in more secluded places. The remainder of the work is left to the hen. She must entice the chicks, which are equipped with claws for climbing, out of the nest and down to the ground and then accompany the family through difficult terrain to the safer ponds.

The Park Environment

More than 200 separate areas within the greater Washington, D.C., area are part of National Capital Parks, administered by the National Park Service. They include such diverse locations as the White House grounds, Washington Monument, Tidal Basin, Theodore Roosevelt Island, Rock Creek Park, and the C & O Canal. Some are less than a city block in size, while others are much larger. Rock Creek Park is 1,754 acres (710 ha), making it one of the world's largest urban parks. And the C & O Canal National Historic Park encompasses 20,781 acres (12,457 ha) within its 184-mile (296-km) route along the Potomac River between Washington, D.C., and Cumberland, Maryland. This route gained considerable recognition as a superb hiking trail following an eight-day March excursion by the late Supreme Court Justice William O. Douglas and 36 colleagues. Douglas wrote about this experience and the canal in his 1961 book, *My Wilderness: East to Katahdin.*

Rock Creek Park was authorized in 1890, at a time when many of the District's significant natural and cultural areas were being set aside for preservation within the growing city. Today, it is a unique gem within the sprawling city of tensions and politics. In his wonderful *Spring in Washington*, Louis Halle wrote, "There is Rock Creek Park, with its forests and fields, which wanders through Washington and remains uncorrupted." The park offers 29 miles (47 km) of hiking trails, 11 miles (18 km) of bridle trails, and an excellent nature center and planetarium. The center houses a museum and interpretive operation where daily programs, including regularly scheduled bird walks, are provided throughout the year. A small but good publications sales outlet is also available.

Theodore Roosevelt Island is another valuable sanctuary within the greater D.C. area, accessible from the George Washington Memorial Parkway, Virginia. The 88 acres (36 ha) of upland forest, marsh, and swamp were set aside as a sanctuary by Congress in 1932 to memorialize President Roosevelt's contributions to conservation.

Its 2½ miles (4 km) of foot trails provide easy access to the island's surprisingly mature and productive forest and adjacent wetlands.

And farther up the Potomac is Great Falls Park, which is accessible from either Maryland or Virginia. The Virginia side is the best birding area and includes a visitor center and hiking trails.

Park brochures are available for each of these areas. *Welcome to Washington* contains a map for the District and greater D.C. area. *A Field List of Birds of the District of Columbia Region* is available from the local Audubon Naturalist Society. But the best guidebook is Claudia Wilds's *Finding Birds in the National Capital Area*, a Smithsonian Nature Guide.

Additional information can be obtained from the Superintendent, National Capital Parks, 900 Ohio Drive SW, Washington, D.C. 20242; (202) 426-7620.

Bird Life

The C & O Canal is unequaled for observing birds in spring. Halle wrote, "If this canal had been designed for the observation of birds rather than for commerce with the West it could not have been better done." The towpath is high enough above the waterways and vegetation that one does not need to strain the neck and eyes to watch birds. The trees and shrubs along the river attract lots of birds and also provide good cover for observing birds moving along the river way.

Green-backed herons were common along the canal in early May, quietly feeding along the shore or flying off with sudden, loud squawks. The only other wading bird encountered was a lone great blue heron flying upriver against the Virginia shore. There, too, was an osprey, making its way northward to some lake or bay where it would fish and probably build a nest of sticks high in an adjacent tree. Also during the course of the morning, I recorded four species of swallows over the river, all moving northward: tree, northern rough-winged, bank, and barn.

A pair of **blue-gray gnatcatchers** was nest building on a bare limb directly over the trail and only four or five feet beyond my reach. I drew back ten feet or so and watched as both birds went about their business of preparing for a family. Pieces of grass and tiny strips of

bark were being added to the cup-shaped structure. After each contribution, the builders would fly off into the woods for a few minutes
before returning with more material. I was able to track their movement by the high-pitched, buzzy "tseee" calls every few seconds.

The gnatcatcher's overall slim shape and grayish color, blue-
gray above and whitish underparts, white eye ring, and long tail,
reminded me of a miniature northern mockingbird. It even has a
similar habit of flipping its tail from side to side and up and down.

A very loud and emphatic "peet, tweet, tweet, tweet" song burst
forth from the edge of the canal just ahead. I knew immediately
that this was a song of a **prothonotary warbler**, but it took me several minutes to locate this golden-headed songster. Then I was able
to admire it as it searched for insects among the dense willows.
There are few birds with the appeal of a male prothonotary. Its brilliant gold, almost orange-colored head is a bold contrast to its
rather heavy black bill, large black eyes, and blue-gray wings. Then I
realized that I also was watching a second bird, a female with duller
plumage, that I had not noticed before. A pair no doubt, and I
wondered if these birds were going to nest nearby. I switched back
to the more colorful male just as it put its head back and sang its
clear, ringing song, all on one pitch, "peet, tweet, tweet, tweet."
What a wonderful song for a beautiful bird! See chapter 28 on
Congaree Swamp for details about this warbler there.

The trees beyond, on the opposite side of the canal, were suddenly alive with birds. I had finally found a bird party on the move,
and for the next hour or more I remained at that one spot while
myriad songbirds passed me by. Most numerous of these was the
yellow-rumped warbler, with its white throat, black ear patches, and
four yellow patches on the rump, sides of the breast, and crown.
Yellow warblers and northern parulas were common that morning,
gleaning the new foliage for insects to supply energy for their continued migration. And there were fewer numbers of great crested
flycatchers; eastern kingbirds; gray catbirds; wood thrushes; house
and marsh wrens; white-eyed, solitary, and warbling vireos; black-
throated blue warblers; American redstarts; and common yellowthroats. I also saw lone examples of the black-billed cuckoo, red-
eyed vireo, cerulean warbler, ovenbird, Louisiana and northern

waterthrushes, yellow-breasted chat, rufous-sided towhee, song and swamp sparrows, and a male northern oriole. All these birds seemed to be part of a comprehensive party of migrants that slowly moved northward, engulfing me for a time and requiring my complete attention to identify as many as I could, and then they were gone.

I recorded several other birds that morning, including those that can be found there all year long. These full-time residents included the red-shouldered hawk, mourning dove, red-bellied and downy woodpeckers, common and fish crows, blue jay, tufted titmouse, white-breasted nuthatch, Carolina chickadee, Carolina wren, European starling, chipping sparrow, brown-headed cowbird, common grackle, and American goldfinch. I found a total of 66 species in a little over three hours that morning, typical perhaps of the avian diversity at that time of year.

Great Falls Park, Virginia, has long been a favorite birding site in the D.C. area. It is a beautiful area with a variety of habitats, including upland forest, open woodland, and freshwater marsh. And the Great Falls of the Potomac is spectacular. This park is good for migrants as well as a number of nesting birds that do not frequent the C & O Canal area in summer. The Swamp Trail is especially good for the Acadian flycatcher, yellow-throated vireo, American redstart, northern parula, Louisiana waterthrush, and Kentucky warbler.

The latter two birds are very different in appearance but have songs that are similar in character. Each song is usually expressed with great enthusiasm and vigor. They can be heard for a considerable distance, and they also tend to be ventriloquistic. They are difficult to pin down to an exact location.

The song of the black-and-white **Louisiana waterthrush** is written as "see-you see-you see-you chew chew to-wee," while the black and yellow Kentucky warbler song is written as "chur-ree, chur-ree" repeated five to ten times, thanks to descriptions by Paul Sykes and Wayne Peterson. The waterthrush song has an extra dimension to it, a penetrating wildness that is difficult to ignore. Halle wrote that its song "is undoubtedly designed to be heard above the roar of tumbling water, for it is loud and piercing, three sharp notes followed by a chatter: tzee-tzee-tzee-tzipplytzippytzip." Kentucky warbler songs, though loud and clear, resemble certain phrases of the songs of the northern cardinal and Carolina wren: "tur-dle tur-dle tur-dle" or "tory tory tory."

A trail behind the rest rooms provides habitat for several other breeding birds of interest. Watch for the eastern wood-pewee; wood thrush; black-and-white, worm-eating, and hooded warblers; scarlet tanager; and rose-breasted grosbeak. In addition, Swainson's warbler has been found to nest there. And the more open woodlands of the picnic area support the yellow-billed cuckoo, yellow-throated and cerulean warblers, and summer tanager.

The Potomac River provides an additional habitat at Great Falls Park that can be very productive. Waterfowl, when present, are best seen above the dam. Wintertime can produce the greatest numbers. Wilds points out, "From November to April Ring-necked Ducks are regular; Buffleheads, Common Goldeneye and Hooded Mergansers are often present, and are sometimes joined by other species."

More water birds are usually found downriver at Dyke Marsh, just below Belle Haven off the George Washington Parkway. The cattail marsh is the only place in the National Capital Parks where the **least bittern** can be expected with regularity in spring and summer. It actually nests there, and in early mornings bitterns can sometimes be found chasing one another in and out of the cattails. The least bittern's yellowish and black wings are its most obvious feature from a distance. When not in flight, it can be extremely difficult to find because of its habit of spending most of its time in the dense marsh cover. On rare occasions, it may perch briefly on a cattail, or if disturbed while feeding along the edge, it will freeze on the spot with its bill pointed upward, yellow eyes forward, and its feathers tightly compressed. Then it looks for all the world like part of the marsh. Its underparts are a buff color, with tan to brown stripes that blend perfectly into its surroundings.

A neighboring marsh bird is the tiny **marsh wren**, a bird with a wonderful "rippling, bubbling, gurgling song," according to Frank Chapman. During spring and summer it oftens sings all day long, and while nesting it may sing long into the night. When disturbed, it will proclaim its concern with a sharp single or double "tsuk" call. In spite of its continuous song, it, too, is a skulker that seldom spends time in the open. It prefers the dense cattail forest. However, it can be enticed into the open with low spishing or squeaking sounds. And if the light is right, it can be a very pretty bird. The five-inch-long marsh wren usually appears buff to reddish, with a black back streaked with white and a bold white line over the eye.

Other summer birds of Dyke Marsh's freshwater habitat include the Canada goose, common gallinule, king rail, willow flycatcher, yellow warbler, common yellowthroat, and red-winged blackbird. And in winter, the marsh area may produce a whole array of water birds: the pied-billed grebe; great blue heron; tundra swan; green-winged teal; American black duck; mallard; wood duck; bufflehead; ruddy duck; common merganser; American coot; herring, great black-backed, and ring-billed gulls; and Caspian tern. The best viewing site is usually from the adjacent picnic area.

Theodore Roosevelt Island is just behind the Kennedy Center, although access is available only from the northbound lanes of George Washington Memorial Parkway. There is something very incongruous about the island completely surrounded by city, with D.C. to the east and Rosslyn, Virginia, to the west. Theodore Roosevelt Bridge (Highway 66) actually crosses the island's southern tip. What's more, airline traffic in and out of National Airport often passes directly overhead. And yet the Woods and Upland trails, as well as the Swamp Trail, seem to be as wild and unaffected as many places far removed from the city. Maybe the monument to President Roosevelt, located near the entrance footbridge, somehow protects the sanctity of the place.

Included in the Roosevelt Monument are four 21-foot (6-m) granite tablets, on which are carved several quotes. Two of those quotes are particularly appropriate. First: "There are no words that can tell the hidden spirit of the wilderness, that can reveal its mystery, its melancholy, and its charm." Second: "The Nation behaves well if it treats the natural resources as assets which it must turn over to the next generation increased and not impaired in value."

The heart of National Capital Parks is Rock Creek Park and the nature center on Glover Road. Just behind the center is Wood Oaks Trail, where Park Interpreters Bill Rudolph and Heather Rosselle lead nature walks. These guided walks, which require reservations, have introduced thousands of people to nature and birds. Typical birds seen by the groups in spring and summer include such spectacular species as the wood duck, barred owl, pileated and red-bellied woodpeckers, eastern kingbird, great crested flycatcher, blue jay, wood thrush, veery, Kentucky warbler, Louisiana waterthrush, scarlet tanager, and indigo bunting. A list of Rock Creek Park birds (available for the asking) contains a total of 142 species, 26 of which are warblers, and 50 of which are known to nest within the 1,754-acre (710-ha) reserve.

Winter birds can be a treat throughout the D.C. area, primarily because of the presence of scattered tracts of natural vegetation administered by the National Park Service. Since 1945, the Christmas Bird Count area has remained the same and includes many of the local hot spots. These annual counts usually total approximately 115 species of 30,000 or more individuals. The dozen most common species on the 1990 Christmas count (in descending order of abundance) were ring-billed gull, European starling, herring gull, mallard, American crow, white-throated sparrow, Canada goose, house sparrow, rock dove, dark-eyed junco, Carolina chickadee, and northern cardinal.

In summary, an ancient checklist for National Capital Parks contains 194 species, 62 of which occur all twelve months of the year. One hundred nine species occur in June, presumably as breeding birds, of which 10 are water birds, 8 are hawks and owls, and 11 are warblers. None of the birds listed occur only in winter.

Birds of Special Interest

Least bittern. This elusive marsh bird nests at Dyke Marsh, where it can best be located early on spring mornings. Its yellowish and black wings are its best identifying feature.

Wood duck. The gaudy drake is difficult to mistake, but the duller hen has only a large, white, elliptic eye ring to help with identification.

Marsh wren. This reddish songbird is particularly common at cattail marshes such as Dyke Marsh. Its continuous gurgling song is unmistakable.

Blue-gray gnatcatcher. It looks like a thin, miniature version of the northern mockingbird, complete with its long tail, which is ever busy.

Prothonotary warbler. Watch for this beautiful warbler at dense, wet areas. Its yellow-gold head, black bill and eye, and blue-gray wings are its best features.

Louisiana waterthrush. This long-legged bird frequents fast-moving streams. It has dark upperparts, except for a bold white eye line, white underparts that are heavily streaked, and buff flanks.

25

Cape Hatteras and Cape Lookout National Seashores, North Carolina

Sanderlings are the most abundant shorebird on the Atlantic Coast beaches during most of the year. These are the comical little "peeps" or sandpipers that run up and down the beach, usually at the very edge of the surf. They are never still in their search for a variety of marine invertebrates. They swiftly probe into the moist sand, with their bills partly open for tiny beach "fleas," crabs, and shrimp burrowing back into the sand after the retreating surf. The next wave may drive them 10 to 40 feet (3-12 m) up the beach before they scamper back in hot pursuit.

These little sandpipers are too often taken for granted because of their abundance and drab appearance. Their nonbreeding plumage, worn on the Outer Banks, is overall pale gray except for a black bill, legs, and feet. In flight, they show black at the bend and on the trailing edge of the wings, an obvious white stripe that extends almost to the wing tip, and a whitish rump divided by a rather broad black line. In spring, their plumage changes dramatically, from the dull winter gray to deep chestnut with dark brown streaks and white on the belly. Their flight pattern remains essentially the same.

Sanderlings that frequent the beaches of Cape Hatteras and Cape Lookout experience a constant turnover. Only in midwinter will their populations stay the same. Otherwise, they include birds en route either south to their wintering grounds or north to nesting sites on the Arctic tundra from Alaska to Labrador. They are truly continental travelers. North America's sanderlings may spend their winters as far south as the southern tip of South America. But by late March they begin their movement northward, usually traveling along the coast or a few miles offshore in flocks of a few individuals to a few hundred. The spring turnover on the Outer Banks can sometimes be detected by the plumage changes one observes in birds arriving from the south. And these migrants may spend a greater than normal amount of time resting, often standing in scattered groups with heads laid on their wings, many perfectly balanced on one leg. When disturbed, they may jump away on the one leg, or they may fly up in flocks, wheel overhead, and quickly settle down out of the way to take up a resting posture again.

Sanderlings

The beaches of the Outer Banks, especially those in the national parks and refuges, are vitally important for the survival of sanderlings and a multitude of other migrant shorebirds. Many are so exhausted from their long, often overwater flights that adequate food and rest are essential if they are going to continue to their wintering grounds or northward to their Arctic breeding grounds. They arrive on the tundra by late May and June, immediately select nesting sites, and by mid-June are incubating three to four eggs. Often they will utilize two nests at the same time, the female tending one and the male the other. Adults may begin their southern journeys by mid-July, while the young of the year remain another several weeks. The earliest postnesting birds reach the Outer Banks by the end of July.

There is never a time when at least a few sanderlings cannot be found at Hatteras and Lookout; nonbreeding birds often remain through the summer. But nothing can compare with the millions of shorebirds that pass along the beaches and inner bays during spring and fall. As many as forty species of plovers, oystercatcher, avocet and stilt, and sandpipers can be found there during migration.

The Park Environment
The two national seashores occupy a significant portion of the 175-mile-long (282-km) chain of barrier islands between Virginia Beach, Virginia, and Cape Lookout, North Carolina. The chain of islands is unique in that it bends 30 miles (48 km) eastward from the mainland, like an elbow into the Atlantic, only partially paralleling the coastline, as do most barrier island systems.

Cape Hatteras National Seashore, established in 1953, occupies 30,320 acres (12,270 ha) on the four northern islands of Bodie, Pea, Hatteras, and Ocracoke. Pea Island National Wildlife Refuge (6,700 acres, or 2,711 ha) runs for 13 miles (21 km) and occupies the greater part of Pea Island. Cape Lookout National Seashore, established in 1966, extends southward on North and South Core islands and Shackleford Banks, comprising 24,400 acres (9,875 ha).

All the barrier islands generally possess similar cross sections but contain somewhat different plant communities. Behind the bare beach are the berm and dunes with a scattering of sea-oats. Next are the grasslands, which usually are dominated by salt meadow cordgrass and pennywort. The thickets and woodlands beyond the grasslands vary considerably, from a maritime forest of live oak, red cedar, and yaupon holly on the northern islands to thickets of waxmyrtle and groundsel-tree to the south. Farther inland along the bay is a salt marsh that is dominated by salt meadow cordgrass and black neddlerush. The maritime woods and shrub thickets are more developed on Hatteras than on Lookout because of the widening of the island near the cape, partly due to man-made dune lines. The more extensive vegetation filters out much of the salt spray and ocean flooding that help give Cape Lookout a more open character.

Access to Cape Hatteras is via 75-mile-long (121-km) Highway 12, which runs southward from Manteo (Highway 64) or Nags Head (Highway 158). Cape Lookout is accessible only by a toll ferry or private boat. Ferries operate out of Ocracoke and four locations along Highway 12 north of Beaufort: Harkers Island, Davis, Atlantic, and Ferry Landing. The ferries at Davis and Atlantic are able to transport four-wheel-drive vehicles and trailers to the Core Banks. Schedules vary with the seasons.

Camping is available at five sites at Cape Hatteras: Oregon Inlet, Salvo, Cape Point, Frisco, and Ocracoke. Only primitive camping is permitted on Cape Lookout. In addition, there are several private campgrounds along Highway 12. Lodging is available at the numerous villages on Cape Hatteras and at the southern access points to Cape Lookout.

The National Park Service operates four visitor centers, north to south, at Bodie Island, Hatteras Island, Ocracoke Island, and Harkers Island. All contain exhibits and publication outlets with bird field guides. A comprehensive bird checklist for the Outer Banks and another for Cape Lookout are available for the asking. Interpretive activities include evening talks and nature walks. Morning bird walks are scheduled for Hatteras and Okracoke, as well as Pea Island Refuge. The full listing of interpretive activities is printed in the newspaper, *In The Park*, available at all the visitor centers and ranger stations.

Additional information can be obtained from the Superintendent, Cape Hatteras National Seashore, Route 1, Box 675, Manteo, NC 27954; (919) 473-2111; or from the Superintendent, Cape Lookout National Seashore, 3601 Bridges Street, Suite F, Morehead City, NC 28557-2913; (919) 473-2111.

Bird Life

Two other shorebirds are almost as numerous in winter as sanderlings, the black-bellied plover and the dunlin. Both are Arctic nesters that winter along the southern coastline. The **dunlin** is another peep that has a drab winter dress and a very different appearance during the breeding season. It can be confused with a sanderling at first sight, but further observation will reveal a very different plumage and personality. This is a somewhat larger, gray-brown bird with faint streakings on the neck and chest and a relatively long, slightly drooping bill. Its flight pattern is similar to that of a sanderling, but the white streak on the wing is less obvious. When feeding, it is very deliberate, probing and picking up food in a much slower fashion than the more active sanderling. Also, dunlins are likelier to be found on the mud flats on the inner bay, walking slowly forward, searching for crustaceans, mollusks, and marine worms.

During the spring migration, they often form huge mixed flocks with sanderlings, sometimes numbering in the thousands. By then, instead of being in their dull winter dress, many appear in their full or emerging breeding plumage: a coal black belly that contrasts with the almost white but faintly streaked chest and head and a reddish back. See chapter 26 on Cumberland Island for additional information on migrating dunlins.

The **black-bellied plover** is a very different bird from either of the smaller peeps. Along the beach and the mud flat and even in the short grass of campgrounds and picnic areas, black-bellies stand upright and feed by running forward and snatching up their prey, often earthworms, which they locate by sight. Unlike the peeps, they are not probers. Also, they rarely occur in pure flocks, as do sanderlings and dunlins, but seem to prefer instead the company of other shorebirds, feeding nearby but usually alone.

Black-bellies also possess very different plumage in winter than during the breeding season. Their winter dress is a mottled brown-gray with a whitish eye line and black bill, legs, and feet. And in flight they show distinct black wing pits (axillaries), a key marking at all times of the year. Lesser golden plovers can look very similar but do not possess the black axillaries. The transformation from winter to spring plumage is spectacular; in a few short weeks black-bellies sport a velvet black face, throat, and chest; silvery-white head, sides, and belly; and black-and-white mottled back. They, too, nest on the tundra but return in numbers by late July. Wintering birds may go as far south as South America, but others may find suitable feeding sites as far north as Cape Cod.

In summer, the vast numbers of migrant shorebirds are reduced to a few nonbreeding individuals that feed alongside only seven shorebird species that nest so far south: the piping and Wilson's plovers, killdeer, American oystercatcher, black-necked stilt, American avocet, and willet.

The endangered **piping plover** is never common, but everyone who wanders the beach in summer should watch out for this little plover. It is not easy to locate because of its sand-colored plumage, which provides perfect camouflage, and its habit of freezing in place when disturbed. Besides its sand-colored back and white underparts, this rather stocky bird possesses a black collar, forehead band from eye to eye, and breastband. Its legs, feet, and bill are bright orange, and its bill has a black tip.

Piping plovers on the Outer Banks have learned to nest on the beaches that are most accessible to the inner bay. Cape Lookout's resource specialist Michael Rikard informed me that 90 percent of the chicks are escorted to the mud flats, instead of being raised on the beaches that are subjected to heavy human use. A three-year study has begun to assess the effects of human use of the seashore on the shorebirds. See chapter 10 on Kouchibouguac about the status of this species in Canada.

None of the many Outer Bank birds are as obvious as the gulls and terns. And the most abundant of these (at least in summer) is the **laughing gull,** so named for its laughing call. John Terres described its call as "a hoarse cheer-ah! cheer-ah! or ka-ha, ka-ha, and a long-drawn hah-ha-ha-ha-hah-hah-hah, the last syllables drawn out in a wail, all sounding like excited laughing." This is the gull that sports a black head, red bill, and dark gray mantle in summer. In winter it loses its black head feathers, and its bill turns black.

The ring-billed gull, the other middle-sized gull, which is especially common in winter, also loses much of its bright breeding plumage but still retains its ringed bill. And the two large gulls, herring and great black-backed, which can be common in winter, retain the yellow bill with a reddish-orange spot on the lower mandible.

There were thousands of gulls and terns feeding off Cape Lookout on an early November visit. I had taken the Harkers Island passenger ferry across Back Sound to the Cape Lookout Lighthouse dock in the morning, and I spent the entire day walking the outer and inner bay beaches and crisscrossing the thickets. Dozens of fishermen were casting into the surf, and an unbelievable number of pickups were scattered along the berm or moving about on the network of roadways.

The majority of the gulls present that day were laughing gulls, although there were also large numbers of herring gulls and smaller numbers of great black-backs and ring-bills. Brown pelicans were fairly common, too, flying back and forth in small groups of three to eight. A few royal and Forster's terns and a pair of gull-billed terns were present as well. And the large white birds with black wing tips, shaped like streamlined torpedoes, were northern gannets. Once I discovered these birds, which were fishing only a few hundred yards off the beach, I started to watch them as they plummeted into the sea. They would disappear for several seconds before emerging either to float a while, to consume their catch, or to take off immediately to try again when they found other suitable prey. Gannets are true seabirds that live their entire lives at sea. They winter along the southern coastline of the United States and nest in huge colonies on small rocky islands in Canada's Gulf of St. Lawrence. See chapter 11 on Forillon and chapter 29 on Canaveral for additional information on this seabird.

The Outer Banks are close to the Gulf Stream and Virginia coastal drift, which provide an extremely rich nutrient base for multitudes of marine species, including an extremely valuable fishery that supplies many of the East Coast restaurants. Because of the food supply that is available from upwellings at the edges of these ocean currents, an especially large number of pelagic birds rarely if ever approach the islands. Birding boat trips 20 to 40 miles (32-64 km) into the Gulf Stream are offered several times each year to find the oceanic species that might occur there. Species found vary with the time of year, just as they do on the mainland.

May and August produce the largest number of pelagics. In May, Cory's, greater, sooty, and Audubon's shearwaters; black-capped petrel; Wilson's storm-petrel; and pomarine and parsitic jaegers are most common. In August, black-capped petrel, band-rumped and white-faced storm-petrels, bridled and sooty terns, and white-tailed tropicbird are most expected.

Of the approximately 30 pelagics that occur off the Outer Banks, **Wilson's storm-petrel** is the best representative. Many ornithologists believe it is the world's most abundant bird. It nests in burrows and rock crevices on islands in the Antarctic and off the southern tip of South America but spends the rest of its life at sea. These storm-petrels come north in spring and can be found all summer long in the Atlantic off the coast of North America. There they often occur in huge swarms, hovering and dancing above the ocean surface, wings upright and long legs forward as if walking on the water. This behavior has provided the name "petrel," after Simon Peter, who, according to the New Testament, walked on water. "Storm" comes from the belief that these birds are more abundant just prior to a storm.

Wilson's storm-petrel is only seven inches in length, with a wingspan double that and a square tail. It is sooty brown overall, with a bold white rump and pale upper wing patch, and weighs only one and a quarter ounces. Surface feeders, storm-petrels feed on plankton in colder waters and small fish and squid in summer. They also feed on waste materials from fishing boats and oil leaking from wounded marine mammals.

During my November visit to the Cape Lookout lighthouse area, I found only a few songbirds among the waxmyrtle thickets. A few could have been late southbound migrants, but, more than likely, they represented winter residents. The most numerous species was the **yellow-rumped warbler**, an active little black, gray, and white bird with four distinct yellow spots on the rump, sides, and crown. This northern breeder is well known for its winter residency among the coastal waxmyrtle thickets. Its earlier name, myrtle warbler, was derived from this dominant shrub of its wintering grounds. The name change occurred after it was discovered that the eastern myrtle and the western Audubon's warblers interbreed where their populations overlap. This makes them the same species; the white throat of the myrtle and yellow throat of the Audubon's are geographic differences only. For information about this bird's nesting habitats, see chapter 8 on Canada's Terra Nova National Park.

Other wintertime songbirds found that day included the ruby-crowned kinglet, yellowish color and always nervous; American robin, with its rusty red belly; gray catbird, slate gray with a rusty undertail covert; orange-crowned warbler, overall olive green; palm warbler, with a yellow belly and habit of tail wagging; common yellowthroat, yellowish with a black mask; savannah sparrow, streaked with yellow lines above and below the eye; song sparrow, streaked with an obvious black breast spot; swamp sparrow, reddish back and clear gray breast; and eastern meadowlark, stocky build and yellow underparts.

The ferry departed Cape Lookout at 4:30 p.m., and as we passed the spoilbank island, just off the Harkers Island terminal, hundreds of brown pelicans were arriving for the night. I counted more than 1,200 birds already roosting along the shore and on the low shrubbery, and there were many more flying in against the dimming skyline. Rikard told me that brown pelicans, as well as laughing gulls, great blue and tricolored herons, American oystercatchers, and black skimmers, nest there in spring and summer.

The greatest spectacle of birds on the Outer Banks, however, occurs in winter and during migration at Pea Island National Wildlife Refuge. Open ponds and grassy fields are visible from the Cape Hatteras highway or along the refuge nature trail. Several thousand water birds of 30 or more species are often present.

One early November day, I stopped along the highway and recorded all of the birds I could find through my binoculars. Of the 25 species found, none were as obvious as the large, all-white tundra swans, with their long necks and coal black bills. Few birds are as graceful. And Pea Island's wintering swans are equally fascinating because of their extensive journey to and from their breeding grounds in Alaska. They migrate all the way across North America to overwinter along the East Coast. See chapter 23 on Assateague for further details.

Other water birds visible in the open pond included the pied-billed grebe, double-crested cormorant, great blue heron, great egret, Canada goose, green-winged teal, northern pintail, northern shoveler, gadwall, American wigeon, ring-necked duck, ruddy duck, American coot, and a few shorebirds, including the semipalmated plover, greater and lesser yellowlegs, least and western sandpipers, and short-billed dowitcher.

The most abundant of all these was the **American wigeon**, a medium-sized duck with a buff body and grayish head; the male possesses a white cap and forehead, which provided its earlier name of "baldpate," and a bold green stripe that runs from the eye back onto the neck. And at close range, the bluish, black-tipped bill is a helpful clue for identification. It can be distinguished in flight by a large square white patch on the wrist of the upper wing and a green patch on the trailing edge.

The American wigeon is a "dabbling" duck that feeds on stems and leafy parts of aquatic plants by tipping its head below the surface with tail pointed skyward. It also feeds on grass and seeds, waddling on land like a pull toy. They arrive at Pea Island in mid-September and stay through the winter; a few can still be found in May. Nesting occurs in the pothole country from Colorado north through central Canada to Alaska.

A flock of ten white ibis flew over while I was admiring a particularly close wigeon drake. A dry rattle call from the far edge of the pond was that of a belted kingfisher. A merlin flew swiftly across the pond and landed briefly on a top railing of the observation tower. A flock of about two dozen snow geese, with bright white bodies and black wing tips, crossed the horizon and settled down in the adjacent field. And then my attention focused on a great black-backed gull that seemed to be struggling in the shallow water in the direction of the tower. It took me a couple of minutes to realize what I was watching: an adult black-back had caught a green-winged teal and was trying to kill it. The gull had a firm grip on the teal's wing and seemed to be trying to force it below water, perhaps to drown it or to obtain a more lethal grip. The teal was making a valiant effort to escape, constantly tugging away from the gull. It took about four minutes before the teal stopped struggling, and the successful predator hauled it to shore. Two other black-backs and a lone herring gull immediately landed nearby, and the first black-back then had to defend its kill against the three marauders. Fifteen minutes later, when I departed, the feast had not yet begun; all of the black-back's attention was focused on the half dozen other gulls just as intent on sharing its success.

I could not help commenting to my wife that we had just witnessed something that happens many times every day in nature, although I had never before seen a gull capture and kill a duck. Predators such as gulls and the wading birds, hawks, owls, and a host of other species survive on what they can capture or steal from others.

Christmas Bird Counts provide a good summary of what species occur during winter. Five counts are undertaken annually within the Cape Hatteras-Cape Lookout area: at Kitty Hawk, Bodie-Pea Island, Cape Hatteras, Morehead City, and Pamlico County. The Cape Hatteras count can be considered the most representative; 41,951 individuals of 134 species were recorded in 1990. The dozen most numerous species, in order of abundance, were the ring-billed gull, yellow-rumped warbler, herring gull, double-crested cormorant, brant, great black-backed gull, Bonaparte's gull, brown pelican, tree swallow, cedar waxwing, European starling, and northern gannet.

In summary, the Outer Banks checklist contains 300 species, 75 of which occur in summer and are known to nest. Of those, more than half are water birds (a grebe, pelican, wading birds, ducks, rails, moorhen, shorebirds, gulls, and skimmer), 5 are hawks and owls, and 6 are warblers (yellow, pine, prairie, prothonotary, common yellowthroat, and yellow-breasted chat). Eighteen species have been found only during the winter months: the great cormorant; king eider; harlequin duck; rough-legged hawk; purple sandpiper; great skua; common black-headed, Iceland, and glaucous gulls; dovekie; razorbill; northern saw-whet owl; hairy woodpecker; tufted titmouse; fox sparrow; Lapland longspur; snow bunting; and evening grosbeak.

Birds of Special Interest

Wilson's storm-petrel. This robin-sized pelagic species rarely is found near shore. It is all sooty brown with a bold white rump and "dances" over the ocean surface while feeding on tiny fish and oil from fishing boats and wounded marine mammals.

American wigeon. A common wintering duck, the male possesses a gray head with a broad white cap. Both sexes show a white square in front and green behind at the wrist of their wings in flight.

Black-bellied plover. This large, upright shorebird is dull gray in winter and black and white in summer. Its best identifying feature is an obvious black wing pit in flight.

Piping plover. Human use of the Atlantic beaches has seriously threatened this little sand-colored shorebird with orange legs and feet and orange and black bill. It has been listed as threatened by the federal government.

Sanderling. This is the park's most abundant shorebird, often seen running here and there at the edge of the surf and less commonly on the back beach and short-grass fields.

Laughing gull. Its summer dress includes an all-black head and red bill; in winter it is overall gray and mottled with a black bill. Its name is derived from its laughlike calls.

Yellow-rumped warbler. This common winter resident and migrant is black, gray, and white, with four yellow spots, on the rump, sides, and cap.

26

Cumberland Island National Seashore, Georgia

The long, green island lay a short distance ahead of us. The morning fog was still clinging to the bluish waters of Cumberland Sound. The scene was surrealistic! Cumberland Island rose above the misty morning, as if beckoning us to partake of its sublime beauty.

I had seen few birds during the half-hour ferry ride, once the *Cumberland Queen* had pulled away from the St. Marys terminal. Laughing gulls had dominated the scene at the dock. A couple of snowy egrets patrolled the nearby shoreline. A lone spotted sandpiper, already sporting its spotted breeding plumage this early in April, searched for insects along a section of the shore. And a dozen white ibis approached from the south, flapping and soaring over St. Marys River and out of sight to the north.

Royal terns flew ahead of us as we crossed Cumberland Sound. I assumed the fog restricted their visibility in these fishing grounds and they were heading elsewhere. A line of about two dozen cattle egrets flew across the horizon, perhaps migrants en route north to summer quarters.

The *Cumberland Queen* moved north along the western edge of the island. The rather extensive salt marsh that forms most of the island's southwestern corner gave way to the higher and drier pine-oak and oak-palmetto communities. When we landed at Dungeness Dock, most of the passengers disembarked. Dungeness is Cumberland's most popular destination. It is preferred by people planning to spend only the day on the island, especially history buffs and beachcombers. Day use-only visitors must depart the island on the late afternoon ferry.

The eight of us who remained on board were going on to Sea Camp, the island's only other dock, one mile farther north and nearer to the park campground. Another half hour, and the ferry arrived at Sea Camp Dock, where the rest of the passengers disembarked and headed for the adjacent park service visitor center, a rather large building that was visible from the dock and dominated by wonderfully huge oak trees. In a very short time, we all had been assigned campsites in the nearby Sea Camp Beach Campground.

This campground is located on the Atlantic side of the island under a beautiful canopy of moss-covered oaks, not as huge as those at the visitor center but gorgeous nonetheless. The ground cover is dominated by saw palmettos, presenting an almost tropical setting. There is almost always a breeze on the Atlantic side of the island, which helps to control mosquitoes after wet periods. Camping is free, although reservations are necessary, even though the campground was only two-thirds filled during my four-day stay. There are four "wilderness" campsites on the island as well. Those more isolated sites lack drinking water, rest rooms, and a bathhouse, comforts that are available at Sea Camp Beach.

The Park Environment

Cumberland Island is one of the largest barrier islands along the Atlantic Coast, slightly more than 17 miles long and up to 3 miles wide (27 by 3 km). Its dunes reach a maximum height of 50 feet (15 m), but the island's overall relief is only 15 to 25 feet (4.5-8 m) above the sea. Soils are mostly derived from quartz sands, so that the beaches and dunes are unusually white and appealing.

The entire island of 36,000 acres (14,569 ha) was included in the authorized Cumberland Island National Seashore in 1972, although a few hundred acres were left in private ownership as life estates for the owners and their children.

In spite of the island's low profile, there are a number of freshwater lakes and ponds. Five of these are considered permanent, and several others hold fresh water during wet periods. Rainfall is the only water source. The largest and most accessible of the permanent ponds are Lake Whitney and Willow Pond.

Most significant of the temporary ponds is Sweetwater Lake. It encompasses 300 acres (121 ha) along the island's outer edge, separated from the Atlantic Ocean by a series of dunes. Sweetwater Lake is comprised of a series of narrow impoundments that drain northward and form a narrow, 4-mile-long (6.4-km) strip. The southern drainage is coupled to the marine environment and produces an extremely nutrient-rich area known as Lake Retta. This area produces an abundance of fish and other creatures that attract the island's greatest densities of wading birds and waterfowl.

The profile of Cumberland Island, from the Atlantic side to Cumberland Sound, includes surf and beach; fore dunes; meadowlike interdunal areas; taller rear dunes; broad flats and depressions with freshwater ponds and sloughs; another series of low, stabilized older dunes with forest on the backside; and, finally, salt marsh that is confined by a natural levee along the edge of Cumberland Sound. A maintained roadway, locally known as "Grand Avenue," runs the entire length of the island from near Terrapin Point south to Dungeness. Secondary roadways and numerous trails lead off Grand Avenue and provide good access to all parts of the island.

The National Park Service brochure describes Cumberland Island in one word: "tranquillity." It would be hard to disagree. The island is unlike any of the other national and state parks along the busy Atlantic Coast, not just because of its island location but primarily because of the park's capacity of 300 individuals per day, as designated in its general management plan. Only two ferries arrive and depart daily. And what's more, 19,000 acres (7,689 ha) have been designated as wilderness, where motorized vehicles and other creature comforts are limited. Rental vehicles are not available on the island.

Cumberland Island's wilderness gives priority to nature study and tranquillity. Nature walks and evening programs are scheduled during the peak visitor season, and a few publications can be acquired at the visitor center. Limited lodging is available at the privately owned Greyfield Inn, one of four original Carnegie homes on the island.

Additional information can be obtained from the Superintendent, Cumberland Island National Seashore, P.O. Box 806, Saint Marys, GA 31558; (912) 882-4335.

Barred owl

Bird Life

A spring night on Cumberland Island can be alive with sounds, especially through the thin canvas walls of a tent. The deep hooting calls of several **barred owls**, at times directly overhead, are among the great sounds of Cumberland Island. The deep, resonant quality of their songs seems almost primordial. And they often carry on their vocalizations with little or no abatement. On my first night there, four to six barred owls whooped away for more than an hour. Then suddenly they were silent; they apparently had moved elsewhere.

The barred owl is one of the most common owls of the eastern forests and is especially common in the Southeast, where it prefers wet, lowland forests. Its name is derived from its barred breast. A fairly large, dark brown to buff owl without the ear tufts of the larger great horned owl, the barred owl has a rounded head and large, all-brown eyes. It preys on rodents and other small mammals but will also take birds, amphibians, reptiles, and even invertebrates. It hunts at night, using its special hearing. Its ear openings are offset to help in locating prey by triangulation. But the barred owl's most outstanding characteristic is its emphatic song, sometimes written as "who cooks for you? who cooks for you all?"

It was not until the barred owls had moved elsewhere that I realized the closeness of a singing chuck-will's-widow. I had heard this nightjar just after dusk but had pretty well forgotten it during the hour-long barred owl chorus. Now it apparently was taking its turn to serenade the campground. Although the "chuck-will's-widow" call of the lone songster was never at the same decibel level of the barred owls' performance, it added a very positive perspective to the nighttime. I wondered how recently this individual had arrived in Georgia from its wintering grounds to the south and whether it would remain to nest on Cumberland Island or continue its migration to a more northerly breeding site.

The next morning I was up and out at dawn, when the first calls of American crows announced the coming daylight. Most of the bird song was that of the common residents. Carolina wren songs seemed to emanate from every direction. Northern cardinal, white-eyed vireo, Carolina chickadee, and tufted titmouse songs were numerous. A pileated woodpecker called from the forest, and

flocks of red-winged blackbirds were talking to one another as they
flew overhead, en route no doubt to feeding sites somewhere along
the seashore.

Dungeness contains some incredibly huge live oak trees. Some
of the monstrous trees possess branches that are larger than a person's waist and must rest on the ground. The numerous scattered
oaks, festooned with ferns, Spanish moss, and other epiphytes, provide yet another habitat for birds. Most of the live oaks were logged
off the island in the early 1800s; those at Dungeness represent some
of the oldest yet remaining.

Dungeness has a fascinating history. Its name came from an
Englishman named Oglethorpe who built a hunting lodge there in
the mid-1700s. In 1783, General Nathanael Greene, of Revolutionary War fame, built a four-story mansion there that was destroyed
by fire during the Civil War. A third Dungeness, grander yet with
more than 40 buildings, was built during the 1880s by Thomas
Carnegie, brother of industrialist Andrew Carnegie. It burned in
1959.

As I walked through the old compound, I discovered that the
area was literally alive with mixed parties of birds, including residents, species that occur only during the nesting season, and still
others that were only passing through. Of all the species there that
morning, the most numerous was the little **northern parula**, a warbler that was present undoubtedly as both a migrant and a nester. It
seemed to me that every oak had two or three individuals, and most
were in full song. Their song, a rising trill that ends with an abrupt
"hic," was heard everywhere. I think I will always associate
Dungeness with northern parulas.

The presence of numerous yellow-rumped and black-and-
white warblers, a few Tennessee and prairie warblers and solitary
vireos, and lone yellow and magnolia warblers suggested that at
least some of the parulas were part of a larger bird party migrating
northward along the coast.

I walked the Dungeness Trail to the beach and skirted the dunes
in search of shorebirds. I discovered thousands of birds feeding
along the shore or over the sea. Seabirds, waders, and shorebirds
were all there. I was able to approach very close to huge flocks of

Northern parula

shorebirds that were dominated by **dunlins**. The majority were already sporting their breeding plumage, reddish backs and black bellies that are much brighter than their dull winter dress. The dunlin is one of the many "peeps" but somewhat larger than the common three: semipalmated, western, and least sandpipers. The dunlin possesses a heavier bill that curves downward slightly at the tip. These birds, I knew, were on their way north to nest on the Arctic tundra. See chapter 25 on Cape Hatteras and Cape Lookout for additional information about dunlin feeding habits.

Dunlin

I estimated that dunlin numbers exceeded a thousand individuals. There also were numerous black-bellied plovers and sanderlings, smaller numbers of least and semipalmated sandpipers, red knots, semipalmated, and threatened piping plovers, and a pair of American oystercatchers.

Between the surf and the dunes was a series of small ponds, the result, no doubt, of recent rains. Each contained an assortment of birds. Short-billed dowitchers and lesser yellowlegs were present in every pond I examined. Numerous killdeers made themselves obvious by their incessant "kill-dee" calls. Three blue-winged teals, two of which were males with distinct white crescent face patches, exploded from one pond when I approached too close.

There were at least a dozen **wild turkeys** behind the ponds on the dunes; they probably had come there to drink. These large birds seemed very much at home on the dunes, but they should be most expected within the forests, where they feed on acorns and a variety of other plant and animal matter.

Savannah sparrows were fairly numerous along the grassy edges and flew ahead of me as I wandered on. These birds were the very light-colored race that was once considered a separate species, known until the 1970s as Ipswich sparrow. They occur along the Atlantic coast south to Georgia only in winter and nest far to the north in Nova Scotia and adjacent Sable Island.

At the extreme southeastern corner of the island is a jetty that extends seaward for several hundred feet. It is made up of hundreds of huge granite boulders brought from a mainland quarry during the island's heyday. Now the jetty is used primarily by the birds and fish. From my brief scoping of the jetty and surrounding waters, it seemed to be a particularly good place to sample seabirds that frequent this part of the coast.

Surprisingly common were brown pelicans, which are making a remarkable recovery since they were declared endangered and the use of DDT was outlawed in the United States. I imagined that the name of this corner of the island—Pelican Banks—was bestowed long before these birds were threatened by man-made chemicals.

Double-crested cormorants were common there as well, in the surf and flying overhead in small flocks. However, gulls and terns were most numerous. Laughing gulls, many already with the solid black heads and red bills that indicate breeding condition, were common. There also were fairly good numbers of royal terns and lesser numbers of Forster's, common, least, and Sandwich terns.

Black skimmers were present as well, flying together as if training for some precision flying mission. And farther out, beyond the end of the jetty, was a raft of dark-colored waterfowl. Walking past the jetty to get a better look, I could see they were scoters: 8 surf and 5 black scoters. These sea ducks probably were wintering birds that had not yet begun their northern migration.

Roller Coaster Trail, accessible from the Kings Bottom Trail that crosses Grand Avenue, follows a north-south ridge around Sweetwater Lake to Lake Whitney and provides an excellent overview of the area. It also is one of the island's best birding routes.

It seemed to me that all the migrants on the East Coast were represented that April morning along the Roller Coaster Trail. Most impressive was the variety of songbirds. Warblers, vireos, and a large variety of other species were moving northward, often in flocks of a hundred or more. The northern parula was still in the majority, but there were substantial numbers of Tennessee, orange-crowned, yellow, magnolia, yellow-rumped, black-throated green, yellow-throated, prairie, black-and-white, and palm warblers, oven-birds, and northern waterthrushes.

I found still more warblers, such as a brightly colored male Cape May warbler, with its chestnut-colored ear patch and "tiger-striped" underparts. There were two male black-throated blues; one sang a buzzy four-note song before moving on. Prothonotary war-blers were present in the undergrowth near water; these gold and blue birds were among the most distinct and colorful I saw that day. A male Kentucky warbler responded to my spishing and approached to within a dozen feet of me before realizing where the sound was coming from. I had an excellent look at this bright yel-low and black songster before it beat a hasty retreat. And at almost the same time, I heard the sharp chips of a hooded warbler that had been attracted by my spishing. This bird, too, was a bright male with a brilliant yellow face and velvet black throat, neck, and cap.

Among other songbirds of interest along the Roller Coaster Trail was a Philadelphia vireo, which I first detected by its song. Yellow-throated and red-eyed vireos put in their appearance; two bright red summer tanagers gleaned insects from newly leafed trees overhead; a male orchard oriole, brown and black, moved by; and I recorded both hermit and wood thrushes along the trail.

The ponds to the south of Sweetwater Lake are brackish and provide nesting habitat for a relative newcomer to Cumberland Island, the **wood stork**. Susan Bratton reported in the 1989 summer issue of *Park Science* that the summer population of wood storks may be as high as 500 birds. She postulated that the Cumberland Island birds may have moved north from the Everglades because of inadequate water supply there. See chapter 31 on the Everglades for further details.

Lake Whitney gleamed like a bright blue jewel, set off by deep green foliage and white dunes. The day was gorgeous! I walked around the lake as best I could, although the swampy edges did not permit a close-up inspection. I was fascinated by the way the dunes came right up to the lakeshore in places or encroached on the pine community elsewhere. I was reminded of the "marching dunes" at Spain's Coto Donana National Park. I walked east onto the dunes to where I could see the Atlantic Ocean less than a quarter mile away and found other similarities to Donana: pines, red cedar, and bright green shrubs surrounded by white dunes.

Bird life at Lake Whitney can be exceptional. The fresh water provides an important stopover site for migrant waterfowl and other water birds during both spring and fall. And in summer, pied-billed grebe, anhinga, least bittern, tricolored heron, cattle egret, black-crowned and yellow-crowned night-herons, white ibis, wood duck, king rail, purple gallinule, common moorhen, and American coot all nest there.

John Mitchell, in a 1984 *Audubon* article, best described the early days of Cumberland Island. He called Cumberland an island that is "floating free," free unto itself, not connected to the mainland by some artificial device. Cumberland Island is indeed free of the encumbrances too often assigned parks and other public places. In a sense, Cumberland has been left to the birds and to those humans who appreciate the very special natural setting that exists there.

In summary, the park's bird checklist contains 264 species, 99 of which are known to nest; of those, 27 are water birds, 9 are hawks and owls, and 8 are warblers. Thirty-six species are listed only for winter: red-throated loon; horned and red-necked grebes; northern gannet; snow goose; gadwall; American wigeon; greater scaup; surf and white-winged scoters; common goldeneye; ruddy duck; purple sandpiper; great black-backed gull; long-eared and short-eared owls; Bewick's and winter wrens; golden-crowned and ruby-crowned kinglets; hermit thrush; water pipit; cedar waxwing; chipping, vesper, savannah, sharp-tailed, fox, song, swamp, and white-throated sparrows; dark-eyed junco; purple finch; pine siskin; American goldfinch; and evening grosbeak. Some of these are undoubtedly also present as migrants.

Birds of Special Interest

Wood Stork. The population of this summer resident of Sweetwater Lake complex may be increasing due to drying of south Florida habitats. This is a large (40-inch, or 102-cm, wingspan), black-and-white wading bird.

Least bittern. A fairly common summer resident at cattails in ponds throughout, this little yellow and black wader is very shy and rarely ventures far from concealment. However, during the breeding season, it often flies out of the cattails in pursuit of its mate.

Wild turkey. This large bird frequents open areas, especially among the southern dunes. Watch for it along the Dungeness Trail. It cannot be mistaken for any other species.

Dunlin. Spring migrants may occur by the hundreds. The dunlin has a reddish back and black belly, and the bill droops slightly at the tip.

Barred owl. A fairly common permanent resident, it is most vociferous during early spring. Its deep, rhythmic hoots are loud and often continuous for long periods of time.

Northern parula. This little songster is common in spring and summer. The male possesses a black to reddish chest band. Its song is an ascending trill ending in a sharp "hic." 🐦

SOUTHEAST AND VIRGIN ISLANDS

With exceeding vision the American people through the National Park Service and other agencies have sequestered these and similar areas. Scientists need them for the study of undisturbed nature. And the generations to come need them for the same breath-taking visitas into the past and into the future. May they remain for all time—islands in time and in space, where living men can detach themselves from their civilization, and walk into eternity.

—Harvey Broome

27

Chattahoochee River National Recreation Area, Georgia

The loud rattle call of a belted kingfisher from only a few yards away, especially on a calm and peaceful early morning on the river, can be startling, to say the least. I was completely absorbed in the misty morning setting as we drifted with the flow. I had not noticed the kingfisher perched on a bare limb that protruded over the river until it suddenly took flight, expressing its disapproval of our presence. I followed its swift flight downriver and watched it alight on another bare limb over the waterway.

The kingfisher apparently frightened a green-backed heron that was probably feeding along the nearby bank. I could see the heron's blue-green back and chestnut throat as it flew across the river. I searched the thick tree canopy along the banks for a nest, but to no avail. It was probably well hidden from predators and other disturbances. I turned my attention back to the kingfisher, which had not moved since it had reached its new perch. Maybe it thought it would not be seen. But I kept watching it as we drifted closer.

Belted kingfishers are extremely well adapted to a life along the riverway. Slightly longer than 12 inches (30 cm), it is a heavy-bodied bird with a short tail and an extremely large, heavy bill. It feeds on fish and other creatures that it captures underwater or on the shore. Its fishing procedure involves spotting prey either by passing over the water or by hovering, then making a quick, headlong dive, sometimes from as high as 40 feet (12 m) above the surface. It may completely submerge itself and stay underwater for several seconds before it literally flies out of the water with a fish held tightly in its bill. Then it flies to a perch over the water, where it may beat its prey first before tossing it into the air and swallowing it headfirst.

We were only about 60 feet (18 m) away now, and I could see the kingfisher's key features very well. It was a female with a rusty belly band (males lack the belly band) below the wider blue breast band that crosses its otherwise snow white underparts. The rest of the bird was solid blue-gray, except for its white collar and barred tail. And then it raised its high crest, and off it streaked again, down the Chattahoochee to another perch very much like the previous two.

Belted kingfisher

Kingfishers nest in dirt banks along rivers, and the Chattahoochee contains a number of suitable sites. This bird actually tunnels as far as 15 feet (4.5 m) into banks at a slightly upward angle. At the end of the tunnel, it constructs a 6- to 10-inch-deep (15-25 cm) nest chamber. Its bill serves as its digging tool, and it pushes the loose dirt out with its small but strong feet. The construction takes three days to three weeks, depending upon the type of soil. The chamber then is lined with grass, feathers, and materials from its pellets.

Like many other birds that swallow their prey whole, kingfishers regurgitate pellets of undigested materials, bones, and scales. There are times when a fish is so large that it is impossible to swallow and literally sticks out of the bird's throat. To compensate for this occurrence, these remarkable birds possess very rapid digestion, so that their prey gradually slips into their gut.

For the third time, we approached the kingfisher. But now, instead of flying farther down the river, it flew across the river and made a large loop, heading back, I was sure, to the perch where we had found it first.

The Park Environment

The Chattahoochee River National Recreation Area is composed of a series of units totaling about 4,200 acres (1,670 ha) of the authorized 6,800 acres (2,752 ha) along 48 miles (77 km) of the riverway on the northern edge of Atlanta, Georgia. Its purpose, according to the park's general management plan, is to "protect the scenic, recreational, and natural values of a 2,000-foot-wide (610-m) corridor adjacent to each bank of the Chattahoochee River." The river supplies 70 percent of the drinking water for the Atlanta region.

Established in 1978, the park lies between the southern edge of the Appalachians and the Atlantic coastal plains in the Piedmont region, which contains an overlap of flora and fauna. There is no original forest left, but some secondary forest habitats contain many of the original species. The dominating Chattahoochee River floodplain contains riverine forest, open fields, and freshwater marsh habitats. Riverine plants, such as those found at Cochran Shoals, are dominated by black walnut, tulip-tree, sycamore, smooth alder, river birch, and several willows. The old fields and forest edges contain numerous grasses and thickets of blackberry, deerberry, sumacs, and briars. Loblolly pines form small stands at various localities. The freshwater marshes are small and scattered; they are dominated by cattails and edged with willows.

The upland forest, such as that found at Gold Branch and Palisades, is dominated by oaks (white, chestnut, and red) and short-leaf pine. Other common trees include pignut and mockernut hickories, beech, white ash, tulip-tree, red maple, sour-gum, and sourwood. Dogwood and redbud are common in the understory.

The river is the centerpiece of the park and almost half of the park's visitation comes from river users who raft, canoe, and kayak. The most popular stretch of river is from Johnson Ferry to Paces Mill. Fishing is of secondary importance, although the cold water, resulting from Buford Dam above the Bowman Island unit, provides good habitat for 22 species of game fish, including trout, bream, catfish, and several other very palatable species. Cochran Shoals has an excellent fitness trail that is extremely popular with local folks. A total of 57 miles (92 km) of hiking trails exist in the park. The most popular of these are at Cochran Shoals, Island Ford, Johnson Ferry, Gold Branch, and Palisades.

The park does not have a visitor center at present, but an interpretive complex is being planned for Paces Mill, within the Atlanta city limits, for the 1996 Olympics. Ranger stations exist at the Island Ford and Palisades units. The private, nonprofit Chattahoochee Nature Center (very near Gold Branch Unit) provides a variety of interpretive and educational activities, including bird walks throughout the year and an excellent selection of bird books, bird houses, feeders, and the like. Although there is no bird checklist for the park per se, an excellent greater Atlanta bird list, developed by the Atlanta Audubon Society, is available on request.

There are no campgrounds inside the park, but there are several private campgrounds in the greater Atlanta area, as well as those operated by the U.S. Army Corps of Engineers at Lake Sidney Lanier, above Buford Dam. The park does offer several picnic areas.

Additional information can be acquired from the Superintendent, Chattahoochee River National Recreation Area, 1978 Island Ford Parkway, Dunwoody, GA 30350; (404) 399-8070.

Bird Life

I will never again hear the rattle call of a belted kingfisher without thinking of that June river trip on the Chattahoochee. Between Johnson Ferry and the Powers Island takeout, we found eight of these handsome birds. My companions, however, were more impressed with the **great blue herons** that we encountered along the shoreline or flying ahead of us with slow beating of their huge wings. One individual remained on the shore, perfectly still to keep from being seen. We floated within 30 feet (9 m) or so. It was an adult in breeding plumage, and we admired the long, black feathers that streamed down its neck. Its bluish body, black-and-white neck and head, and huge, yellowish-green bill were spectacular. This bird is sometimes confused with a crane, because of their similar size and long necks. But sandhill cranes are very different birds, visiting Chattahoochee only for a day or so in spring. An adult sandhill is all gray with a red crown and flies with its neck straight out; a heron usually flies with its neck doubled and head drawn in. See chapter 7 on Prince Edward Island for additional information on great blue herons.

Three kinds of waterfowl occur along the river in summer: the fairly common Canada goose, mallard, and wood duck, especially at Palisades. Canada geese, or "honkers," as they are sometimes called because of their honking calls, may occur anywhere along the riverway. They are easily identified by their large size and black necks with a white throat patch. A male mallard is readily identified by its metallic green head, narrow white collar, rusty breast, and yellow bill. The female is very drab overall, but both possess the mallard's bright blue wing speculum.

The male **wood duck** is one of a kind, one of the river's most spectacular creatures. Its long crest is iridescent green to purple bordered with white, and its blood red eye stands out against a velvet black face with a white line running from its white throat onto the cheek. Combined with its chestnut-colored chest and multicolored body, it has an almost unreal appearance. The female is mottled gray-brown with an elliptic white eye ring. This bird has done very well along the Chattahoochee, particularly since the state installed nest boxes along the floodplain. See chapter 24 on National Capital Parks for details about the wood duck's life history.

I recorded a number of smaller birds along the river that summer day. The low, moaning calls of mourning doves were commonplace. Chimney swifts, recognized by their swept-back wings and gray, cigar-shaped bodies, twittered overhead. Black-and-white eastern kingbirds were calling their harsh "dzeet" calls from the tip-top of several tall sycamores and occasionally dashing out to capture flying insects. The fork-tailed barn swallows were common along the waterway. Tufted titmice were present within the forested shoreline; there was seldom an instance when their "peter, peter, peter" calls were not in evidence. The "wheedle, wheedle, wheedle" songs of Carolina wrens, with a slightly different accent from their northern cousins, were abundant. Bright red summer tanager males crossed the river on a number of occasions. Indigo buntings flashed their bright blue color from the tops of shrubs and trees. And rufous-sided towhees called "chreee" time and again from the dense underbrush.

Other, less obvious songbirds recorded on that river trip included the great crested and Acadian flycatchers, blue jay, Carolina chickadee, white-breasted nuthatch, northern mockingbird, blue-gray gnatcatcher, white-eyed and red-eyed vireos, yellow and yellow-throated warblers, common yellowthroat, yellow-breasted chat, northern cardinal, orchard oriole, and common grackle.

Soaring birds are usually common along the river as the day warms enough to produce thermals over the adjacent ridges. The all-black turkey vultures, with their bare, red heads, can be numerous. Red-tailed hawks, with their dull- to brick-red tails, are commonplace, too. Less numerous are the small broad-winged hawks and the resident red-shouldered hawks; both possess banded tails.

Nighttime predators are rarely seen, but three owls make their presence known with their distinct calls. The larger great horned owl prefers the adjacent fields; its call is a series of three to eight loud hoots, like "who, who, who-who-who." Barred owls prefer wetlands and streamsides; their calls are most varied and impressive, often "who cooks for you, who cooks for you all." And the smaller eastern screech-owl lives in the denser forest. Its call is a series of quavering whistles, descending in pitch. In addition, two nightjars, chuck-will's-widow in the moist lowlands and whip-poor-will in the higher, drier sites, can be heard in spring and summer.

The cattail marshes and open water of Bull Sluice Lake contain an additional group of birds of interest. This is the best place to find resident and visiting wading birds, waterfowl, and marsh birds. None are as abundant as the **red-winged blackbirds** that nest within the cattails in spring and summer. Dozens can usually be found singing from the cattails and adjacent vegetation. Their song is like a liquid gurgle, "konk-quer-reee." Males possess all-black bodies with bright red shoulder patches or epaulets. Females are streaked with dark lines and possess only a hint of the red epaulets. In winter they often occur in huge flocks, sometimes in the hundreds and mixed with European starlings, common grackles, and brown-headed cowbirds.

A visitor to these areas is likely to find other marsh birds, as well. The pied-billed grebe is noted for its stubby pied or banded bill; the tall great egret is all-white with a yellow bill. The upright, buff bird with a banded belly and long bill that haunts the cattails is a king rail. Both northern rough-winged and barn swallows can be numerous, feeding on insects over the water's surface. Song sparrows, little brown birds with a noticeable breast spot, frequent the shrubbery at the edge of the marsh.

The Gold Branch Unit trails, accessible from Lower Roswell Road, form a network across the ridge to Bull Sluice Lake beyond. This reasonably small area serves as a good representative of the upland forest. A visit to this area in spring will more than likely produce a dozen or more birds that rarely occur along the floodplain. An early morning walk can produce as many as six or seven warblers, usually in full song and actively involved with family matters. Pine warblers stay high in the pines, but their twittering musical trills can be heard throughout the area. Black-and-white warblers are almost as vocal, and their thin, high-pitched warbling notes emanate from the broadleaf canopy.

Three warblers prefer the forest understory—worm-eating, hooded, and ovenbird. A worm-eating warbler is a very plain, buff warbler with four blackish head stripes and a song that is like a dry, insectlike trill. Hooded warblers are bright yellow and black songsters that sing their emphatic "weeta, weeta, wee-tee-o" song at any time of the day. And ovenbirds spend even more time on the forest floor, walking about in a jerky manner, searching for insects in every nook and cranny. They, too, have a very distinct song: "teacher, teacher, teacher." The ovenbird is brown above and white below with wide streaks of black. It has a bold white eye ring and a russet-orange head stripe.

Finally, two warblers are often found at Gold Branch which prefer streamside habitats and produce marvelous songs. The louder of the two is the black-and-white Louisiana waterthrush, which prefers the banks of the fast-flowing stream. It has a grayish back, streaked underparts, and a bold white eye line. Its song has been described as "see-you, see-you, see-you, chew chew to-wee." The Kentucky warbler prefers swampy areas and sings its "chur-ree, chur-ree" song over and over. It has bright yellow underparts, a black and yellow head with yellow "spectacles," and an olive green back.

The loveliest song of the upland forest, however, is the flutelike "ee-o-lay" of the **wood thrush**, which it will repeat over and over. But it is never in a hurry, taking its time to make sure that each song is better than the one before. Frank Chapman described its song as a "hymn of praise rising pure and clear from a thankful heart, 'ee-o-lay, ee-o-lay.'"

The wood thrush is a reasonably large thrush with a rufous back, head, and tail and white underparts with fairly large black spots. It often feeds on the ground like its first cousin, the American robin, but it also feeds on berries from fruiting shrubs. See chapter 16 on Mammoth Cave for further details about the wood thrush.

Other summer resident songbirds of the upland forest include the eastern wood-pewee, blue jay, American crow, Carolina chickadee, tufted titmouse, white-breasted nuthatch, Carolina wren, American robin, red-eyed vireo, and scarlet tanager.

There, too, is where six woodpecker species can be found. Most abundant of these is the red-bellied woodpecker, with grayish underparts, except for a tinge of red on the belly; black-and-white barred back; and bright red cap, forehead, and nape. Its call is a rolling "churr," sometimes repeated several times. Also common is the northern flicker. Its barred back is buff with black markings, and it has a very noticeable white rump, black crescent on its chest, and spotted breast. In flight its wings show yellow shafts. The black-and-white hairy and downy woodpeckers look very much alike, except that the hairy is larger and has a noticeably larger bill. The least common woodpecker is the red-headed woodpecker, which has an all-red head, noticeable white rump, and white patches on the trailing edges of its wings, most evident in flight. The largest of the park's woodpeckers is the pileated, a Woody Woodpecker look-alike. This black-backed woodpecker has a great, bright red crest.

Wintertime produces a different set of birds, and there is no better place to find these than along the Cochran Shoals fitness trail. One morning in mid-November, I found 36 species along the loop trail. Most numerous were the blue jay, American crow, Carolina chickadee, tufted titmouse, Carolina wren, American robin, ruby-crowned and golden-crowned kinglets, yellow-rumped warbler, northern cardinal, rufous-sided towhee, swamp and song sparrows, and house finch. Smaller numbers of the mallard; turkey vulture; red-tailed hawk; killdeer; mourning dove; belted kingfisher; northern flicker; red-bellied, hairy, and downy woodpeckers; eastern phoebe; house wren; northern mockingbird; brown thrasher; hermit thrush; eastern bluebird; chipping, field, and white-throated sparrows; red-winged blackbird; common grackle; and American goldfinch were encountered.

In summary, the park's bird list contains 241 species, 102 of which are known to nest. Nine of those are water birds, 9 are hawks and owls, and 16 are warblers. Four species are considered winter residents or visitors only: tundra swan, snow goose, common merganser, and Bewick's wren.

Birds of Special Interest

Great blue heron. This is the tall blue, gray, and white bird with long legs and a six-foot wingspan seen along the river and at marshy areas.

Wood duck. The male possesses a long crest colored with greens and purples and bordered with white, a red eye, and a black face with white lines. These birds use nest boxes placed on the river floodplain.

Belted kingfisher. This is the bluish bird with a huge bill and a loud, dry rattle call that lives along the river, diving headfirst after fish in the river.

Wood thrush. Its beautiful, flutelike "ee-o-lay" song is common in the forest all spring and summer. The bird is robin-sized, with a reddish back and white underparts with large spots.

Red-winged blackbird. It is most common at cattails along the river during the nesting season but flocks with other blackbirds in winter. Males are all black with bright red wing patches.

28

Congaree Swamp National Monument, South Carolina

There is no better representative of the southern swamps than the prothonotary warbler. Its loud and penetrating song is the embodiment of the cypress-dominated wetlands. On one morning in May, its very explicit song, "peet, zweet, zweet, zweet," exploded from near the boardwalk. And a second later, a golden ball of feathers landed on the edge of the boardwalk just ahead of me. It stayed only a second before flying to a nearby cypress knee, where it perched a foot above the water and sang again, "peet, zweet, zweet, zweet." What an incredibly lovely bird.

It was obvious why this rather tame warbler is sometimes called the golden swamp warbler. Its entire head and breast are bright yellow tinged with orange. Its coal black bill and eyes are a marked contrast. And its olive-gray back and blue-gray wings and tail help emphasize its golden countenance. It is an orange-yellow ball of energy. Larger than most warblers, prothonotaries hop about when feeding, searching in crevices and debris for insects and larvae.

Prothonotary comes from the Latin word *protontarius*, for the yellow hood or robe worn by some church officials. It seemed most appropriate as I watched this gorgeous creature. It did somehow serve as the leading official of the Congaree congregation. I was but a visitor to the chapel.

Yet the prothonotary warbler resides at Congaree only part of the year, from April to mid-August. The brightly colored males and their duller mates build their nests in tree cavities, often in cypress knees or abandoned woodpecker holes, a few feet to 30 feet (9 m)

Prothonotary warbler

high. They fill the cavity with mosses, lichens, dry leaves, and a variety of other materials. They usually construct two nests, one for the female, in which she will lay three to eight yellowish eggs spotted with dark brown, and a second nest for the male. The second or dummy nest helps to fool the common brown-headed cowbird, which often lays its eggs in the nests of smaller birds.

Prothonotary warblers winter in Central America and northern South America, utilizing wetland habitats similar to their breeding grounds. In winter they may use communal roosts, which is very unlike their behavior on their breeding grounds, where they aggressively defend an established territory. Populations of this golden warbler generally seem to be declining, probably due to increased levels of pollution that have serious consequences for wetlands and also to the destruction of wetlands for grazing and developments. The protection of places like Congaree Swamp is essential for the long-term survival of this golden songster.

The Park Environment

The lifeblood of the Congaree Swamp is the Congaree River and its Cedar Creek tributary. Approximately ten times each year, these streams overflow their banks and deposit yellow-brown silt, rich in nutrients, over the vast, swampy floodplain. The Congaree is very different from the nutrient-poor black water swamps found farther north. The result is an incredibly diverse bottomland hardwood forest at Congaree Swamp with 87 tree species. Because of their great size, 7 species of these trees have been listed as national champions, 25 were state champions, and more than 60 additional trees measured at least 80 percent of the national record. The last two national champions—overcup and Shumard oaks—were lost to Hurricane Hugo in 1989. John Dennis described Congaree Swamp and its extraordinary forest trees in his beautiful book, *The Great Cypress Swamps*.

There are good reasons for the exceptional size of the floodplain forest trees. Trees tend to grow large and tall when they consistently are fed rich nutrients from the cycle of flooding. This type of forest is relatively immune to fire and infestations, and so the trees are long-lived. And much of the Congaree area contains forest that experienced little or no logging. The more than 15,000-acre (6,070-

ha) Beidler tract, which became the centerpiece of the park, was long recognized as the most extensive mature bottomland hardwood forest remaining in the southeastern United States. It was under one ownership since the Civil War and, except for some selective cypress logging at the turn of the century, was relatively undisturbed.

Congress recognized the value of this ecologically important freshwater wetland in 1976 and authorized 22,200 acres (8,942 ha) north of the Congaree River as Congaree Swamp National Monument. Located 20 miles (32 km) southeast of Columbia, South Carolina, the park entrance is off State Highway 48, near Gadsden. Although the park is relatively small by national park standards, it contains a 25-mile (40-km) trail system, including two boardwalks, that provides good access onto the floodplain. Also, approximately 20 miles (32 km) of Cedar Creek provide excellent canoeing opportunities. Primitive camping is allowed by permit only. No other camping or lodging is available within the park; these can be found in the local communities.

The park's ranger station/visitor center, near the entrance, contains an information desk and a small publications sales rack that includes bird field guides. A bird checklist, developed and maintained by the Columbia Audubon Society, is available on request. Interpretive activities are limited to a ranger-guided walk at 1:30 p.m. on Saturdays, group tours on request, and evening "owl prowls" during the spring and fall. The "owl prowls" are advertised in the local newspapers and are extremely popular; reservations are necessary. Two trails, the Boardwalk and Bluff trails, are self-guided.

The park topography varies only slightly, from the broad flat floodplain to a slightly elevated and undulating terrain to the north, with low ridges and swales. The ridges possess sandy, well-drained soils that support huge loblolly pines and communities of sweet-gum, laurel oak, American elm, basket and Spanish oaks, and beech. The floodplain contains communities of baldcypress and tupelo in standing water, baldcypress and sour-gum along the water's edge, and overcup oak and water hickory at areas subject to regular flooding.

The word "Congaree" comes from an Indian tribe of that name that once lived in the area. They utilized the abundant resources provided by these swamplands, which have the highest productivity of any natural forest in North America. Today, of all the great fresh-water swamps that once existed along much of the southern coast-line from Texas to the Carolinas, Congaree represents one of the few reasonably intact systems and is the only representative of that ecosystem within the National Park System.

Additional information can be obtained from the Superinten-dent, Congaree Swamp National Monument, 200 Caroline Sums Road, Hopkins, SC 29061; (803) 776-4396.

Bird Life

There were a number of birds in full song that morning along the boardwalk. But only one was singing as consistently as the pro-thonotary warbler—the little **northern parula**, which is partial to various trees draped with Spanish moss. Its song is very distinct, although never so loud and explosive as that of the much larger prothonotary. The parula's song is most often written as "zzzzzzeee-yip," a rather slow and slightly ascending buzz that ends (usually) with a distinct "hic." Not only does it have a very distinct song but it is one of the most colorful of the nesting birds. The parula sports a bright yellow breast and throat (the male has a rusty black chest band), a blue-gray back with a green-yellow patch, and a white belly, eye ring, and two wing bars.

I watched a very bright male flitting in and out of a drapery of moss almost directly above the boardwalk. I assumed its nest was concealed within the Spanish moss, and that a female was incubat-ing four or five whitish eggs inside. The male was feeding in the gray-green moss, at times hanging upside down like a chickadee as it crept and flitted about. Then the male flew up onto the branch, put its head back, and sang again, "zzzzzzeee-yip."

Nearby, a red-eyed vireo sang a series of deliberate, short whis-tle phrases. A second red-eye was singing from the upper canopy foliage a hundred yards beyond. Since only male vireos sing, I rec-ognized that here were two territorial red-eyes, each defending a certain nesting and feeding area. These vociferous songsters, which usually remain in the highest foliage, are well suited for the green world in which they live. Their whitish underparts, olive green backs, white eye line bordered with black, and ruby red eyes are difficult to find in the high canopy of Congaree's tall forest.

The thin, melodious but wheezy warble song of a blue-gray gnatcatcher attracted my attention to the right. And I was able to locate this very thin, long-tailed bird working the foliage of an oak tree at midelevation. A gnatcatcher looks much like the larger northern mockingbird, blue-gray above with a black head, bold white eye ring, and grayish underparts. And a male white-eyed vireo added its scolding song to the morning chorus. Its song has been described as an emphatic "chick-a-per-weeoo-chick" or "quick, take me to the railroad, quick."

The white-eyed vireo is another of Congaree's tiny songbirds, this one preferring thickets in the river bottoms and forest edges to the taller deciduous vegetation. It is particularly fond of the dense vegetation that appears in openings created by tree falls, a common occurrence within the park's mature forest. Although it often stays well hidden, low spishing sometimes brings it into the open. Then its gray-green back, whitish underparts, yellow eye ring and lores, and white eyes help identify this very personable bird. No other bird has this song: "quick, take me to the railroad, quick."

Other songbirds present along the boardwalk that day included the yellow-billed cuckoo, Acadian and great crested flycatchers, Carolina chickadee, tufted titmouse, white-breasted nuthatch, Carolina wren, wood thrush, yellow-throated vireo, yellow-throated and Kentucky warblers, summer tanager, and northern cardinal.

Much of the time a pair of **red-shouldered hawks** circled overhead, sometimes barely above the tops of the highest trees. Their high-pitched call, an extended "kee-ah," echoed down onto the boardwalk. Every now and then I could see one or the other as they wheeled overhead, calling continually. I recognized their very reddish underparts and rather long, banded tails, but their unique call is one of their best identifying features. When perched, the red-shouldered hawk is a blackish-brown bird with reddish shoulders and a tendency to sit upright. This is the park's only common nesting hawk; it is a full-time resident that can be found all twelve months of the year.

The other large, common and full-time resident raptor of the Congaree Swamp is the **barred owl**. Because of its loud calls, which can be heard at any time of day or night, it may be the park's best-known bird. This is the owl responsible for the park's "owl prowls." Several individuals can sometimes be located during one evening. And once its song is identified, it will never be forgotten. Its most common rendition is a series of deep hoots: "who cooks for you, who cooks for you all?" But it also screams, chuckles, and moans. And, especially during springtime, it will continue calling for more than an hour at a time. Or it may move elsewhere and start all over again. And if it is silent, it can often be coaxed to start again with like-sounding calls. There is no other bird that compares with an active barred owl. See chapter 26 on Cumberland Island for additional information about this owl.

Woodpeckers are also common at Congaree and can generally be found on the floodplain as well as on the drier uplands. The most numerous species is probably the red-bellied woodpecker, although the little downy woodpecker can also be common within the thickets along the river and forest edges. The hairy and red-headed woodpeckers are less common but can be plentiful at various times of the year.

Perhaps the park's best-known woodpecker is the large **pileated woodpecker**, a Woody Woodpecker look-alike. At times it seems reasonably tame and allows a close approach, but at other times it will fly off with its very broad wings flapping almost like those of a bat. The pileated woodpecker's crown is entirely red on males and red and black on females. Its other key features include a white throat and a bold white stripe that runs from the bill across the head and down its neck. And its loud, rising and falling call, "wuck-a-wuck-a-wuck-a," can usually be heard throughout the park at any time of the day. These woodpeckers can excavate great holes in both standing and downed trees in search of insects. They also peck out nesting cavities high in standing trees. See chapter 15 on Big South Fork for additional information on this large woodpecker.

Only the **red-cockaded woodpecker** gets more attention. This is the park's only resident bird that has been given official endangered status by the federal government. Park Ranger Kathryn Brett told me that three pairs reside in one isolated portion of the park, using open stands of longleaf pines. This is a small woodpecker with a black-and-white barred back, black cap and hind neck, and large, white cheek patch. Males possess small tufts of red feathers on either side of their heads, a characteristic from which their name was derived.

The most fascinating thing about red-cockaded woodpeckers is their unique nesting behavior. These birds require open mature pine woodlands, where they occur in small family groups, nesting only in live pines usually infected with red-heart fungus, which softens the tree's heartwood. Nest and roost cavities, gourd-shaped and 8 to 12 inches (20-30 cm) deep with a 2-inch opening, are constructed usually 12 to 20 feet (4-6 m) high. Several one-inch pits are maintained around the opening so that resin flows down the trunk like a huge melting candle. This gooey material helps protect the nest from predators such as ants and snakes. The "candle-trees" usually are readily visible in a forest of normally all-dark trunks.

Red-cockaded woodpeckers maintain rather large territories and spend a good deal of time away from their roosting sites. They feed almost exclusively on wood-boring insects and beetle larvae in pine trees, often spiraling upward on the trunk and to the crown. However, they also feed on the ground, among berry thickets, and even on standing corn, from which they extract corn earworms. John Terres reports that a family group of red-cockaded woodpeckers "may eat up to 8,000 earworms per acre" during summer.

Of the park's five main trails, the 6-mile (10-km) Oak Ridge Trail provides the best overview of the old growth hardwood forest. Here is where the wild turkey is sometimes seen. And all of the woodpeckers frequent these woods as well. The eastern wood-pewee, blue jay, American crow, brown-headed nuthatch, brown thrasher, pine and hooded warblers, American redstart, blue grosbeak, indigo bunting, rufous-sided towhee, and chipping sarrow are also present in summer, as are many of the species mentioned for the floodplain.

The **hooded warbler** might best represent the park's uplands. It is one of the showiest of warblers. The male has a coal black head with bright yellow cheeks and forehead, yellow breast and belly, and olive green back and tail. The female is a much duller version without the black head. This warbler's white under tail coverts are often visible when feeding, because it will spread its tail, redstart-fashion, perhaps to startle insects that it will feed on. This is another warbler of the forest floor and understory, rarely feeding above 15 feet (4.5 m). It often will walk over the forest floor, searching crevices and peeking into holes, frequently fanning its tail. It will occasionally utter a loud chip to communicate with its mate, who may be sitting on a clutch of eggs in its well-hidden ground nest.

It is perhaps the male's song, as much as its contrasting colors, that is its special hallmark. It will announce its territory with a loud and emphatic "weeta, weeta, wee-tee-o," with emphasis on the "tee." Its song is a clear and ringing proclamation. Frank Chapman described the song as "sweet and graceful" and transcribed it as "you must come to the woods, or you won't see me."

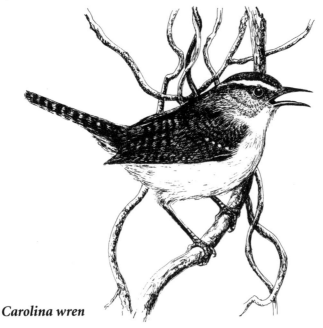

Carolina wren

But of all the bird songs of the uplands and floodplain, none are as consistent all year long as that of the **Carolina wren**. And what more appropriate species for a South Carolina park than this wonderful bird that not only is the official state bird but also graces its award-winning license plate. This wren possesses an array of songs and calls that range from scoldings and rattles to clinking, musical trills, and toadlike squeaks. But its most common song is "tea-kettle, tea-kettle, tea-kettle" or the softer "whee-udel, whee-udel, whee-udel." Terres adds "which jailer, which jailer" to its vast repertoire.

Paul Ehrlich and colleagues point out that male Carolina wrens "sing 27 to 41 different song types, singing one song repeatedly before switching to a different song type; neighboring males frequently match song types. Males and females duet."

The Carolina wren is nervous and secretive, a skulker that frequents the densest thickets and undergrowth. When it finally comes out into the open it is revealed as a rufous to buff bird with a bold white eye line. Its stubby body and reasonably long, barred tail are never still, always bobbing and poking into this and that in a most curious manner. It nests in cavities or depressions, even utilizing flowerpots, mailboxes, and birdhouses.

Wintertime bird life at Congaree is very different from that in summer. A visit on one cold November day produced most of the typical wintering birds. Most abundant were American robins, with smaller numbers of northern flickers, cedar waxwings, and common grackles high in the trees. A lone American kestrel harrassed these birds on one occasion. And as I followed the Bluff Trail loop, I encountered substantial numbers of blue jays, Carolina chickadees, tufted titmice, ruby-crowned and golden-crowned kinglets, swamp and white-throated sparrows, and dark-eyed juncos. I also recorded the great blue heron, hairy and downy woodpeckers, yellow-bellied sapsucker, eastern phoebe, white-breasted nuthatch, hermit thrush, northern mockingbird, yellow-rumped warbler, and northern cardinal.

In summary, the park's 1990 bird checklist contains 140 species, 72 of which are known to nest. Of those, only 4 are water birds, 6 are hawks and owls, and 11 are warblers. Seven species are listed as winter residents or visitors only: common loon, pied-billed grebe, American bittern, hooded merganser, rusty blackbird, pine siskin, and evening grosbeak.

Birds of Special Interest

Red-shouldered hawk. The park's only common resident hawk, it has reddish shoulders and underparts and a fairly long, barred tail.

Barred owl. This is the large, gray-brown owl of the swamp, with dark barring on the upper breast. It has a wonderful series of loud hoots and other calls that can be heard night and day.

Pileated woodpecker. This is the largest of our woodpeckers and can be easily identified by its size, black back and underparts, white stripe from bill to neck, and bright red crest.

Red-cockaded woodpecker. There is only one family still present in the park, in an out-of-the-way area where it can continue to survive without the impact of pollution and logging so common on the outside.

Carolina wren. Its "tea-kettle" song is its trademark, but it can be identified by its stubby body, rusty back, and bold white eye line.

Northern parula. This is among the smallest of the warblers and sports yellow underparts and a yellow-green back. It has a very distinct song, a slow, buzzy, slightly ascending trill that ends in a distinct "hic."

Prothonotary warbler. It is common in spring and summer along the boardwalk. Its bright yellow head and underparts contrast with its black eye and bill and its blue-gray wings and tail.

29

Canaveral National Seashore, Florida

The Florida scrub jay is not a rare or particularly secretive bird. Instead, it seems well adjusted to areas within and adjacent to human habitation. It frequents roadsides, gardens, and other human-made edges and often is fairly numerous in these artificial habitats. But this is not to suggest that it does better after its natural habitat has been destroyed or altered. Just the opposite is probably the case. David Breininger, biologist with the John F. Kennedy Space Center, reported in the May 1989 issue of *Florida Field Naturalist*, that the Florida scrub jay population "has declined by nearly half the size it was a century ago." He stated, "Approximately half of the scrub and slash pine habitat appeared to be unused by Florida scrub jays, probably because the slash pine cover was too dense or the oak cover was too sparse." This condition is at least partly due to excessive fire control. Breininger also pointed out that more than 80 percent of the known Florida scrub jay population occurs within the Cape Canaveral and Ocala National Forest region of central Florida.

The tremendous range separation between the Florida population of scrub jays and their cousins in the western United States, which range from West Texas to the Pacific Coast, suggests that the two populations should be separate species. This is probably the case, although the two birds look very much alike. The Florida birds differ only in possessing lighter foreheads and backs than the darker western birds. Both are blue above with gray underparts and white lines above the eyes.

Florida scrub jay

One of the best profiles of the Florida scrub jay was prepared by Alexander Sprunt, Jr., as a contribution to Bent's classic book, *Life Histories of North American Jays, Crows and Titmice*. Sprunt pointed out that this bird is restricted to Florida's "scrub" habitat along the east and west coasts. He described that habitat as follows: "The characteristic plants of the scrub are the sand pine and shrubby oaks of several species. These oaks, with saw palmetto and rosemary, form dense and almost impenetrable thickets."

Good examples of Canaveral National Seashore's scrub habitat occur immediately behind the primary dunes, especially along the approach roads to Apollo Beach on the north end and Playalinda Beach, to the south.

The Park Environment

Canaveral National Seashore, administered by the National Park Service, encompassses 57,627 acres (23,321 ha) of relatively stable barrier beaches and a sheltered and productive lagoon. The park service claims that the national seashore contains "the major remaining unaltered barrier beach along Florida's Atlantic coast" and is "one of the very last sections of undeveloped beachfront in Florida." The beaches are relatively steep and possess an extraordinary high berm. The barrier dunes are 40 to 65 feet (12-20 m) wide and average about 12 feet (4 m) in height. Mosquito Lagoon averages only three feet (1 m) in depth and experiences daily fluctuations of only six to eight inches (15-20 cm).

It is almost impossible to separate park service lands from those of Merritt Island National Wildlife Refuge, an area almost three times the size of the national seashore and administered by the U.S. Fish and Wildlife Service. And to make matters even more complicated, Kennedy Space Center, which is administered by the National Aeronautics and Space Administration (NASA), owns the largest acreage (180,000 acres, or 72,845 ha) that is located south of the park and refuge. What's more, NASA retains "principal authority" over all the federal lands with the right to restrict all entry in pursuit of the U.S. space program. So a visitor to the national seashore, particularly the southern unit, may find it closed during the preparation and launching of a spacecraft.

The national seashore and the refuge maintain close relations because of their combined responsibilities for managing wildlife and recreational activities. These two Department of the Interior agencies share the same information brochure as well as a checklist of the birds. This is most practical, although well-conditioned park and refuge visitors may need some reorientation.

Access to the national seashore and the entire outer beach that lies south of the principal NASA lands is possible only via Highway 402 from Titusville and Highway 44 from New Smyrna Beach. The seashore roadways are open only for 6 miles on the south and 6 miles (10 km) on the north end. The approximately 12 miles (19 km) between the two road terminals is accessible only by hiking or riding horseback along the beach. However, that portion of the seashore is one of the wildest sections of the Florida coastline. In fact, the area was studied for possible inclusion in the National Wilderness System in 1979 but was not proposed because of limited overall size.

Highway 402, the southern entrance, is the most popular route for wildlife enthusiasts for three very good reasons. The route passes through the heart of Merritt Island National Wildlife Refuge and allows for a visit to the refuge's visitor information center; open ponds adjacent to the roadway provide excellent viewing of waterfowl during winter; and Black Point Wildlife Drive, which is a self-guiding auto tour route, and the 5-mile (8 km) Cruickshank (walking) Trail lead off of Highway 402.

The Merritt Island Visitor Information Center contains several exhibits of the area's bird life and an outdoor boardwalk. It also houses a small sales outlet for bird books, and the checklist is available for the asking. Interpretive talks and environmental education programs are undertaken by both agencies.

There are no campgrounds or accommodations within the national seashore or refuge, but both are readily available nearby in the local communities.

Additional information can be obtained from the Superintendent, Canaveral National Seashore, P.O. Box 2583, Titusville, FL 32780; (407) 267-1110.

Bird Life

From November to March, up to 200,000 waterfowl gather in the wetlands of the national refuge and seashore. Hunting is allowed from about Thanksgiving to mid-January. Especially during the hunting season, waterfowl gather to feed in the protected impoundments along the highway where they are easily observed. Thousands of ducks are usually present. Dabbling ducks—especially the American wigeon, ring-necked duck, northern shoveler, mottled duck, and green-winged and blue-winged teal—are most numerous. The diving ducks—especially the lesser scaup, bufflehead, and hooded merganser—are usually present in smaller numbers.

The most abundant of the wintering waterfowl is the **American wigeon**, a middle-sized duck with a large, rectangular white patch on the upper wing of the drake that is visible in flight. It is less obvious on the hen. The drake also has a bright white crown and a bold green line that runs from the eye to the back of the neck. This species nests on the tundra and south through the Dakotas and marshes of the Rocky Mountain states.

The most appealing of the wintering waterfowl is the little **hooded merganser**. The male is most attractive with its fan-shaped white crest bordered in black, black face, golden eyes, and white chest with a vertical black bar. The female is a brownish color. Unlike most other ducks, this species tends to stay in single groups in winter, sometimes with as many as 200 hooded mergansers. It feeds on fish, a wide variety of other creatures, and even plant life, including acorns, that it finds in quiet pools. It is, however, very adept at fishing underwater. It also is able to sink until only its head is above the surface. It remains on its wintering grounds until March, then returns to its nesting grounds.

Other water birds that usually are present in winter include the pied-billed grebe; American white pelican; great blue, little blue, tricolored, and green-backed herons; great, snowy, and cattle egrets; wood stork; glossy ibis; common moorhen; and American coot.

One January morning of observation along the Playalinda Beach roadway produced 22 species of land birds and an assortment of waders and seabirds. Most numerous were American robins, winter visitors that were feeding on the abundant berries of rosemary and other shrubs. Boat-tailed grackles were also common, as were gray catbirds, whose nasal squeaks arose from almost every thicket. A few house wrens were detected within the thickets as well. And I was surprised by the abundant songs of Carolina wrens. Blue-gray gnatcatchers, numerous yellow-rumped and a few palm warblers, an eastern phoebe, and northern mockingbirds were also present. The weedy patches produced the melodic songs of common yellowthroats and loud chips of swamp sparrows. A pair of red-bellied woodpeckers flew across the horizon, heading for a line of low trees. And at one time the sky was filled with more than a hundred tree swallows. I almost stepped on a pair of common ground-doves behind the ranger station.

Mosquito Lagoon, the open shallow water west of the scrub habitat, produced a very different group of birds. Most of these were waders and seabirds. Gulls and terns were most obvious. Flying ring-billed gulls were common, but there also were a few laughing gulls and an equal number of Forster's, royal, and Caspian terns. One reddish-billed Caspian tern was carrying a small fish that it obviously had caught somewhere, but the reason for carrying it around like some kind of trophy was anyone's guess. It was the wrong time of the year for feeding young, and I wondered how long it would take before some predatory gulls would discover this catch and attempt to take it away. Maybe the tern was simply taunting the abundant gulls.

Brown pelicans were fairly common within the lagoon, mostly flying back and forth between the lagoon and the gulf, but I counted eight or nine lone individuals sitting here and there on the water. Three white pelicans were sitting together on the far edge of the lagoon. And perched on an open shrub along the near edge of the lagoon was a single anhinga. I wondered why this bird was not with those farther south at Everglades National Park, where there is a trail named for it.

While I was scoping the far edge of the lagoon, I found a **bald eagle**, a fully white-headed adult, sitting on top of a tall snag. I watched it only briefly before it took flight, flapping very low over the water and disappearing from view. I later visited with John Stiner, resource management specialist at Canaveral National Seashore, about this endangered species. John told me that he was involved with a long-term bald eagle monitoring program, and that at least one pair nests annually within the park. A few other pairs nest within the adjacent refuge.

Wading birds were in the majority around Mosquito Lagoon. Great and snowy egrets and little blue, tricolored, great blue, and green-backed herons were all present in numbers. And beyond the lagoon was a flock of white ibis in flight; their black-and-white wing patterns were obvious even from a distance.

My wife and I walked the outer beach for about a mile. Her attention was focused downward to examine the abundant seashells, while mine was out to sea and along the surf. Shorebirds were few and far between. I recorded only a few ruddy turnstones and a couple of sanderlings. But out to sea about one-quarter to one-half mile, along the edge of the deeper water, was considerable seabird activity. Gulls and terns were most numerous. I identified many ring-billed and laughing gulls, numerous royal and Caspian terns, lone herring and great black-backed gulls, a common tern, and at least six **northern gannets**.

I watched the gannets for some time as they were feeding, sometimes coming as close as a few hundred yards off the beach. Five of the six were immature birds, which was obvious from their overall black brown plumage. The adult bird was bright white with coal black wing tips. Their body shapes appeared tapered on each end, like rolled tortillas. I was fascinated by their headlong dives into the sea while fishing, especially by the height of their dives, which would begin 60 or 80 feet (18-24 m) above the water's surface. Their plunges created high splashes that were easily visible from a quarter mile. They would totally disappear for 10 to 20 seconds before emerging from the sea. I never did see any sign of a successful catch, although I recalled that this seabird usually swallows its prey before surfacing. Alexander Wetmore claimed that a gannet may descend more than 50 feet (15 m) below the surface in its attempt to capture its prey.

Northern gannets are winter visitors only to this portion of the Atlantic Coast and nest far to the north on rocky islands of Newfoundland and Quebec (see chapter 11 on Forillon for additional information). Canaveral provides an excellent location to find this species and many more of Florida's wintertime visitors.

Canaveral once was a place to find the unique race of seaside sparrow known as the "dusky" seaside sparrow. But this little sparrow disappeared from Merritt Island during the 1960s. According to Allan Cruickshank (1980), its extirpation was caused by excessive impoundments of the natural marshes. An expanded explanation of the bird's demise is included in the *Black Point Wildlife Drive* brochure. The U.S. Fish and Wildlife Service wrote,

> The dusky's demise began in the 1940's when man began spraying the marshes with DDT for mosquito control. The pesticide entered the bird's food chain and the dusky population plummeted from 2,000 to 600 breeding pairs. From the mid-1950's to 1963, dikes were constructed to impound the

marsh. The ground-feeding dusky could not tolerate prolonged periods of flooding, and their population dwindled to
70 pairs. In 1963, the refuge began managing a small portion
of NASA's lands, including the joint management of the
marshes with the mosquito control district. During this era,
America was caught up in a "race for space" and any movement to curtail mosquito control was met with resistance.
Despite support of the local mosquito control director to do
something for the dusky, little was accomplished by the refuge
and the downward spiral continued.

Annual Christmas Bird Counts have been undertaken at Merritt
Island Refuge for many years and normally account for approximately 52,500 individuals of about 170 species. In 1990, the dozen most
numerous species (in descending order of abundance) were the tree
swallow, yellow-rumped warbler, American coot, American robin,
American wigeon, fish crow, northern pintail, white ibis and blue-
winged teal (same number), double-crested cormorant, boat-tailed
grackle, European starling, and western sandpiper.

In summary, the Merritt Island bird checklist contains 314
species, of which 84 are known to nest in the refuge and park.
Thirty-four of the 84 are water birds, 7 are hawks and owls, and 3
are warblers. Seven species have been recorded only in winter: the
red-throated loon, northern gannet, Canada goose, brant, surf and
white-winged scoters, and black-legged kittiwake.

Birds of Special Interest

Northern gannet. This visitor from the north is present only in
winter, and small numbers can often be found well offshore. Its
large size, black-and-white wing pattern, and habit of diving for
prey help to identify this seabird.

American wigeon. One of the most common of the wintering
waterfowl, it frequents the roadside ponds. The drake's white crown
and green bar through the eye are the most obvious identifying
characteristics.

Hooded merganser. This little diving duck seldom joins the flocks of waterfowl, preferring its own kind. The drake possesses a showy white crest bordered with black and a black face with golden eyes.

Bald eagle. It is most likely to be seen along the western edge of Mosquito Lagoon or soaring overhead from the southern portion of Highway 3.

Florida scrub jay. Watch for this noncrested jay in the scrub habitats along the entrance roads. It may even perch on utility poles and wires.

30

Gulf Islands National Seashore, Florida and Mississippi

Brown thrashers will forever more remind me of my springtime visit to Gulf Islands National Seashore. Although this bird is fairly common in gardens and fields throughout the East, I had never before seen the numbers that were present at Davis Bayou Campground. The birds literally were everywhere. On one brief stroll around the campground, I counted 24 individuals, from the very treetops to almost every shady patch along the edge.

The brown thrasher more properly should be called "rufous" thrasher. In full sunlight, it can be a gorgeous, bright rufous color. Its breast has heavy streaks of black against an almost pure white background. Its horn-colored bill is typical of the thrasher family's bills and is reasonably stout and long, like that of its cousin, the northern mockingbird. Also like the mockingbird, it possesses long legs, which it can use for running as well as hopping, scratching, and other useful functions. But its most outstanding characteristic is its singing ability.

I had long thought the mockingbird was the supreme songster in the bird world. Mockers can imitate most any bird, not to mention house cats and a lot of other creatures. But brown thrasher songs possess a deeper and richer quality, and they can be just as loud and obnoxious. At Davis Bayou Campground, thrasher songs were far and away the most obvious sound of the day.

The flutelike songs of wood thrushes, especially at dawn and dusk, would undoubtedly win many votes as the favorite songs at Davis Bayou. (See chapter 16 on Mammoth Cave for a further

Brown thrasher

description of those songs.) But there were only a few wood thrush-es that morning, and their songs did not continue all through the day as did the brown thrasher chorus. The loud squawks of blue jays were commonplace but lacked the finesse of the brown thrash-ers' vocalizations. The bright red northern cardinals were loud enough, but their songs were too repetitious. Tufted titmice and Carolina chickadees sang their songs from the higher foliage. And overhead, the loud "auk" or "auk auk" of fish crows was occasional-ly heard. But all in all, brown thrashers came away as the clear win-ners among the Davis Bayou songsters.

My April visit to the upper Gulf Coast was timed to coincide with one of the outstanding "fallouts" of the spring migration that often occur there. A migrant fallout requires a weather front from the north strong enough to stall further progress of the northbound migrants. But the days were sunny and bright, and the winds, when they blew at all, were from the south or southeast. In a sense, the most comfortable weather is least likely to provide conditions favorable for a fallout. Stormy weather is most likely to produce the necessary conditions.

The Park Environment

The northern coast of the Gulf of Mexico extends from the Mississippi River eastward to Florida's Suwanee River, a distance of about 400 miles (644 km). Gulf Islands National Seashore, established in 1971, is the only national park in that entire area. It is divided into two separate mainland units and six barrier islands, all within the states of Mississippi and Florida. The combined 140,000 acres (56,000 ha) represent the Gulf Coast in microcosm.

One of the park's most obvious features is its wide, gently sloping white sand beaches. The white quartz sand originates in the southern Appalachians, is carried to the gulf by numerous rivers, and arrives with a westerly current. Inland is an equally gentle landscape. The low, rolling hills contain many drainages with numerous streams and ponds. The plant life that covers this landscape is all secondary vegetation. The virgin forests were logged long ago, and a variety of pines and hardwoods cover the ancient scars. Only the islands possess any resemblance to undisturbed conditions. Two of the islands, Mississippi's Horn and Petit Bois, both within the national seashore, were given official wilderness designation in 1978.

The principal habitats on the islands—dune strand, swales, forest-marsh, and salt marsh—are described in an excellent NPS brochure, *Gulf Islands Wildflowers and Barrier Island Plants*. The dunes run parallel to the coastline, sometimes reaching 30 feet (9 m) in height, and the dominant dune plants are sea oats and sea rocket. Swales occur behind many of the dunes and usually possess freshwater wetlands. Florida rosemary, yaupon holly, and woody goldenrod are common in the dry dune habitat.

Inland from the dunes are the taller pines and oaks, shrubs, and other woody plants; sawgrass and cattails can be abundant in wetter areas. Along the bay side is a salt-tolerant wetland that is dominated by black rush and cordgrass.

Most of these habitats also occur on the mainland, where another, somewhat drier, woodland exists. These drier sites are usually dominated by a number of hardwoods interspersed with pines. And isolated stands of southern magnolia, which produce huge, showy blooms in early April, occur close to the open gulf.

Florida's Gulf Islands National Seashore is reached from either Highway 87 at Navarre or Highway 98 from Pensacola. Both routes cross Santa Rosa Sound by high bridges to Santa Rosa Island. Highway 399 runs the length of the island and provides easy access to the outer beaches. Park headquarters and the adjacent Naval Live

Oaks Area are on the mainland in east Gulf Breeze. Nature trails within the Naval Live Oaks Area and at park headquarters are well worth the time and effort.

Mississippi's Gulf Islands National Seashore has only one mainland site, the Davis Bayou Area at Ocean Springs. There one can find a visitor center, nature trails, and the Davis Bayou Campground. Each visitor center provides orientation programs and exhibits as well as a publication sales desk that offers books and videos on birds. A comprehensive bird checklist is also available for the asking.

Interpretive programs are offered in each unit during all seasons of the year. Talks and walks, including bird walks, are scheduled on a regular basis. And a Junior Ranger program for kids 12 years old and under is also available at both units.

Camping is offered in both units, although lodging and supplies must be acquired outside the park within the various communities.

Additional information can be obtained from the Superintendent, Gulf Islands National Seashore, 1801 Gulf Breeze Parkway, Gulf Breeze, FL 32561; (904) 934-2600.

Bird Life

The best bird-viewing area in Florida's Gulf Islands park is at the Fort Pickens area of Santa Rosa Island. Historic Fort Pickens commands the far western end of the island, just beyond a marshy area that separates the fort from the area's principal campground. A bike trail runs between the fort and Langdon Picnic Area. Bob Duncan, in his book, *The Birds of Escambia, Santa Rosa and Okaloosa Counties, Florida*, described this trail as one of the best wintertime birding areas in the park and also one of the "best migrant traps" on the Gulf Coast in both spring and fall. I spent one early winter morning birding the marsh.

Dawn at Fort Pickens marsh was full of bird song. Even in winter, when night temperatures often drop into the 40s, the bird chorus was exciting. Red-winged blackbird song came from all parts of the marsh; their obvious liquid gurgle seemed to start the morning. Marsh wrens were in full song, too, though they stayed deep in the cattails as if they were not quite ready to emerge from their sleeping places for the day. Swamp sparrows were active, but only their loud chips were evident. And finally, close to the trail, the loud "witchity, witchity, witchity" song of a common yellowthroat joined the chorus.

Several northern mockingbirds began their varied songs. At least seven of these aggressive birds were evident atop woody plants along the marshy edge. One suddenly darted after an eastern phoebe that had been perched on the railing of the little wooden bridge that crosses one arm of the marsh. The phoebe easily escaped, and the mocker alighted on the railing to sing. Apparently, the railing was a favorite perch that had been appropriated at least briefly by the wintertime visitor from the north. The mocker did not stay long before it charged one of the many yellow-rumped warblers that had come too close. As I looked around to assess the bird life, it was evident that yellow-rumps dominated the morning. An estimate of 45 to 50 individuals would not have been too high a count.

The **yellow-rumped warbler** is one of the few warblers that overwinters in the United States in large numbers. Its breeding range is far north of the Gulf Coast, within the spruce-fir forests of Canada and isolated spruce-fir zones in the United States, such as the Appalachian highlands. The yellow-rump is an active little bird, catching insects over the marsh as well as feeding on whatever berries are available. It is easily identified by its white throat and four yellow markings; on the crown, sides, and rump.

Farther away, along the edge of the marsh, where the tall, green slash pines form a backdrop to the wetlands and stand between the marsh and the pure white dunes beyond, were several additional birds. American robins were the most obvious; two or three dozen individuals were chipping loudly in the treetops or flying to the water's edge to drink. And then the full, deep-throated song of a Carolina wren erupted from the pines; I detected a second songster farther away. Gray catbirds were squawking along the edge of the woods, as were a number of blue jays. Several rufous-sided towhees were calling rather halfheartedly, while a couple of others were in full song. I could not help but wonder which birds were singing, since both resident birds and northern migrants were present. Bob Duncan had pointed out that the "red-eyed towhee is a migrant; our local resident birds have straw-colored eyes."

There were very few water birds about the marsh that morning. I found a lone pied-billed grebe on the open water, and there were five great blue herons perched along the marsh's edge. That was it, except for the numerous gulls, terns, brown pelicans, and double-crested cormorants that were flying back and forth over the sound to the north. I had expected to hear some rails, which spend their winters in this marsh, but to no avail. Duncan told me that at least three species winter at Fort Pickens Marsh: clapper and Virginia rails and sora.

I was attracted away from the marsh by a series of grunting noises that seemed to be coming from the slash pines. The sound reminded me at first of the barklike song of the greater roadrunner in the Southwest, but it was a little higher pitched and more drawn out. Then from across the marsh flew a great blue heron, its bill full of sticks. It flew directly into the pine tops, where I had been searching for the creature that was making the strange sounds. It was then that I located the heron's mate, the originator of the grunts. Sure enough, the two huge herons were nest building in the pine. They had a long way to go, in both construction and in time, before their youngsters would be fledged from that pile of sticks.

On the mainland, the park headquarters provides another good birding area. The picnic area at the end of the parking lot can contain a good variety of birds. The tall longleaf pines often have **brown-headed nuthatches.** These little tree huggers walk up and down the trunks, sometimes upside down on branches, searching for insects. A wintertime visit there may also produce sightings of the red-bellied and downy woodpeckers; yellow-bellied sapsucker; northern flicker; eastern phoebe; blue jay; fish crow; American robin; house wren; tufted titmouse; Carolina chickadee; ruby-crowned kinglet; pine warbler; northern cardinal; rufous-sided towhee; chipping, song, swamp, and white-throated sparrows; and American goldfinch.

Across the highway in the Naval Oaks section is a network of trails that circles a pretty little freshwater pond with an active beaver population. I added red-tailed hawk, pileated woodpecker, golden-crowned kinglet, orange-crowned warbler, and field sparrow to my mainland list of birds there. But most memorable were the thousands of American robins within the forest and along the edge of the pond. There were so many robins bathing on that January morning that the entire area was filled with splashing noises.

The **American robin** is one of America's most loved songbirds. Its red breast and cheery song are well known. Although it is rare in summer along the Gulf Coast, it is usually abundant during wintertime, when birds from the northern forests are present. This is when these robins occur in huge flocks, and they feed on the usually abundant berries from the native and introduced shrubs and trees.

Davis Bayou is the best bird-finding area on the mainland within Mississippi's Gulf Islands National Seashore. Local bird expert Judy Toups, author of the very informative *Birds and Birding on the Mississippi Coast*, told me that the best places to visit include the campground edges, the Fence Trail just outside the campground entrance on Hanley Road, the adjacent lawns and forest edges, the boat dock area, and the Nature's Way Nature Trail. A good variety of birds can also be seen over the marsh from the end of the boardwalk behind the visitor center.

I found 50 species one April morning in the above area. Besides those birds seen in the campground, at the boat dock, I recorded several common loons; little blue, tricolored, and green-backed herons; white pelican; double-crested cormorant; many laughing gulls and one immature ring-billed gull; a few least, Forster's, and royal terns; mottled duck; several very noisy clapper rails; and a lone belted kingfisher.

The wooded edges echoed with the songs of **northern parulas**. At one point I could hear five birds singing in the Spanish moss-draped live oaks. Although most of these birds were probably migrants, they also nest in that habitat. This short-tailed warbler has a yellow breast and white belly. The male possesses a black and reddish band across the chest, giving it a unique marking. The upperparts are blue-gray with a yellowish-green back, obvious white eye ring broken by a black stripe that runs from the bill through the eye, and two white wing bars. It is a very colorful little warbler.

The song of the northern parula is also special. It is a rising buzzy trill that usually ends with an abrupt and distinct "hic." It has been written as "pree-e-e-e-e-e, yip." And unlike most warblers, the parula will sing all year long, even on sunny days during the winter months.

The Fence Trail produced the largest number of migrants, including the yellow-billed cuckoo; great crested flycatcher; eastern kingbird; hermit thrush; blue-gray gnatcatcher; red-eyed and solitary vireos; yellow-rumped, worm-eating, prothonotary, and hooded warblers; ovenbird; summer tanager; blue grosbeak; and indigo bunting.

Park Service Biologist Ted Simons has been studying migrant birds at Gulf Islands for several years and nets spring arrivals annually on Horn and East Ship islands. These barrier islands lie 8 to 16 miles (13-26 km) off the mainland and are the first land that many trans-gulf migrants find. Therefore, these sites provide important opportunities to learn more about patterns of migration, habitat preferences, and population trends of songbirds when they first arrive from their 20-hour or longer flights across the gulf from Mexico's Yucatan Peninsula or from farther south in Central America or South America. Simons and his helpers net and band as many as 3,000 birds of 80 or more species during a six-week period each year.

Until about 1945, when ornithologists proved the theory of cross-gulf migration by literally watching migrants through a telescope at night against the light of the moon, most people assumed that northbound migrants simply followed the coastline. Later research with radar observations suggested that when a strong front is positioned over the northern Gulf Coast, as many as 80,000 northbound migrants reached the Louisiana coast per mile per day. Southerly winds are likely to carry them many miles inland. But the greatest fallout occurs during periods of strong northerly winds, when the migrants are forced down to rest and restock their energy supplies before continuing northward.

Simons' studies indicate that most trans-gulf migration occurs from mid-April through early May, although some migrants may appear as early as mid-March; the high point is April 18 to 28. The length of their stay varies from a day to more than a week, depending on the local weather and their condition. Spring arrivals are often emaciated from their long journey and require rest and a good food supply before they can continue. The strategic location of Gulf Islands National Seashore, where natural habitats and an adequate food supply are available, is becoming increasingly important. The loss of habitats to development and changing land use patterns along the entire northern Gulf Coast has multiplied the value of the protected landscapes of the national seashore.

Winter birds along the Gulf Coast have been monitored for several years through various Christmas Bird Counts. Two counts include national seashore areas. The Pensacola, Florida, counts usually record approximately 25,000 individuals of about 115 species; the South Hancock County, Mississippi, counts usually record approximately 28,000 individuals of about 150 species. In 1990, the dozen most abundant species in Florida (in descending order of abundance) were the fish crow, American robin, yellow-rumped warbler, tree swallow, mourning dove, laughing gull, European starling, double-crested cormorant, ring-billed gull, white-throated sparrow, Bonaparte's gull, and rock dove. The dozen most abundant Mississippi birds were the lesser scaup, tree swallow, yellow-rumped warbler, American robin, American coot, ring-necked duck, dunlin, greater scaup, brown-headed cowbird, killdeer, mallard, and savannah sparrow.

In summary, the comprehensive bird checklist contains 304 species, of which approximately 100 nest; 22 of those are water birds, 7 are hawks and owls, and 10 are warblers. Seven species are winter visitors only: black, surf, and white-winged scoters; glaucous gull; white-winged dove; golden-crowned kinglet; and fox sparrow.

Birds of Special Interest

Bald eagle. Reintroduction efforts on Horn Island resulted in the release of more than 60 birds into the wild. Some of these birds have returned to nest. Watch for the brilliant white head and tail of this large raptor.

Clapper rail. Its "kuk kuk" calls are commonplace within the salt marshes. But it is not easy to see. Watch for it during very early mornings and at dusk when it feeds along the edges of the marsh.

Brown-headed nuthatch. This little bird is threatened within much of its range, but it is fairly common among the pine stands at Gulf Islands National Seashore.

American robin. It can be abundant in winter. Its reddish breast, cheery songs, and alert posture help to identify this well-known species.

Brown thrasher. It is most common in spring, but this long-tailed, rufous songster can usually be found throughout the year.

Northern parula. This is the little warbler with a yellow breast that frequents the moss-draped woodlands. Its song is a rising buzz that ends with a sharp "hic."

Yellow-rumped warbler. One of the park's most common winter residents, it has four yellow markings, on its crown, both sides, and rump.

31

Everglades and Biscayne National Parks and Big Cypress National Reserve, Florida

The first rays of dawn were just beginning to lighten the scene as I started down the Anhinga Trail; I was the first human to arrive that January day. By midmorning the trail would be crowded, but now I was alone with hundreds of birds, the most spectacular and abundant of which was the anhinga. The 50 or so perched on the willows and cocoplums seemed like sentinels guarding an ancient moat. No wonder the boardwalk built over the Everglades is named Anhinga Trail. There is no better place in all the national parks to find and watch this unusual bird.

Though I could not yet catch sight of them, many birds were already greeting the morning with a variety of songs, calls, and squawks. A northern cardinal was singing off to the right, and beyond it a Carolina wren was in full song. A white-eyed vireo joined the chorus nearby. And the "witchity witchity" songs of common yellowthroats exploded along the trail side. American crows were off and running as well, maybe chasing a barred owl before it settled in for the day.

The water's edge was a living mass of little fishes, an important food base for many of the larger creatures. Strange, sucking noises came from the pond's surface, which I attributed to a large fish that I could only partly see. Bill Loftus, park service biologist and ichthyologist, later told me that the native gar was responsible; it is an air breather and must surface and suck in its oxygen. Most of the other fish there, such as the largemouth bass and sunfish, obtain their oxygen from the water.

A dozen or so yellow-crowned night-herons sat in the open, preening themselves after a successful night of feeding. Soon after sunup these nocturnal birds move into the darker shrubbery for the daylight hours of sleep.

Great blue herons were already fishing among the cattails along the pond's edge. The Everglades is famous for its all-white version of the great blue heron that is locally called the "great white heron." For many years it was thought to be a separate species but is now regarded only as a white morph. Its breeding range does not extend north of southern Florida, although it often wanders northward. This bird and the smaller, all-white egrets, the snowy and great egrets, were instrumental in the initial development of Everglades National Park.

Great numbers of these beautiful birds were being killed for the feather industry during the late 1800s. The long, plumelike feathers of the breeding birds were prized as decorations for ladies' hats, and south Florida and the Keys were principal collecting sites. The National Audubon Society was first organized to stop the wanton destruction of these plumed waders, and Congress eventually passed protective legislation.

Several little blue herons were present around the pond. And two tricolored herons were perched on the boardwalk railing when I first arrived. Almost immediately they flew off across the pond and disappeared into the swamp. But the most numerous wading birds that morning were the little green-backed herons. A very colorful bird, adult green-backs possess a chestnut-colored neck and sides. Most of these herons sat crouched along the water's edge, poised to strike a fish, frog, or other prey.

It was light enough now to see the subtler colors of the anhingas; the mature males are all black, and the females and immatures possess brown chests and necks. During the breeding season, the breast and neck of the adult male has a beautiful, velvet green sheen. Its lores, the soft parts surrounding the eyes, turn bright turquoise. Each adult possesses a silvery-white cape on its upper back and shoulders.

Another characteristic that sets the anhinga apart from its neighbors is its long, very sharp beak, which the bird uses to spear its prey. The anhinga fishes underwater, where it swims down a fish and impales it. Then it surfaces and positions the prey so that it

Anhinga

slides headfirst down the bird's long, skinny neck. The bird may then sit still for an hour or more, wings spread, to dry its plumage.

Watching an anhinga, it is difficult not to think of its other names, "water turkey" and "snake bird." It is nicknamed water turkey because of its dark, shiny plumage, long neck, and tail with a buff tip, like a turkey. The name snake bird comes from its ability to swim underwater with only its long neck and beak above the surface as well as its amazing ability to strike its prey like a serpent.

The other main character along the Anhinga Trail is the alligator. A dozen or more can always be seen there, usually sprawled on the bank or swimming slowly from one side of the pond to the other. If these ancient reptiles did not occasionally blink an eye, they would seem more like Hollywood props. But they are the real thing.

Suddenly, from the row of cypress trees beyond the pond came a red-shouldered hawk, flying directly toward me. It uttered a loud, high-pitched "kee-ah" call as it crossed the pond and disappeared to the south. But I was able to see its reddish, barred breast and barred tail very well from my vantage point. For some inexplicable reason, the hawk seemed to trigger other aerial activity, and the sky was soon filled with birds in flight. At least 250 swallows appeared next from the north; they were mostly tree swallows, but there were a few northern rough-wings, as well. A dozen or so boat-tailed grackles, accompanied by a few common grackles and red-winged blackbirds, came next. And a flock of about 30 American goldfinches flew over, en route no doubt to some choice field of seed plants. And then the black and turkey vultures that had been perched on the royal palms near the visitor center began to soar. And last, a solitary osprey joined in and began to circle the pond in search of breakfast.

The strange "erk erk erk erk" calls of the anhingas brought my attention back to the pond. The day was under way, and people were already beginning to admire and photograph the array of wildlife along the Anhinga Trail.

The Park Environment
The Everglades is undoubtedly the finest of the national parks for wading birds. But the Everglades is more than the southern tip of the

Florida peninsula that has been designated as a national park. Everglades National Park, about 1.5 million acres (607,042 ha), is but one piece of a much larger ecosystem, the parts of which are closely interrelated so that the impairment of one part can threaten the others. That natural system is dependent on the fresh water, derived solely from the annual rainfall of approximately 60 inches (152 cm), that flows through it north to south. The resultant runoff has been described as a 50-mile-wide (80-km) river but one so shallow that, even during the wettest year, one can wade the entire width.

It is easier to understand this amazing ecosystem when the state's geography is understood. Simply put, the entire southern peninsula is underlain by ancient limestone, which is covered with fine sediments that retard seepage. All the rainfall either gathers in depressions, such as Lake Okeechobee and Anhinga Pond, or runs off into the nearest estuary. The southern half of the state is a little like a huge, shallow spoon, deeper in the center and rimmed on both sides. It is tipped very slightly (only 2 in., or 5 cm, per mile) toward the south, so that all the fresh water flows ever so slowly southward. The flow into the estuaries must be constant, so that the saline waters from the gulf and bays do not encroach farther inland. If that system were damaged, saltwater encroachment could literally destroy the Everglades.

The ecological balance of the Everglades supports myriad wildlife within each of the various habitats created. One of the best brief descriptions of how the natural system works was presented by William B. Robertson, Jr., in "The Everglades," a chapter in the book, *The Bird Watcher's America.*

The key to the Everglades is its annual cycle of flooding and desiccation. Most of the rain falls from May through October. The water spreads across miles of marsh, and food chains of freshwater organisms flourish in the warm shallows. The summer flood poured into brackish coastal bays feeds nutrients into other cycles. As the water recedes with the onset of the dry season, aquatic life is forced into an ever-diminishing volume of water. At various points of optimum food concentration, the summer's production of lesser creatures is translated into an increase of alligators, otters, egrets, ibis,

Anhingas, Limpkins, all the rest. Near the end of the dry season, lightning storms often set fires that sweep over large areas of the marsh. Then come the summer rains and repetition.

The road into the heart of Everglades National Park begins at Homestead. Park headquarters and the park's main visitor center are situated just beyond the entrance. The environmental differences at the boundary are like night and day—from heavily sprayed farmlands to semiwilderness. The park's principal information center, museum, and sales outlet can be found in the visitor center. Available literature includes a good assortment of bird books and a bird checklist.

Additional visitor centers are located at Royal Palm, Flamingo, and Shark Valley; each provides orientation programs and publication sales. Each also is a center for interpretive programs, which include a variety of bird activities. The park also operates a significant environmental education program in which more than 13,000 students participate annually.

A free, up-to-date *Visitor's Guide* to south Florida's national park interpretive programs and other activities is available at all park service facilities. The *Visitor's Guide* also includes a Wildlife Activity Calendar to keep everyone aware of the changing seasons. According to the winter calendar, December is when the bald eagle chicks hatch at Flamingo and ducks increase on Florida Bay. January is when ospreys begin nesting, barred owls are courting in mangroves and hammocks, and black skimmers frequent boat ramps at Flamingo and Everglades City. Reddish egrets and red-shouldered hawks begin nesting in February; swallow-tailed kites return from South America in March; and in April, the wintering birds begin to leave and the mosquito populations begin to increase.

Camping is available at Lone Pine Key and Flamingo. And primitive camping, by permit only, is allowed at various other sites accessible by water. Lodging is available in the park only at Flamingo.

Additional information can be obtained from the Superintendent, Everglades National Park, Box 279, Homestead, FL 33030; (305) 247-6211.

Bird Life

Royal Palms and its Anhinga Trail are located four miles beyond the park entrance. The less popular Gumbo Limbo Trail begins there, too. This trail provides the first good introduction to the tropical hardwood hammock habitat that occurs at scattered sites throughout the park, wherever the land is elevated enough that vegetation can grow without being waterbound. Especially after a visit to Anhinga Trail, the Gumbo Limbo Trail can seem like a tropical jungle. It provides an excellent place to find land birds all year.

Northern songbirds are the key avian attractions on the trail in winter. They can usually be found by tracking down the wheezy calls of blue-gray gnatcatchers. Winter residents are almost always in parties of a few to several dozen individuals, and the most vocal member of these groups usually is the gnatcatcher. A morning walk on the Gumbo Limbo Trail will usually produce a number of warblers. I walked the trail following my dawn visit to the Anhinga Trail.

My first warbler sighting was a black-and-white warbler that was literally creeping around the upper branches of a strangler fig, searching for insects in its special probing manner. Then a loud chip attracted my attention to the lower vegetation where a well-marked black-throated green warbler was gleaning its food from the foliage of a little wild coffee tree. It did not stay still for long but flitted from branch to branch, and then moved off onto a tangle of ferns. A moment later, it was back at another wild coffee. Then I noticed the movement of another bird that was feeding even closer to the ground but slightly behind some ferns and a saw palmetto. It came into view and sat on a bare branch for several seconds. It was a male hooded warbler! A really gorgeous bird, and one that is not often seen in the Everglades in winter.

The loud call of a great crested flycatcher attracted my attention to an adjacent tree. The bird had just captured a large dragonfly, and I watched it gulp down its winged prey. For just a second or two, I wondered if the dragonfly continued to wiggle inside, and for how long? Then, just a couple of feet to the left, were two or three smaller birds. Two turned out to be gnatcatchers, but the third was a solitary vireo. This was a brightly marked, yellowish bird with a bold white eye ring. But like solitary vireos everywhere, it was methodical in its behavior of gleaning the branches and foliage for insects.

I returned to the hooded warbler, which I rediscovered after a few minutes' search, and continued to admire this lovely creature. It is one of the many North American warblers that have declined in recent years, due in part to the massive destruction of rain forest in its normal wintering grounds in the West Indies, Central America, and northern South America. I could not avoid thinking how important the national parks and other protected reserves are for the survival of so many of our land birds. Much more land must be protected from overuse and abuse if we are going to save these important resources.

As I walked along the trail, I detected other birds. Two species of woodpeckers were present, red-bellied and pileated. And bright red northern cardinals were active as well. Then a flock of blue jays put in an appearance, and I noticed their smaller size in comparison with those that occur farther north. Bergman's Rule came to mind, the ecological principle that states that animal body size increases with higher latitudes. The concept is that body size is more important for northern critters than for residents of more tropical climates.

As I walked along the trail I appreciated the variety of vegetation around me. The tallest trees, those that actually rose above the canopy, were the oldest royal palms, a really magnificent native species. Most of the canopy foliage seemed to consist of live oak and gumbo limbo. Everglades' live oaks are the same species that occur throughout the eastern half of the United States. But the gumbo limbo is something really special! This tree is easily identified by its reddish color and smooth, often peeling, bark. This same tree in the West Indies is called the "tourist tree," because, as the locals say, it is red and peeling.

I was near the far bend of the trail when all of a sudden two hawks appeared very low and close to me. I knew immediately that I was seeing a pair of **short-tailed hawks**, which apparently I had frightened off a nearby perch. As they soared over me to gain elevation, I had a wonderful view of these Florida specialties. One was in dark plumage and the other was a very light-colored bird. They were low enough that I could easily see their yellow feet and ceres (soft parts above the bill). Both birds possessed subtly banded tails. The light bird had an immaculate white breast, while the second was all black except for its checkered wing pattern. I watched these two raptors circle higher and higher until they were hidden from view by the surrounding vegetation. This is a relict tropical species in south Florida; it is more numerous in southern Mexico and Central America. The entire U.S. population winters in south Florida, although a few nest as far north as northern Florida.

Walking back to Royal Palm in late morning, I continued to watch for additional bird parties. Gnatcatchers were still doing their thing, and I found more black-and-white warblers, another solitary vireo, and a white-eyed vireo. Carolina wrens sang from the undergrowth at one stop. And at another stop, as I was trying to entice a prairie warbler closer, I noticed a couple of tree snails on the branch of a little tree above my head. In a couple of minutes of searching the ground below the tree, I discovered two empty spiral shells, each about an inch in length. One was quite faded, but the other was fresh and bright. It possessed colorful yellow, red, and black bands, a really beautiful shell. I read later that there are 52 color forms, or morphs, of the species *Liquus fasciatus*, and some of the hammocks possess their own unique forms. I also remembered a story that I heard years ago about how an early shell collector, after gathering all of the shells (both dead and live tree snails) from one hammock, burned the hammock so that no one else could ever collect there. He had increased the value of the collected shells but had destroyed the hammock. What kind of people destroy such a special environment for their personal gain?

A little farther south along the highway is Mahogany Hammock, where one can walk out into the hammock via a short self-guided loop trail. This hammock is more typical of the tropical hardwood hammock habitats that exist in the coastal prairie. It is an excellent place, at least during wintertime, to find another avian specialty of the Everglades, the **white-crowned pigeon**. This species is known only in the Caribbean Basin, including the southern part of Florida. It usually nests and roosts in the mangroves but feeds on figs and other tropical fruits in the hardwood hammocks during the daytime. This large, rather streamlined pigeon is overall slate gray with a snow white cap, red legs, and purplish bill. See chapter 33 on Virgin Islands National Park for additional information on this species. Across the highway from the Mahogany Hammock entrance (to the east) is a scattering of Florida slash pines. Although pine stands are common along the entrance route, the pine area near Mahogany Hammock is special. One of the pines, some distance from the highway, contains the large, bulky nest of a **bald eagle**. And eagles often perch in full view from the highway. Park Biologist Bill Robertson told me that this nest and several earlier ones in this area are "play" nests built by birds that are associated with a nearby eagle roost. There is no evidence that eggs were ever laid in any of these nests.

The bald eagle, America's best-known symbol, declined throughout its range during the 1950s. But since the late 1970s, it has begun to increase in the Everglades. The decline was attributed to habitat destruction as well as pesticides, especially DDT, which causes eggshell thinning. In addition, before the park was established, most of the old pine stands were logged. Only those so remote that logging was not economically feasible went untouched. Since the park was established and DDT was banned, the bald eagle and several other top-level predators have begun to recover.

Logging of the Everglades' pine stands and removal of the old growth timber affected several other birds as well. Most affected were the species at the southern edge of their breeding range, and two of those—the red-cockaded woodpecker and brown-headed nuthatch—disappeared from Everglades National Park altogether. These two species still exist in small numbers in Big Cypress National Park. See the Big Cypress section below. And also see chapter 6 on Cape Breton Highlands for a description of the bald eagle in Canada.

On the park road south to Flamingo from Mahogany Hammock, the scene begins to change from prairie grassland, an environment that is dependent on the annual freshwater flow, to the area most influenced by seawater. The first clue to this change is the presence of mangroves, usually stunted red mangroves, with their bare taproots and bright green leaves. Paurotis Pond, Nine Mile Pond, West Lake, and Mrazek Pond, encountered on the Flamingo Road, are good examples of mangrove-edged ponds.

Mrazek Pond is the most often visited of the four because it borders the main road, and even the most casual visitor is attracted by
the high concentration of wading birds usually found there. During
most of the winter, until the late spring rains commence, the water
depth at Mrazek Pond is usually just right to attract waders.

When I visited this pond with Bill Robertson one morning in
January, it was raining so hard that we had to remain inside the car
and wait for the morning show to commence. Already, 13 **wood
storks** were standing in the center of the pond; they undoubtedly
had been there all night. They seemed frozen in time, and I wondered if they were asleep. As the dawn crept into the pond, it was
evident that they were the pond's sole residents. Robertson pointed
out that only one was an adult, evident from its dark bill, clean
white back, and distinct white plume below the tail. The immature
birds possessed yellowish bills and dirty plumage. Bill guessed that
these youngsters had fledged the previous year outside of the park
and were winter visitors only.

Bill explained that the park's wood stork population has dramatically declined in recent years. South Florida birds have declined
from an estimated high of 20,000 nesting pairs during the 1930s to
about 5,800 by 1974. There is an excellent article in the January
1983 issue of *Audubon* about the plight of this bird, which author
John Ogden, another of the park's knowledgeable biologists, refers
to as "the endangered flinthead." John explains the bird's decline
thus:

> The food supply is not sufficient to support the nesting
> colonies over the long haul. The food supply is being depleted
> by the draining of freshwater wetlands and manipulation of
> water supplies that create the habitat in which the storks feed,
> and in which those outside the mangroves nest. The decrease
> in the numbers of wood storks seems to parallel the rate at
> which the wetlands have been damaged.

We were startled by the sudden arrival of a flock of white ibis.
Forty to 50 birds settled into the pond, and another dozen or so
perched on the surrounding mangroves. Like a chain reaction,
other waders began to arrive, and in the following 20 minutes or so,
in spite of the rain, Mrazek Pond came alive with birds. We

Wood stork

remained inside the car—our viewing blind—and admired their antics. We were equally amazed at their varied feeding behaviors. Each species seemed to utilize a slightly different technique.

The wood storks are touch feeders and probe underwater for their food. Their delicate mouthparts detect fish and other prey, which they grab without ever seeing into the water. The herons and egrets were not as active as the touch feeders. They must first see their prey, and with the rain roiling the water, it was difficult for them to feed. The little snowy egret sometimes used a slightly different technique of flying low over the water with its yellow feet dangling, like a lure, and grabbing whatever it came upon.

By the time we left Mrazek Pond there were more than 800 waders of 8 species in the pond, an area of about one acre: wood storks; white ibis; great blue, little blue, tricolored, and green-backed herons; and great and snowy egrets. In addition, there were several double-crested cormorants, a couple of belted kingfishers, and a lone laughing gull. The next day when I drove by, there were almost as many bird photographers as birds at the pond.

Although Mrazek Pond consistently provides the best opportunity in the park for close-up observation and photography of most of the waders, it somehow lacks the naturalness of Eco Pond at Flamingo, despite the fact that Eco Pond is artificial and requires an occasional cleaning by the park service to keep it from being totally overgrown by cattails. Flamingo, 38 miles (61 km) south of park headquarters, is the final destination for most park visitors, since the highway ends there. The area provides at least three good birding sites: Eco Pond, Florida Bay, and the Coastal Prairie Trail.

The dawn bird chorus at Eco Pond is quite different from that at Mrazek Pond. One reason is the abundance of red-winged blackbirds that roost at Eco Pond. But it is more than that. Eco Pond is the only freshwater pond along the southern coast, and so it attracts a wide variety of birds. Most notable are the rails. The loudest of these are the king rails. There were at least three individuals calling that early morning in January. A few Virginia rails and a lone sora were heard as well.

However, common moorhens were probably the loudest and most abrasive; they sound a little like someone trying, very loudly, to clear his throat. Pied-billed grebes joined the chorus as well, with their assortment of strange, slurred whistles. But the most obvious wading bird present at dawn was the green-backed heron, which seemed continuously busy scolding its neighbors.

As daylight began, I could see several additional birds perched in the willows around the pond. There were a dozen or so anhingas and eight black-crowned night-herons. I wondered why this species was here instead of the yellow-crowned species that was at Anhinga Pond.

A large bird suddenly approached from the left and flew directly across the pond and on to the east. It was evident even without the aid of binoculars that it was an adult bald eagle. There, too, were the ospreys; one had already caught a surprisingly large fish, which it was carrying to a favorite perch nearby.

There was lots of activity among the cattails. Marsh wrens and common yellowthroats were most obvious, and I found a lone prairie warbler there as well. At the far bend of the pond was a purple gallinule, an incredibly beautiful bird even in the subdued morning light. Then a pair of least bitterns emerged from the cattails, one chasing the other for only a few seconds before they plopped back into the marsh.

More wading birds were moving now, crossing over the pond en route to their feeding grounds. A few snowy and great egrets, and a small flock of white ibis settled on the willows. And there also was a lone **cattle egret**. I realized it was the first cattle egret I had seen in the park, in spite of its common occurrence along the highways in central and northern Florida. When I later asked Bill Robertson about this, he told me that most of the Everglades population of cattle egrets migrates south into the Yucatán and Central America each winter. Why this population has chosen to do this is anyone's guess, but I found it strange that the Everglades' population developed such a pattern while those in northern Florida are full-time residents.

Cattle egret invasion of the United States is one of the most interesting recent stories in the bird world. This Old World species was first reported in South America during the 1930s. It took another 18 years before it was discovered in Florida. And today it is common throughout the southeastern United States and seems to be progressing northward each year. Roger Tory Peterson and James Fisher wrote a delightful chapter, "World Invader—The Cattle Egret," about this invader of Florida in their 1955 book, *Wild America*. The book should be in every nature lover's library.

Two large, pinkish birds suddenly appeared overhead flying fairly low across the pond. These were **roseate spoonbills,** one of the park's most beautiful and charismatic waders. This species can only be confused with flamingos, which generally occur only in Florida Bay. The flamingo possesses an all-pink neck and breast, while the spoonbill has a white neck and breast. And their heads are altogether different. A flamingo has a huge beak that is curved down at the front. This feature is evident from a considerable distance. A roseate spoonbill possesses a rather flat, spatulate bill that, at least in flight, is quite apparent. Spoonbills nest in Florida Bay, and most move north for the summer months. At least a few individuals can usually be found year-round at Flamingo.

Florida Bay provides yet another exciting and completely different bird habitat, but it is not so easily observed as at Eco Pond. However, the various mud flats, especially at low tide, provide the best bet for wintering shorebirds. There are two good viewing sites: the porch of the Flamingo Visitor Center/Coffee Shop and the observation platform at the end of Snake Bight Trail.

Scoping the muddy flats from the visitor center in winter can produce an incredible array of water birds. Most obvious are the larger species: white and brown pelicans, double-crested cormorants, and all of the waders. A bald eagle is often perched on the sign near the little mangrove-clad islands offshore. Middle-sized birds usually include the gulls (ring-billed and laughing and the larger herring gull), terns (Forster's and the larger royal and Caspian), black skimmers, belted kingfishers, and some of the larger shorebirds such as black-bellied plovers, greater yellowlegs, and marbled godwits. The smaller shorebirds require a spotting scope for positive identification and can include almost any of the two dozen or so species that occur along the East Coast in winter; dunlins and least and western sandpipers are usually the most numerous.

Farther up the bay at Snake Bight is an even better place for observing shorebirds. It can be reached by a 1.8-mile (2.9-km) trail through the mangroves. The trail follows the remains of dredged materials from a canal that was dug prior to park establishment. Snake Bight Trail ends at the bay, where a short boardwalk leads to a railed platform. It makes a wonderful site for a dawn visit, but because of the angle of the sun during the morning hours, it is next to impossible to scope the broad mud flats after the first couple of hours of daylight.

Bill Robertson and I walked the trail in the dark, arriving at Snake Bight just as dawn was beginning to creep up the eastern horizon. The bay was glassy calm. The sight of the sun creating its crimson morning glow, the lines of white pelicans and double-crested cormorants, and the scattering of shorebirds, herons and egrets, gulls and terns, all forming a fascinating natural mosaic, will not soon be forgotten. There were birds everywhere. We estimated the numbers as high as 7,000 to 9,000 individuals that January morning.

We did not, however, see the greater flamingos that Sonny Bass had found in that area a few days earlier. The flamingos that frequent Florida Bay are probably from colonies in the Bahamas. As many as 30 individuals are occasionally seen in the northern Florida Bay area; Snake Bight is the likeliest spot for seeing these amazing birds. Robertson says that although he had doubted the birds' wild character when they first began to appear, he is now convinced they are a natural part of a northern Caribbean Basin population.

After about two hours of gazing eastward and identifying every species we could find, we started back toward the highway, birding our way through the black mangrove-dominated habitat. Snake Bight Trail provides another good area for land birds, and we recorded 31 species. Once again, blue-gray gnatcatchers were the most common and obvious species. The only additional species added to my growing Everglades bird list were a lone American redstart and ovenbird and two yellow-bellied sapsuckers. Also, when we began our predawn excursion at the highway, we heard a pair of eastern screech-owls from the roadway. A chuck-will's-widow had called briefly at the start of the trail, and far off toward the bay a barred owl added its deep song of the swamps.

We stopped at the junction of Rowdy Bend Road and Snake Bight Trail to look for a stripe-headed tanager that had been seen there a few days earlier. This is a West Indian bird that only rarely visits south Florida. In spite of a diligent search, it eluded us. But it is this kind of possibility that makes the hobby of birding so exciting. The chance of finding a bird new to the state or even new to the United States helps to create dedicated birders. And Snake Bight Trail has a long history of avian surprises!

Snake Bight Trail is where the fifth record of the Key West quail-dove occurred in 1979. Lee Snyder and Wes Biggs wrote an article in *WildBird* about the sixth record, in 1987 in the Keys, and provided some interesting background about this West Indian species. They reported that John James Audubon first gave it recognition when, in 1832, he wrote that the bird was "sufficiently abundant on Key West to shoot as many as a score in a day." However, by 1889 it was considered rare, and for nearly 70 years, the bird "virtually disappeared from North America." The recent set of six records has occurred since 1933.

South Florida is a natural place for accidentals like the stripe-headed tanager and Key West quail-dove, as well as for new invaders from the south, such as the cattle egret and others. One of those "others" arrived as recently as the 1980s—the shiny cowbird. Already these aggressive birds seem to be established at Flamingo. The species is expected to invade most of the United States; sightings have been reported in Alabama, Louisiana, and Texas. P. William Smith and Alexander Sprunt IV reported its Florida occurrence in 1987.

Biscayne National Park

The numerous islands along the eastern and southern edge of Florida undoubtedly are first to greet exploring or lost birds. Forty-four of Florida's southeastern islands have been included within the boundary of Biscayne National Park. Established in 1968 and enlarged in 1980 to 181,500 acres (73,452 ha), the park is intended "to protect a rare combination of terrestrial and undersea life, to preserve a scenic subtropical setting, and to provide an outstanding spot for recreation and relaxation," according to the park's brochure.

Seven-mile-long (11-km) Elliott Key is 9 miles (14 km) across the channel from the park's Convoy Point Visitor Center and Headquarters on the mainland and 10 miles (16 km) from downtown Homestead. Elliott Key is the principal site for an outstanding assortment of sightings, many of which first occurred during the park's annual Christmas Bird Counts. The first U.S. sighting of La Sagra's flycatcher was recorded during the 1982 Christmas Count, and the species has been found there occasionally ever since.

Christmas counts have taken place in the park every year since 1979, but bird numbers are always low. For example, according to Sonny Bass, seven counters found only 1,754 individuals of 59 species during the December 18, 1990, count. Twelve of those were water birds, 11 were shorebirds, 9 were seabirds (gulls and terns), and the rest were land birds.

There is a good article about Biscayne Bay and the fight to establish the national park in the September 1970 issue of *Audubon*, by Brooks Atkinson and with excellent photographs by James A. Kern. It is well worth reading.

Big Cypress National Preserve
The northern portion of the Everglades ecosystem did not become part of the National Park System until 1974, when 570,000 acres (230,676 ha) of the Big Cypress "swamp" were established as Big Cypress National Preserve. It has since been enlarged to 716,000 acres (289,761 ha). Both terms, "swamp" and "preserve," need further explanation. As the park's brochure states, swamp "is a misnomer, for the land consists of sandy islands of slash pine, mixed hardwood hammocks (tree islands), wet prairies, dry prairies, marshes, and estuarine mangrove forests." And "preserve" is a term used in the park's enabling legislation to signify that the "wild country is protected, but certain preexisting human uses, not allowed in most National Park System areas, are permitted to continue here." Those preexisting rights include certain types of hunting, residency, off-road vehicle use, mineral exploration, and grazing.

The intent of that legislation was greater protection for the wildlands and their significant resources. It was an important step in providing environmental integrity to the greater system, at least more than previously existed.

Big Cypress National Preserve is cut in two by the Tamiami Trail (U.S. Highway 41), a wedge of concrete that serves as the only route from Miami to Naples on the Gulf Coast. Big Cypress Preserve Headquarters, near the western boundary, and Oasis Visitor Center, near the center of the park, are on the Tamiami Trail. And two very different motor nature routes, which provide exciting bird and other wildlife observations, exist as loop routes off the Tamiami Trail.

The most popular of the two routes is the Loop Road, a round-trip of 42 miles (68 km), which can be entered at Monroe Station on the west or from the Tamiami Ranger Station on the east. The wildest portion of the area is on the west side, below Monroe Station. Here, huge bald cypress trees still grow as they did long before the Tamiami Trail dissected the landscape. I half expected to see the last ivory-billed woodpecker fly out of the forest and alight on one of the gigantic cypress trees. I could almost hear the unique bugle call it would make from the cypress swamp. It is too late to save that extinct species, but it is not too late to save other south Florida species in danger of extinction—the wood stork, snail kite, short-tailed hawk, and red-cockaded woodpecker.

At one place on the Loop Road a great white heron stood among the cypress knees, providing a memory that will last a long time. There is something symbolic about that great white bird in its threatened habitat. At another open place, where we crossed over a large culvert, there was obvious turmoil in the adjacent water. We stopped and walked back to see what was causing the fuss. There were a number of 7- to 10-inch-long fish, roiling the water in a very strange manner, almost as if they were swimming in tight circles, surfacing slightly at the top of each circle. Then suddenly, from the center of the turmoil, the head and upper shoulders of a river otter popped out of the water. In an instant, on seeing me, it was back underwater and gone. Then, just across the little creek on the opposite bank, I spotted two more individuals. I focused my binoculars on them just in time to watch them slide into the water and disappear. An exciting moment, one that I have never before experienced.

The fish were walking catfish, another of Florida's many non-native species. They have increased rapidly since they were first discovered in the Shark River Valley in the 1970s. Walking catfish, Park Service Biologist Bill Loftus explained, use a special mode of aerial respiration in which members of a group rise rapidly to the surface to breath in synchrony. This strange behavior enables the species to survive in low dissolved oxygen situations, but it also attracts predatory wading birds. It was this behavior that had attracted the river otters, much to my advantage.

Bob Rogers, a retired high school biology teacher from Michigan and one of the park's winter volunteers, was my guide at Big Cypress. Rogers takes visitors on bird walks and tours. He suggested a second, shorter birding route, Turner River Road, 10 miles (16 km) west of Monroe Station. I found it had more variety than the Loop Road but lacked the spectacular and mysterious cypress pools and swamps.

Turner River Road is a lesser-known area that can provide a surprisingly rich birding experience. The road runs north from the Tamiami Trail at H. P. Williams Wayside Park (state park), 4 miles (6 km) east of Big Cypress National Park Headquarters and about 10 miles (16 km) west of the Monroe Station junction. It can be taken as a loop trip by starting either at Turner River Road or at Birdon Road to the west, near park headquarters. Both roads follow old drainage channels through prairie habitats and occasional cypress swamps and are linked by a county road running east to west. Besides seeing all the regular waders that are so numerous throughout the Everglades, we got good close-up views of wood storks and a lone limpkin. We also found the tufted titmouse and eastern bluebird, species that disappeared from the Everglades 20 to 30 years ago.

I talked with a couple who are only casual birders and who had taken the Turner River Road-Birdon Road loop one early morning in January. They said that without getting off the road, they easily identified 32 species, including raptors, songbirds, and an abundance of waders feeding in the shallow waters of the drainage ditches.

The red-cockaded woodpecker and brown-headed nuthatch occur in the Big Cypress, too, but only at a few of the old pine stands that are not so accessible. Small populations along the Florida Trail can be visited by foot from the Oasis Ranger Station. Obtain further directions from a park ranger.

Another choice Everglades National Park birding location is Shark Valley, which is on the northern edge of the park and accessible only from the Tamiami Trail. You can hike, bike (rentals are available), or take a concession-operated tram tour. The 15-mile (24-km), two-hour tram ride into the Shark Valley Slough is well worth the effort, and each trip provides another opportunity for good close-up views of most of the park's waders, lots of alligators, and an additional assortment of birds that may not be so visible elsewhere.

I took the last tour of the day, beginning at 4:00 p.m., and had an outstanding guide who knew about the wildlife and ecology of the area. Red-shouldered hawks were surprisingly common along the route, but we did not see a snail kite, one of the specialties of this part of the Everglades. Our visit coincided with a drought that had dried up many of the kite's regular feeding grounds, places where the large apple snail is common. Florida's snail kite was listed as endangered in 1966; their numbers fluctuate widely due to droughts and dispersals.

The view over the Everglades from the 65-foot-high (20-m) Shark Valley Tower, located at the end of the 7-mile (11-km) road, can be spectacular. It is one of the best places to get a true perspective of the flatness and extent of the Everglades, to see the vast "river of grass" with its hammock islands, and to watch the incredible cloud formations that are so interrelated with the Everglades. I recalled a quote from William O. Douglas's book, *My Wilderness: East To Katahdin*. Douglas wrote,

> Clouds race overhead, streaking the grass with their shadows. Clouds receive new importance and new dignity in this vast level country of the Everglades. In most parts of America we look up at peaks or mountain ranges, at undulating hills and pleasant valleys. Clouds over the Everglades take their place. The eyes are raised to them; it is from them that man gets a new measure of the universe.

In summary, Everglades National Park's 1990 bird checklist contains 350 species, 86 of which are known to nest. Twenty-five of those are water birds, 12 are hawks and owls, and 4 are warblers. Thirty-five species are listed as winter residents/visitors only: the red-necked grebe; great cormorant; snow and Canada goose; American black and wood ducks; mallard; gadwall; oldsquaw; surf scoter; common goldeneye; bufflehead; American oystercatcher;

parasitic jaeger; Franklin's and great black-backed gulls; burrowing owl; lesser nighthawk; red-headed woodpecker; vermilion flycatcher; horned lark; fish crow; tufted titmouse; white-breasted nuthatch; brown creeper; winter wren; black-throated gray, Kirkland's, and Canada warblers; stripe-headed tanager; vesper, Lincoln's, and white-throated sparrows; lark bunting; and purple finch.

Birds of Special Interest

Anhinga. It is fairly common at ponds, especially at Anhinga Pond. It is identified by its long neck, sharp beak, and black or brown plumage with a silver-white "cape."

Roseate spoonbill. This large, pink-bodied wader is seen best in winter at Flamingo. Its wide, spatulate bill is evident in flight or close up.

Wood stork. This large wader is best seen at Mrazek and similar ponds in winter. It often soars. Its black-and-white color and large beak help identify this bird.

Bald eagle. This large raptor with a bright white head and tail can be fairly common at Flamingo and over Florida Bay, where it nests.

Red-shouldered hawk. The park's most common hawk, it is often found sitting on snags or flying low. Notice the red shoulders on sitting birds and the rather long, banded tail of birds in flight.

Short-tailed hawk. It is resident throughout but most often seen soaring over the Everglades from Royal Palm south. It is a reasonably small, broad-winged hawk with a banded tail and a white spot behind the bill.

White-crowned pigeon. The only large pigeon of the coastal mangroves, it feeds in the hardwood hammocks and is often seen crossing the highway between West Pond and Flamingo. Its body is slate gray with a snowy white crown.

Mangrove cuckoo. A resident of coastal mangroves all year, it is rarely seen in winter. It is usually first detected by its gutteral call and is distinguished from the yellow-billed cuckoo by its very buff chest and sides.

Smooth-billed ani. A resident of thickets and weedy places, including Eco Pond at Flamingo, this is an ink black bird with a long, floppy tail and a large bill that is ridged on the top.

Gray kingbird. A summer resident from April to September, especially along the coast, it shows all shades of gray, with a blackish mask, pale yellow on its belly, and a heavy beak.

Black-whiskered vireo. A summer resident from April to October, found in coastal mangroves and hammocks, it is similar to the red-eyed vireo but has a dark line running from its beak to below its cheeks. It is usually detected by its deliberate, four-note song.

32

Fort Jefferson National Monument, Florida

The specks of land grew larger as we approached the islands, jutting out of the blue-green Caribbean Sea like the backs of gigantic sea turtles. Ahead was Garden Key, identified by the low brick walls of Fort Jefferson. And soaring overhead, like a great umbrella, was a milling canopy of birds, all magnificent frigatebirds. They reminded me of a "kettle" of Mississippi kites I had once found above a lone grain elevator outside a small Kansas town surrounded by miles and miles of flat prairie. They were utilizing the thermals from that one structure just as this mass of seabirds was riding the thermals rising over the historic walls of Fort Jefferson.

We had seen several other frigatebirds, singly or in pairs, all the way from Key West, but at Garden Key there were at least 300 birds visible at one time. It was impossible to tell their exact number because of their continuous circling. I counted 78 individuals in one photograph that I took from directly beneath the birds. They were so low that my 50mm lens could take in only about a quarter of the total number.

Frigatebirds are incredible creatures! Their size and shape alone make them extraordinary. A frigatebird has a wingspan of up to 96 inches (2.4 m), a body length less than half that, and a long, forked tail reminiscent of a pair of curved scissor blades. Both males and females, adults and juveniles, were among the soaring mass of birds that May day at the Dry Tortugas. An adult male is glossy black with metallic purple and glossy green on the back and wings and a blood red throat, or gular sac, that it inflates like a huge balloon

Magnificent frigatebird

during courtship. Adult females are brownish black with white chests. Juveniles possess white chests and throats.

Frigatebirds are the most aerial of all the seabirds, and, except when nesting, they spend their entire life at sea. They never swim or rest on the ocean surface. Their long, narrow, pointed wings have a greater surface area in relation to their body weight than those of any other bird. And the skeleton of a frigatebird weighs only four ounces, less than the weight of its feathers. Therefore, they are able to soar with a minimal amount of uplift, usually at about 50 feet (15 m) above the ocean's surface. But sightings have been reported at more than 4,000 feet (1,219 m). Years earlier at Los Mochis, Mexico, I had recorded the fascinating behavior pattern of a dozen or so magnificent frigatebirds that were soaring over a hotel where I was staying along the bay. I had found the same birds there all day and evening and late that night. I checked the birds again at midnight and at 2:00 a.m., and they still were soaring over the hotel. I assumed that they were able to sleep on the wing.

Frigatebirds feed in flight by "dipping," a method by which they pick up prey above or just below the ocean surface with their long, hooked bills. They may hardly break the surface of the water or may submerge both bills and heads in rough water. Frigatebirds use this method to snatch squid, small sea turtles, jellyfish, and various other food items off the surface. They are able to catch flying fish in the air or to capture food dropped by gulls and other birds they harass before it hits the water. They also prey on seabird colonies, especially those of sooty terns, actually picking chicks and eggs off the nests. Their piracy has provided them with two common names: frigatebird and man-o'-war bird.

Although magnificent frigatebirds are usually seen in flight, roosting birds often perch on shrubs on the little islands near Garden Key. Nesting occurs on Marquessas Keys near Key West, in the Bahamas and Bermuda, and south and east throughout the West Indies to islands off Venezuela and Brazil. Most birds are territorial and remain in their breeding territories throughout their lifetime. Nonbreeders wander extensively and in summer can regularly be found along the Atlantic Coast as far north as Cape Hatteras or along the entire coastline of the Gulf of Mexico.

The Park Environment

Approximately 70 miles (113 km) west of Key West, Florida, are seven tiny coral islands known as the Dry Tortugas, all part of Fort Jefferson National Monument. The park covers an area of approximately 47,000 acres (19,021 ha), but only a fraction of that is land. Spanish explorer Ponce de Leon, who is credited with their discovery in 1513, is said to have bestowed their original name, Las Tortugas, for the sea turtles he found there. It was later changed to Dry Tortugas to illustrate the fact that no fresh water occurs there. The seven islands are all part of one coral atoll, which is mostly submerged.

The Dry Tortugas' fascinating history stretches from their days as a port for early pirates to their present status as one of America's favorite birding sites, especially during the spring migration. After Florida became part of the United States in 1821, a lighthouse was built on Garden Key. And in 1846, the U.S. Army Corps of Engineers began the construction of Fort Jefferson, a project that continued for 30 years. That fort was to become the largest link in a chain of seacoast fortifications in the Western world. By the time it was completed, however, it was obsolete. Nevertheless, it was used during the Civil War, primarily as a military prison. Dr. Samuel Mudd, who set the broken leg of John Wilkes Booth, President Abraham Lincoln's assassin, was imprisoned there. Mudd was pardoned in 1869 after helping to fight the 1867 yellow fever epidemic that took the lives of 38 of the 300-man Fort Jefferson garrison. The fort was abandoned in 1874 but was used during the Spanish-American War as a coaling station. In 1908, it became a wildlife refuge; in 1935, it was designated a national monument. The park is under the administration of Everglades National Park, but a park ranger lives at the fort.

Fort Jefferson is probably the most isolated spot in the eastern United States. Not only is it far from the mainland but these tiny islands are not on the way to anywhere. Visitors must plan to go there, either by boat or by airplane. Commercial boats make round-trip tours daily, and arrangements can be made to stay overnight and catch the boat back at a later date. Those day trips, however, allow only about two hours to visit the fort and little, if any, time to snorkel at the surrounding coral reef or study adjacent Bush Key and its abundant wildlife. The other way to visit the Dry Tortugas is to fly there via locally available seaplanes. Camping is permitted on Garden Key just outside the fort, but since drinking water and other provisions are unavailable on the islands, everything must be brought along, and all refuse must be hauled out.

My wife and I visited the Dry Tortugas in early May as participants in a Victor Emanuel Nature Tour. Our group had leased a boat out of Key West that slept 40 people; we stayed three nights. Special tours of this kind are the best way to see the Dry Tortugas and their fascinating wildlife.

Additional information can be obtained from the Superintendent, Everglades National Park, P.O. Box 279, Homestead, FL 33030; (305) 247-6211.

Bird Life

There were three key birding interests in the Dry Tortugas on our May visit: the abundant terns that nest on Bush Key, other seabirds that may be in the area, and the migrant land birds that occur on the grounds of the fort. All three can be spectacular!

Probably as much has been written about the long-term studies of terns in the Tortugas as has been written about the wading birds of the Everglades. And there is a good reason for that. Everglades' Park Biologist Bill Robertson and his colleagues have been banding terns, primarily sooties and brown noddies, that nest nowhere else in the United States, every year since 1959. The sooty tern colony has fluctuated from a low of about 5,000 adults in 1903 to a peak of about 190,000 birds in 1950. The brown noddy population was 35,000 in 1919 but declined to only 400 adults in 1938. Current populations are about 100,000 sooties and 2,500 brown noddies.

The Dry Tortugas tern monitoring project is one of the oldest and most consistent seabird colony studies anywhere and is built on a 1937-1941 program. From 1959 to 1979, nearly 200 of those banded in the first years were recaptured. At least 2 individuals had reached 32 years of age. And juvenile sooty terns banded in the Tortugas have been recovered from as far away as Cameroons, Nigeria, and Sierra Leone in Africa.

Sooty tern

The **sooty tern** is our only tern that is all black above, except for its white forehead; its underparts are snow white. It has a deeply forked tail with white outer tail feathers. The **brown noddy** is over-all brown with a silvery white cap and a wedge-shaped tail. Brown noddies build their nests of seaweed and little sticks on bay cedar and prickly pear, while the sooties nest on the beach, sometimes directly below overhanging nests of the noddies. Smaller colonies of roseate terns exist on Hospital, Bush, and Long keys. Sooty terns acquire their food by snatching small fish and other marine life from the ocean surface. Noddies fish the surface and occasionally dive for fish; roseate terns fish almost exclusively by diving.

Other seabirds usually present at Fort Jefferson include the brown pelican, double-crested cormorant, and masked and brown boobies. **Brown pelicans** spend most of their time fishing the clear waters around the islands or perching on various structures about the Garden Key Harbor. This huge pelican possesses an enormous throat pouch that it uses as a net to gather fish after diving on them, often from 20 to 30 feet (6-9 m) above the water's surface. On surfacing, it points its bill downward and forces the excess water out through its mandibles before throwing its head upward to swallow its catch.

Brown pelicans are without doubt one of nature's most unusual creatures. Unlike the slim frigatebirds, a pelican has a bulky body and an awkward-looking beak. Its plumage is all brown, except for the white or yellowish head and neck of an adult. See chapter 23 on

Assateague Island National Seashore for additional information on this fascinating bird.

A few pairs of masked boobies nest on Hospital and Middle keys. But the **brown booby** can often be found sitting on one of the channel markers or buoys or fishing in the shallow waters near Garden Key. This large, brown and white bird is built like a torpedo with long, tapered wings. The adult is all brown with a white belly and underwing linings and a heavy, horn-colored bill. It flies with strong but stilted wing beats, sometimes very close to the surface. It fishes by plunging after its prey, often in a spectacular dive from 30 to 50 feet (9-15 m) above the surface, and by chasing down its prey underwater. It can remain underwater for up to 40 seconds.

Boobies sometimes fly in front of a boat to locate flying fish, which often fly ahead of a fast-moving boat. These birds sometimes get so close that they can be caught in nets, thus the reason for their scientific name, *bubo*, Spanish for dunce.

Another seabird that we found at Fort Jefferson in May was a lone **white-tailed tropicbird**. It perched on the fort walls a good part of the time, as if searching for a suitable nesting site, but without a partner. In flight it is an amazing creature! Its plumage is snow white except for coal black streaks on the wings and primaries; it possesses a distinct and extremely long tail. Actually the two white, central tail feathers, extending far beyond the tail proper, are longer than the bird's body. Its wingspan is about 36 inches (91 cm), and its length is 43 to 48 inches (109-122 cm); two-thirds of that is tail. It undoubtedly is one of the truly glamorous birds of the West Indies.

Tropicbirds are extremely graceful in flight, but they fish much like the larger, heavier-bodied boobies, by diving on small fish, squid, and crabs that they sight from 50 to 100 feet (15-30 m) above the surface. They dive with half-closed wings, often spiraling downward, and plunge below the surface to capture their prey. They then surface, where they remain afloat to swallow their catch.

Then there are the spring migrants that begin to appear in mid-February, starting with waders and shorebirds and the various raptors that live off these earlybirds. The peak of the northbound migration is mid-April to mid-May. At that time of year, almost any of North America's migrants are possible.

The spring migrants can be so exhausted from their nonstop journey across the Gulf of Mexico from the Yucatán Peninsula that they can do little more at first than remain motionless wherever they land. Heads droop, eyes close, and it is often possible to pick them up with little or no protest. Shortly, or sometimes as long as a couple of hours later, they stir and begin to search for food and fresh water. Food usually is in short supply because of the minimal amount of vegetation on the islands, and what little drinking water is available is rather salty. It is not unusual to find bird carcasses scattered here and there around the fort grounds.

Inside the fort grounds is a lone watering area, a fountain that recycles fresh water for the birds. It attracts a continuous stream of birds, including predators that take advantage of the available prey. I watched a pair of cattle egrets capture three smaller songbirds that were perched on the adjacent vegetation. Two were a female American redstart and a male indigo bunting; I was not able to identify the other bird.

During one two-hour visit inside the fort, I found a really strange assortment of migrants, birds from the northern forests to the southern lowlands. I recorded the cattle egret, purple gallinule, sharp-shinned hawk, mourning dove, common nighthawk, yellow-billed cuckoo, barn swallow, gray-cheeked thrush, indigo bunting, and fourteen species of warblers: northern parula, yellow, magnolia, Cape May, yellow-rumped, black-throated green, Blackburnian, palm, bay-breasted, blackpoll, black-and-white, American redstart, Connecticut, and common yellowthroat. My brief census produced more species of warblers than many places on the mainland receive in an entire season.

Two species of nighthawks occur in late spring: the migrating common nighthawk (it nests at the Everglades) and the **Antillean nighthawk**, a West Indian specialty that summers along the Keys. They appear only during evening and early morning, flying around the various islands. The two species can best be distinguished by their very different calls. The Antillean nighthawk's call is a "pity-pit-pit," while that of the common nighthawk is "pleet." They may roost on top of or in the crevices of the fort walls during the daytime.

The majority of the spring migrants that pause at Fort Jefferson National Monument are en route to breeding grounds far beyond south Florida. Most stop for only brief periods before moving on toward their final destinations. Fort Jefferson and other protected areas along the coastline, including Gulf Islands National Seashore and various national refuges, are vitally important as stopovers for the millions of spring and fall migrants.

In summary, the bird checklist for Fort Jefferson National Monument lists 284 species, of which only a handful occur other than as migrants. Only 8 species are known to nest: the brown pelican; laughing gull; roseate, least, and sooty terns; brown noddy; mourning dove; and house sparrow. An additional 9 species are suspected to nest: the common moorhen, royal and common terns, mangrove cuckoo, smooth-billed ani, gray kingbird, barn swallow, northern mockingbird, and black-whiskered vireo. Only larger Loggerhead Key, west of Garden Key, contains adequate vegetation (coconut and date palms, tamarind, Australian pine, gumbo limbo, and century plant) to support nesting land birds. During the winter months, only 6 species of land birds can be expected with confidence: the American kestrel, belted kingfisher, gray catbird, yellow-rumped and palm warblers, and savannah sparrow.

Birds of Special Interest

Brown pelican. This large bird with a huge bill and pouch fishes the clear waters by diving headfirst to net a pouch full of fish.

White-tailed tropicbird. Watch for this snow white seabird with its extremely long, white tail feathers. It occurs only occasionally and is one of the real avian treats.

Brown booby. A few individuals are usually present around Garden Key, fishing the clear waters by diving in headfirst and chasing down their prey.

Magnificent frigatebird. Hundreds of these huge, scissor-tailed birds with wingspans of up to 96 inches can often be found soaring over Fort Jefferson.

Sooty tern. It is the only tern with an all-black back. It has a white forehead, snow white underparts, and a long, forked tail. These terns nest in great numbers on Bush Key, laying eggs in scrapes on the beach.

Brown noddy. This species is all brown with a silver-white crown. Noddies build their nests in the shrubs on Bush Key.

Antillean nighthawk. A late spring and summer visitor only, it is distinguished from the common nighthawk by its very different call, which is a "pity-pit-pit" rather than "pleet."

33

Virgin Islands National Park, Buck Island Reef National Monument, and Salt River Bay Historical Park and Ecological Preserve, U.S. Virgin Islands

Leinster Bay was entirely calm, like a sheet of glass. The only things moving were a lone brown pelican flying across the bay and a pair of magnificent frigatebirds circling above Mary Point. The dawn chorus of songbirds was still under way in the adjacent forest; it was dominated by the very loud squawks of pearly-eyed thrashers. This large, aggressive species can be found almost everywhere on St. John. Only the diminutive bananaquit was of equal abundance on that day's Christmas Bird Count.

Bananaquits and pearly-eyed thrashers stand in stark contrast to one another. The large, very plain, white-eyed thrasher is an opportunist that feeds on everything from garbage to lizards. Anoles, the bright green lizards that are so abundant in the islands, are often hunted by these pearly-eyed predators. But the brightly colored bananaquits, with their rasping but cheerful "see-e-e-e-te" songs, feed almost exclusively on fruit, nectar, and sugar. The introduction of sugarcane to the islands and the subsequent production of cane syrup, sugar, and rum undoubtedly enhanced the numbers of this little honeycreeper. The bananaquit later became the official

Bananaquit

bird of the Virgin Islands, where it is best known as "sugarbird" or "yellow-breast."

To most visitors from the mainland, bananaquits are the most memorable of all the Virgin Islands' birds. They are as abundant as the flowers, and they frequent the many outdoor restaurants, where they feed on the available sugar. It is a special treat to have one or several of these tiny, colorful songsters at one's table during breakfast or lunch.

The Park Environment

St. John is one of the three major islands (the other two are St. Thomas and St. Croix) and numerous cays that make up the U.S. Virgin Islands, a territory since 1918, when the islands were purchased from Denmark. The Virgin Islands have a total land mass of only 133 square miles (51 sq km), only one-tenth the size of Rhode Island. St. John is the smallest of the three, with only 20 square miles (8 sq km). But three-quarters of St. John is included in Virgin Islands National Park, established in 1956.

The park's extensive tropical moist forest, dry evergreen woodland habitats, small areas of mangroves, some of the finest beaches in all the West Indies, and underwater resources attract more than 400,000 visitors annually. The forests are recovering very well from the years when sugar was king (early 1700s to early 1900s), when almost all of the vegetation was cut for sugarcane fields and for fuel to operate the mills.

Park visitors reach St. John by air, cruise ship, or sailboat. The majority spend only a few hours on the island, arriving at the town of Cruz Bay and touring the park by taxi or open bus. Car rentals are also available at Cruz Bay, and driving on the left side, up and down the steep roadways, can be an unnerving experience. Visitor accommodations vary greatly, from the very adequate Raintree Inn in downtown Cruz Bay to the exclusive Caneel Bay Plantation inside the park. Cinnamon Bay Campground, operated by the park service, provides tent and cottage sites, a store, a restaurant, and water recreation equipment for rent on the bay. Maho Bay Camps is concession operated and provides tent-cabins and a restaurant tucked into the forest overlooking Maho Bay.

Visitors arriving by airline from the continent go through St. Thomas or St. Croix. St. Thomas's Redhook Dock, on the eastern end of that island, is only a 20-minute ferry ride from Cruz Bay. From St. Croix, 40 miles (64 km) to the south, one can fly to St. Thomas or go directly to Cruz Bay via a seaplane shuttle from Christiansted.

The park offers a wide range of activities, such as hiking the various trails, soaking up rays on one of the clean white sand beaches, boating, fishing, wind sailing, snorkeling, visiting the many historic sites, birding, and nature study. Afternoon and evening programs, including bird walks, are scheduled on a regular basis. The Cruz Bay Visitor Center contains an information station, sales outlet, and museum on the area's natural and cultural history. Available there is a little book, *Virgin Islands Birdlife*, by this author, which describes the various habitats and common birds and includes a complete checklist.

Additional information can be obtained from the Superintendent, Virgin Islands National Park, P.O. Box 7789, Charlotte Amalie, VI 00801; (809) 775-6238; or, on St. Croix, from the Superintendent, Christiansted National Historic Site, P.O. Box 160, Christiansted, VI 00821; (809) 773-1460.

Bird Life

That early December morning, I was most interested in birding the Annaberg mangroves that grow along the edge of Leinster Bay. Mangrove habitats support a surprisingly high population of North American songbirds during the winter months. Many of these valuable mangrove areas in the West Indies have been destroyed for developments of one kind or another, but the mangroves within Virgin Islands National Park are fully protected.

I walked along the roadway that runs between the mangroves and bay. The sun was still below the horizon. Yellow warbler songs blended with the hoarse squawks of the pearly-eyed thrashers. And then a **mangrove cuckoo** sounded off fairly close to the roadway. I made a low, squeaking sound, and almost immediately the cuckoo moved closer. It perched in the top of a red mangrove, clearly visible from where I stood. I admired its very buff underparts, broad white bars on its blackish tail, and the black marking behind the eye. It remained very quiet, allowing me a careful examination; I wondered if it was looking me over as well. This species is rare in winter but fairly common during the summer months, and most numerous in the dry forest habitats on the hills.

Loud chips from among the mangrove roots attracted my attention. I enticed two northern waterthrushes into the open with another series of squeaks. And there, too, were a pair of American redstarts, lone prairie and black-and-white warblers, and a northern parula. These birds apparently were all members of a bird party that was overwintering in the Annaberg mangroves.

The faint "cheeery" call from the mangrove foliage came from a **Caribbean elaenia**. It took me a couple of minutes to locate this little resident bird. But then it stayed surprisingly close for several minutes and allowed me a good look. This flycatcher is one of the park's true Caribbean specialties, and it also is one of the local favorites, in spite of its rather drab appearance. Virgin Islanders call it "John Phillips" and "pee whistler." John Phillips is derived from one of its songs that is interpreted as "John Phillips." Its more commonly heard call is a distinct "che-eup." The Caribbean elaenia is a drab flycatcher with two whitish wing bars and a seldom-seen yellowish line on the crest of its head.

A larger bird moved farther back into the mangroves; apparently it had been sitting much closer, but I had not seen it until it moved. I located it in my binoculars immediately, but it took me several more minutes to identify it for sure. It was an immature night-heron, but from a distance it was difficult to be sure whether it was yellow- or black-crowned. The shorter length of the wings relative to the legs, dark body and bill, and fairly long, thin neck convinced me it was the more common yellow-crowned night-heron, a bird that is often missed on the St. John Christmas count.

The sun had begun to touch the hilltops as I walked back to my vehicle. The day would warm up very fast now, and I needed to visit nearby Mary Point Pond early on. This pond is one of the park's best birding areas; Thelma Douglas, a local volunteer for the national park, has been leading bird walks there for many years. It also is one of the places that Herb Raffaele describes in his excellent book, *A Guide to the Birds of Puerto Rico and the Virgin Islands.*

Pearly-eyed thrasher

I parked at the trailhead, just below the entrance to Maho Bay Camps, and slowly made my way along the interpretive trail that circles the pond. I could hear a pair of black-necked stilts calling from the pond's shallow edge. A greater yellowlegs joined the fuss. Maybe a mongoose had disturbed these birds, or perhaps a pere-

SOUTHEAST AND VIRGIN ISLANDS

grine falcon was hunting nearby. I searched the sky as best I could but to no avail.

Caribbean elaenias, pearly-eyed thrashers, bananaquits, yellow warblers, gray kingbirds, and Zenaida doves were all present within the forest along the trail. I soon reached a place where I could partially see the pond. I crawled through some of the undergrowth to get a better look, ever watchful of jack Spaniards, the tiny wasps that are so common in the Virgin Islands. There are no poisonous snakes on the islands, but one must beware of jack Spaniards, which build small paper nests on shrubs two to eight feet above the ground. The sting of these little wasps can be very painful.

I could see a great blue heron feeding along the opposite shoreline. A pair of common moorhens was present as well, and far to the right I could barely see some ducks. A green-backed heron squawked farther on. It took me several more minutes to carefully maneuver to get a better view of the waterfowl. Finally in a more strategic position, I counted a total of 15 white-cheeked pintails, 3 blue-winged teals, and 4 American wigeons. The teal and wigeon were visitors from the states, but the **white-cheeked pintails** were local ducks that frequent this and similar ponds throughout the Virgin Islands. They are the only full-time resident ducks in the islands. Although they appear to be declining in their broader West Indian range, they seem to be holding their own in the Virgin Islands, where they are known to nest all twelve months of the year. Occasionally one visits south Florida, where it creates quite a stir among birders.

The white-cheeked pintail is well named; it has a very noticeable white cheek and upper throat. Less obvious is a bright red patch at the base of its bill. Its tail is similar to that of the northern pintail but never so long and spectacular. Also, the body markings of the white-cheeked pintail are more like those of the female northern pintail, complete with a green speculum.

I turned to make my way back to the trail when, almost at my feet, I startled a little bird that was walking along the dry forest floor. It flew only a few yards away before it landed and continued its search for food among the leaves and other debris. It was an ovenbird, another North American winter resident, perhaps an individual that nests in Great Smoky Mountains National Park or along the Blue Ridge Parkway.

I continued on the loop trail to an opening onto the adjacent beach. Maho Bay was serenely beautiful. I found a lone little blue heron and two black-bellied plovers along the shoreline and a brown booby fishing over the bay. The aqua bay waters reflected on the booby's underwings, giving it an overall aqua color.

I left the lowland area shortly and drove up to Centerline Road, which runs along the east-west crest of the island. I stopped several places along the road to check the bird life on the adjacent slopes. Both the green-throated Carib and Antillean crested hummingbird were added to the day's list. These hummingbirds are the only two normally found in the Virgin Islands, but both are fairly common there. They are easily distinguished by their size and shape. The **green-throated Carib,** the largest of the two, is all green with a purplish belly and under tail coverts. It often seems to be all black, but in good light its green throat can be spectacular. The **Antillean crested hummingbird** is much smaller, and the male possesses a tall crest that can also be bright green in the sunlight. Both hummers utilize the abundant flowers on the islands but seem to like especially the red-flowering ixora shrub and the white blossoms of the white manjack tree. They also occasionally feed on ginger thomas, the Virgin Islands' official flower.

I had already counted a number of black-faced grassquits, tiny, heavy-billed birds with black faces, but finding the similar but larger **Lesser Antillean bullfinch** was a surprise. I first heard its very distinct song: a series of "seep" notes followed by a distinct buzz. A lone female was soon discovered sitting on a little tan-tan tree at the edge of the roadway. This species is much more numerous in the eastern Lesser Antilles but has recently moved into the Virgin Islands. It has been on St. John only since the early 1960s and appears to be increasing; it began to appear on St. Croix in the mid-1980s.

The best bird of the morning was the **bridled quail-dove.** I recorded a total of five individuals along the slopes from Centerline Road, although I saw only one. The other four were identified by their mournful calls. This very low-pitched "who-whooo" is easy to identify once you tune into the pitch and frequency. Raffaele fur-

Bridled quail-dove

ther describes the call as "on one note or descending toward the end, getting loudest in the middle of the second syllable and then trailing off." Sometimes the first syllable is omitted. I have been able to imitate this bird by whistling inward as low as possible.

This West Indian specialty is more commonly seen near Cinnamon Bay Campground, which is located at the base of a steep forested slope where the birds spend most of their time. However, it also can be found along the edges of the roadway and campground entrance parking lot. It rarely flies but will walk away from a disturbance or freeze until the annoyance disappears. The bridled quail-dove is a fairly large bird with a rufous back and buff underparts. Its most obvious feature is a bold white line on each cheek, like a bridle.

By the end of the day's census, the twenty-five count participants had recorded a total of 66 species and 1,902 individuals. Seventeen of the 66 species are considered West Indian specialties that normally do not occur elsewhere. Eighteen are full-time residents of both the Virgin Islands and the Continent: pelican, herons, egrets, red-tailed hawk, American kestrel, royal tern, common ground-dove, among others. And 27 species are winter visitors to the Virgin Islands only: merlin, blue-winged teal, American wigeon, sora, 7 shorebirds, swallows, yellow-throated vireo, and 11 warblers.

It is this latter group that provides the fascinating connection between North America and the West Indies.

More than half of all the birds that spend their summers in the northern latitudes fly south for the winter months. The largest group of these are the warblers, of which more than two dozen species use the West Indies. Some species, such as the blackpoll warbler, only pass through on their southward journey to South America. Others depend on the various forest types in the western West Indies for their survival. Since many of the forests in Jamaica, Cuba, Haiti, the Dominican Republic, Puerto Rico, and the Virgin Islands have been eliminated or reduced, the few natural areas that still exist, such as Virgin Islands National Park, are vital to the long-term survival of those North American songbirds.

Christmas Bird Counts are important ways to acquire a long-term understanding of the changes that occur in bird populations, and counts undertaken in the Virgin Islands are extremely worth-while. Rob Norton and his associates have monitored Virgin Islands' bird populations in this way for many years; they have found a gradual decline of certain winter visitors.

Other bird-finding areas on St. John include a few of the park's hiking trails. A park service trail guide brochure lists 21 separate routes, varying from very short walks to the more extensive 2½-mile (4-km) Reef Bay Trail. Each has its own appeal. For instance, the Lind Point Trail, just behind the Cruz Bay Visitor Center, is one of the best places in the park to find the Lesser Antillean bullfinch. An overlook at the end of the trail also provides an excellent view of Cruz Bay and nearby St. Thomas.

The Bordeaux Mountain Trail provides access to the highland forest habitat where the largest number of North American song-birds can usually be found in winter. The wetter areas along the slopes of Bordeaux Mountain (1,270 ft., or 387 m elev.) usually contain magnolia, Cape May, black-throated blue, worm-eating, and Kentucky warblers, and rarely a Swainson's warbler.

Reef Bay Trail is the longest of the park's trails and descends through a variety of habitats from Centerline Road to Reef Bay, ending in a little valley with a historic sugar mill. The rare Puerto Rican fly-catcher is most often seen near the junction with the Petroglyph Trail.

In addition to land birds, the adjacent cays provide a very different environment and a different set of species. Although the majority of the birds are the same as those found on the bays and estuaries, the breeding season produces a few terns (Sandwich, roseate, bridled, and sooty) and tropicbirds (both white-tailed and red-billed), which are extremely rare in winter.

Buck Island Reef National Monument

Most visitors to Buck Island Reef, just off the north-central coast of St. Croix, go there to see the underwater treasures. The coral gardens in the park are some of the finest in all the Virgin Islands. However, this little island of only 298 acres (121 ha) also has a fascinating littoral forest habitat along the south shore. The numerous manchineel trees produce applelike fruits that are poisonous to anyone who may confuse them with the real thing. The leaves, too, are toxic, and rainwater dripping from their leaves can create sores on bare skin.

Buck Island's bird life is similar to that of the dry forest on St. John. However, the presence of nesting white-crowned pigeons in late spring and summer and chuck-will's-widows in winter is of special interest. Black-whiskered vireos are also present during wintertime, while they are seldom found on St. John that time of year. Why this species is more common on St. Croix in winter is difficult to determine. During the summer months it is common on all the islands.

The trail to the top of the island provides an excellent perspective of the forest habitat, and the lookout tower at the summit is a good place to scope the surrounding vegetation and waters. Some years brown pelicans nest on the stunted vegetation along the island's northeast slope, and the nests are visible from the tower. Brown pelicans, ospreys, and royal terns are always present in the surrounding waters. Brown boobies and ring-billed gulls are less numerous.

Salt River Bay Historical Park and Ecological Preserve

This 1,000-acre (405-ha) park, located along the north-central coast of St. Croix, was established in 1992 to protect one of the most diverse areas in all of the national parks. Within this pocket-sized area are pre-Columbian burials, an old Carib Indian village, and remnants of the only ceremonial ball court found anywhere in the Lesser Antilles, the only positively identified site under the U.S. flag where the Christopher Columbus party landed, and a European fortification (the oldest earthen fort in the Americas) that was occupied by the English, Dutch, and French. Here, too, is an ecological continuum, or series of interconnecting, unique habitats that range from upland forest, freshwater stream and marsh, salt pond, mangrove forest, and shallow estuary with extensive sea grass beds to deep water corals and a biologically rich submarine canyon.

This area at the mouth of Salt River is considered one of the best birding areas in all the Virgin Islands. A total of 110 bird species have been recorded at Salt River, 21 of which are considered threatened or endangered. Six are federally listed species: the brown pelican, peregrine falcon, snowy and piping plovers, and roseate and least terns. Twenty-six of the 110 species nest at Salt River.

The Salt River mangrove forest is one of the largest in the Virgin Islands, although the area was hard hit by Hurricane Hugo in 1989. Fred Sladen and I conducted bird censuses in these mangroves prior to the storm (1987), and we found the area to be an extremely valuable wintering ground for North American songbirds. Twenty-three species were found to utilize this area in winter; 13 of these were warblers. In descending order of abundance, they were the northern waterthrush, northern parula, black-and-white, American redstart, prairie, Cape May, hooded, worm-eating, blue-winged, common yellowthroat, ovenbird, magnolia, and yellow-rumped.

The mangrove forest also supports breeding populations of several West Indian species, including the scaly-naped and white-crowned pigeons, Zenaida dove, mangrove cuckoo, green-throated Carib, Antillean crested hummingbird, gray kingbird, Caribbean elaenia, bananaquit, and black-faced grassquit.

In summary, the Virgin Islands checklist contains 210 species, of which 55 nest. Of those, 29 are water birds (grebe, seabirds, herons, egrets, moorhen, and shorebirds), 2 are hawks (red-tailed hawk and American kestrel), and only 1 is a warbler (yellow warbler).

Birds of Special Interest

Scaly-naped pigeon. This is the largest of the Virgin Islands' pigeons and is most numerous on St. Croix, especially in the Salt River mangroves.

Bridled quail-dove. It is fairly common along the forested slopes, especially near Cinnamon Bay Campground. It is a heavy-bodied, quaillike bird with a bold white stripe below the eye.

Mangrove cuckoo. This long-tailed bird with a buff front and black patch behind the eyes can be fairly common in the dry forest habitats and less numerous in the mangroves.

Green-throated Carib. Common throughout the Virgin Islands, this is the large, green-throated hummingbird with a purplish body.

Antillean crested hummingbird. This is the tiny, crested hummingbird with an all-green body.

Caribbean elaenia. It is most common within the dry forest and littoral forest habitats and is usually first detected by its mournful whistle calls.

Pearly-eyed thrasher. It is abundant in the forests and gardens and is easily identified by its robin-size, plain color, long tail, and white eye. It is an aggressive bird that will eat almost anything.

Bananaquit. This is the Virgin Islands' official bird and one of the islands' most gregarious and easily recognized species. Its all-yellow belly and preference for sugar and fruits make it the most obvious of all birds.

Checklist of Birds Occurring Regularly in the Eastern National Parks

LOONS

__ Red-throated loon
__ Common loon

GREBES

__ Pied-billed grebe
__ Horned grebe
__ Red-necked grebe
__ Eared grebe

SHEARWATERS

__ Northern fulmar
__ Black-capped petrel
__ Cory's shearwater
__ Greater shearwater
__ Sooty shearwater
__ Manx shearwater
__ Audubon's shearwater

STORM-PETRELS

__ Wilson's storm-petrel
__ White-faced storm-petrel
__ Leach's storm-petrel
__ Band-rumped storm-petrel

TROPICBIRDS

__ White-tailed tropicbird
__ Red-billed tropicbird

BOOBIES and GANNET

__ Masked booby
__ Brown booby
__ Red-footed booby
__ Northern gannet

PELICANS

__ American white pelican
__ Brown pelican

CORMORANTS

__ Great cormorant
__ Double-crested cormorant

ANHINGAS

__ Anhinga

FRIGATEBIRDS

__ Magnificent frigatebird

BITTERNS AND HERONS

__ American bittern
__ Least bittern
__ Great blue heron
__ Great egret
__ Snowy egret
__ Little blue heron
__ Tricolored heron
__ Reddish egret
__ Cattle egret
__ Green-backed heron
__ Black-crowned night-heron
__ Yellow-crowned night-heron

IBIS

__ White ibis
__ Glossy ibis

SPOONBILL

__ Roseate spoonbill

WOOD STORK

__ Wood stork

FLAMINGO

__ Greater flamingo

SWANS, GEESE, and DUCKS

__ Fulvous whistling-duck
__ Tundra swan
__ Mute swan
__ Greater white-fronted goose
__ Snow goose
__ Ross' goose
__ Brant
__ Canada goose
__ Wood duck
__ Green-winged teal
__ American black duck
__ Mottled duck
__ Mallard
__ White-cheeked pintail
__ Northern pintail
__ Blue-winged teal
__ Northern shoveler
__ Gadwall
__ Eurasian wigeon
__ American wigeon
__ Canvasback
__ Redhead
__ Ring-necked duck
__ Greater scaup
__ Lesser scaup
__ Common eider
__ King eider
__ Harlequin duck
__ Oldsquaw
__ Black scoter
__ Surf scoter
__ White-winged scoter
__ Common goldeneye
__ Barrow's goldeneye
__ Bufflehead

__ Hooded merganser
__ Common merganser
__ Red-breasted merganser
__ Ruddy duck

VULTURES

__ Black vulture
__ Turkey vulture

HAWKS and EAGLES

__ Osprey
__ American swallow-tailed kite
__ Mississippi kite
__ Black-shouldered kite
__ Snail kite
__ Bald eagle
__ Northern harrier
__ Sharp-shinned hawk
__ Cooper's hawk
__ Northern goshawk
__ Red-shouldered hawk
__ Broad-winged hawk
__ Short-tailed hawk
__ Red-tailed hawk
__ Swainson's hawk
__ Rough-legged hawk
__ Golden eagle

FALCONS

__ American kestrel
__ Merlin
__ Peregrine falcon
__ Gyrfalcon

GROUSE, TURKEY, and QUAIL

__ Gray partridge
__ Ring-necked pheasant
__ Spruce grouse
__ Willow ptarmigan
__ Rock ptarmigan
__ Ruffed grouse

__ Wild turkey
__ Northern bobwhite

RAILS, GALLINULES, AND COOTS

__ Yellow rail
__ Black rail
__ Clapper rail
__ King rail
__ Virginia rail
__ Sora
__ Purple gallinule
__ Common moorhen
__ American coot
__ Caribbean coot
__ Limpkin
__ Sandhill crane

SHOREBIRDS

__ Black-bellied plover
__ Lesser golden-plover
__ Snowy plover
__ Wilson's plover
__ Semipalmated plover
__ Piping plover
__ Killdeer
__ American oystercatcher
__ Black-necked stilt
__ American avocet
__ Greater yellowlegs
__ Lesser yellowlegs
__ Solitary sandpiper
__ Willet
__ Spotted sandpiper
__ Upland sandpiper
__ Whimbrel
__ Long-billed curlew
__ Hudsonian godwit
__ Marbled godwit
__ Ruddy turnstone
__ Red knot
__ Sanderling
__ Semipalmated sandpiper
__ Western sandpiper

__ Least sandpiper
__ White-rumped sandpiper
__ Baird's sandpiper
__ Pectoral sandpiper
__ Purple sandpiper
__ Dunlin
__ Curlew sandpiper
__ Stilt sandpiper
__ Buff-breasted sandpiper
__ Ruff
__ Short-billed dowitcher
__ Long-billed dowitcher
__ Common snipe
__ American woodcock
__ Wilson's phalarope
__ Red-necked phalarope
__ Red phalarope

JAEGERS, GULLS, AND TERNS

__ Pomarine jaeger
__ Parasitic jaeger
__ Long-tailed jaeger
__ Great skua
__ South polar skua
__ Laughing gull
__ Little gull
__ Common black-headed gull
__ Bonaparte's gull
__ Ring-billed gull
__ Herring gull
__ Iceland gull
__ Lesser black-backed gull
__ Glaucous gull
__ Great black-backed gull
__ Black-legged kittiwake
__ Sabine's gull
__ Gull-billed tern
__ Caspian tern
__ Royal tern
__ Sandwich tern
__ Roseate tern
__ Common tern
__ Arctic tern

__ Forster's tern
__ Least tern
__ Bridled tern
__ Sooty tern
__ Black tern
__ Brown noddy
__ Black noddy
__ Black skimmer

AUKS AND ALLIES

__ Dovekie
__ Common murre
__ Thick-billed murre
__ Razorbill
__ Black guillemot
__ Atlantic puffin

PIGEONS AND DOVES

__ Rock dove
__ Scaly-naped pigeon
__ White-crowned pigeon
__ White-winged dove
__ Zenaida dove
__ Mourning dove
__ Common ground-dove
__ Ruddy quail-dove
__ Key West quail-dove
__ Bridled quail-dove

PARROTS

__ Brown-throated parakeet

CUCKOOS

__ Black-billed cuckoo
__ Yellow-billed cuckoo
__ Mangrove cuckoo
__ Smooth-billed ani
__ Groove-billed ani

OWLS

__ Barn owl
__ Eastern screech-owl

__ Great horned owl
__ Snowy owl
__ Northern hawk owl
__ Burrowing owl
__ Barred owl
__ Long-eared owl
__ Short-eared owl
__ Boreal owl
__ Northern saw-whet owl

NIGHTJARS

__ Lesser nighthawk
__ Common nighthawk
__ Antillean nighthawk
__ Chuck-will's-widow
__ Whip-poor-will

SWIFTS

__ Black swift
__ Chimney swift

HUMMINGBIRDS

__ Ruby-throated hummingbird
__ Green-throated Carib
__ Antillean crested hummingbird

KINGFISHERS

__ Belted kingfisher

WOODPECKERS

__ Red-headed woodpecker
__ Red-bellied woodpecker
__ Yellow-bellied sapsucker
__ Downy woodpecker
__ Hairy woodpecker
__ Red-cockaded woodpecker
__ Three-toed woodpecker
__ Black-backed woodpecker
__ Northern flicker
__ Pileated woodpecker

FLYCATCHERS

___ Caribbean elaenia
___ Olive-sided flycatcher
___ Eastern wood-pewee
___ Yellow-bellied flycatcher
___ Acadian flycatcher
___ Alder flycatcher
___ Willow flycatcher
___ Least flycatcher
___ Black phoebe
___ Eastern phoebe
___ Vermilion flycatcher
___ Great crested flycatcher
___ Brown-crested flycatcher
___ La Sagra's flycatcher
___ Puerto Rican flycatcher
___ Tropical kingbird
___ Western kingbird
___ Eastern kingbird
___ Gray kingbird
___ Scissor-tailed flycatcher

LARKS

___ Horned lark

SWALLOWS

___ Purple martin
___ Tree swallow
___ Northern rough-winged swallow
___ Bank swallow
___ Cliff swallow
___ Cave swallow
___ Barn swallow

JAYS AND CROWS

___ Gray jay
___ Blue jay
___ Scrub jay
___ American crow
___ Fish crow
___ Common raven

TITMICE

___ Black-capped chickadee
___ Carolina chickadee
___ Boreal chickadee
___ Tufted titmouse

NUTHATCHES

___ Red-breasted nuthatch
___ White-breasted nuthatch
___ Brown-headed nuthatch

CREEPERS

___ Brown creeper

WRENS

___ Carolina wren
___ Bewick's wren
___ House wren
___ Winter wren
___ Sedge wren
___ Marsh wren

KINGLETS AND GNATCATCHERS

___ Golden-crowned kinglet
___ Ruby-crowned kinglet
___ Blue-gray gnatcatcher

THRUSHES

___ Eastern bluebird
___ Veery
___ Gray-cheeked thrush
___ Swainson's thrush
___ Hermit thrush
___ Wood thrush
___ American robin

THRASHERS

___ Gray catbird
___ Northern mockingbird
___ Brown thrasher

__ Pearly-eyed thrasher

PIPITS

__ Water pipit

WAXWINGS

__ Bohemian waxwing
__ Cedar waxwing

SHRIKES

__ Northern shrike
__ Loggerhead shrike

STARLINGS

__ European starling

VIREOS

__ White-eyed vireo
__ Bell's vireo
__ Solitary vireo
__ Yellow-throated vireo
__ Warbling vireo
__ Philadelphia vireo
__ Red-eyed vireo
__ Black-whiskered vireo

WOOD WARBLERS

__ Blue-winged warbler
__ Golden-winged warbler
__ Tennessee warbler
__ Orange-crowned warbler
__ Nashville warbler
__ Northern parula
__ Yellow warbler
__ Chestnut-sided warbler
__ Magnolia warbler
__ Cape May warbler
__ Black-throated blue warbler
__ Yellow-rumped warbler
__ Black-throated green warbler

__ Blackburnian warbler
__ Yellow-throated warbler
__ Pine warbler
__ Prairie warbler
__ Palm warbler
__ Bay-breasted warbler
__ Blackpoll warbler
__ Cerulean warbler
__ Black-and-white warbler
__ American redstart
__ Prothonotary warbler
__ Worm-eating warbler
__ Swainson's warbler
__ Ovenbird
__ Northern waterthrush
__ Louisiana waterthrush
__ Kentucky warbler
__ Connecticut warbler
__ Mourning warbler
__ Common yellowthroat
__ Hooded warbler
__ Wilson's warbler
__ Canada warbler
__ Yellow-breasted chat

BANANAQUITS

__ Bananaquit

TANAGERS

__ Summer tanager
__ Scarlet tanager
__ Western tanager

CARDINALS, GROSBEAKS, AND
ALLIES

__ Northern cardinal
__ Rose-breasted grosbeak
__ Blue grosbeak
__ Indigo bunting
__ Painted bunting
__ Dickcissel

TOWHEES, SPARROWS, AND ALLIES

___ Rufous-sided towhee
___ Black-faced grassquit
___ Lesser Antillean bullfinch
___ Bachman's sparrow
___ American tree sparrow
___ Chipping sparrow
___ Clay-colored sparrow
___ Field sparrow
___ Vesper sparrow
___ Lark sparrow
___ Lark bunting
___ Savannah sparrow
___ Grasshopper sparrow
___ Henslow's sparrow
___ Le Conte's sparrow
___ Sharp-tailed sparrow
___ Seaside sparrow
___ Fox sparrow
___ Song sparrow
___ Lincoln's sparrow
___ Swamp sparrow
___ White-throated sparrow
___ White-crowned sparrow
___ Dark-eyed junco
___ Lapland longspur
___ Snow bunting

BLACKBIRDS AND ORIOLES

___ Bobolink
___ Red-winged blackbird
___ Eastern meadowlark
___ Yellow-headed blackbird
___ Rusty blackbird
___ Brewer's blackbird
___ Boat-tailed grackle
___ Common grackle
___ Shiny cowbird
___ Brown-headed cowbird
___ Orchard oriole
___ Northern oriole

FINCHES

___ Pine grosbeak
___ Purple finch
___ House finch
___ Red crossbill
___ White-winged crossbill
___ Common redpoll
___ Hoary redpoll
___ Pine siskin
___ American goldfinch
___ Evening grosbeak

OLD WORLD SPARROWS

___ House sparrow

COMMON AND SCIENTIFIC PLANT NAMES

Alder, mountain. *Alnus crispa*
Alder, speckled. *Alnus rugosa*
Apple, domestic. *Pyrus malus*
Arrowwood. *Viburnum recognitum*
Ash, white. *Fraxinus americana*
Azalea, flame. *Rhododendron calendulaceum*
Azalea, rhodora. *Rhododendron canadense*
Azalea, swamp. *Rhododendron viscosum*
Baldcypress. *Taxodium distichum*
Basswood. *Tilia americana*
Basswood, white. *Tilia heterophylla*
Bayberry, northern. *Myrica pennsylvanica*
Bearberry. *Arctostaphylos uva-ursi*
Beech. *Fagus grandifolia*
Bilberry. *Vaccinium*
Birch, black. *Betula lenta*
Birch, gray. *Betula populifolia*
Birch, river. *Betula nigra*
Birch, white. *Betula papyrifera*
Birch, yellow. *Betula lutea*
Blackberry. *Rubus allegheniensis*
Blueberry. *Vaccinium*
Blueberry, highbush. *Vaccinium corymbosum*
Brazilian-pepper. *Schinus terebinthifolius*
Broomsedge. *Andropogon virginicus*
Buckeye. *Aesculus*
Bullbriar. *Smilax rotundifolia*
Butternut. *Juglans cinerea*
Cattail. *Typha latifolia*

Cedar, Atlantic white. *Chamaecyparis thyoides*
Cedar, red. *Juniperus virginiana*
Cherry, black. *Prunus serotina*
Cherry, pin. *Prunus pennsylvanicus*
Chinquapin, eastern. *Castanea pumila*
Coco-plum. *Chrysobalanus icaco*
Cordgrass, salt marsh. *Spartina alterniflora*
Creeper, Virginia. *Parthenocissus quinquefolia*
Crowberry. *Empetrum*
Dogwood, flowering. *Cornus florida*
Dogwood, red-panicle. *Cornus racemosa*
Dusty miller. *Artemsia stellariana*
Elderberry, red. *Sambucus racemosa*
Elm, American. *Ulnus americana*
Fig, strangler. *Ficus aurea*
Fir, balsam. *Abies balsamea*
Ginger Thomas. *Tecoma stans*
Goldenrod, seaside. *Solidago sempervirens*
Goldenrod, woody. *Chrtsoma pauciflosculosa*
Grape. *Vitis*
Grape, muscadine. *Vitis rotundifolia*
Grass, marram. *Ammophila brevigulata*
Grass, salt meadow. *Spartina petens*
Greenbriar, common. *Smilax rotundifolia*
Groundsel-tree. *Baccharis halimifolia*
Gumbo limbo. *Bursera simaruba*

* Reference: Petrides, George A. *A Field Guide to Trees and Shrubs*. Boston: Houghton Mifflin Co., 1972.

Heather, golden. *Hudsonia ericoides*
Hemlock, eastern. *Tsuga canadensis*
Hickory, bitternut. *Carya cordiformis*
Hickory, mockernut. *Carya tomentosa*
Hickory, pignut. *Carya glabra*
Hickory, water. *Carya aquatica*
Holly, American. *Ilex opaca*
Holly, deciduous. *Ilex decidua*
Holly, yaupon. *Ilex vomitoria*
Honeysuckle. *Lonicera*
Huckleberry. *Gaylussacia*
Ixora. *Ixora*
Ivy, poison. *Rhus radicans*
Laurel, mountain. *Kalmia latifolia*
Laurel, sheep. *Kalmia angustifolia*
Leatherleaf. *Chamaedaphne calyculata*
Lichen, reindeer. *Cladina rangiferina*
Locust, black. *Robinia pseudoacacia*
Locust, honey. *Gleditsia triancanthos*
Loosestrife, purple. *Lythrum salicaria*
Magnolia, bigleaf. *Magnolia macrophylla*
Magnolia, earleaf. *Magnolia fraseri*
Magnolia, Southern. *Magnolia grandiflora*
Mahogany. *Swietentia mahogani*
Mangrove, black. *Avicennia germinans*
Mangrove, red. *Rhizophora mangle*
Mangrove, white. *Languncularia racemosa*
Manjack, white. *Cordia dentata*
Maple, ashleaf. *Acer negundo*
Maple, mountain. *Acer spicatum*
Maple, red. *Acer rubrum*
Maple, silver. *Acer saccharinum*
Maple, sugar. *Acer saccharum*
Marsh-elder. *Iva frutescens*
Myrtle, wax. *Myrica cerifera*
Neddlerush, black. *Juncus*
Oak, basket. *Quercus michauxii*

Oak, black. *Quercus velutina*
Oak, chestnut. *Quercus prinus*
Oak, live. *Quercus cerifera*
Oak, overcup. *Quercus lyrata*
Oak, red. *Quercus rubra*
Oak, scrub. *Quercus ilicifolia*
Oak, Shumard. *Quercus shumardii*
Oak, Spanish. *Quercus falcata*
Oak, Virginia live. *Quercus virginiana*
Oak, white. *Quercus alba*
Olive. *Elaeagnus*
Palm, royal. *Roystonea elata*
Palmetto, saw. *Serenoa repens*
Pennywort. *Obolaria*
Pine, Australian. *Casuarina equitifolia*
Pine, jack. *Pinus banksiana*
Pine, loblolly. *Pinus taeda*
Pine, longleaf. *Pinus palustris*
Pine, pitch. *Pinus rigida*
Pine, red. *Pinus resinosa*
Pine, shortleaf. *Pinus echinata*
Pine, slash. *Pinus elliottii*
Pine, Virginia. *Pinus virginiana*
Pine, white. *Pinus strobus*
Pitcher plant. *Sarracenia purpurea*
Plum, beach. *Prunus maritima*
Poplar, balsam. *Populus balsamifera*
Ragweed. *Ambrosia artemesifolia*
Redbud. *Cercis canadensis*
Rhododendron, catawba. *Rhododendron catawbiense*
Rhododendron, great. *Rhododendron maximum*
Rhododendron, rosebay. *Rhododendron lapponicum*
Rose, salt spray. *Rosa rugosa*
Rose, Virginia. *Rosa virgiania*
Rosemary, Florida. *Ceratiola ericoides*
Rush, black. *Juncus roemerianus*
Sassafras. *Sassafras albidium*
Sawgrass. *Cladium albidium*

Seaside lavender. *Limonium carolinianum*
Sea-oats. *Uniola paniculata*
Sea rocket. *Cakile constricta*
Serviceberry. *Amelanchier*
Silverbell-tree. *Halesia carolina*
Sour-gum. *Nyssa sylvatica*
Sourwood. *Oxydendrum arboreum*
Spanish dagger. *Yucca aloifolia*
Spice bush. *Lindera benzoin*
Spirea. *Spiraea*
Spruce, red. *Picae rubens*
Spruce, white. *Picae glauca*
Sumac, smooth. *Rhus glabra*
Sumac, staghorn. *Rhus typhina*
Sumac, winged. *Rhus copallina*
Sundew. *Drosera rotundifolia*
Sweetgum. *Liquidambar styraciflua*
Sycamore. *Platanus occidentalis*
Tamarack. *Larix laricina*
Tamarind, wild. *Lysiloma latisiliquum*
Tea, Labrador. *Ledum groenlandicum*
Tulip-tree. *Liriodendron tulipifera*
Tupelo. *Nyssa aquatica*
Walnut, black. *Juglans nigra*
Waxmyrtle, common. *Myrica cerifera*
Witch-Hazel, common. *Hamamelis virginiana*
Willow. *Salix caroliniana*
Wrack, knotted. *Ascophyllum nodosum*

ᴮIBLIOGRAPHY

Able, Kenneth P. 1991. Migration biology for birders. *Birding* April: 64-72.

Allen, Robert Porter. 1947. *The flame birds*. New York: Dodd, Mead & Co.

Alsop, Fred J., III. 1991. *Birds of the Smokies*. Gatlinburg, Tenn.: Great Smoky Mts. Natl. Hist. Assoc.

American Ornithologists' Union. 1983. *Check-list of North American birds*. AOU, Kan.: Allen Press.

Arbib, Robert S., Jr., Olin Sewall Pettingill, Jr., and Sally Hoyt Spofford. 1966. *Enjoying birds around New York City*. Boston: Houghton Mifflin Co.

Ardrey, Robert. 1976. *The hunting hypothesis*. New York: Atheneum.

Armistead, Henry T. 1983. Hooded warbler. In *The Audubon Society master guide to birding*, ed. John Farrand, Jr. New York: Alfred A. Knopf.

Atkinson, Brooks. 1970. Biscayne Bay, the splendor, the endless fight to save it. *Audubon* (Sept.):36-57.

Bake, William A. 1975. *Along the Blue Ridge Parkway*. Washington, D.C.: USDI, NPS.

Bellrose, Frank C. 1976. *Ducks, geese and swans of North America*. Harrisburg, Penn: Stackpole Books.

Berry, Ken. 1969. Wildlife checklist of Mammoth Cave National Park. Photocopy: 12pp.

Biderman, John O. 1983. Food for flight. *Audubon* (May):112-119.

Bierly, Michael Lee. 1980. *Bird finding in Tennessee*. Nashville: Michael Lee Bierly.

Bond, James. 1985. *Birds of the West Indies*. Boston: Houghton Mifflin Co.

Bratton, Susan B. 1989. Wood storks move in on Cumberland Island. *Park Science* (Summer):16.

Buhlmann, Kurt Andrew. 1990. *A naturalist's view of the New River Gorge National River*. East. Natl. Parks and Mon. Assoc.

Burleigh, Thomas D. 1944. The bird life of the Gulf Coast region of Mississippi. Occas. Papers Mus. Zool., LSU, no. 20: 329-490.

Burton, Maurice & Robert. 1977. *Inside the animal world*. New York: Quadrangle/NY Times Book Co.

Butcher, Russell D. 1977. *Field guide to Acadia National Park*. New York: Reader's Digest Press.

Canadian Parks Service. 1990. *State of the parks 1990 report*. Gloucester, Ont.: T&H Printers.

Canadian Parks Service. 1990. *State of the parks 1990 profiles*. Gloucester, Ont.: T&H Printers.

Carson, Rachel. 1955. *The edge of the sea*. Boston: Houghton Mifflin Co.

Catlin, David T. 1984. *A naturalist's Blue Ridge Parkway*. Knoxville: Univ. Tennessee Press.

Catton, Bruce. 1960. *The American Heritage short history of the Civil War*. New York: Dell.

Chadwick, Douglas H. 1990. The biodiversity challenge. *Defenders* (May/June): 19-31.

Chapman, Frank M. 1966. *Handbook of birds of eastern North America.* New York: Dover Publ., Inc.

Christensen, Norman L. 1988. Vegetation of the southeast coastal plain. In *North American terrestrial vegetation,* ed. Michael G. Barbour and William Dwight Billings. New York: Cambridge Univ. Press.

Clark, Jim. 1991. Silent chorus. *Birder's World* (Oct.):25-29.

Clark, William S., and Brian K. Wheeler. 1987. *A field guide to hawks of North America.* Boston: Houghton Mifflin Co.

Coleman, Brenda D., and Jo Anne Smith. 1989. *Hiking the Big South Fork.* Knoxville: Univ. Tennessee Press.

Cook, Francis R., and Dalton Muir. 1984. The committee on the status of endangered wildlife in Canada (COSEWIC): History and progress. *The Canadian Field-Naturalist* 98:63-70.

Council on Environmental Quality and Dept. of State. 1980. *The global 2000 report to the president.* Washington, D.C.: GPO.

Craighead, F. C., Sr. 1969. Is man destroying South Florida? In *The environmental destruction of South Florida,* ed. William Ross McCluney. Coral Gables: Univ. Miami Press.

DeLaughter, Jerry. 1986. *Mountain roads and quiet places.* Gatlinburg: Great Smoky Mts. Natural History Assoc.

Dennis, John V. 1988. *The great cypress swamps.* Baton Rouge: Louisiana State Univ. Press.

Douglas, William O. 1961. *My wilderness: East to katahdin.* Garden City, New York: Doubleday & Co.

Duncan, Robert A. 1988. *The birds of Escambia, Santa Rosa and Okaloosa Counties, Florida.* Gulf Breeze, Fla: Bob Duncan.

Duncan, Bob. 1990. Weather and birding. *Birding* (Aug.):173-175.

Dunne, Pete, David Sibley, and Clay Sutton. 1988. *Hawks in flight.* Boston: Houghton Mifflin Co.

Elliott-Fisk, Deborah L. 1988. The boreal forest. In *North American terrestrial vegetation,* ed. Michael G. Barbour and William Dwight Billings. New York: Cambridge Univ. Press.

Emmons, Louise H. 1990. *Neotropical rainforest mammals: A field guide.* Chicago: Univ. Chicago Press.

Erskine, Anthony J. 1977. *Birds in boreal Canada: Communities, densities and adaptations.* Canadian Wildlife Ser. Report No. 41, Ottawa, Canada.

Forman, Richard T. T. 1980. An introduction to the ecosystems and plants on St. Croix, U.S. Virgin Islands. In *Guidebook to the geology and ecology of some marine and terrestrial environments,* ed. H. Gray Multer and Lee C. Gerhard. Spec. Publ. No. 5, West Indies Lab., St. Croix.

Freeman, Judith. 1986. The parks as genetic islands. *National Parks* (Jan./Feb.):12-17.

George, Jean Craighead. 1988. *Everglades wildguide.* Washington, D.C.: USDI, NPS.

Graham, Frank, Jr. 1990. 2001: Birds that won't be with us. *American Birds* (Winter):1074-1081 + 1194-1199.

1221

Greller, Andrew M. 1988. Deciduous forest. In *North American terrestrial vegetation*, ed. Michael G. Barbour and William Dwight Billings. New York: Cambridge Univ. Press.

Grossman, Mary Louise, and John Hamlet. 1964. *Birds of prey of the world.* New York: Clarkson N. Potter, Inc.

Haig, Susan M. 1988. Beach battle. *Birder's World* (March/April): 10-13.

Halliday, Hugh M. 1965. Bonaventure Island. In *The bird watcher's America*, ed. Olin Sewall Pettingill, Jr. New York: McGraw- Hill Book Co.

Hillestad, Hilburn O., J. R. Bozeman, A. S. Johnson, C. W. Berisford, and J. I. Richardson. 1975. The ecology of the Cumberland Island National Seashore, Camden County, Georgia. Georgia Marine Sci. Center, Univ. Georgia, Skadaway Island, GA, report.

Holt, Harold R. 1989. *Lane's a birder's guide to Florida.* Colorado Springs: Amer. Birding Assoc.

Hutto, Richard L. 1988. Is tropical deforestation responsible for the reported declines in Neotropical migrant populations? *American Birds,* (Fall):375-379.

Jadan, Doris. 1985. *A guide to the natural history of St. John.* St. Thomas, V.I.: Environ. Studies Program, Inc.

Johnsson, Robert G., and John D. Dawson. 1984. *A naturalist's notebook, Great Smoky Mountains National Park.* Gatlinburg: Great Smoky Mts. Natural History Assoc.

Jorgensen, Neil. 1978. *A Sierra Club naturalist's guide to southern New England.* San Francisco: Sierra Club Books.

Kale, Herbert W. II., ed. 1978. *Rare and endangered biota of Florida.*Vol. 2, Birds. Gainesville: Univ. Presses of Florida.

Kaufman, Kenn. 1990. *Advanced birding.*Boston: Houghton Mifflin Co.

Kilham, Lawrence. 1989. *The American crow and the common raven.* College Station: Texas A&M Univ. Press.

Kirkpatrick, Roy. 1991. Chronology and population trends Chincoteague weekly waterfowl census. Typed report to NPS, 17pp.

Kricher, John C., and Gordon Morrison. 1988. *Eastern Forests.* Boston: Houghton Mifflin Co.

Kushlan, James A., and Deborah A. White. 1977. Nesting wading bird populations in Southern Florida. *Florida Scientist* 40(1):65-72.

Laycock, George. 1987. Keeping a Key pigeon in the Keys. *Audubon* March:76-80.

Leonard, Jonathan Norton. 1972. *Atlantic beaches, the American wilderness.* New York: Time-Life Books.

Leopold, Aldo. 1966. *A sand county almanac.* New York: Oxford Univ. Press.

Loftus, William F. 1986. Distribution and ecology of exotic fishes in Everglades National Park. *Proc. Conf. on Science in the Natl. Parks 1988.* Vol. 5, Managt. of exotic species in natural communities. Ed. L. K. Thomas, Jr., NPS and George Wright Soc.:24-34.

Loughlin, Maureen H., J.C. Ogden, W.B. Robertson, Jr., and R. Wood. 1990. *Everglades National Park checklist a habitat guide to birds of the Everglades.* Homestead, Fla. Evergl. Natl. Parks and Mon. Assoc.

Meisel, John S. 1991. Piping plover monitoring report, Cape Cod National Seashore 1991. Typed report. 34 pp.

Merritt Island Natl. Wildf. Refuge. undated. *Birds Merritt Island National Refuge.* USDI, USFWS.

Mitchell, John G. 1984. Cumberland, floating free. *Audubon* (July):48-61.

Mittlehauser, Glen, and Judy Hazen. 1990. Monitoring harlequin ducks at Acadia. *Park Science* (Winter):18.

Monroe, Burt L. 1951. Kentucky. In *A guide to bird finding east of the Mississippi*, 2d ed., ed. Olin Sewall Pettingill, Jr. New York: Oxford Univ. Press:190-210.

Moore, John R. 1988. A Gulf of Mexico migration. *Mississippi Outdoors* (Sept./Oct.):13-15.

Moore, John R. 1988. Utilization of Gulf Coast barrier islands by migrating birds. Report to NPS.

Morris, Arthur A. 1989. Birding hot spots Jamaica Bay Wildlife Refuge. *Birder's World* (Aug.):42-46.

National Audubon Society. 1980. The Eightieth Audubon Christmas Bird Count. *American Birds* 34, no. 4. New York: Nat'l. Aud. Soc.

National Audubon Society. 1990. The Ninetieth Christmas Bird Count. *American Birds* 44, no. 4. New York: Nat'l. Aud. Soc.

National Audubon Society. 1991. The Ninety-First Christmas Bird Count. *American Birds* 45, no. 4. New York: Nat'l. Aud. Soc.

National Fish and Wildlife Found. 1990. Proposal for a Neotropical migratory bird conservation program. Photocopied report.

National Geographic Society. 1987. *Field guide to the birds of North America.* 2d ed. Washington, D.C.: Natl. Geogr. Soc.

National Park Service. 1981. *General management plan Canaveral National Seashore Florida.* USDI, NPS, Denver Ser. Center.

Ogburn, Charlton. 1975. *The southern Appalachians: a wilderness quest.* New York: William Morrow & Co., Inc.

Ogden, John C. 1983. The abundant, endangered flinthead. *Audubon* (Jan.):90-101.

Palmer, Ralph S. 1988. *Handbook of North American birds.* Vol. 4. New Haven: Yale Univ. Press.

Parks Canada. 1987. *Management plan summary for Cape Breton Highlands National Park.* Environment Canada.

Pasquier, Roger F. 1983. The eastern seaboard: Avian highway. *The Nat. Cons. News* (Sept./Oct.):16-19.

Perry, Bill. 1985. *A Sierra Club naturalist's guide to the middle Atlantic coast Cape Hatteras to Cape Cod.* San Francisco: Sierra Club Books.

Peterson, Roger Tory, and James Fisher. 1963. *Wild America.* Boston: Houghton Mifflin Co.

Peterson, Wayne R. 1983. Louisiana waterthrush. In *The Audubon Society master guide to birding*, ed. John Farrand, Jr. New York: Alfred A. Knopf.

Petrides, George A. 1972. *A field guide to trees and shrubs*. Boston: Houghton Mifflin Co.

Pettingill, Olin Sewall, Jr. 1977. *A guide to bird finding east of the Mississippi*. New York: Oxford Univ. Press.

Ridgley, Robert S., and Guy Tudor. 1989. *The birds of South America*. Vol. 1, *The oscine passerines*. Austin: Univ. Texas Press.

Robbins, Chandler S., John R. Sauer, Russell S. Greenberg, and Sam Droege. 1989. Population declines in North American birds that migrate to the Neotropics. *Population Biology* 86:7658-7662.

Robertson, William B., Jr. 1964. The terns of the Dry Tortugas. *Bull. Fl. State Mus.* 8:1-94.

Robertson, William B., Jr. 1965. The Everglades. In *The Bird Watcher's America*, ed. Olin Sewall Pettingill, Jr. New York: McGraw Hill.

Robertson, William B., Jr. 1973. *Everglades—The park story*. Coral Gables: Univ. Miami Press.

Robertson, William B., Jr. 1986. *Birds of Fort Jefferson National Monument*. Homestead, Fla.: Fl. Natl. Parks and Monuments Assoc.

Robertson, William B., Jr., and C. Wesley Biggs. 1983. A West Indian Myiarchus in Biscayne National Park, Florida. *American Birds* (July-Aug.):802-804.

Robertson, William B., Jr., L.L. Breen, and B.W. Patty. 1983. Movement of marked roseate spoonbills in Florida with a review of present distribution. *Jour. Field Ornith.* 54:225-236.

Robertson, William B., Jr., and James A. Kushlan. 1974. The southern Florida Avifauna. In *Memoir 2: Environments of south Florida: Present and past*. Miami Geol. Soc.

Ryan, A. Glen. 1978. *Native trees and shrubs of Newfoundland and Labrador*. Parks Div., Govt. Newfound. & Labrador, St. John's.

Serle, W., G. J. Morel, and W. Hartwig. 1980. *A field guide to the birds of West Africa*. London: William Collins Sons & Co. Ltd.

Shafer, Craig L. 1990. *Nature reserves island theory and conservation practice*. Washington, D.C.: Smithsonian Inst.

Shelton, Napier. 1975. *The nature of Shenandoah*. USDI, NPS.

Simons, Ted, John Peine, and Richard Cunningham. 1989. Proposed migratory bird watch to encompass research, monitoring, and interpretation. *Park Science* 9:8.

Simons, Ted, S. K. Sherrod, M. W. Collopy, and M. A. Jenkins. 1988. Restoring the bald eagle. *American Scientist* (May-June): 252-260.

Smith, P. William, and Alexander Sprunt IV. 1987. The shiny cowbird reaches the United States. *American Birds* (Fall):370-371.

Smith, Richard M. 1989. *Wild plants of America*. New York: John Wiley & Sons.

Snyder, Lee F., and Wesley Biggs. 1988. Key West quail-dove spotted! *WildBird* (June):14-17.

St-Amour, Maxime. 1985. *Forillon National Park*. Vancouver: Douglas & McIntyre.

Stolzenburg, William. 1991. The fragment connection. *Nature Conservancy* (July/Aug.):19-25.

Stupka, Arthur. 1963. *Notes on the birds of Great Smoky Mountains National Park*. Knoxville: Univ. Tennessee Press.

Sutton, Ann, and Myron Sutton. 1986. *Eastern forests: Audubon Society nature guides*. New York: Alfred A. Knopf, Inc.

Torrey, Bradford. 1896. *Spring notes from Tennessee*. Cambridge: The Riverside Press.

Toups, Judith A., and Jerome A. Jackson. 1987. *Birds and birding on the Mississippi Coast*. Jackson: Univ. Press of Miss.

Turner, Frederick Jackson. 1990. The significance of the frontier in American history. In *Milestone of thought*, ed. Harold P. Simonson. New York: The Continuum Publ. Co.

Udall, James R. 1991. Launching the natural ark. *Sierra* (Sept./Oct.):80-89.

United States Department of Agriculture. 1949. *Trees, the yearbook of agriculture*. Washington, D.C.: USDI, GPO

Venezia, Kathryn, and Robert P. Cook. 1991. Flora of Gateway National Recreation Area. Report to NPS.

Virginia Society of Ornithology. 1979. *Virginia's birdlife an annotated checklist*. Virginia Soc. Ornithology, Inc.

Wallace, Elaine. No date. *Fact sheet Cape Breton Highlands National Park*. Parks Canada.

Walton, Richard K. 1988. *Bird finding in New England*. Boston: David R. Godine.

Wauer, Roland H. 1988. *Virgin Islands birdlife*. St. Croix: Univ. V.I. Coop. Ext. Ser.

Wauer, Roland H., and Fred W. Sladen. 1992. Importance of Virgin Islands mangrove habitats to migrant and wintering birds. *Ornithologia Caribena* (in press).

Welty, Joel Carl. 1963. *The life of birds*. New York: Alfred A. Knopf.

Wharton, Charles H. 1978. *The natural environments of Georgia*. Atlanta: Georgia Dept. Natural Resources.

Whatley, Michael E. 1988. *Common trailside plants of Cape Cod National Seashore*. Eastham, Mass.: Eastern Natl. Parks and Mon. Assoc.

Wilcove, David. 1990. Empty skies. *The Nature Conservancy Magazine* (Jan./Feb.):4-13.

Wilds, Claudia. 1983. *Finding birds in the national capital area*. Washington, D.C.: Smithsonian Inst.

Wilson, Gordon. 1968. *Birds and their habitats in Mammoth Cave National Park*. Eastham, Mass.: Eastern Natl. Park and Mon. Assoc.

Worthington, Gary, J. D. Phillips, and Don Kodak. 1990. *A guide to the birds of New River Gorge area*. West Virginia Dept. Nat. Resources.

ℐNDEX

murre, thick-billed, 46, 92
Neotropical migrants: Acadia, 31; decline, 13; program, 19; scarlet tanager, 141; red-eyed vireo, 182; blackpoll warbler, 363; black-throated blue warbler, 196; blue-winged warbler, 125; prairie warbler, 150-51; yellow-throated warbler, 207-08
nighthawk: Antillean, 352, 354; common, 55, 352; lesser, 343
night-heron: black-crowned, 220, 279, 335; yellow-crowned, 201, 220, 279, 323, 359
noddy, brown, 349, 354
nuthatch: brown-headed, 299, 317, 320, 331, 341; red-breasted, 30, 43, 44, 46, 72, 87, 102, 112, 143, 153, 164, 183, 194, 195, 288; white-breasted, 53, 121, 129, 134, 141, 149, 155, 157, 163, 171, 181, 187, 199, 203, 207, 233, 252, 290, 297, 301, 343
oldsquaw, 32, 65, 70, 114, 233, 342
oriole: northern, 45, 121, 134, 245, 251; orchard, 208, 278, 288 osprey, 4, 32, 73, 74-76, 75, 81, 82, 91, 93, 95, 96, 103, 170, 209, 250, 325, 327, 335, 364
ovenbird, 13, 30, 42, 51, 55, 65, 73, 87, 102, 114, 128-29, 135, 141, 160, 173, 181, 197, 198, 199-200, 201, 222, 233, 251, 278, 289, 319, 337, 360, 365
owl: barred, 55, 151-52, 255, 272-73, 280, 288, 287-98, 302, 322, 325, 327, 337; boreal, 73; burrowing, 343; great horned, 151, 273, 288; long-eared, 126, 143, 246, 279; northern saw-whet, 126, 143, 194, 267; short-eared, 35, 143, 153, 279; snowy, 35, 46, 102, 114, 143, 223, 234, 246
oystercatcher, American, 230-31, 234, 243, 262, 265, 276, 342
parula, northern, 13, 30, 42, 45, 51, 65, 102, 114, 181, 197, 199-200, 208, 245, 251, 274, 275, 278, 280, 296, 302, 318-19, 321, 352, 358, 365
pelican: American white, 307, 308, 318, 336, 337; brown, 235-36, 246, 263, 265, 267, 277, 308, 317, 336, 350, 353, 355, 364, 365
Peterson, Wayne (in *The Audubon Society master guide to birding*): eastern kingbird song, 53; Lincoln's sparrow song, 101-02; sharp-tailed sparrow song, 100; Swainson's thrush song, 42-43; Louisiana waterthrush song, 252; northern waterthrush song, 87;
Pettingill, Olin Sewall (*A guide to bird finding east of the Mississippi*): hawk flight over Kittatinny Ridge, 123
petrel, black-capped, 263
phalarope, northern, 31
phoebe, eastern, 142, 156, 162, 197, 199, 203, 233, 291, 301, 307, 316, 317
pigeon: passenger, 236; scaly-naped, 365, 366; white-crowned, 330-31, 343, 364, 365
pintail: northern, 35, 125, 220, 233, 242, 246, 265, 310; white- cheeked, 360
pipit, water, 279
plover: black-bellied, 70, 231, 242, 243, 260, 261, 268, 336, 361; lesser golden, 261; piping, 10, 55, 70-71, 73, 96, 98-99, 103, 220-21, 231, 243, 268, 276, 365; semipalmated, 70, 78, 99, 231, 242, 243, 265, 276; snowy, 365; Wilson's, 243, 261
pollution: acid rain at Kejimkujik, 49; DDT and bald eagles, 81, 331; DDT and ospreys, 75; DDT and pelicans, 236; DDT and peregrines, 12, 133, 170; DDT and razorbills, 108; DDT and dusky seaside sparrow, 309-10
ptarmigan: rock, 90-91, 93; willow, 81, 82, 90
puffin, Atlantic, 32
quail-dove: bridled, 361-62, 366; Key West, 338
rail: clapper, 317, 318, 320; king, 254, 279, 289, 334; Virginia, 317, 334
raven, common, 6, 45, 46, 81, 82, 114, 170, 173, 174, 185-87, 186, 187, 197
razorbill, 108-09, 115, 223, 267
redhead, 242
redpoll: common, 35, 65, 103, 126, 174, 201, 223, 246; hoary, 73, 114
redstart, American, 30, 35, 42, 45, 51, 65, 79, 102, 114, 129, 135, 160, 172, 177, 181, 182-83, 188, 197, 231, 233, 244, 245, 252, 299, 337, 352, 358, 365
research: Acadia, 18; Assateague, 18; Cape Breton Highlands, 18; Fort Jefferson, 18, 349; Cape Cod, 222; Great Smoky Mountains, 13; Gulf Islands, 18, 319-20; Kejimkujik, 18; Outer Banks, 18; Shenandoah, 173
restoration project: Acadia, 35; Assateague, 35; Fundy, 46; Great Smoky Mountains, 12, 35; New River Gorge, 133; Shenandoah, 170; Cumberland Gap; 143
robin, American, 4, 30, 34, 52, 53, 54, 79, 87, 102, 114, 128, 132, 134, 136, 140, 149, 156, 173, 174, 181, 184, 194, 195, 197, 198, 209, 222, 231, 233, 244, 264-65, 290, 291, 301, 307, 310, 316, 317, 318, 320, 321
sanderling, 70, 242, 243, 246, 257-58, 259, 260, 268, 276, 308,
sandpiper: least, 31, 70, 78, 231, 242, 243, 265, 276, 336; pectoral, 70, 242, 243; purple, 65, 82, 92-93, 233, 267, 279; semipalmated, 31, 45, 70, 231, 242, 243, 276; spotted, 31, 70, 78-79, 82,

Other Books from John Muir Publications

Parenting Series

Being a Father: Family, Work, and Self, *Mothering* Magazine 176 pp. $12.95

Preconception: A Woman's Guide to Preparing for Pregnancy and Parenthood, Aikey-Keller 232 pp. $14.95

Schooling at Home: Parents, Kids, and Learning, *Mothering* Magazine 264 pp. $14.95

Teens: A Fresh Look, *Mothering* Magazine 240 pp. $14.95

"Kidding Around" Travel Guides for Young Readers

Written for kids eight years of age and older.

Kidding Around Atlanta, Pedersen 64 pp. $9.95

Kidding Around Boston, Byers 64 pp. $9.95

Kidding Around Chicago, Davis 64 pp. $9.95

Kidding Around the Hawaiian Islands, Lovett 64 pp. $9.95

Kidding Around London, Lovett 64 pp. $9.95

Kidding Around Los Angeles, Cash 64 pp. $9.95

Kidding Around the National Parks of the Southwest, Lovett 108 pp. $12.95

Kidding Around New York City, Lovett 64 pp. $9.95

Kidding Around Paris, Clay 64 pp. $9.95

Kidding Around Philadelphia, Clay 64 pp. $9.95

Kidding Around San Diego, Luhrs 64 pp. $9.95

Kidding Around San Francisco, Zibart 64 pp. $9.95

Kidding Around Santa Fe, York 64 pp. $9.95

Kidding Around Seattle, Steves 64 pp. $9.95

Kidding Around Spain, Biggs 108 pp. $12.95

Kidding Around Washington, D.C., Pedersen 64 pp. $9.95

"Extremely Weird" Series for Young Readers

Written for kids eight years of age and older.

Extremely Weird Bats, Lovett 48 pp. $9.95

Extremely Weird Birds, Lovett 48 pp. $9.95

Extremely Weird Endangered Species, Lovett 48 pp. $9.95

Extremely Weird Fishes, Lovett 48 pp. $9.95

Extremely Weird Frogs, Lovett 48 pp. $9.95

Extremely Weird Primates, Lovett 48 pp. $9.95

Extremely Weird Reptiles, Lovett 48 pp. $9.95

Extremely Weird Spiders, Lovett 48 pp. $9.95

Masters of Motion Series

For kids eight years of age and older.

How to Drive an Indy Race Car, Rubel 48 pages $9.95 paper (avail. 8/92)

How to Fly a 747, Paulson 48 pages $9.95 (avail. 9/92)

How to Fly the Space Shuttle, Shorto 48 pages $9.95 paper (avail. 10/92)

Quill Hedgehog Adventures Series

Green fiction for kids. Written for kids eight years of age and older.

Quill's Adventures in the Great Beyond. Waddington-Feather 96 pp. $5.95

Quill's Adventures in Wasteland, Waddington-Feather 132 pp. $5.95

Quill's Adventures in Grozzieland, Waddington-Feather 132 pp. $5.95

X-ray Vision Series

For kids eight years and older.

Looking Inside Cartoon Animation, Schultz 48 pages $9.95 paper (avail. 9/92)

Looking Inside Sports Aerodynamics, Schultz 48 pages $9.95 paper (avail. 9/92)

Looking Inside the Brain, Schultz 48 pages $9.95 paper

Other Young Readers Titles

The Indian Way: Learning to Communicate with Mother Earth, McLain 114 pp. $9.95

The Kids' Environment Book: What's Awry and Why, Pedersen 192 pp. $13.95

Kids Explore America's Hispanic Heritage, Westridge Young Writers Workshop 112 pp. $7.95

Rads, Ergs, and Cheeseburgers: The Kids' Guide to Energy and the Environment, Yanda 108 pp. $12.95

Automotive Titles

How to Keep Your VW Alive, 14th ed., 440 pp. $21.95

How to Keep Your Subaru Alive 480 pp. $21.95

How to Keep Your Toyota Pickup Alive 392 pp. $21.95

How to Keep Your Datsun/Nissan Alive 544 pp. $21.95

The Greaseless Guide to Car Care Confidence: Take the Terror Out of Talking to Your Mechanic, Jackson 224 pp. $14.95

Off-Road Emergency Repair & Survival, Ristow 160 pp. $9.95

Ordering Information

If you cannot find our books in your local bookstore, you can order directly from us. Please check the "Available" date above. If you send us money for a book not yet available, we will hold your money until we can ship you the book. Your books will be sent to you via UPS (for U.S. destinations). UPS will not deliver to a P.O. Box; please give us a street address. Include $3.75 for the first item ordered and $.50 for each additional item to cover shipping and handling costs. For airmail within the U.S., enclose $4.00. All foreign orders will be shipped surface rate; please enclose $3.00 for the first item and $1.00 for each additional item. Please inquire about foreign airmail rates.

Method of Payment

Your order may be paid by check, money order, or credit card. We cannot be responsible for cash sent through the mail. All payments must be made in U.S. dollars drawn on a U.S. bank. Canadian postal money orders in U.S. dollars are acceptable. For VISA, MasterCard, or American Express orders, include your card number, expiration date, and your signature, or call (800) 888-7504. Books ordered on American Express cards can be shipped only to the billing address of the cardholder. Sorry, no C.O.D.'s. Residents of sunny New Mexico, add 5.875% tax to the total.

Address all orders and inquiries to:
John Muir Publications
P.O. Box 613
Santa Fe, NM 87504
(505) 982-4078
(800) 888-7504